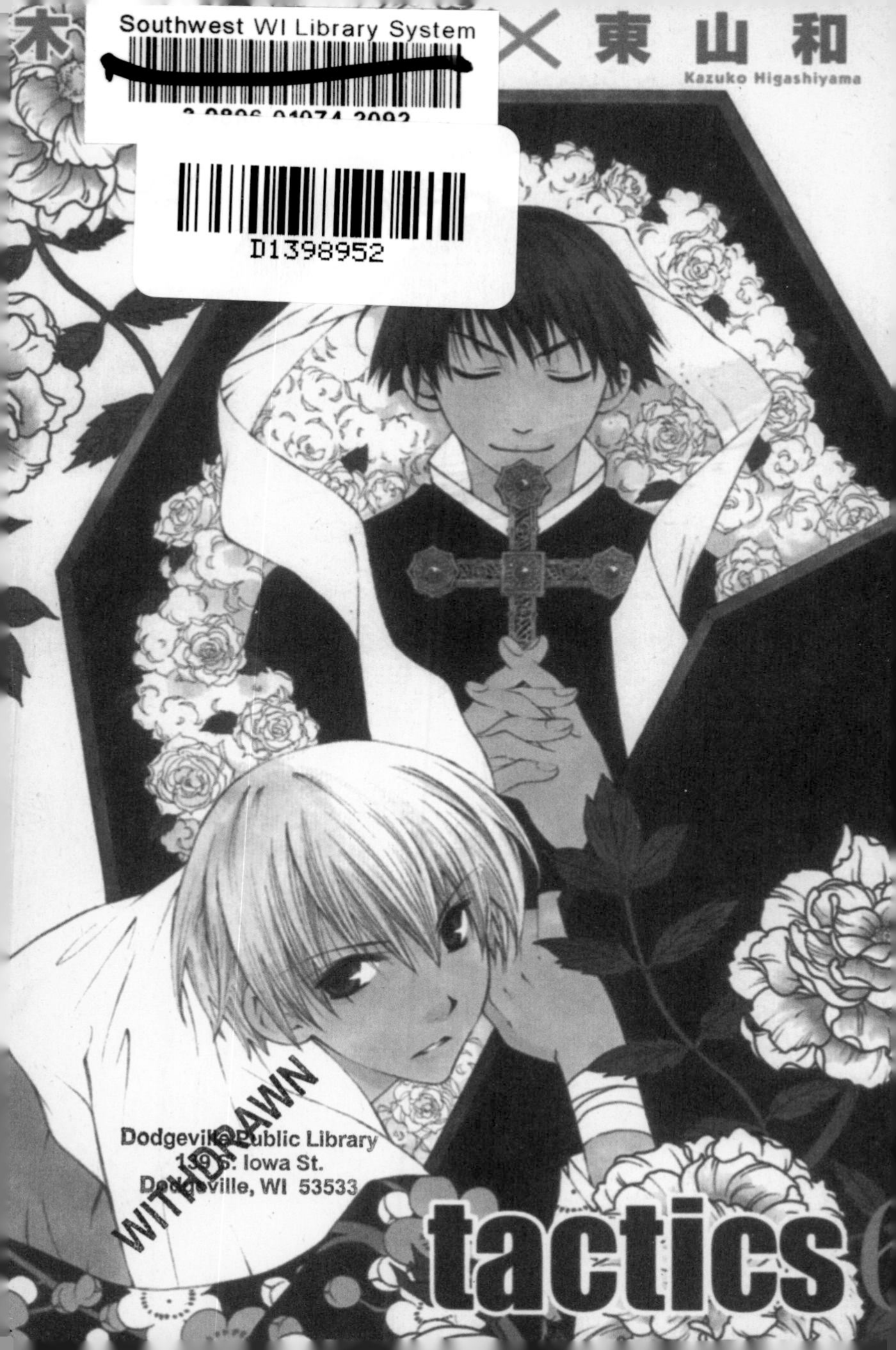
木
×東山和
Kazuko Higashiyama
tactics

tactics

Sakura Kinoshita ✕ *Kazuko Higashiyama*

6

tactics

**Volume 6
by Sakura Kinoshita and
Kazuko Higashiyama**

HAMBURG // LONDON // LOS ANGELES // TOKYO

tactics Volume 6
Art & Story by Sakura Kinoshita x Kazuko Higashiyama

Translation - Christine Schilling
English Adaptation - Lianne Sentar
Retouch and Lettering - Star Print Brokers
Production Artist - Lauren O'Connell
Cover Design - James Lee

Editor - Stephanie Duchin
Digital Imaging Manager - Chris Buford
Pre-Production Supervisor - Vicente Rivera, Jr.
Production Specialist - Lucas Rivera
Managing Editor - Vy Nguyen
Art Director - Al-Insan Lashley
Editor-in-Chief - Rob Tokar
Publisher - Mike Kiley
President and C.O.O. - John Parker
C.E.O. and Chief Creative Officer - Stu Levy

A  Manga

TOKYOPOP and  are trademarks or registered trademarks of TOKYOPOP Inc.

TOKYOPOP Inc.
5900 Wilshire Blvd. Suite 2000
Los Angeles, CA 90036

E-mail: info@TOKYOPOP.com
Come visit us online at www.TOKYOPOP.com

ISBN: 978-1-59816-965-2

First TOKYOPOP printing: September 2008
10 9 8 7 6 5 4 3 2 1
Printed in the USA

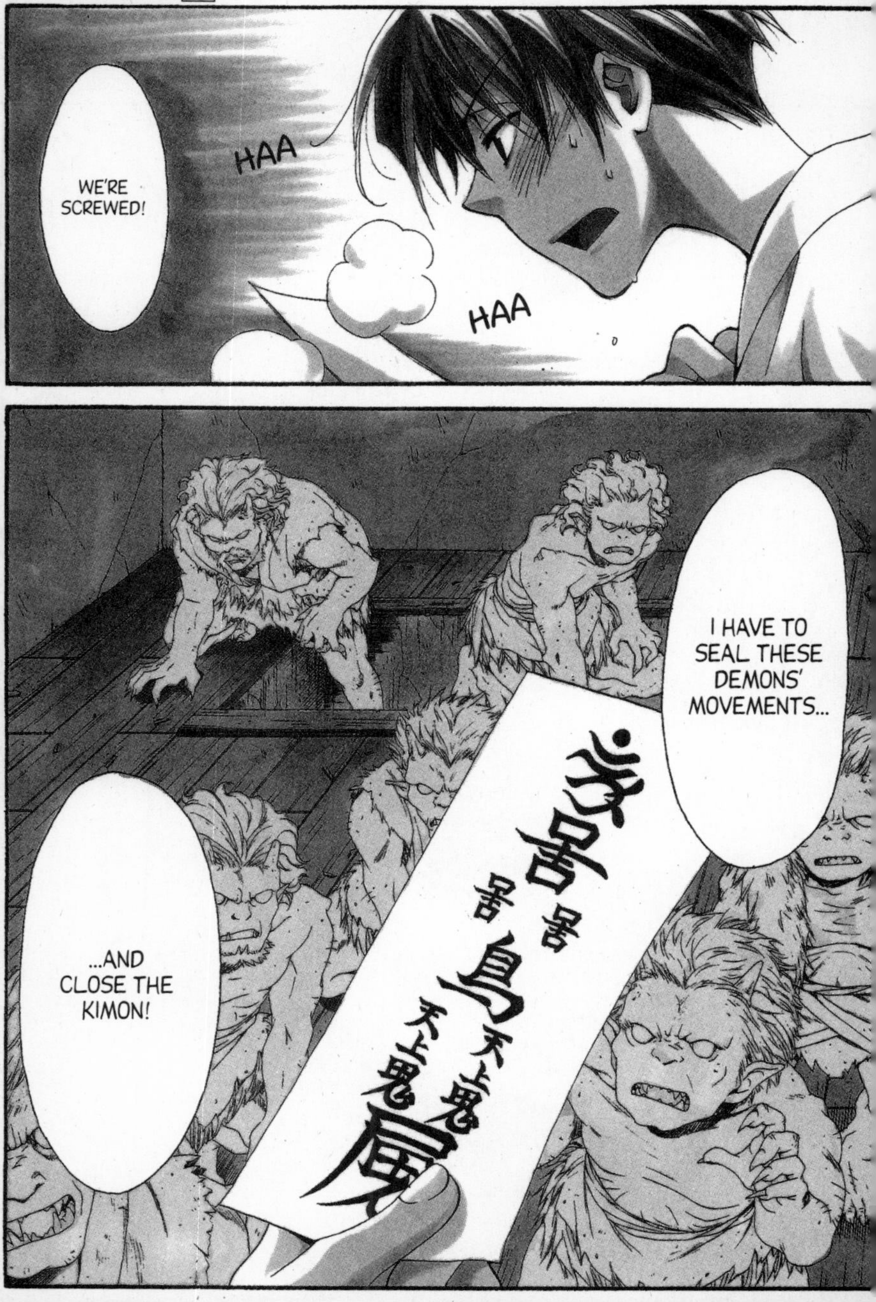
HAA
WE'RE SCREWED!
HAA
I HAVE TO SEAL THESE DEMONS' MOVEMENTS...
...AND CLOSE THE KIMON!

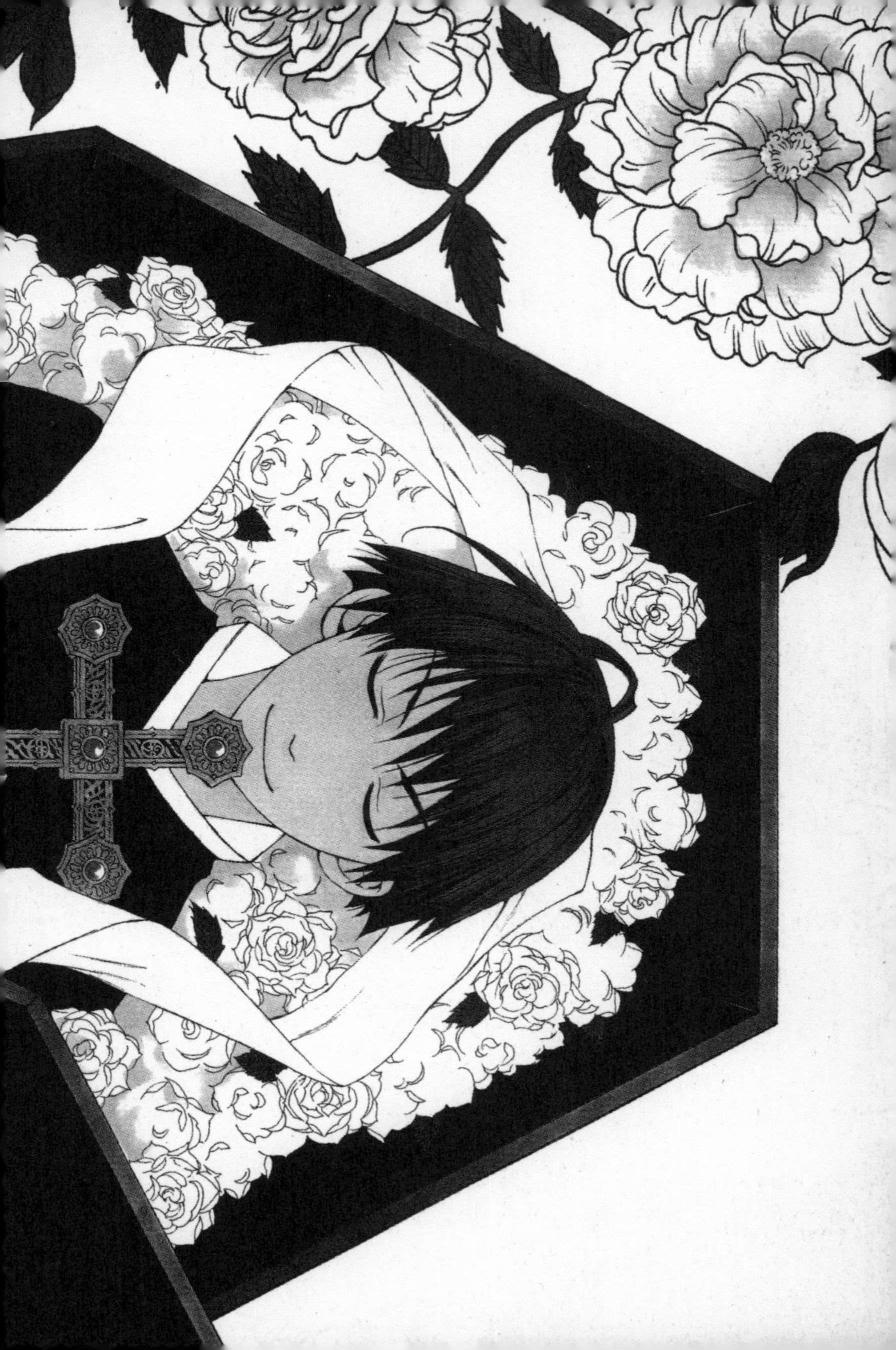

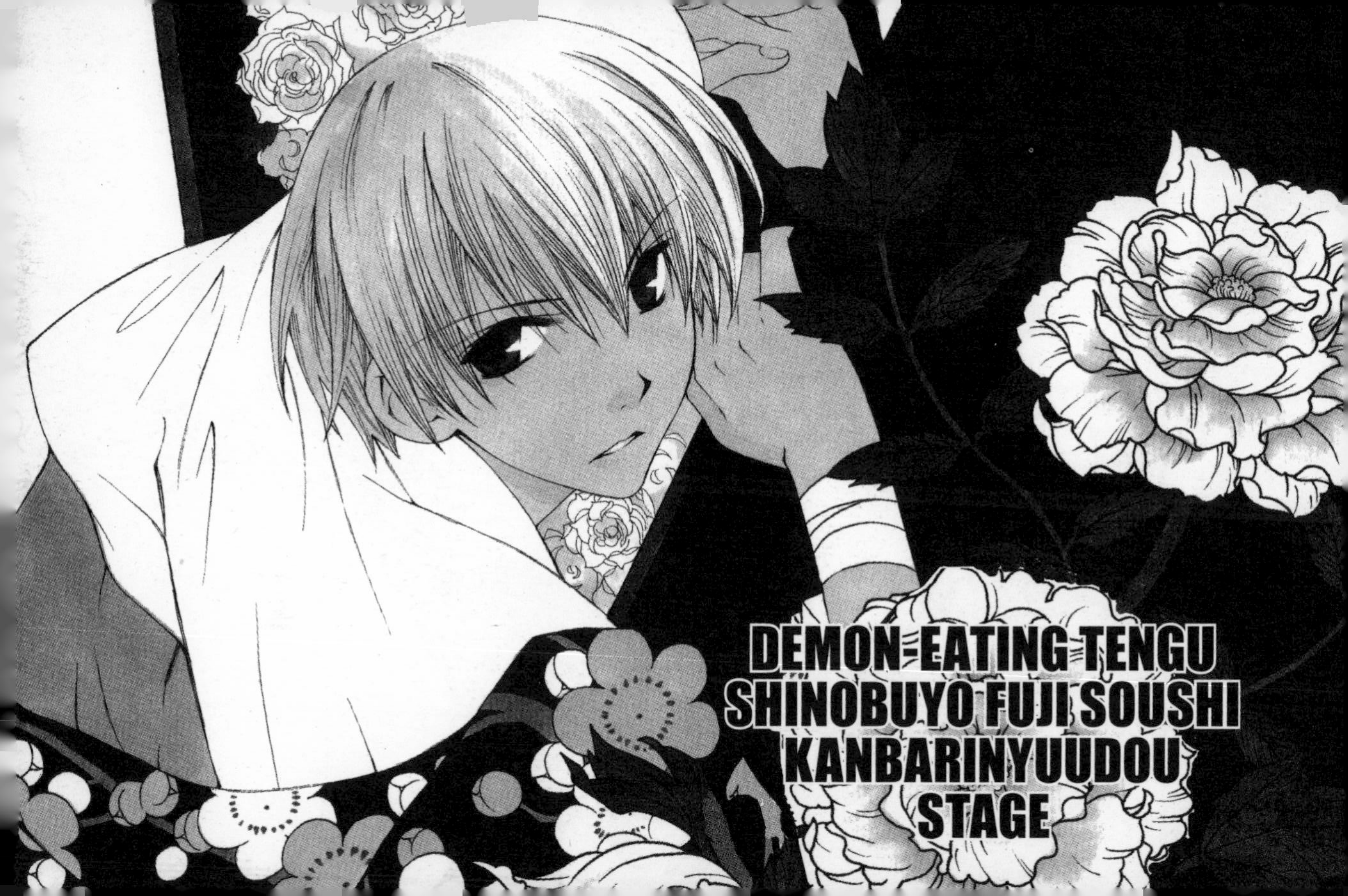
DEMON-EATING TENGU
SHINOBUYO FUJI SOUSHI
KANBARINYUUDOU
STAGE

FORTUNE COMES TO A MERRY HOME !!!!

SMILE! SMILE! SMILE! tactics

tactics

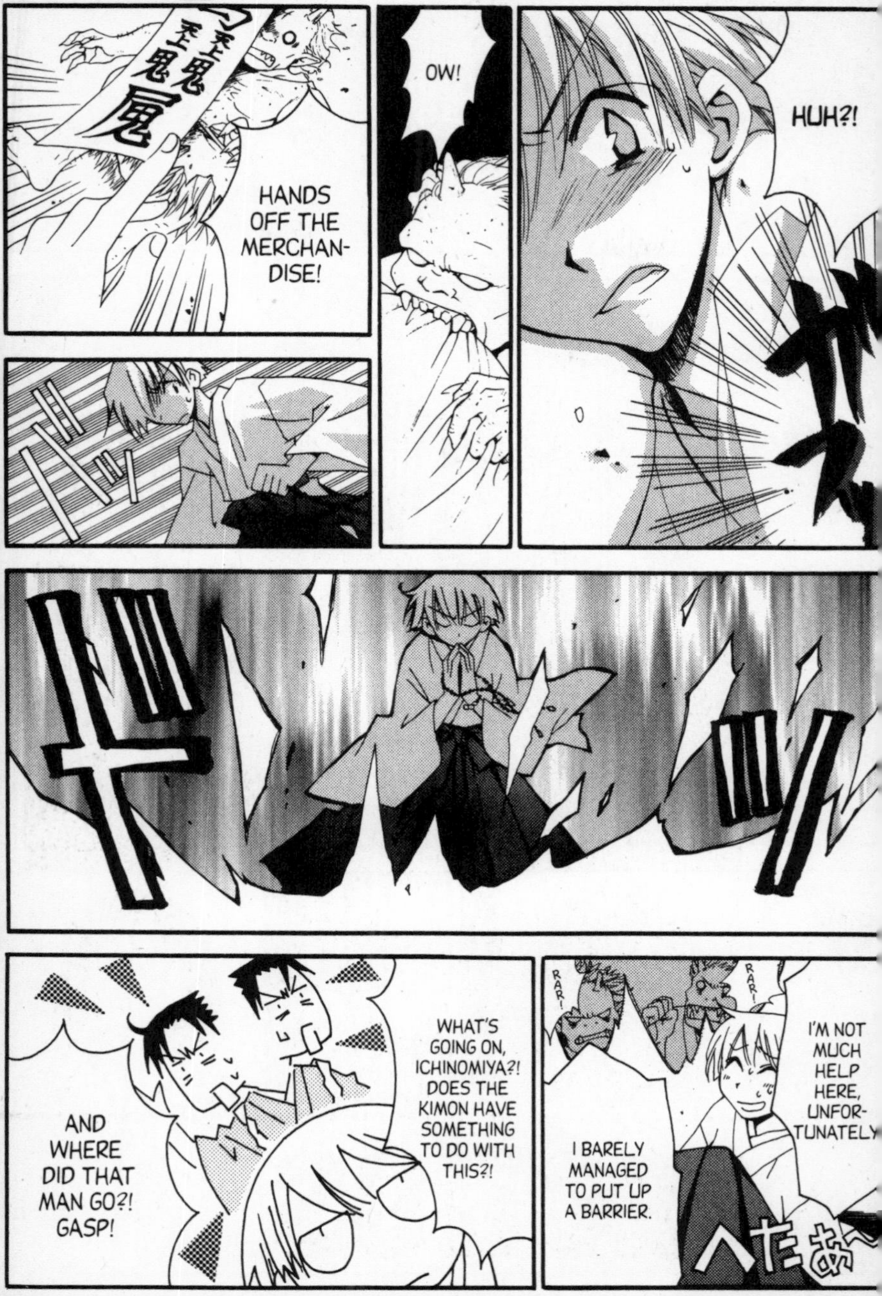
HUH?!
OW!
HANDS OFF THE MERCHANDISE!
RAR!
RAR!
I'M NOT MUCH HELP HERE, UNFORTUNATELY
I BARELY MANAGED TO PUT UP A BARRIER.
へたぁ~
WHAT'S GOING ON, ICHINOMIYA?! DOES THE KIMON HAVE SOMETHING TO DO WITH THIS?!
AND WHERE DID THAT MAN GO?! GASP!

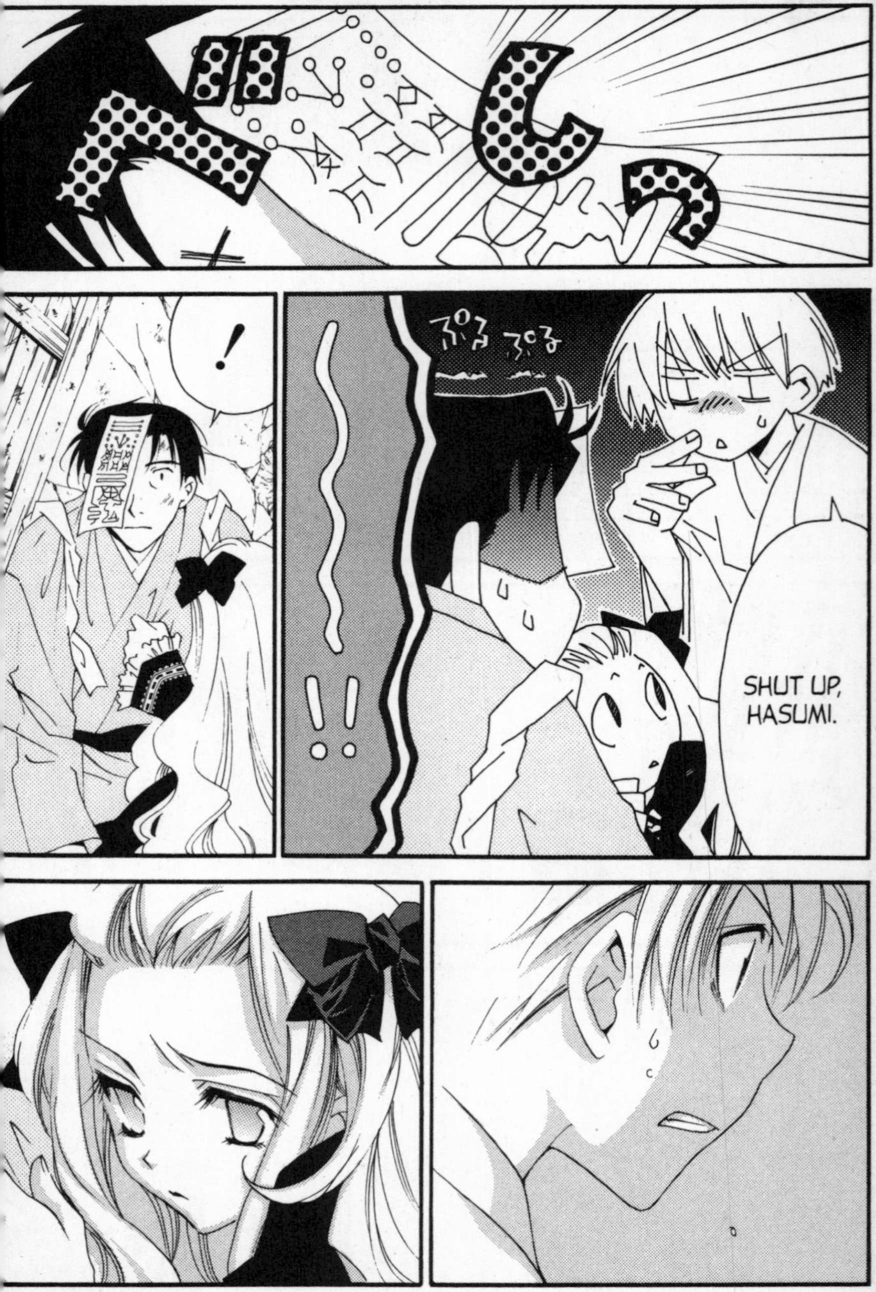

ドしっ
ぷるぷる
!!
SHUT UP, HASUMI.
!

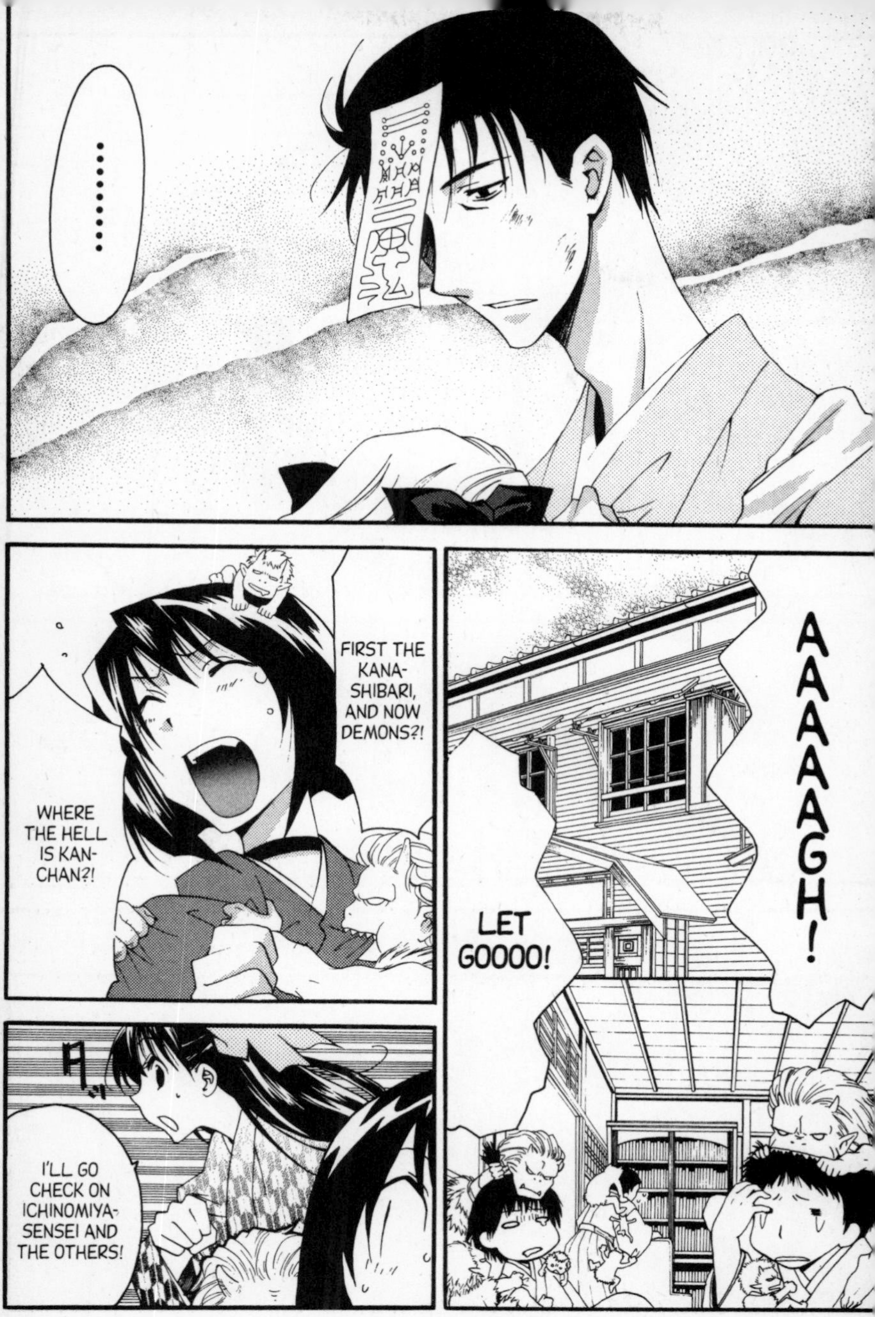
……
AAAAAGH!
LET GOOOO!
FIRST THE KANA-SHIBARI, AND NOW DEMONS?!
WHERE THE HELL IS KAN-CHAN?!
I'LL GO CHECK ON ICHINOMIYA-SENSEI AND THE OTHERS!

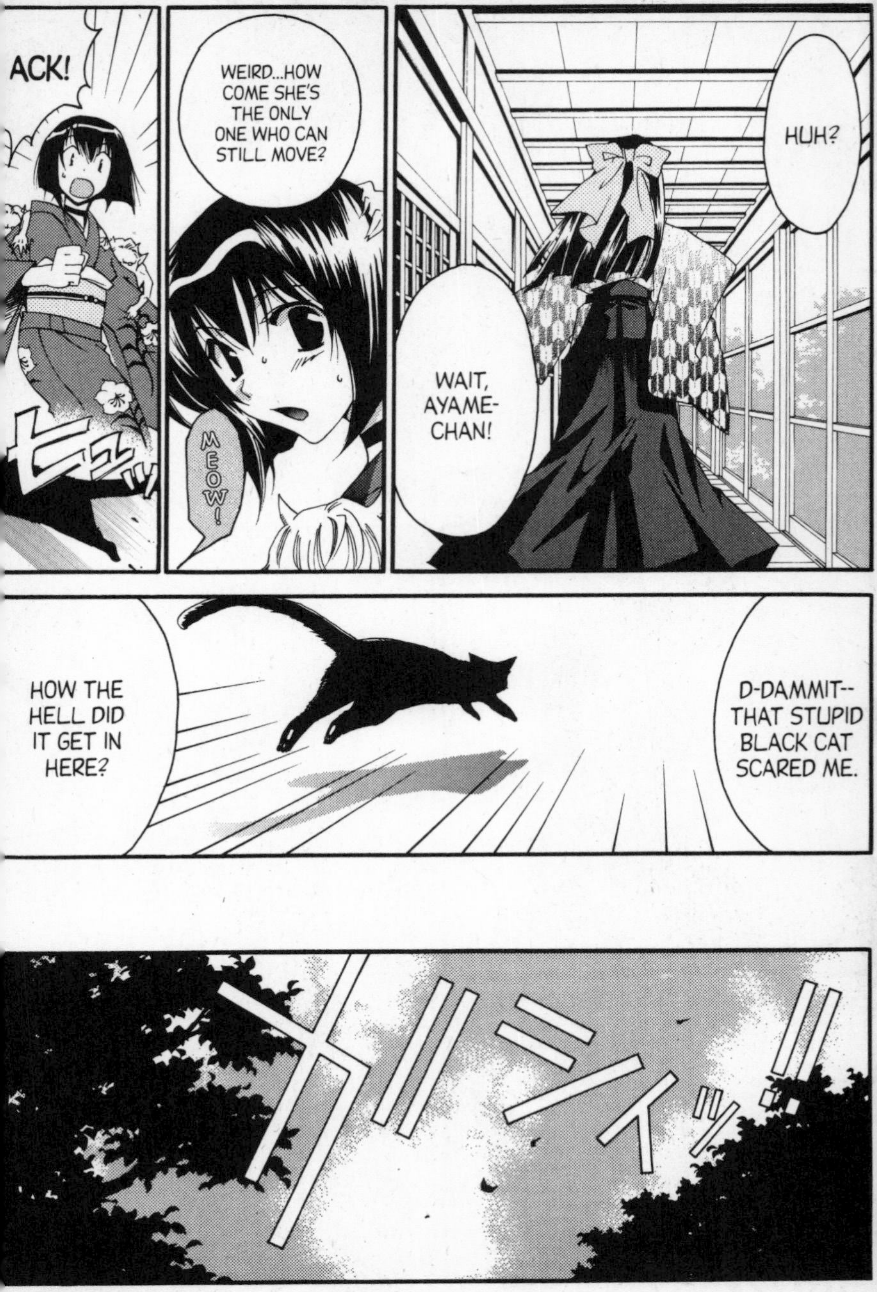
HUH?
WAIT, AYAME-CHAN!
WEIRD...HOW COME SHE'S THE ONLY ONE WHO CAN STILL MOVE?
MEOW!
ACK!
D-DAMMIT--THAT STUPID BLACK CAT SCARED ME.
HOW THE HELL DID IT GET IN HERE?

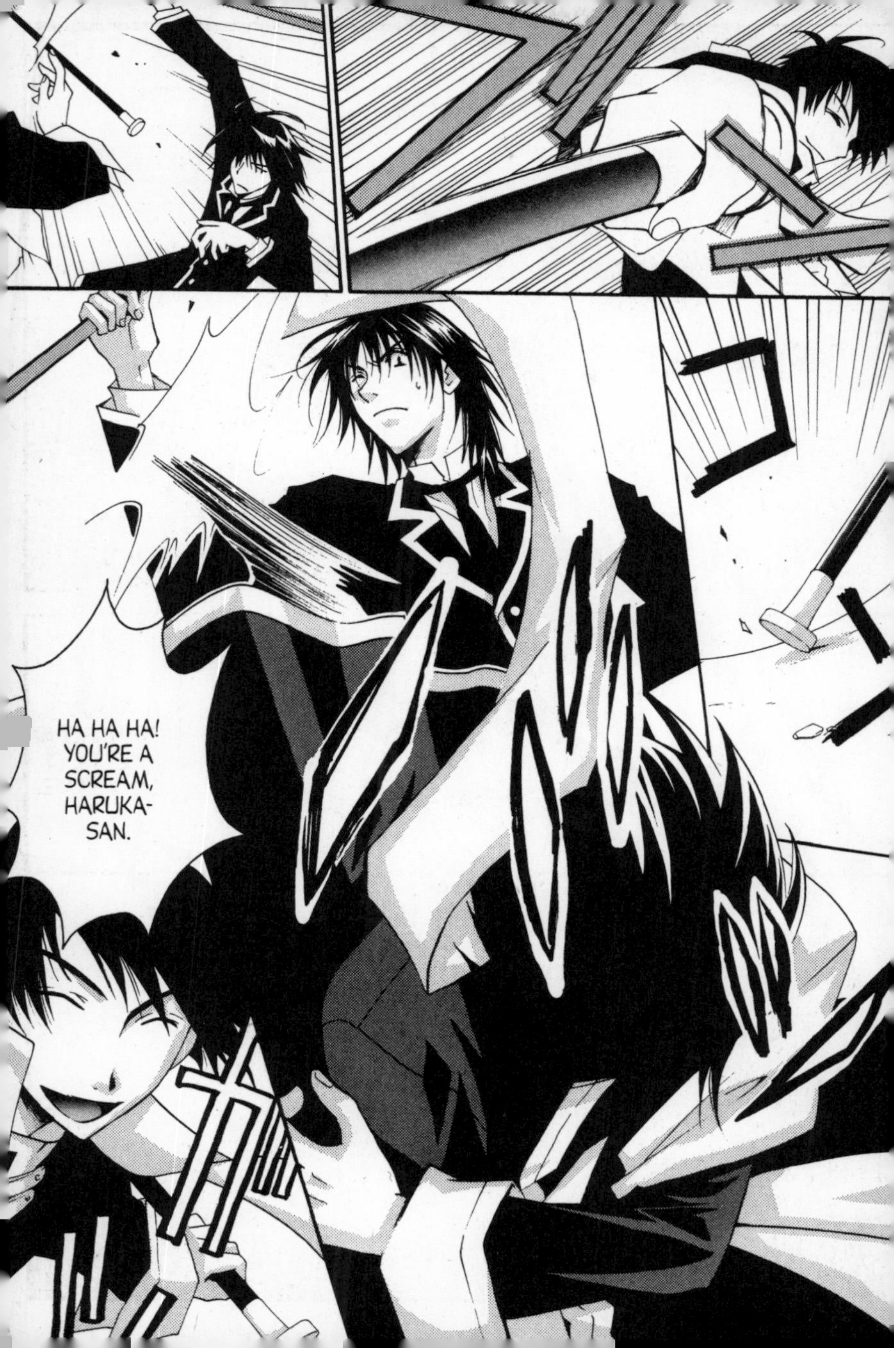
HA HA HA! YOU'RE A SCREAM, HARUKA-SAN.

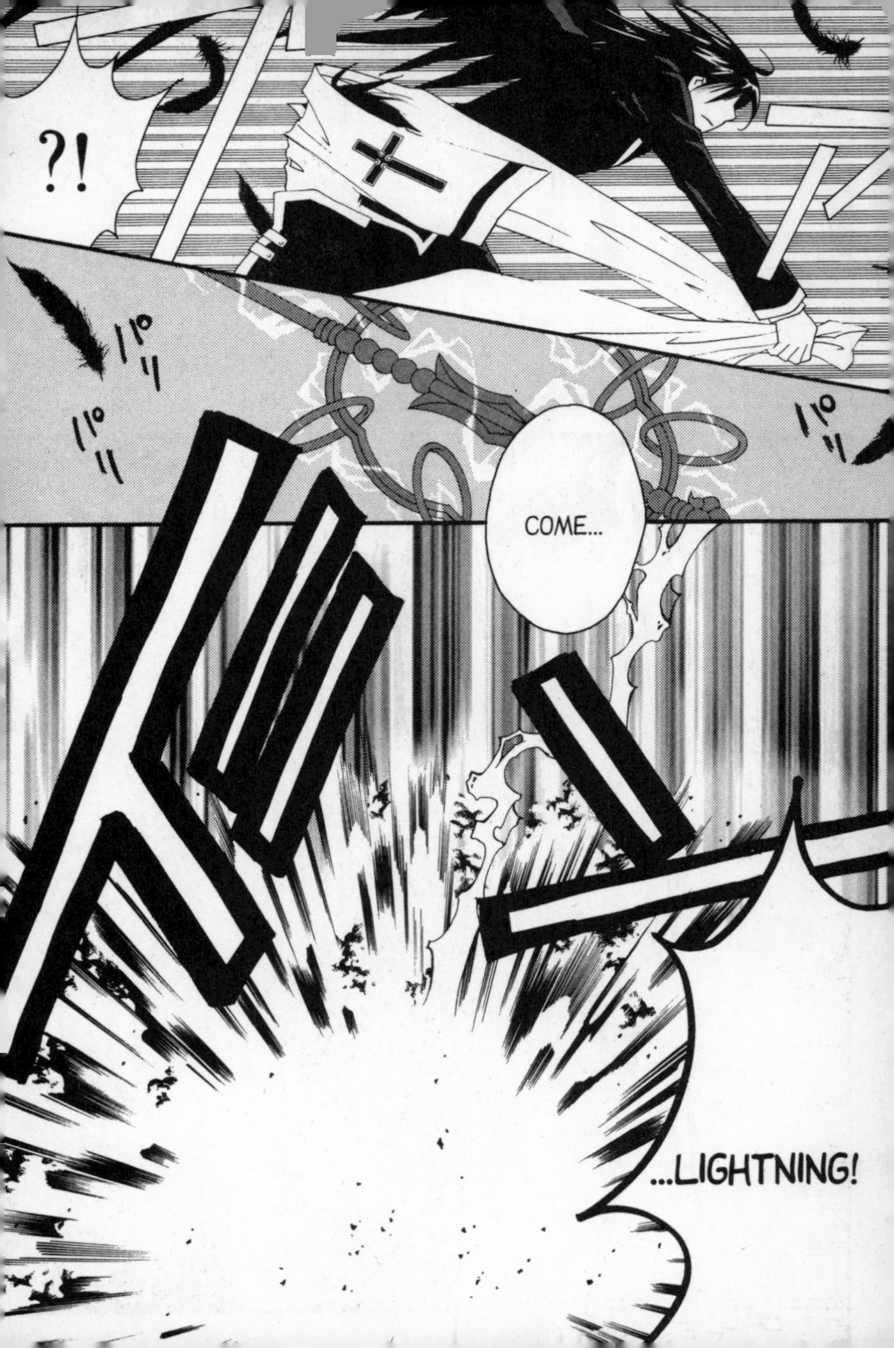
?!
パリ
パリ
パリ
COME...
...LIGHTNING!

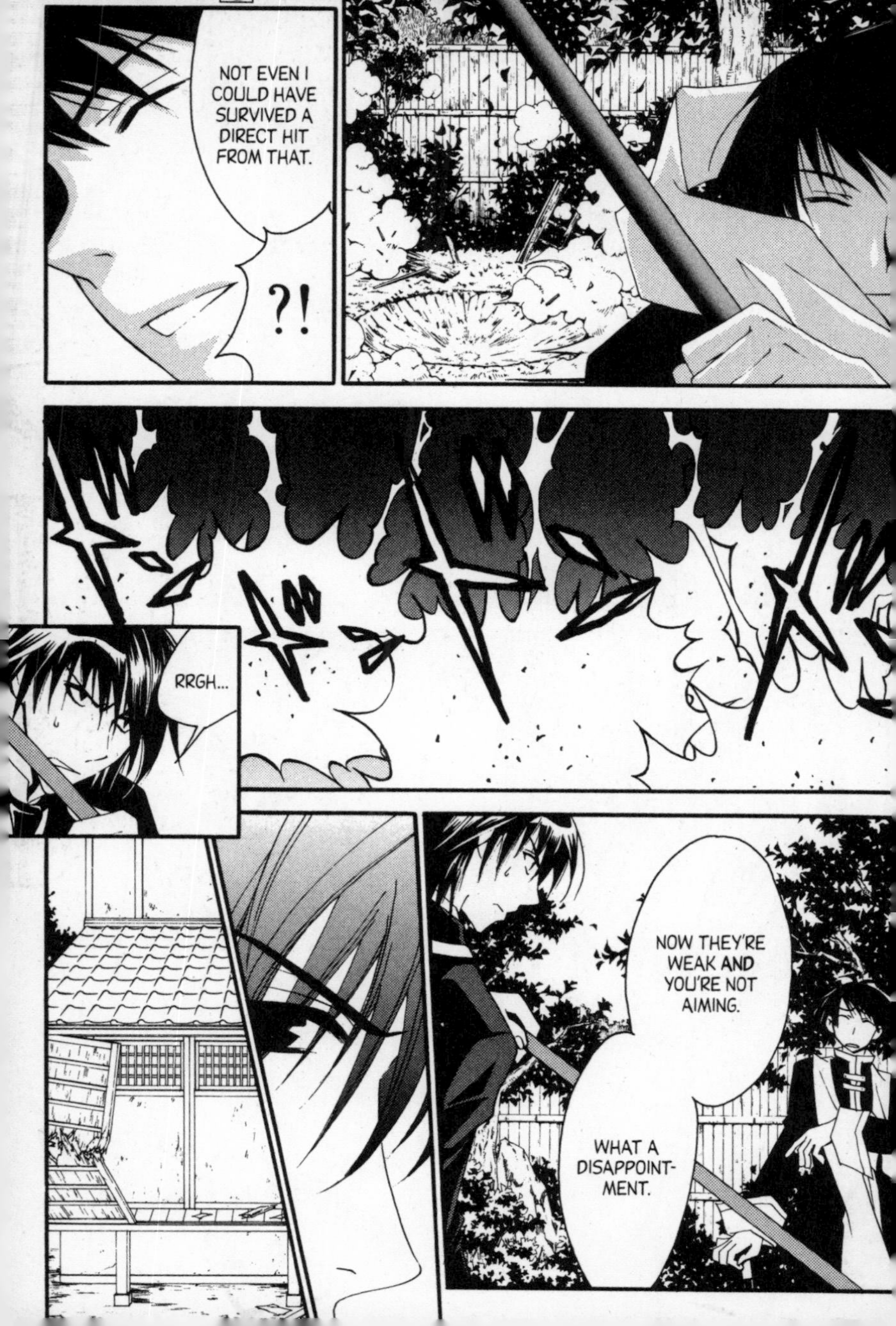
NOT EVEN I COULD HAVE SURVIVED A DIRECT HIT FROM THAT.
?!
RRGH...
NOW THEY'RE WEAK AND YOU'RE NOT AIMING.
WHAT A DISAPPOINTMENT.

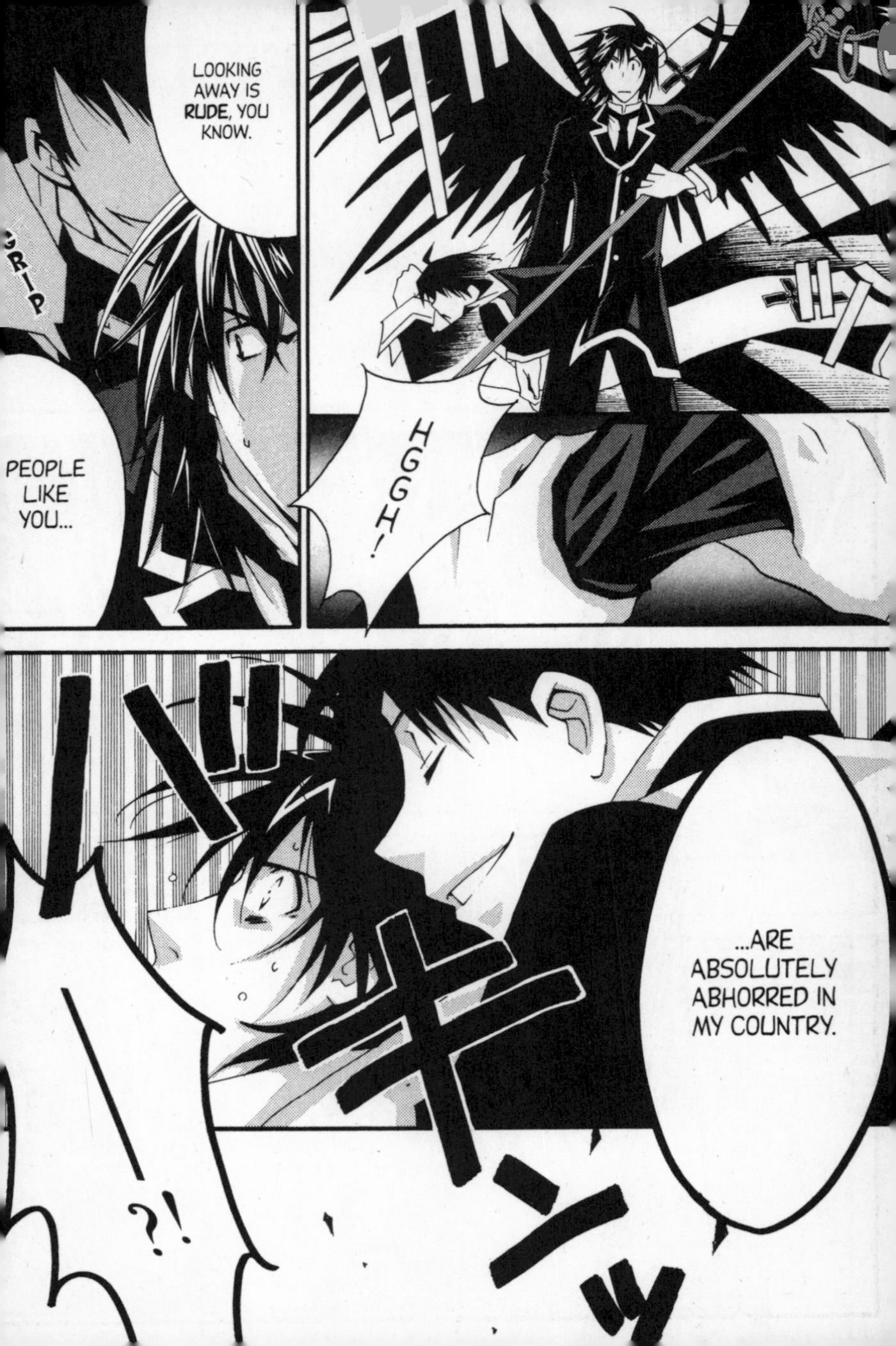
HGGH!
LOOKING AWAY IS RUDE, YOU KNOW.
GRIP
PEOPLE LIKE YOU...
...ARE ABSOLUTELY ABHORRED IN MY COUNTRY.
?!

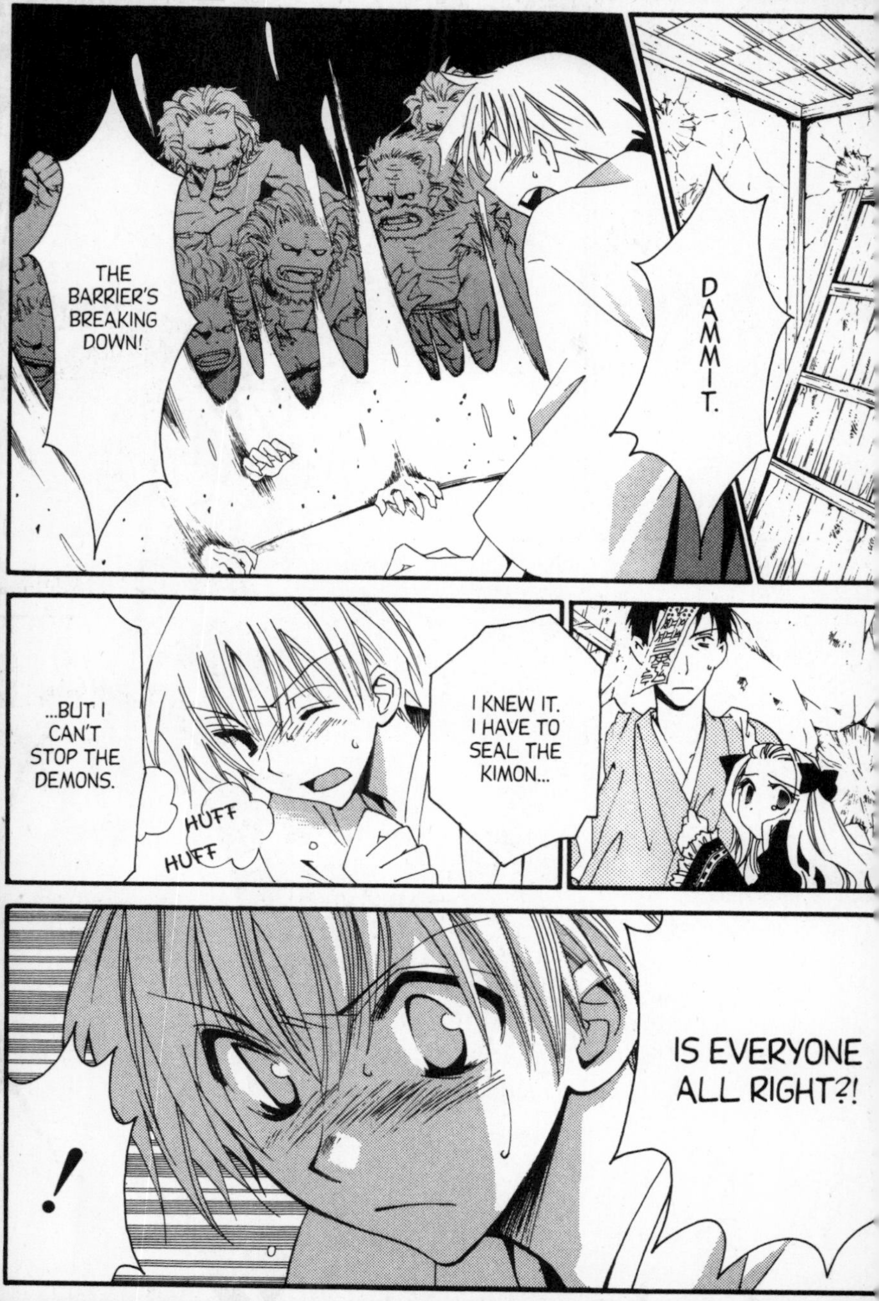
DAMMIT.
THE BARRIER'S BREAKING DOWN!
I KNEW IT. I HAVE TO SEAL THE KIMON...
...BUT I CAN'T STOP THE DEMONS.
HUFF HUFF
IS EVERYONE ALL RIGHT?!
!

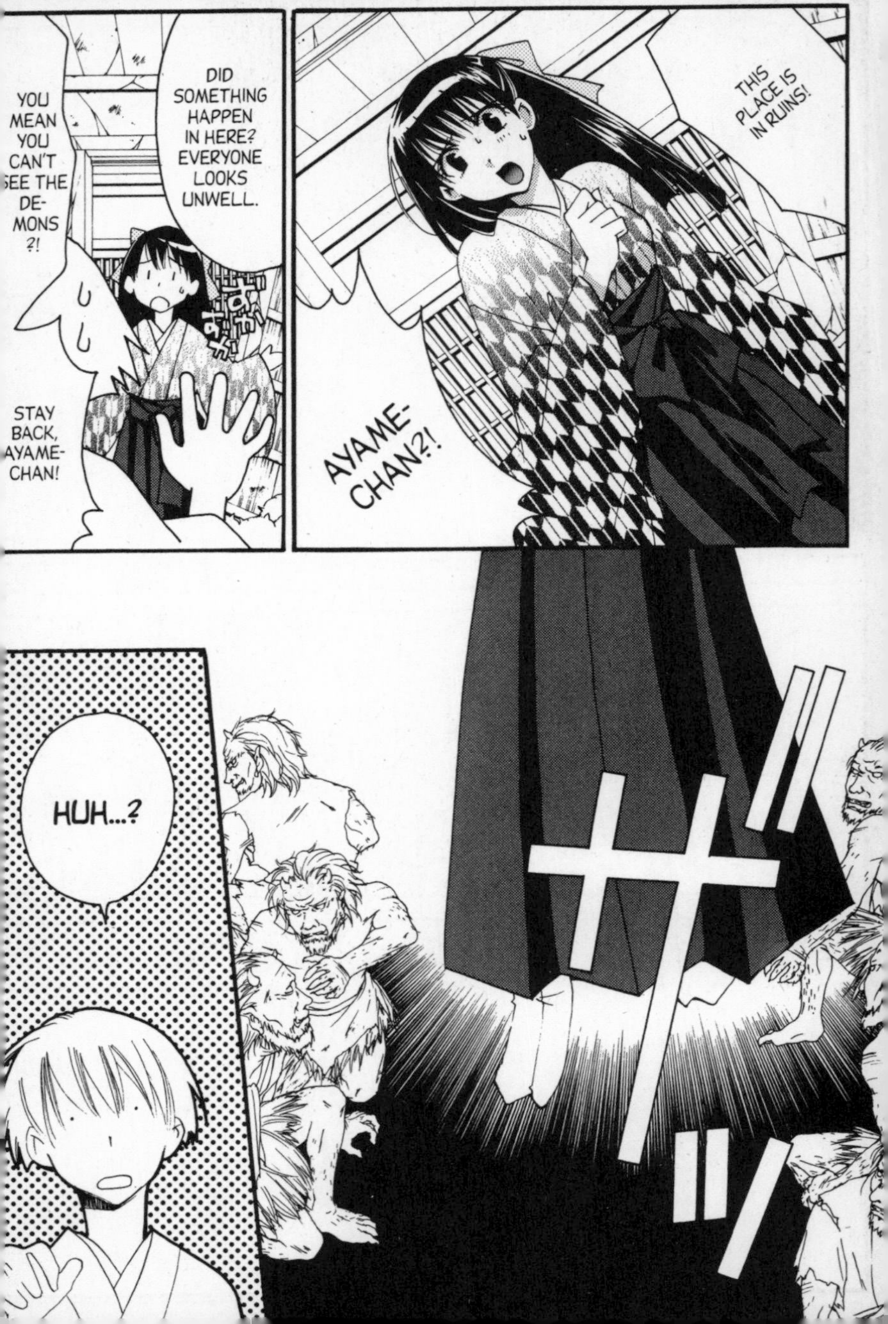
THIS PLACE IS IN RUINS!
AYAME-CHAN?!
DID SOMETHING HAPPEN IN HERE? EVERYONE LOOKS UNWELL.
YOU MEAN YOU CAN'T SEE THE DEMONS?!
STAY BACK, AYAME-CHAN!
HUH...?

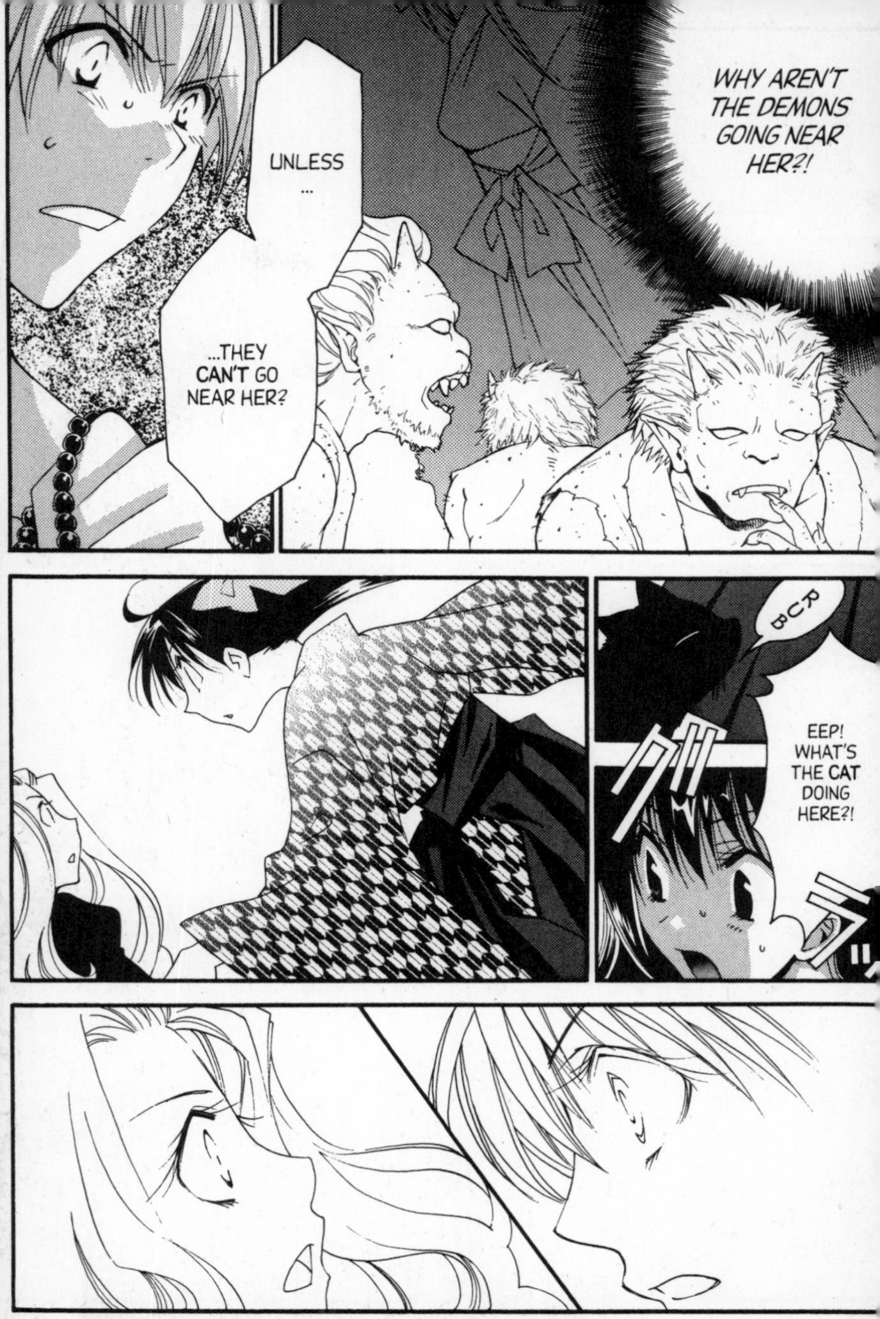
WHY AREN'T THE DEMONS GOING NEAR HER?!
UNLESS ...
...THEY CAN'T GO NEAR HER?
BCR
EEP! WHAT'S THE CAT DOING HERE?!

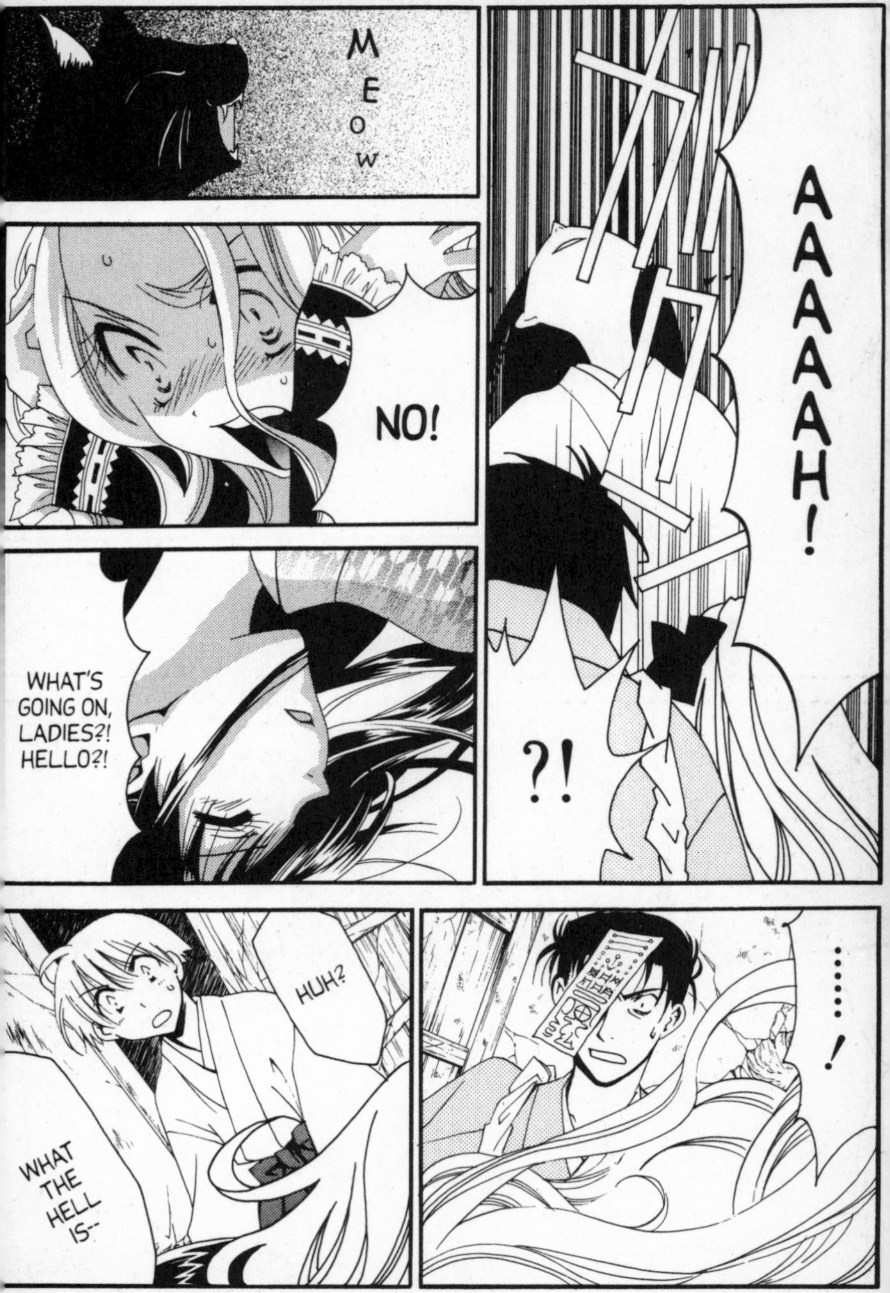
AAAAAH!
?!
MEOW
NO!
WHAT'S GOING ON, LADIES?! HELLO?!
.....!
HUH?
WHAT THE HELL IS-

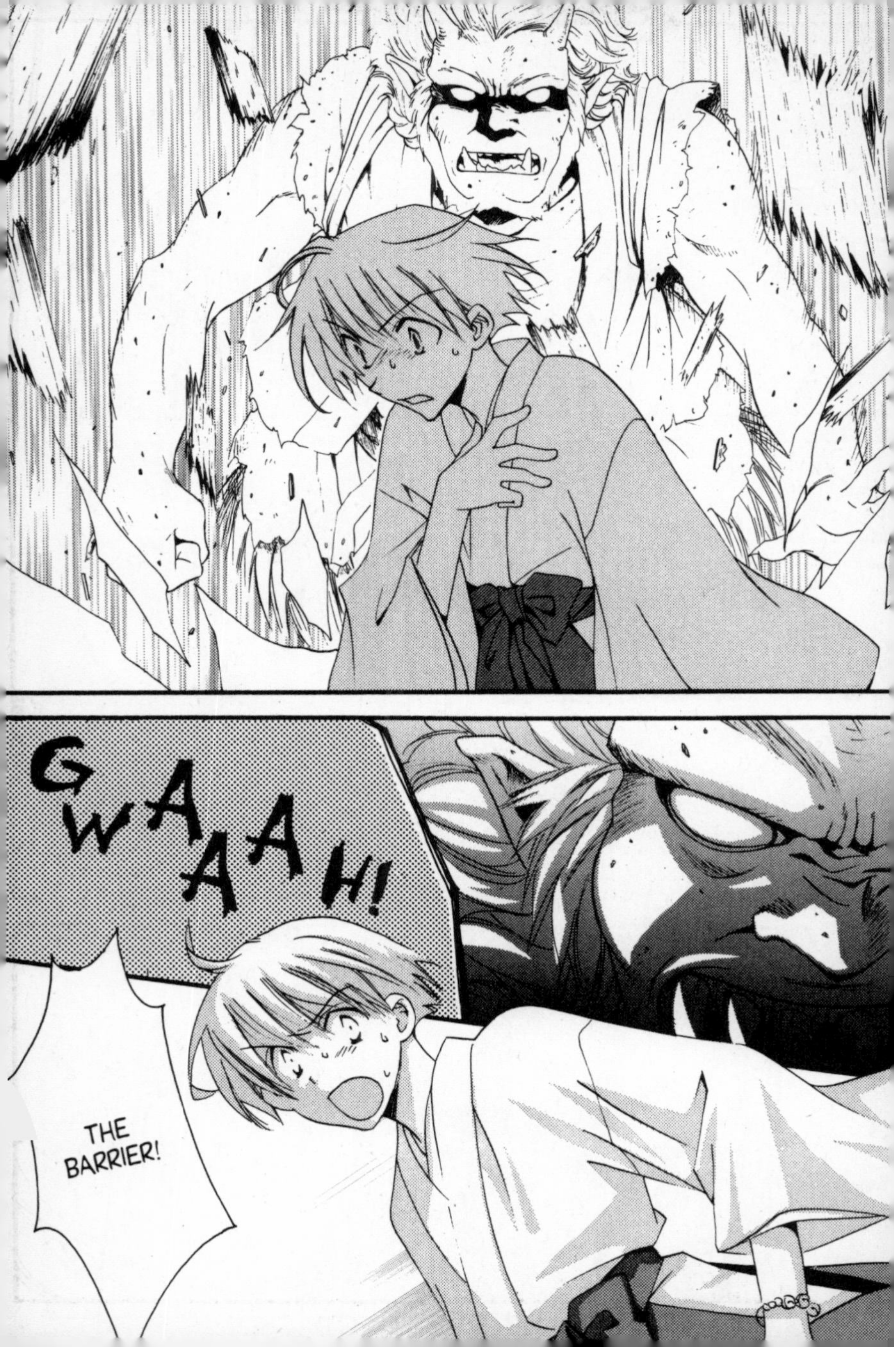
GWAAAH!
THE BARRIER!

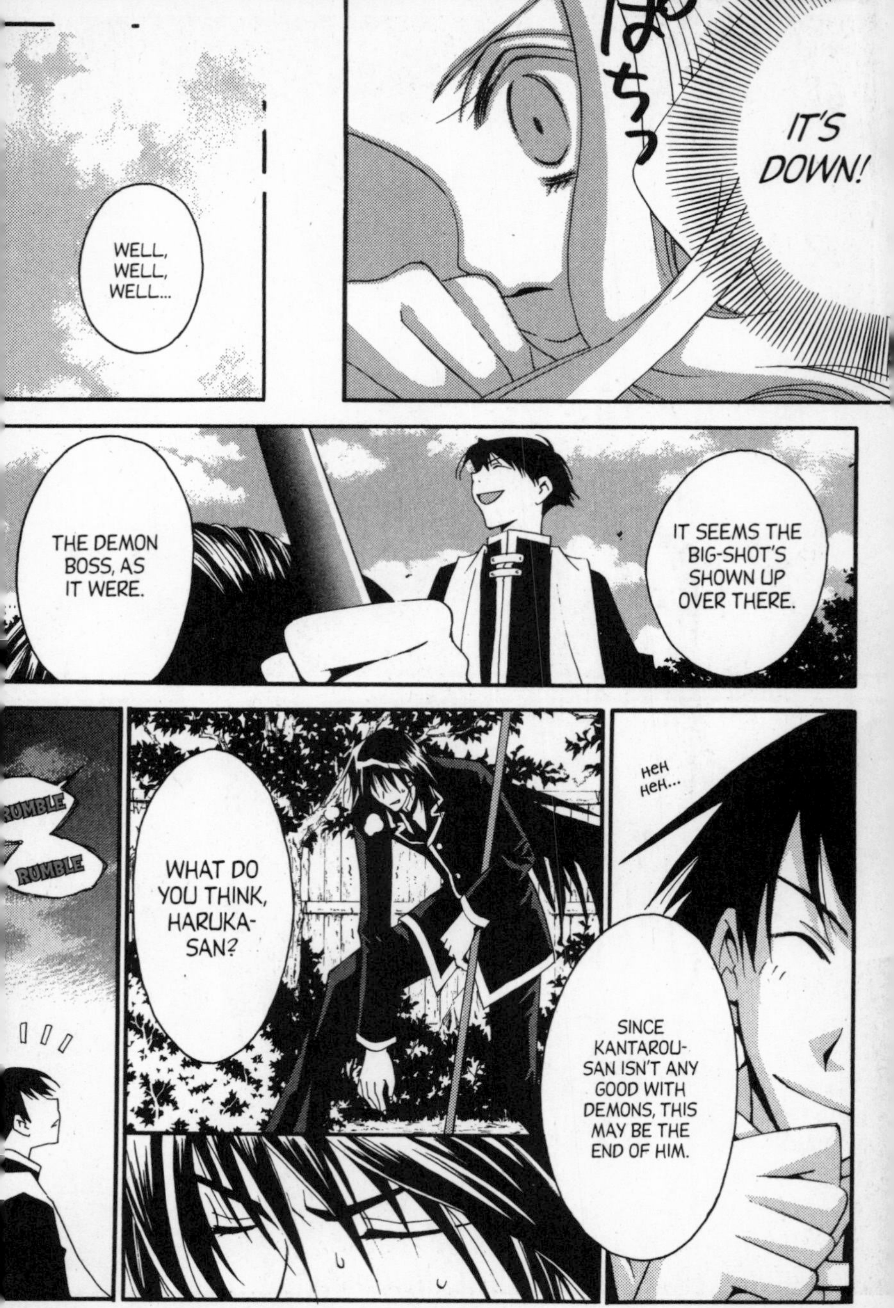
ぱちっ
IT'S DOWN!
WELL, WELL, WELL...
IT SEEMS THE BIG-SHOT'S SHOWN UP OVER THERE.
THE DEMON BOSS, AS IT WERE.
HEH HEH...
SINCE KANTAROU-SAN ISN'T ANY GOOD WITH DEMONS, THIS MAY BE THE END OF HIM.
WHAT DO YOU THINK, HARUKA-SAN?
RUMBLE
RUMBLE

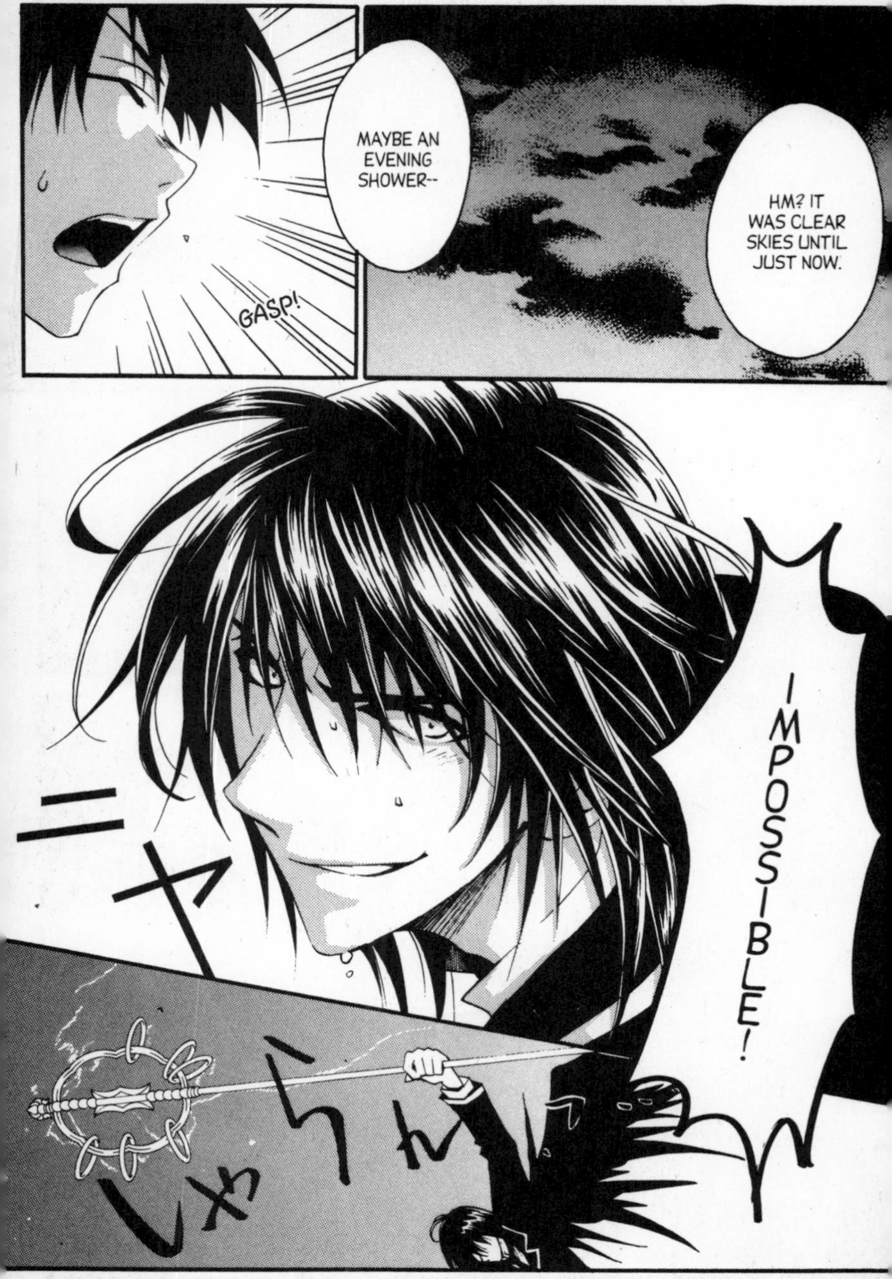
HM? IT WAS CLEAR SKIES UNTIL JUST NOW.
MAYBE AN EVENING SHOWER--
GASP!
IMPOSSIBLE!

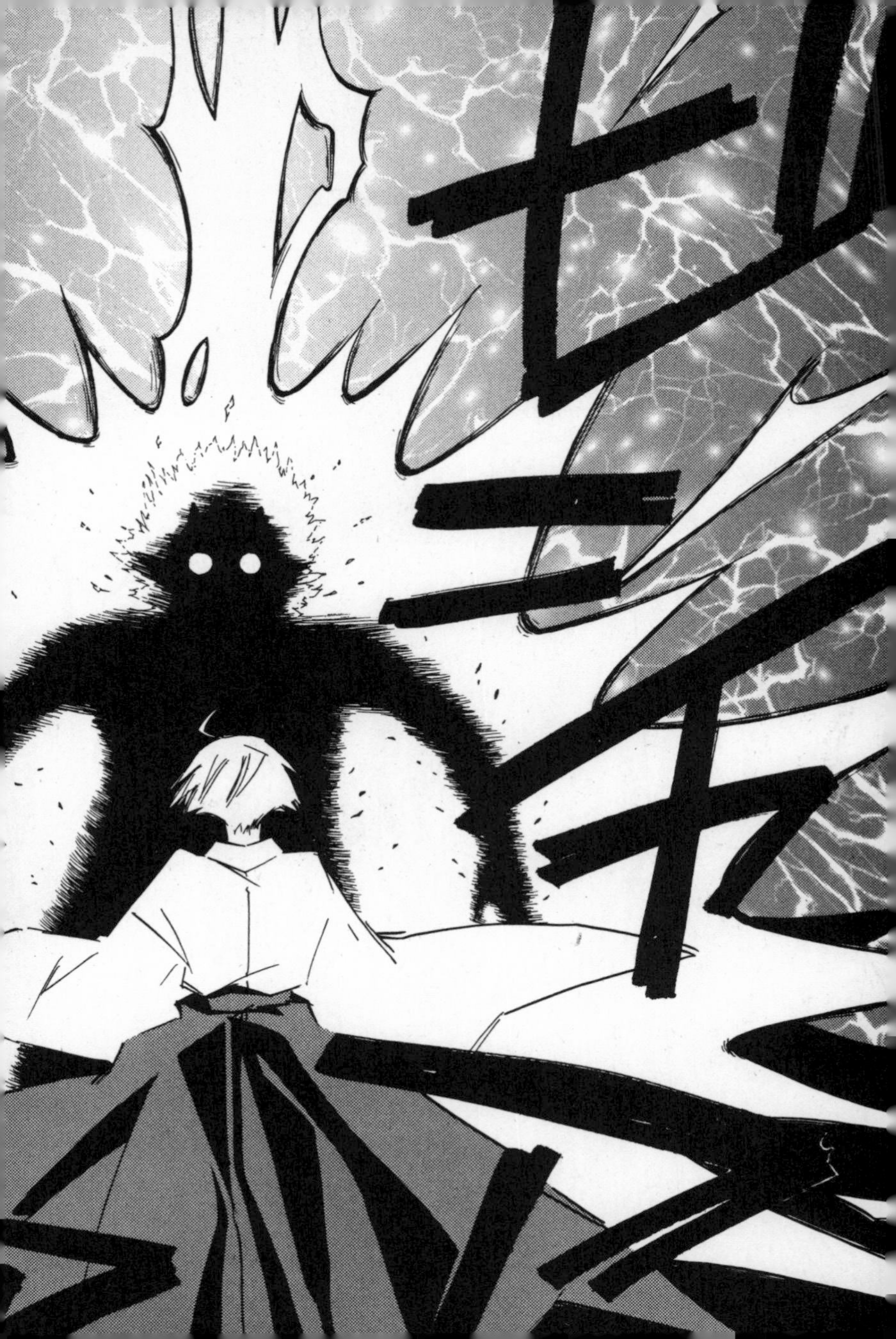

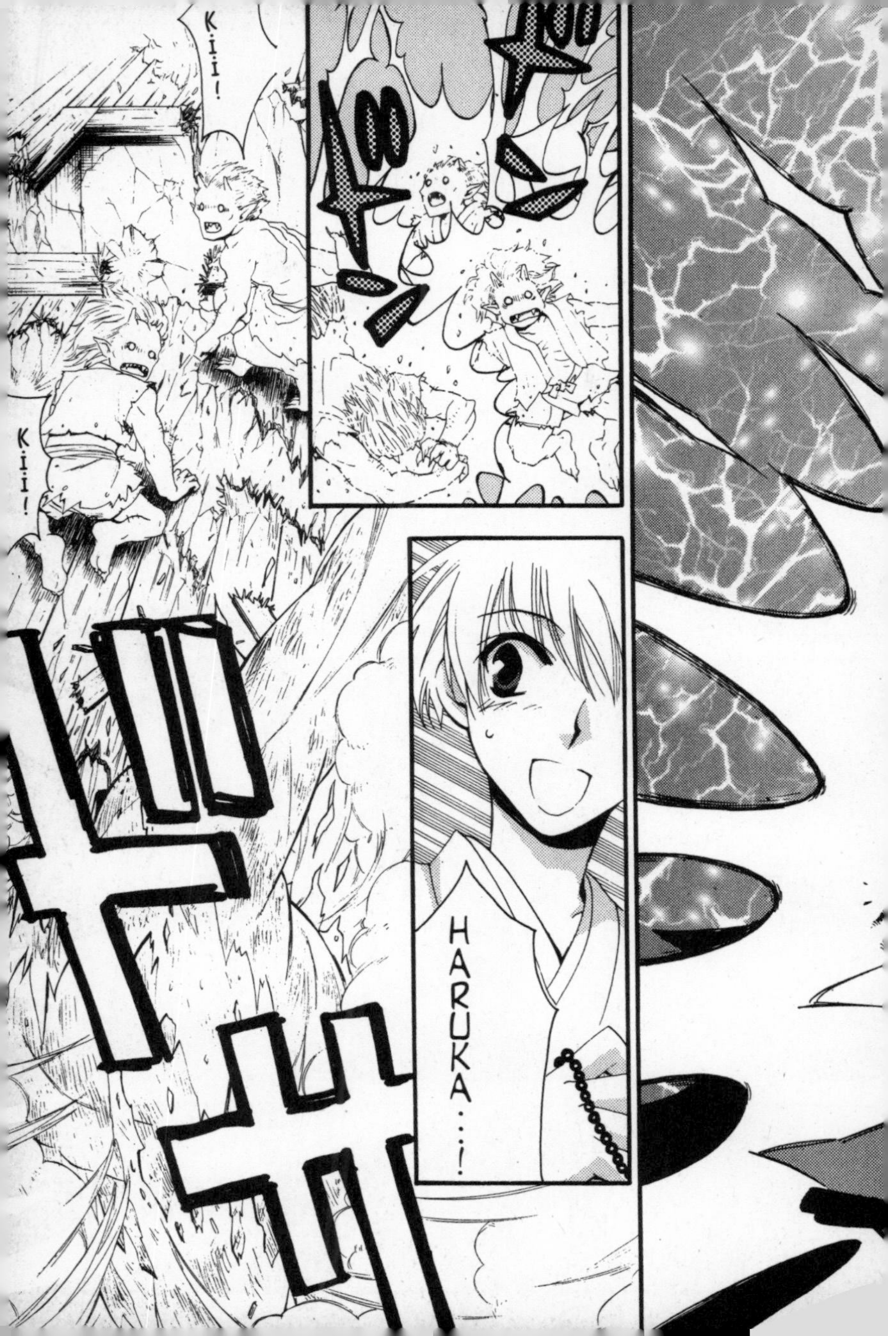
HARUKA...!
K-I-I!
K-I-I!

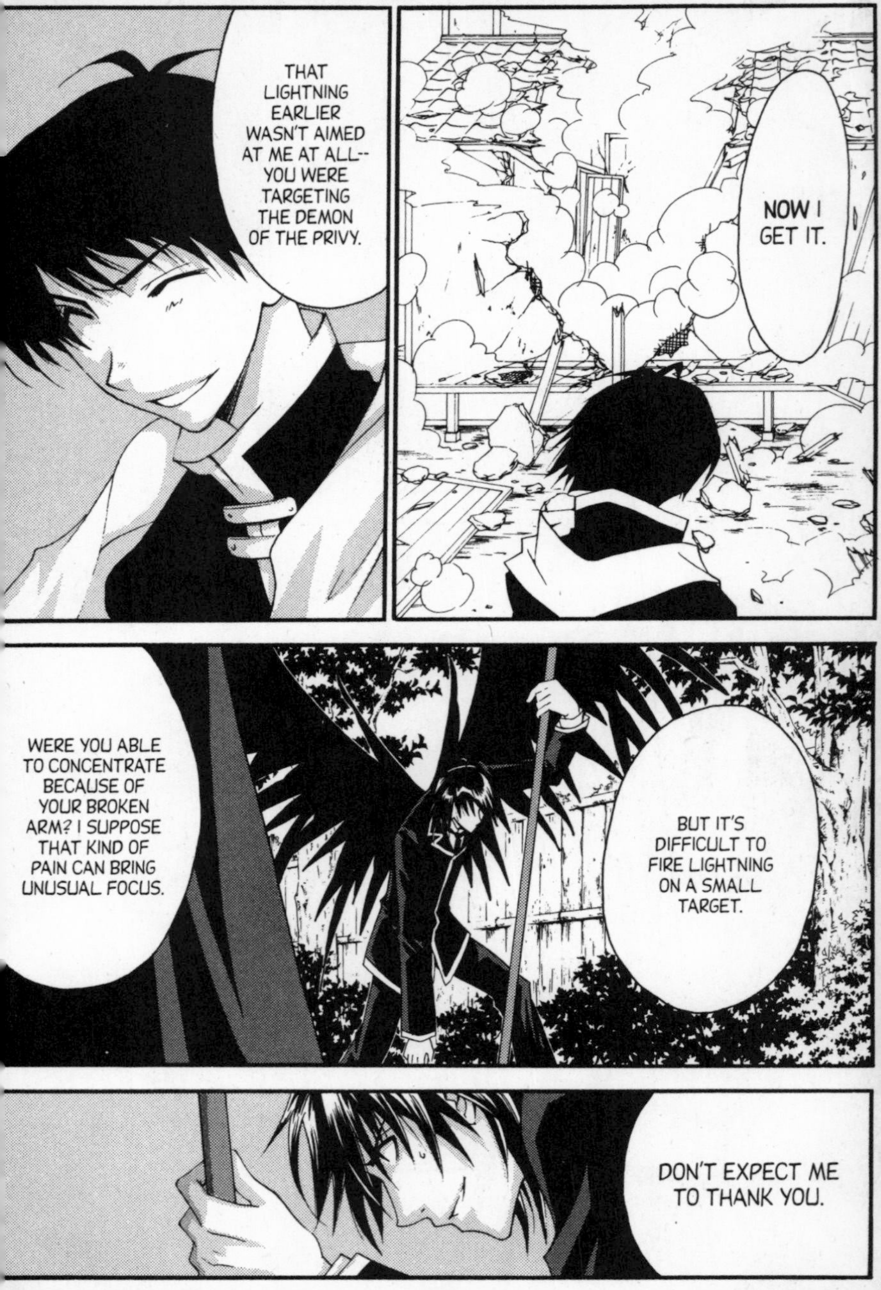
NOW I GET IT.
THAT LIGHTNING EARLIER WASN'T AIMED AT ME AT ALL-- YOU WERE TARGETING THE DEMON OF THE PRIVY.
BUT IT'S DIFFICULT TO FIRE LIGHTNING ON A SMALL TARGET.
WERE YOU ABLE TO CONCENTRATE BECAUSE OF YOUR BROKEN ARM? I SUPPOSE THAT KIND OF PAIN CAN BRING UNUSUAL FOCUS.
DON'T EXPECT ME TO THANK YOU.

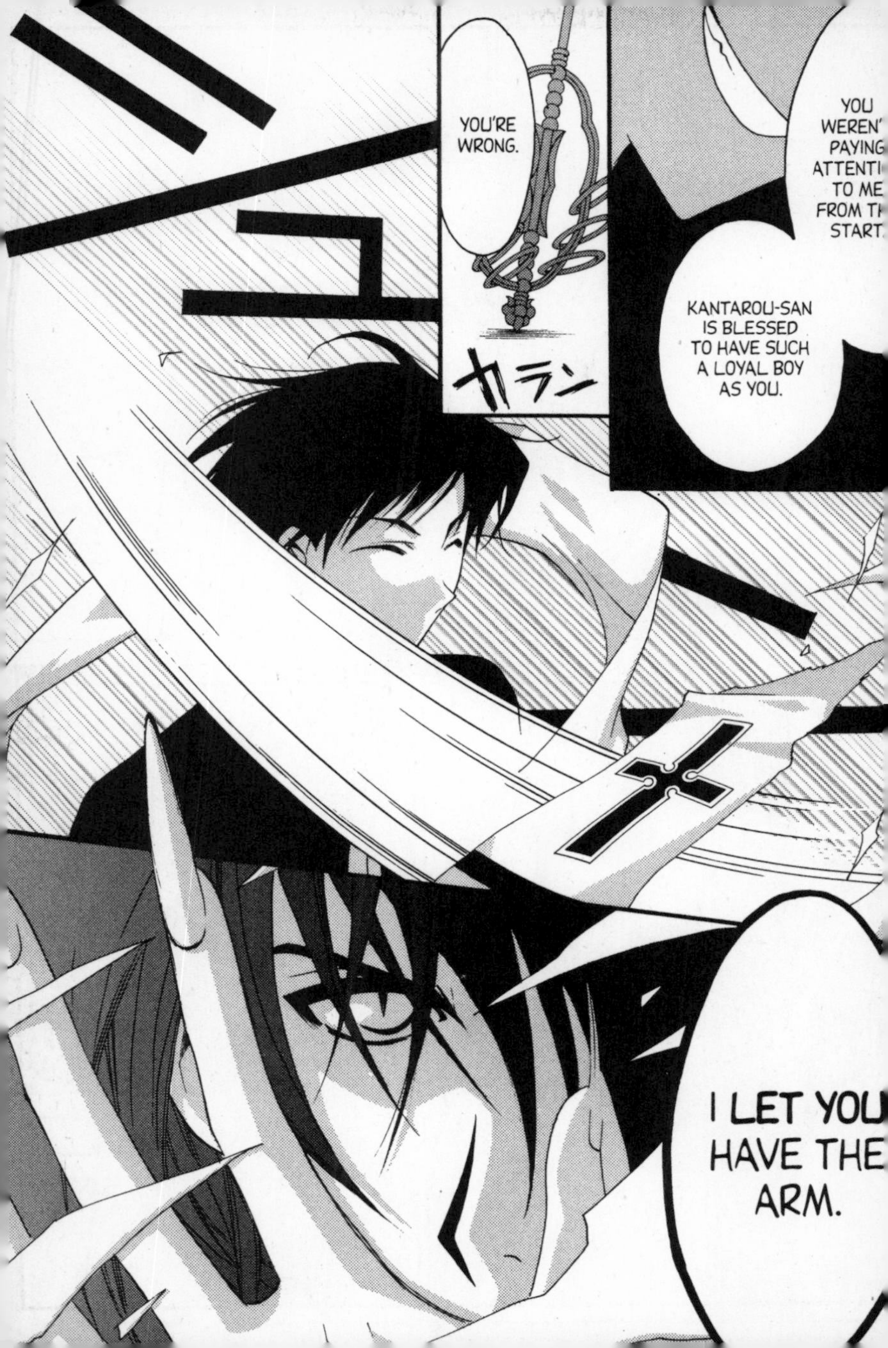
YOU WEREN' PAYING ATTENTI TO ME FROM TH START.
KANTAROU-SAN IS BLESSED TO HAVE SUCH A LOYAL BOY AS YOU.
YOU'RE WRONG.
カラン
I LET YOU HAVE THE ARM.

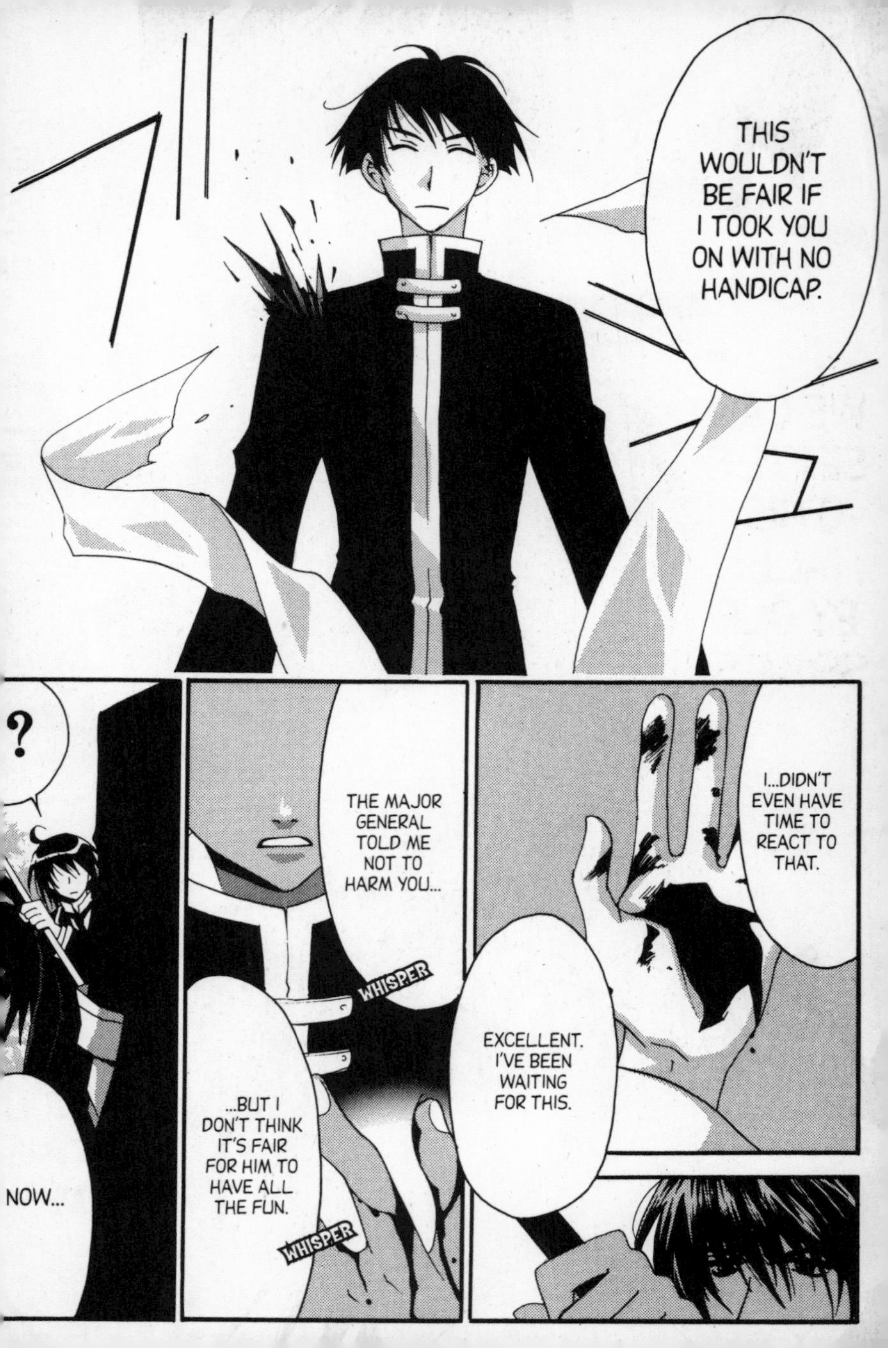
THIS WOULDN'T BE FAIR IF I TOOK YOU ON WITH NO HANDICAP.
I...DIDN'T EVEN HAVE TIME TO REACT TO THAT.
EXCELLENT. I'VE BEEN WAITING FOR THIS.
THE MAJOR GENERAL TOLD ME NOT TO HARM YOU...
WHISPER
...BUT I DON'T THINK IT'S FAIR FOR HIM TO HAVE ALL THE FUN.
WHISPER
?
NOW...

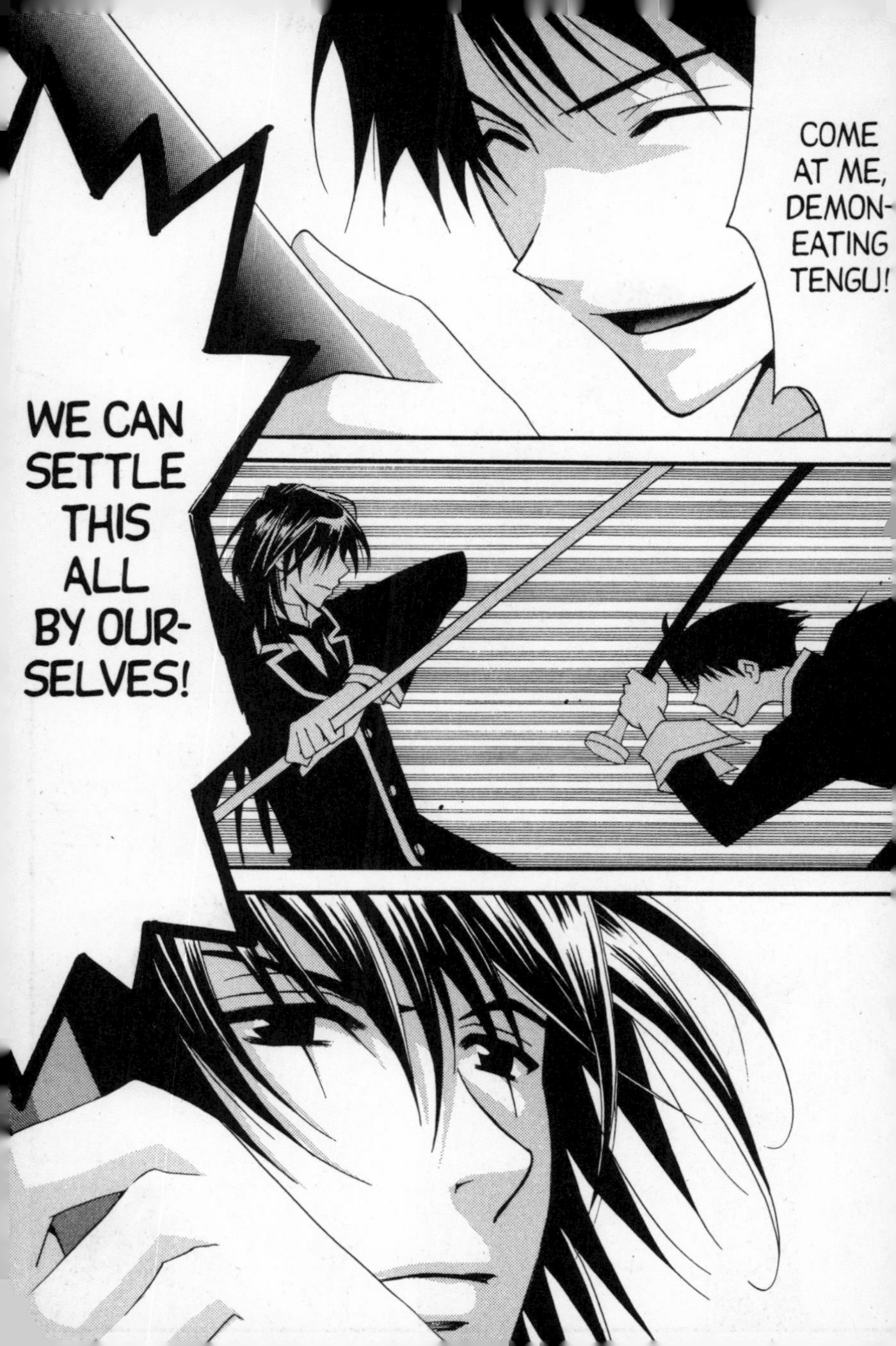
COME AT ME, DEMON-EATING TENGU!
WE CAN SETTLE THIS ALL BY OURSELVES!

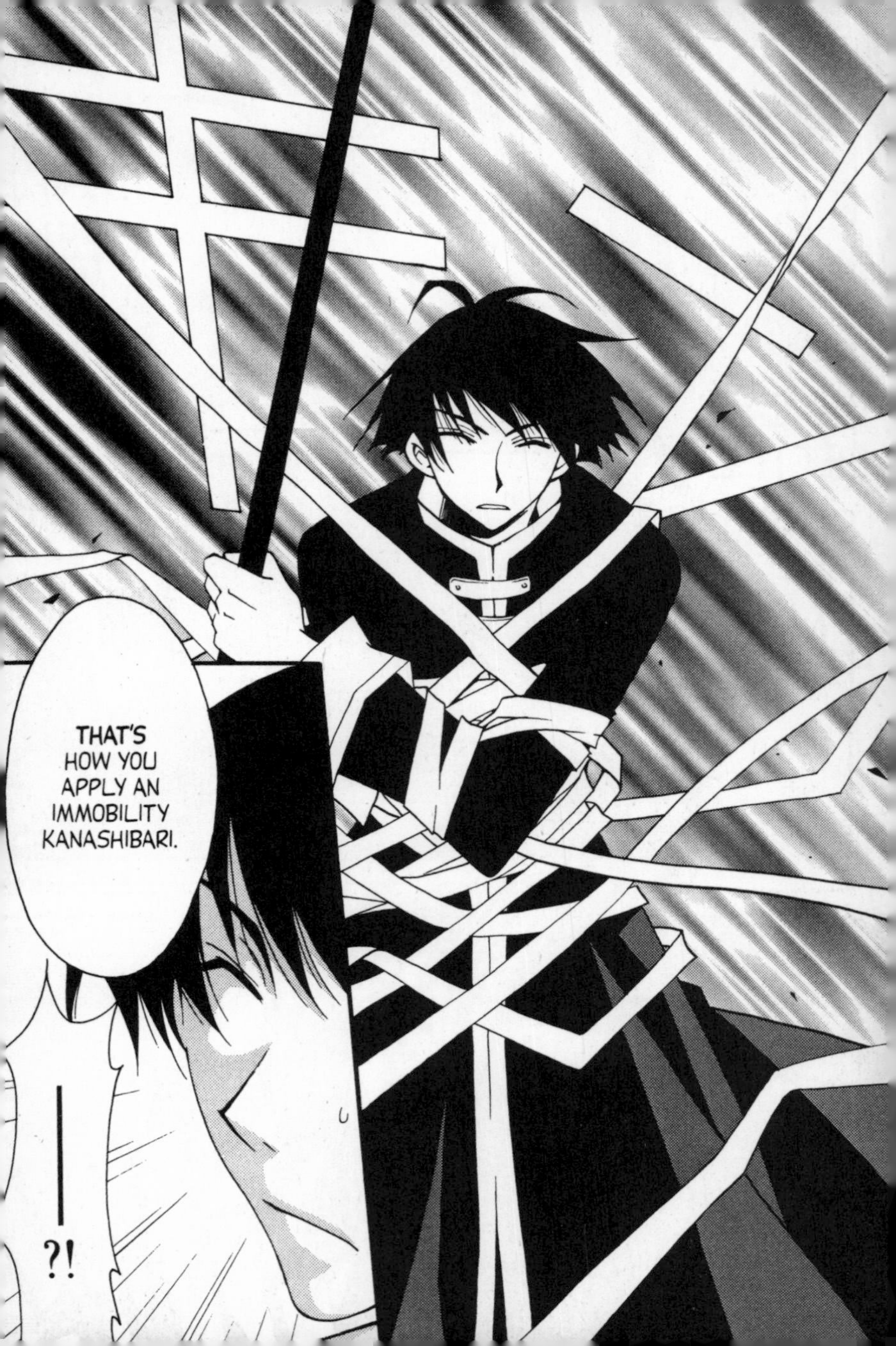
THAT'S HOW YOU APPLY AN IMMOBILITY KANASHIBARI.
— — ?!

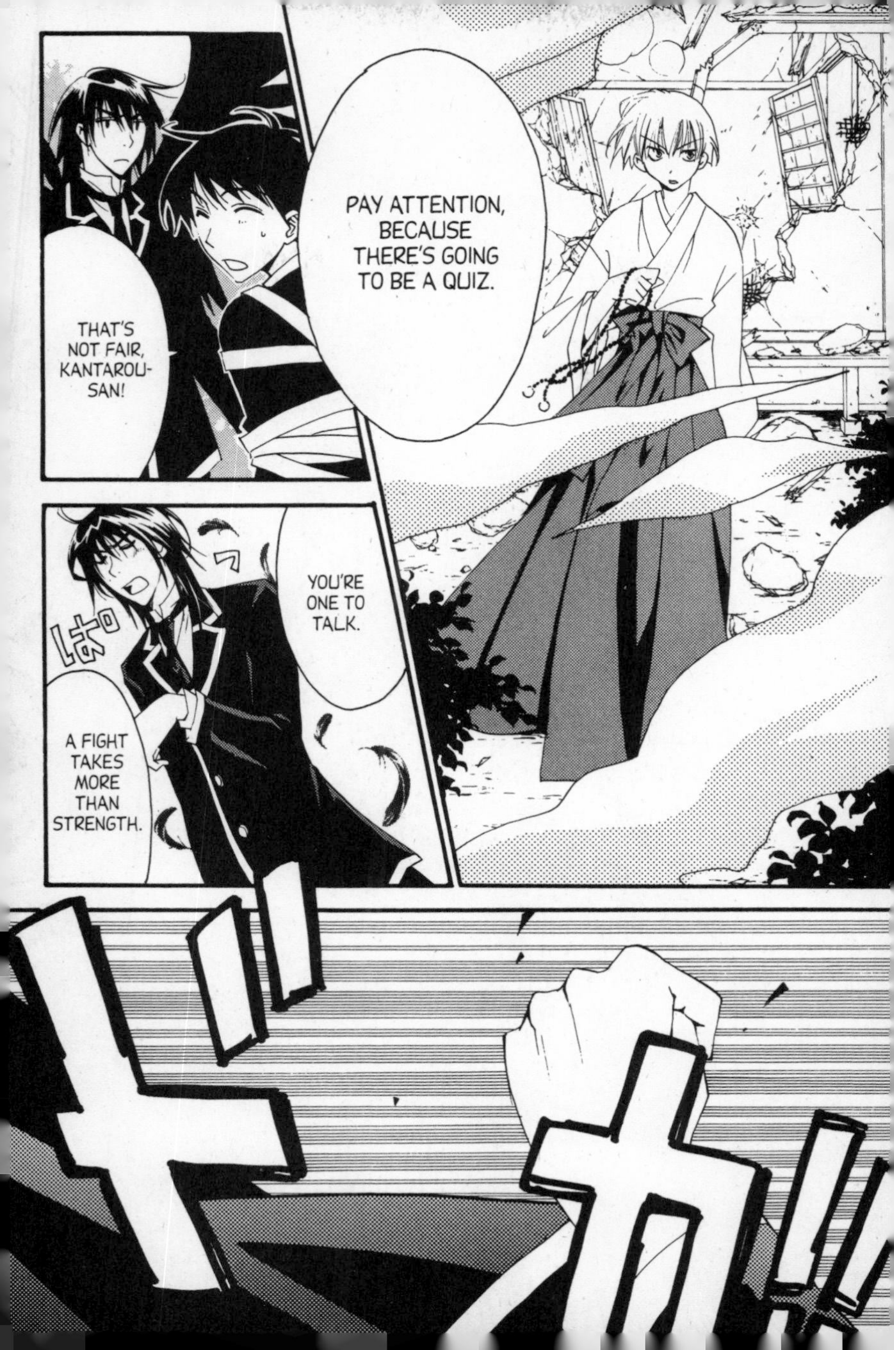
PAY ATTENTION, BECAUSE THERE'S GOING TO BE A QUIZ.
THAT'S NOT FAIR, KANTAROU-SAN!
YOU'RE ONE TO TALK.
A FIGHT TAKES MORE THAN STRENGTH.

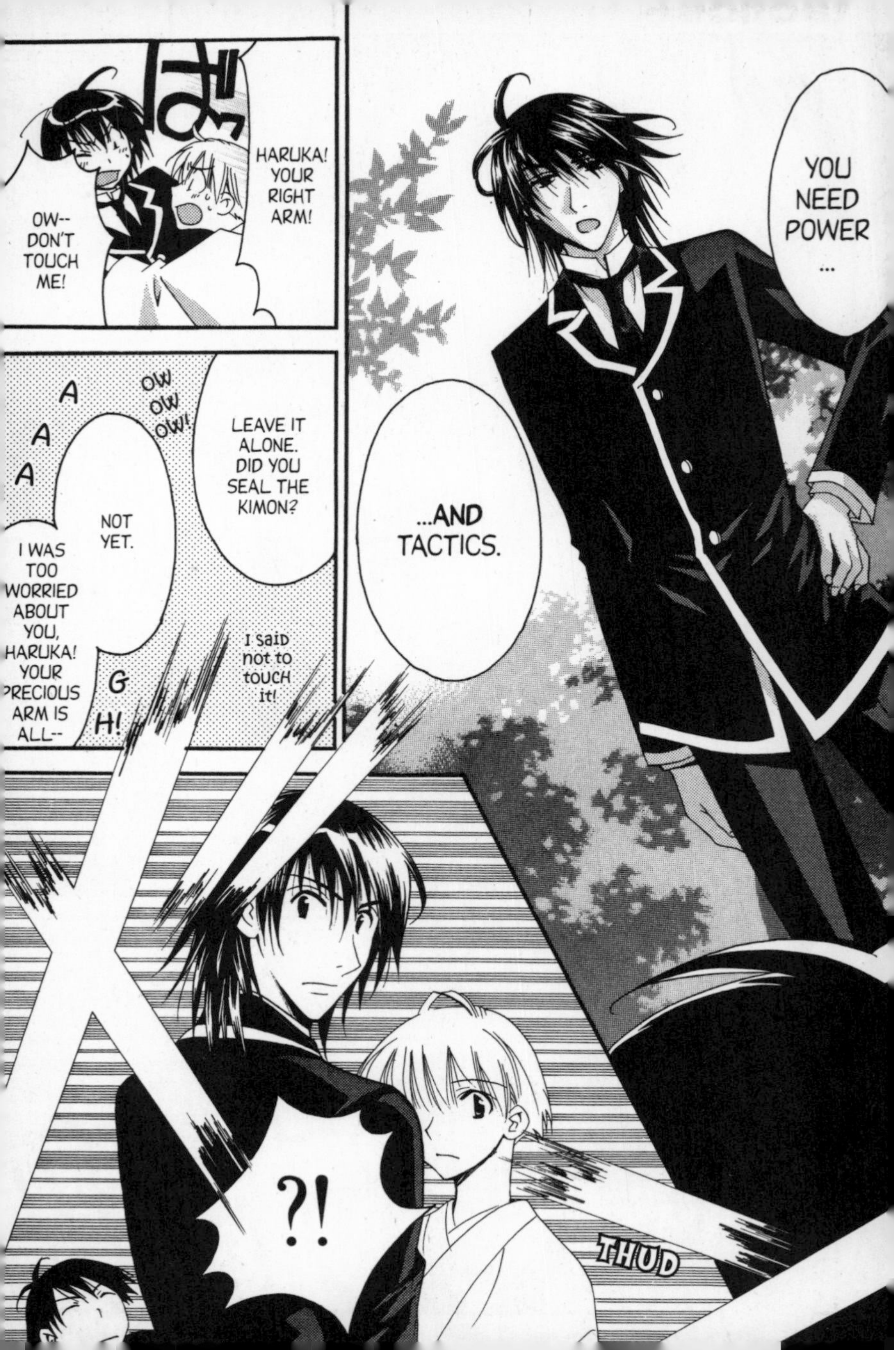
YOU NEED POWER ...
...AND TACTICS.
ばっ
HARUKA! YOUR RIGHT ARM!
OW-- DON'T TOUCH ME!
LEAVE IT ALONE. DID YOU SEAL THE KIMON?
OW OW OW!
NOT YET.
AAAGH!
I WAS TOO WORRIED ABOUT YOU, HARUKA! YOUR PRECIOUS ARM IS ALL--
I said not to touch it!
?!
THUD

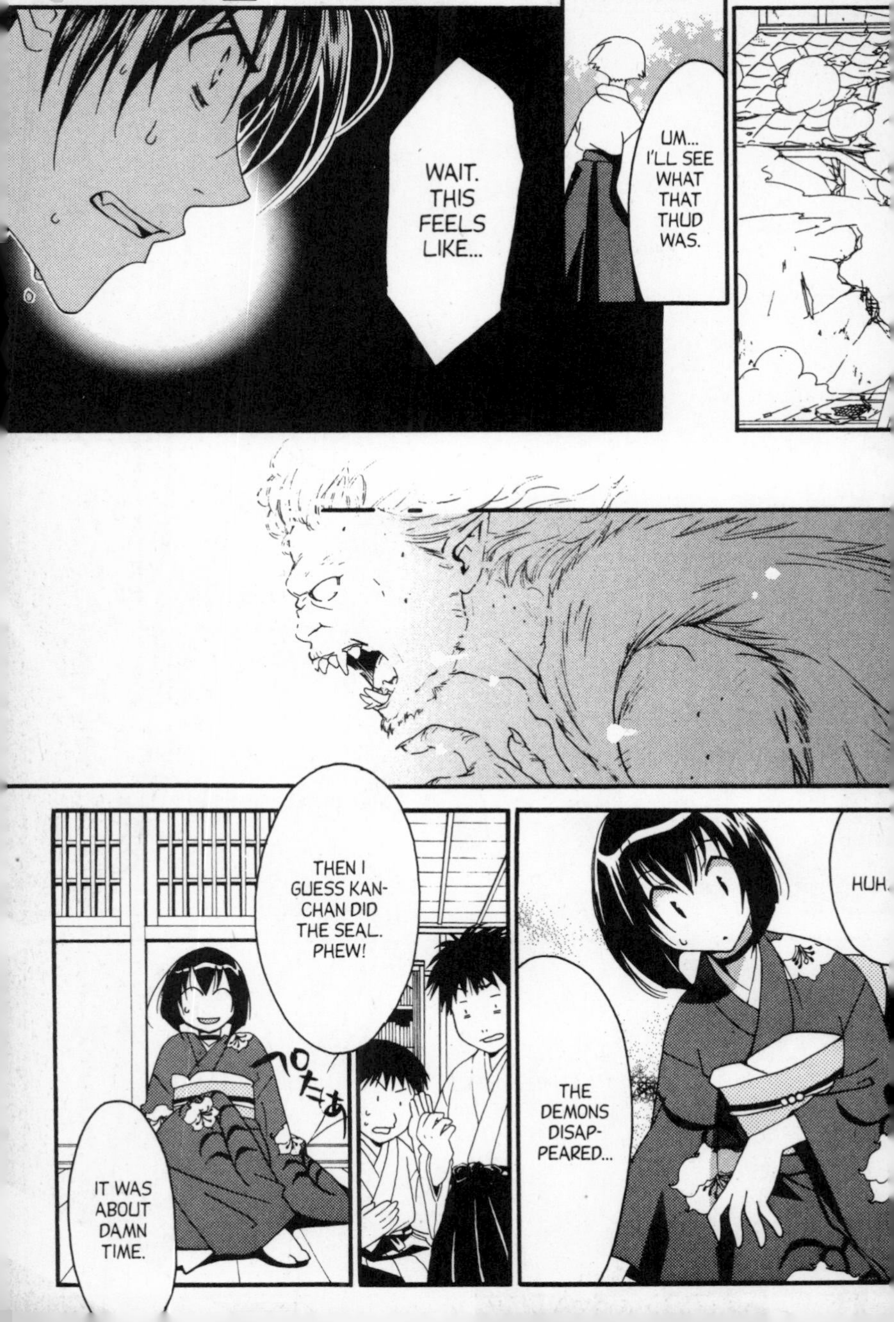
UM... I'LL SEE WHAT THAT THUD WAS.
WAIT. THIS FEELS LIKE...
HUH.
THE DEMONS DISAPPEARED...
THEN I GUESS KAN-CHAN DID THE SEAL. PHEW!
IT WAS ABOUT DAMN TIME.

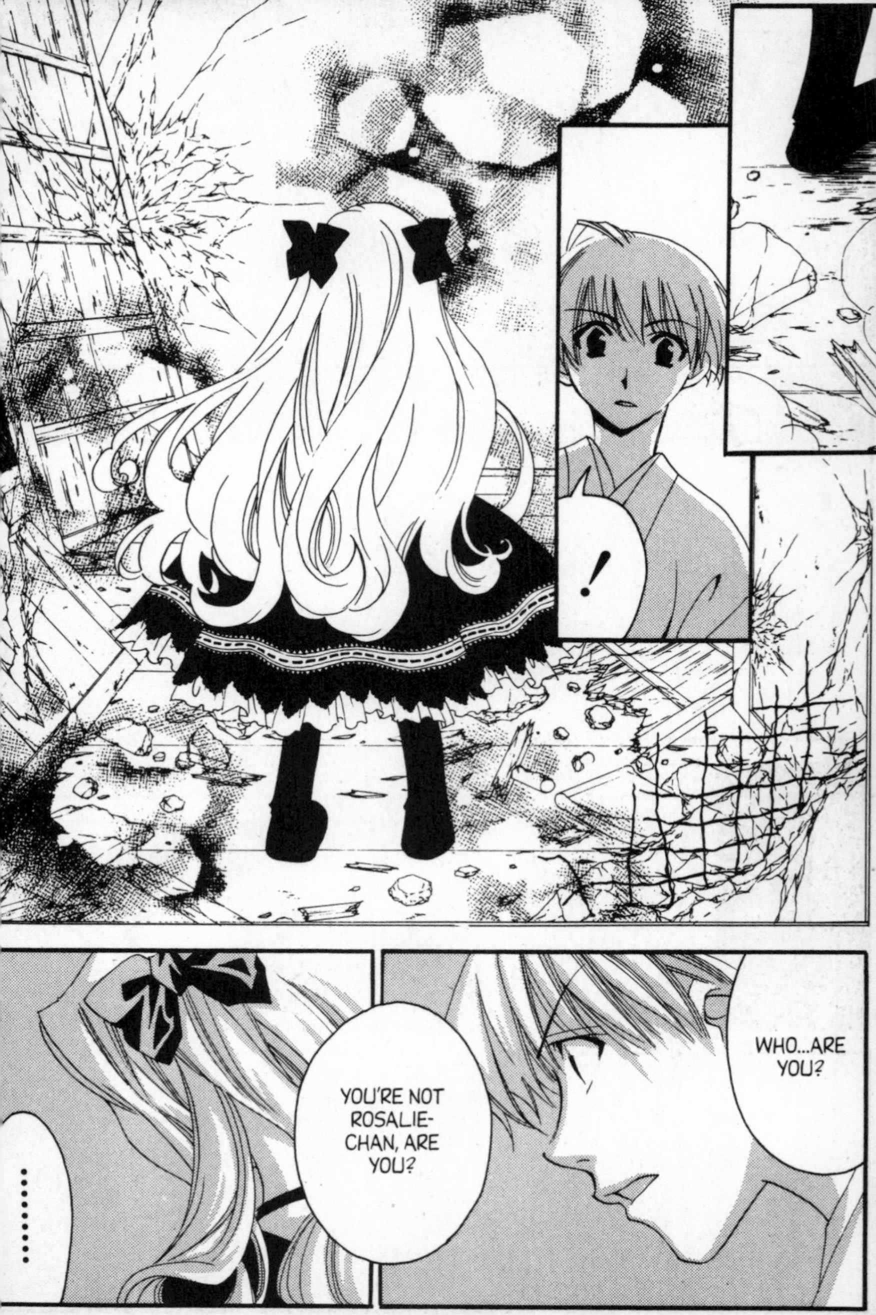
!
WHO...ARE YOU?
YOU'RE NOT ROSALIE-CHAN, ARE YOU?
....

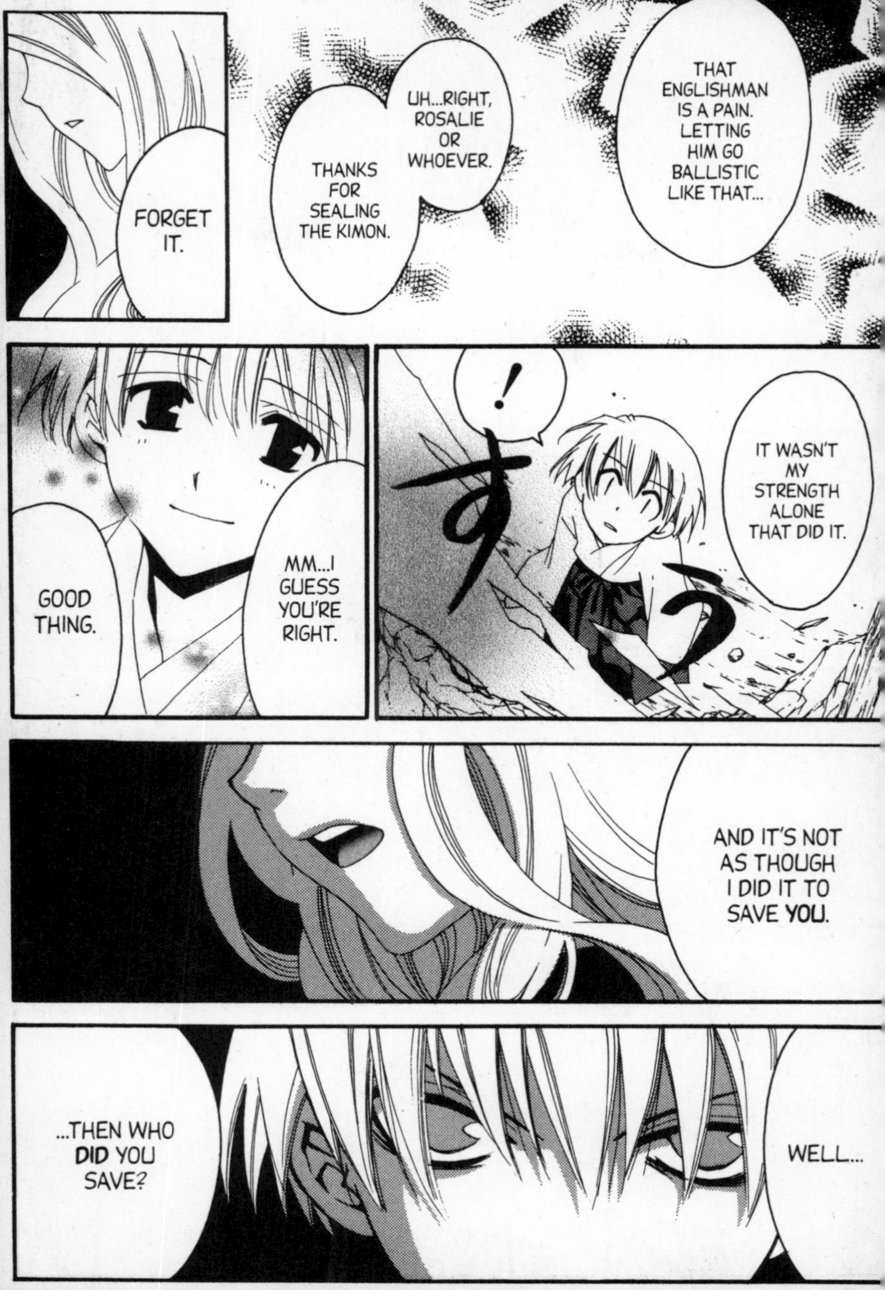
THAT ENGLISHMAN IS A PAIN. LETTING HIM GO BALLISTIC LIKE THAT...
UH...RIGHT, ROSALIE OR WHOEVER.
THANKS FOR SEALING THE KIMON.
FORGET IT.
IT WASN'T MY STRENGTH ALONE THAT DID IT.
!
すっ
MM...I GUESS YOU'RE RIGHT.
GOOD THING.
AND IT'S NOT AS THOUGH I DID IT TO SAVE **YOU**.
WELL...
...THEN WHO **DID** YOU SAVE?

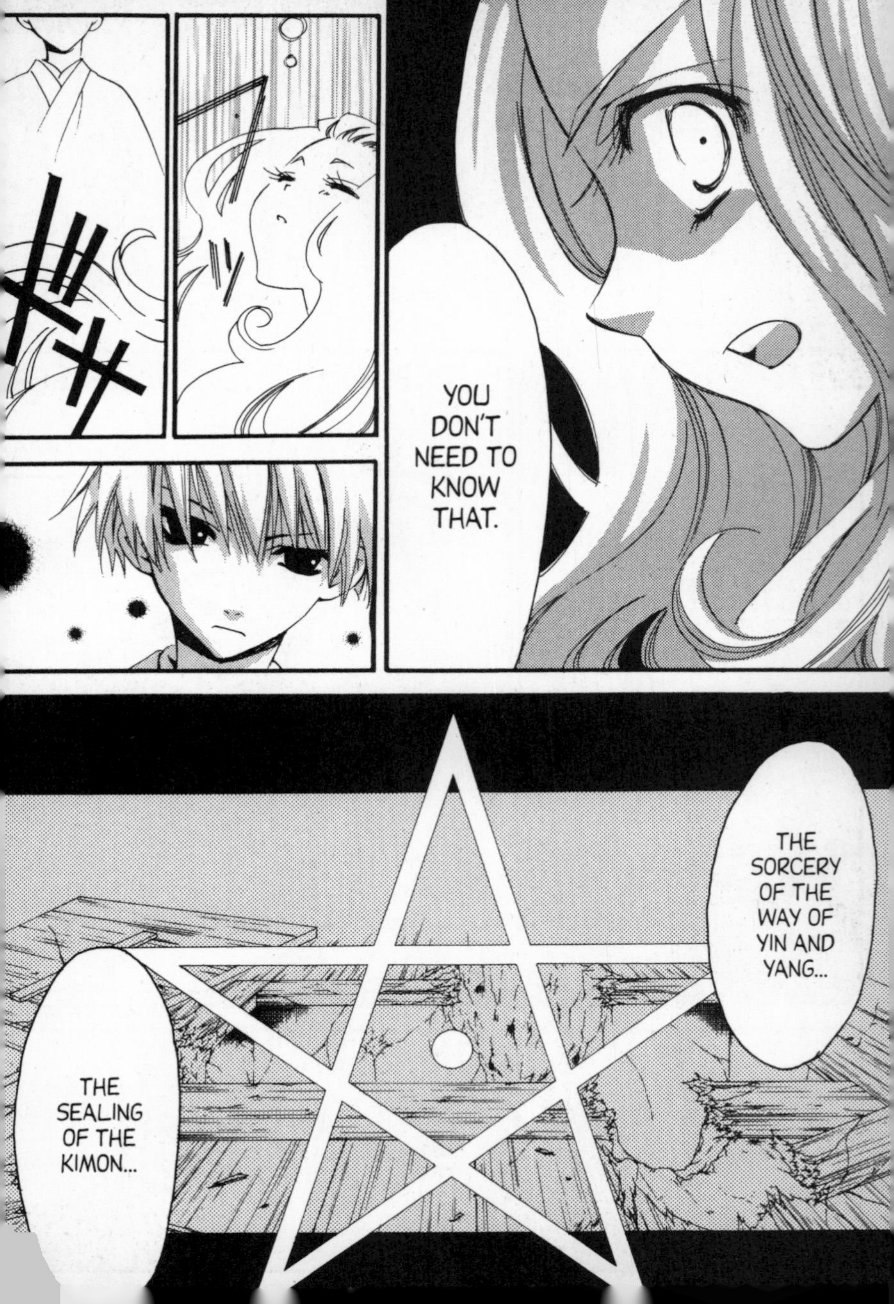
YOU DON'T NEED TO KNOW THAT.
THE SORCERY OF THE WAY OF YIN AND YANG...
THE SEALING OF THE KIMON...

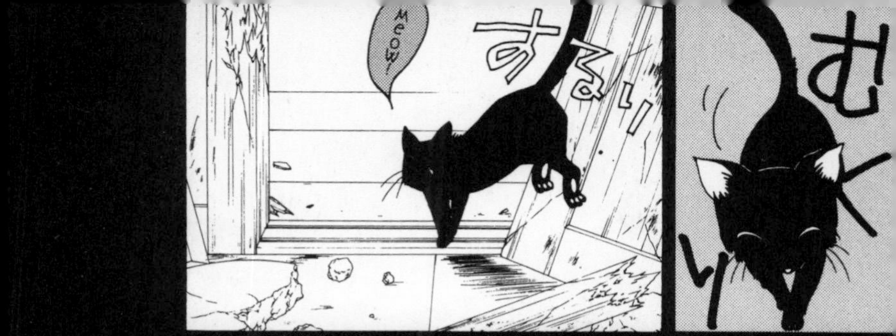

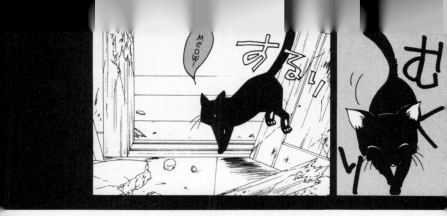

むい
MEOW!
するい

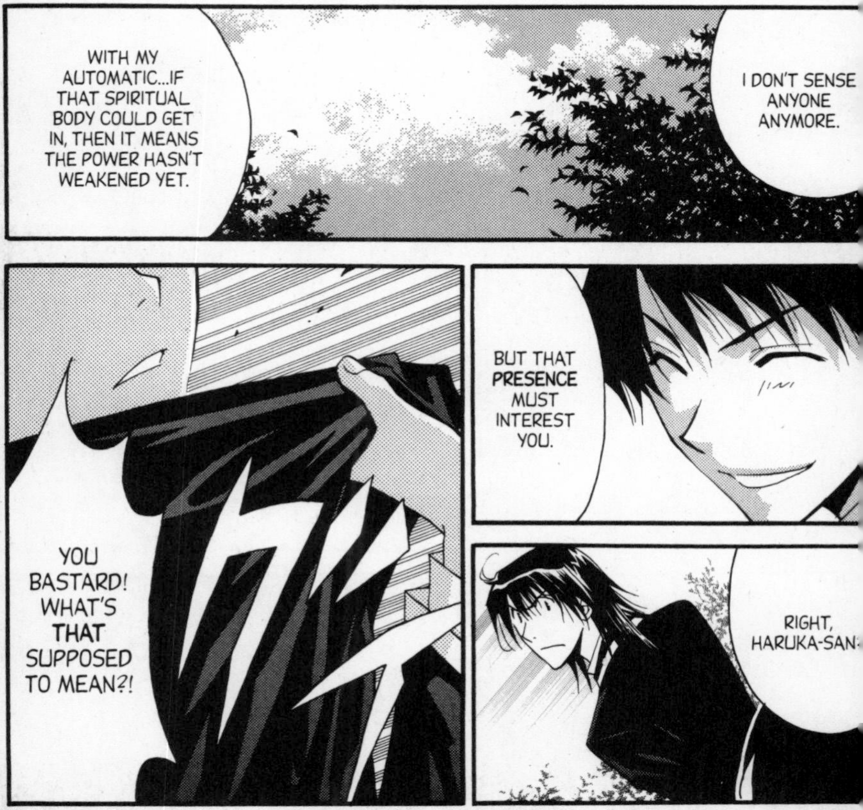

I DON'T SENSE ANYONE ANYMORE.
WITH MY AUTOMATIC...IF THAT SPIRITUAL BODY COULD GET IN, THEN IT MEANS THE POWER HASN'T WEAKENED YET.
BUT THAT **PRESENCE** MUST INTEREST YOU.
RIGHT, HARUKA-SAN?
YOU BASTARD! WHAT'S **THAT** SUPPOSED TO MEAN?!

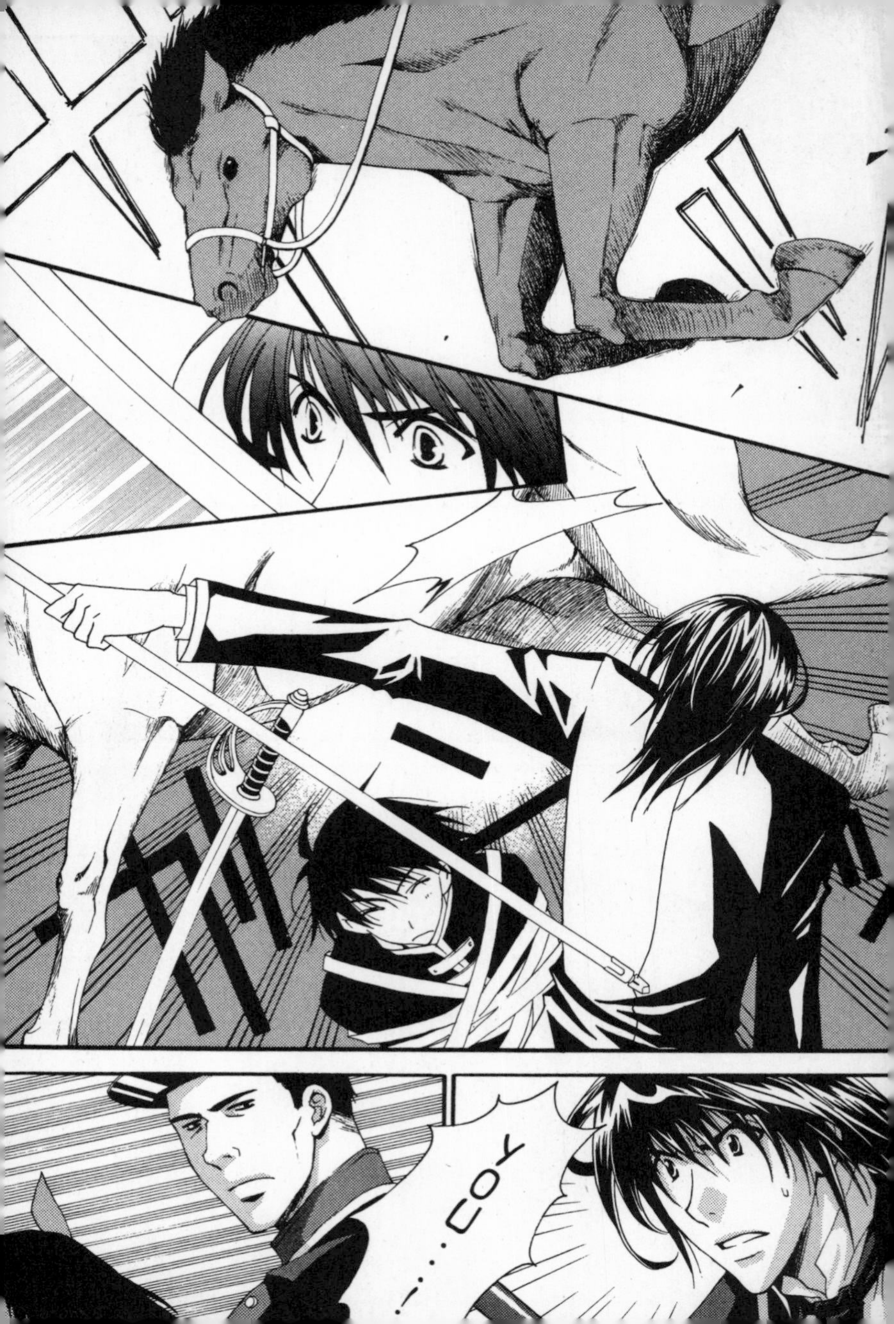
YOU...!

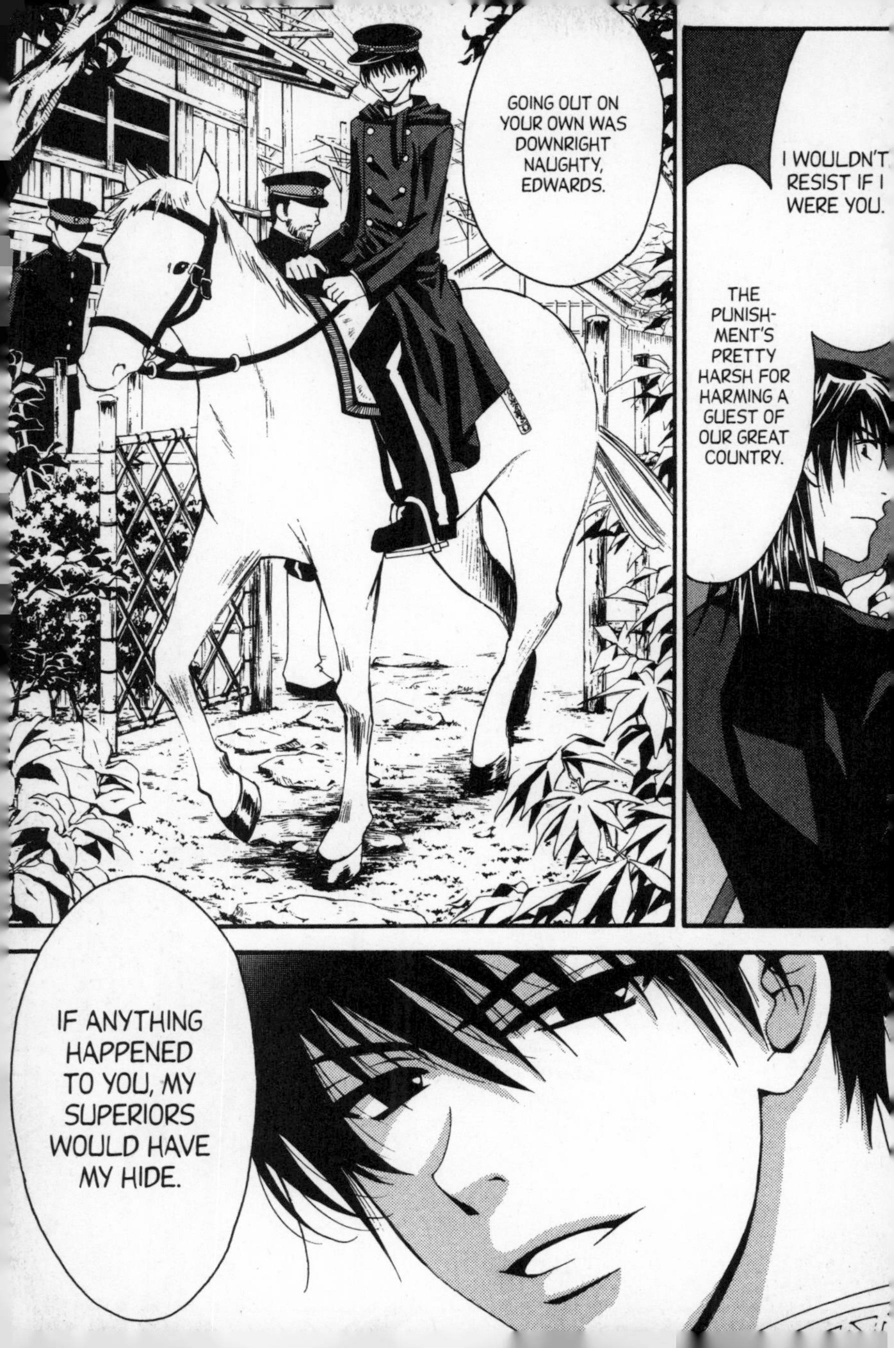
I WOULDN'T RESIST IF I WERE YOU.
THE PUNISHMENT'S PRETTY HARSH FOR HARMING A GUEST OF OUR GREAT COUNTRY.
GOING OUT ON YOUR OWN WAS DOWNRIGHT NAUGHTY, EDWARDS.
IF ANYTHING HAPPENED TO YOU, MY SUPERIORS WOULD HAVE MY HIDE.

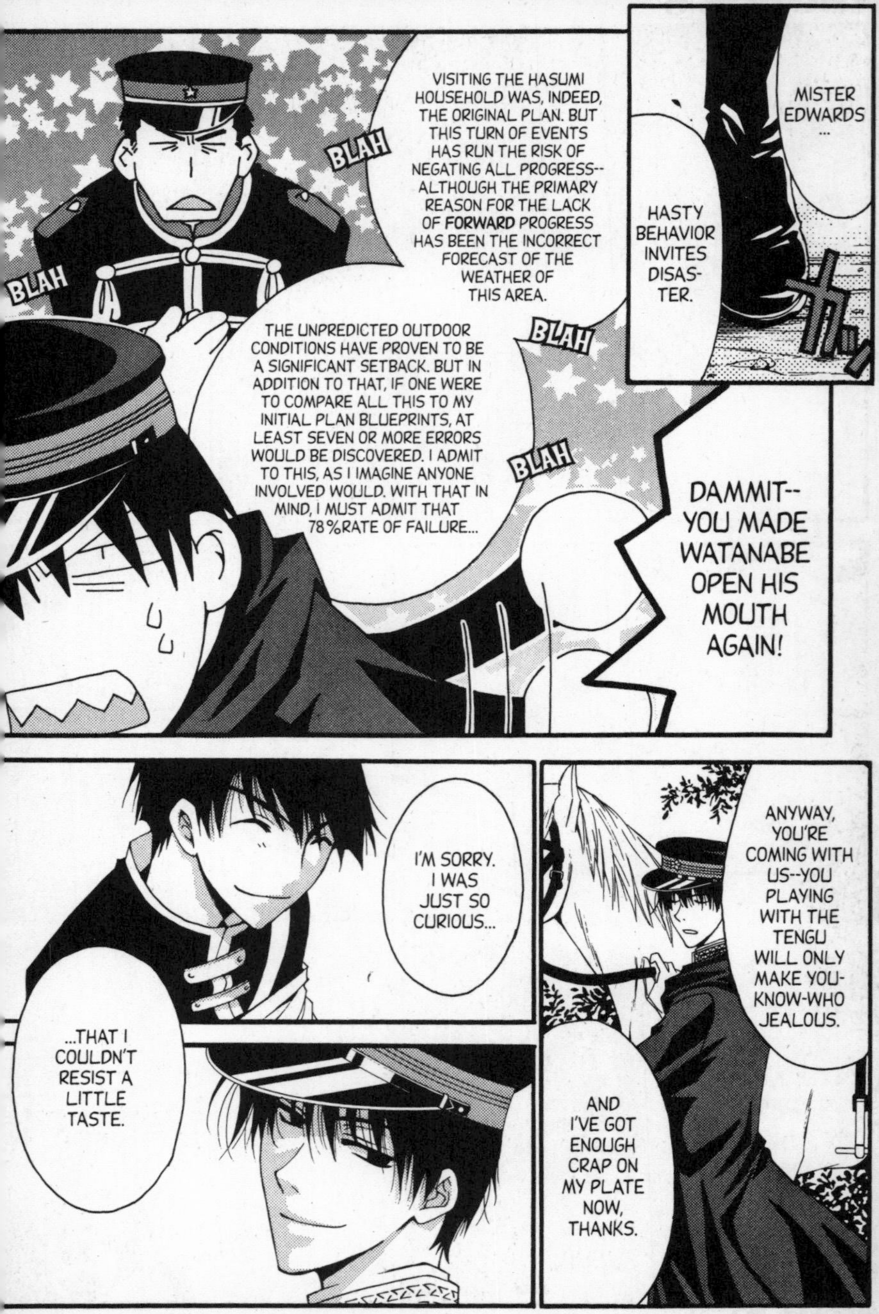
MISTER EDWARDS ...
HASTY BEHAVIOR INVITES DISASTER.
VISITING THE HASUMI HOUSEHOLD WAS, INDEED, THE ORIGINAL PLAN. BUT THIS TURN OF EVENTS HAS RUN THE RISK OF NEGATING ALL PROGRESS--ALTHOUGH THE PRIMARY REASON FOR THE LACK OF **FORWARD** PROGRESS HAS BEEN THE INCORRECT FORECAST OF THE WEATHER OF THIS AREA.
BLAH
BLAH
THE UNPREDICTED OUTDOOR CONDITIONS HAVE PROVEN TO BE A SIGNIFICANT SETBACK. BUT IN ADDITION TO THAT, IF ONE WERE TO COMPARE ALL THIS TO MY INITIAL PLAN BLUEPRINTS, AT LEAST SEVEN OR MORE ERRORS WOULD BE DISCOVERED. I ADMIT TO THIS, AS I IMAGINE ANYONE INVOLVED WOULD. WITH THAT IN MIND, I MUST ADMIT THAT 78%RATE OF FAILURE...
BLAH
BLAH
DAMMIT--YOU MADE WATANABE OPEN HIS MOUTH AGAIN!
ANYWAY, YOU'RE COMING WITH US--YOU PLAYING WITH THE TENGU WILL ONLY MAKE YOU-KNOW-WHO JEALOUS.
AND I'VE GOT ENOUGH CRAP ON MY PLATE NOW, THANKS.
I'M SORRY. I WAS JUST SO CURIOUS...
...THAT I COULDN'T RESIST A LITTLE TASTE.

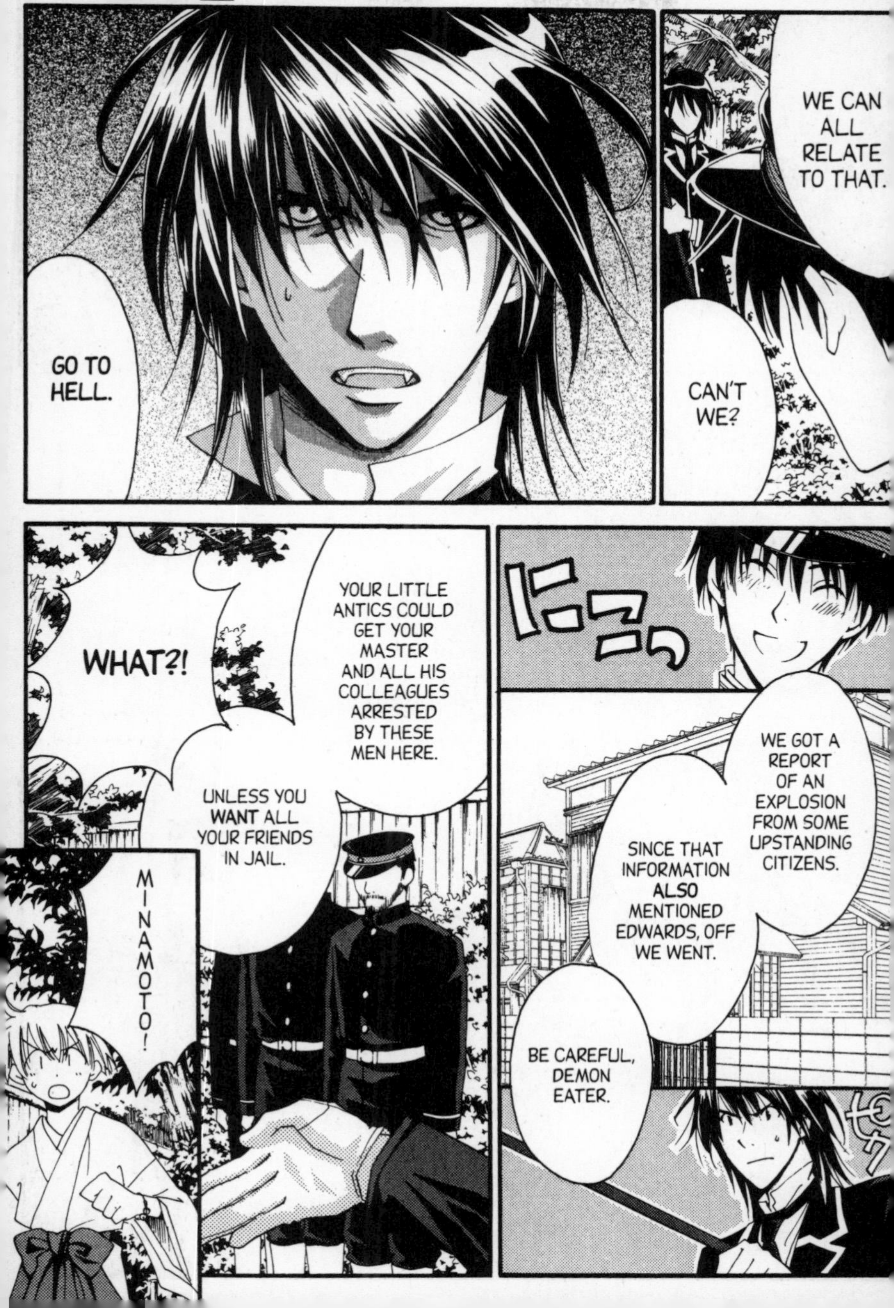
WE CAN ALL RELATE TO THAT.
CAN'T WE?
GO TO HELL.
にこっ
WE GOT A REPORT OF AN EXPLOSION FROM SOME UPSTANDING CITIZENS.
SINCE THAT INFORMATION ALSO MENTIONED EDWARDS, OFF WE WENT.
BE CAREFUL, DEMON EATER.
YOUR LITTLE ANTICS COULD GET YOUR MASTER AND ALL HIS COLLEAGUES ARRESTED BY THESE MEN HERE.
WHAT?!
UNLESS YOU WANT ALL YOUR FRIENDS IN JAIL.
MINAMOTO!

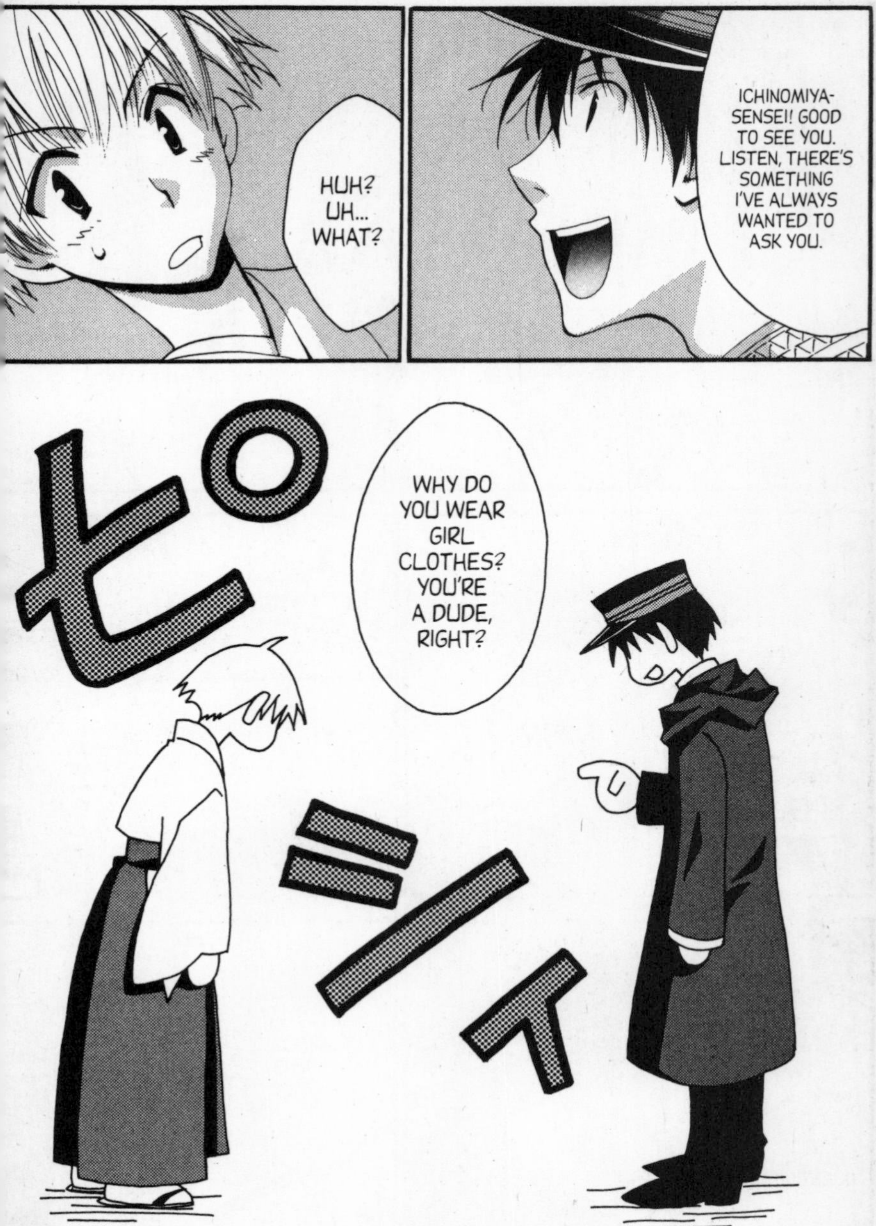
ICHINOMIYA-SENSEI! GOOD TO SEE YOU. LISTEN, THERE'S SOMETHING I'VE ALWAYS WANTED TO ASK YOU.
HUH? UH... WHAT?
WHY DO YOU WEAR GIRL CLOTHES? YOU'RE A DUDE, RIGHT?

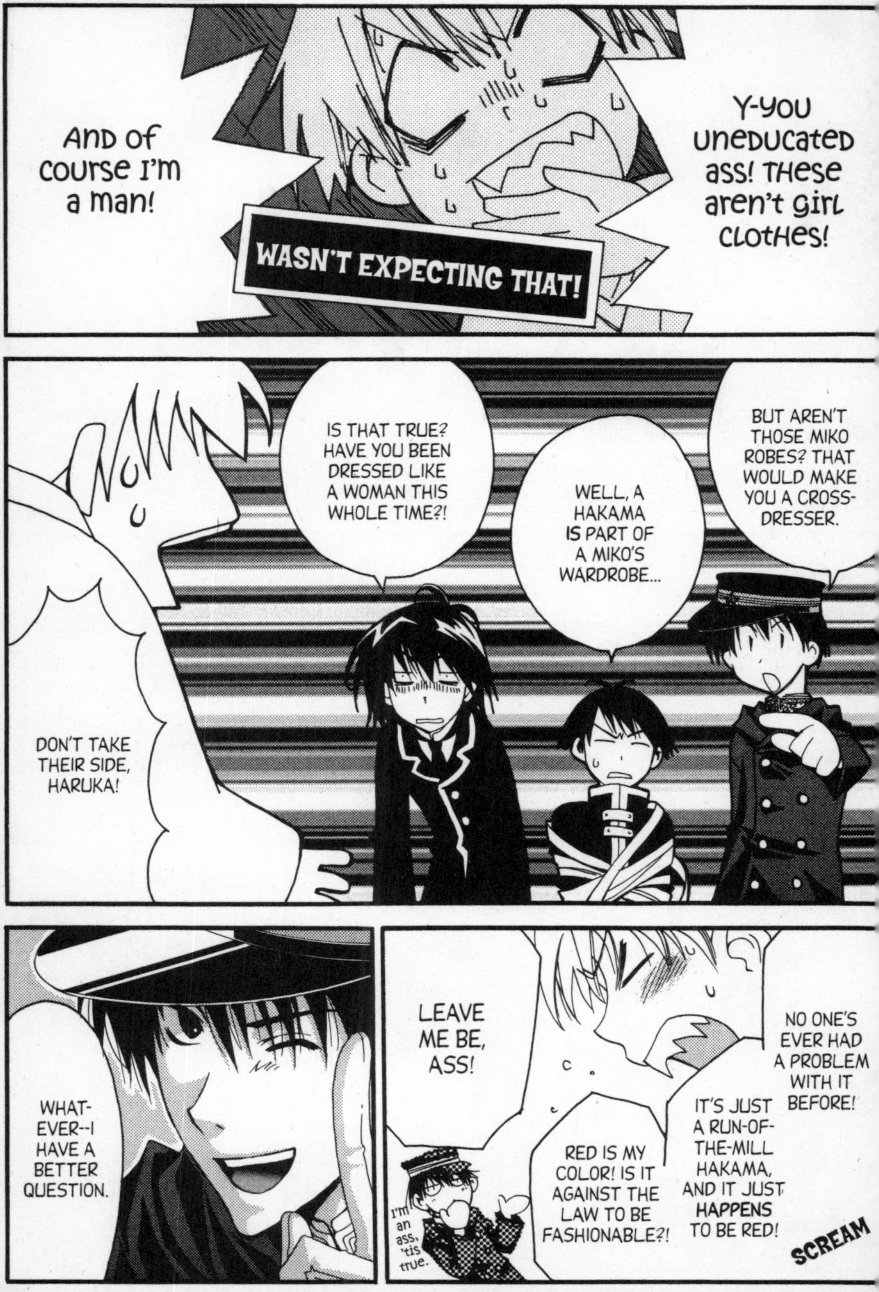
Y-YOU UNEDUCATED ASS! THESE AREN'T GIRL CLOTHES!
And of course I'm a man!
WASN'T EXPECTING THAT!
BUT AREN'T THOSE MIKO ROBES? THAT WOULD MAKE YOU A CROSS-DRESSER.
WELL, A HAKAMA IS PART OF A MIKO'S WARDROBE...
IS THAT TRUE? HAVE YOU BEEN DRESSED LIKE A WOMAN THIS WHOLE TIME?!
DON'T TAKE THEIR SIDE, HARUKA!
NO ONE'S EVER HAD A PROBLEM WITH IT BEFORE!
LEAVE ME BE, ASS!
IT'S JUST A RUN-OF-THE-MILL HAKAMA, AND IT JUST HAPPENS TO BE RED!
RED IS MY COLOR! IS IT AGAINST THE LAW TO BE FASHIONABLE?!
SCREAM
I'm an ass, 'tis true.
WHAT-EVER--I HAVE A BETTER QUESTION.

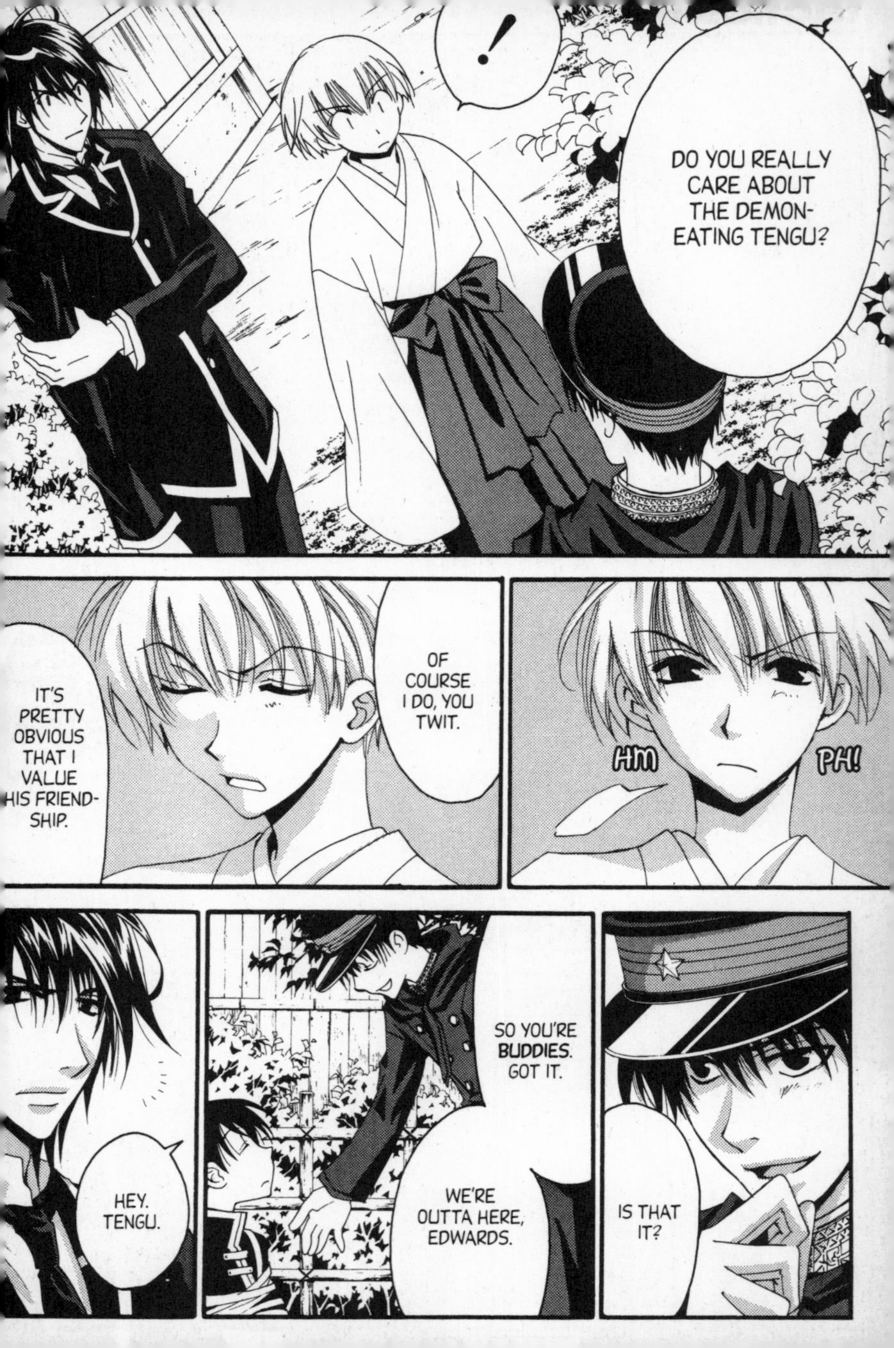
DO YOU REALLY CARE ABOUT THE DEMON-EATING TENGU?
!
HM PH!
OF COURSE I DO, YOU TWIT.
IT'S PRETTY OBVIOUS THAT I VALUE HIS FRIEND-SHIP.
IS THAT IT?
SO YOU'RE **BUDDIES**. GOT IT.
WE'RE OUTTA HERE, EDWARDS.
HEY. TENGU.

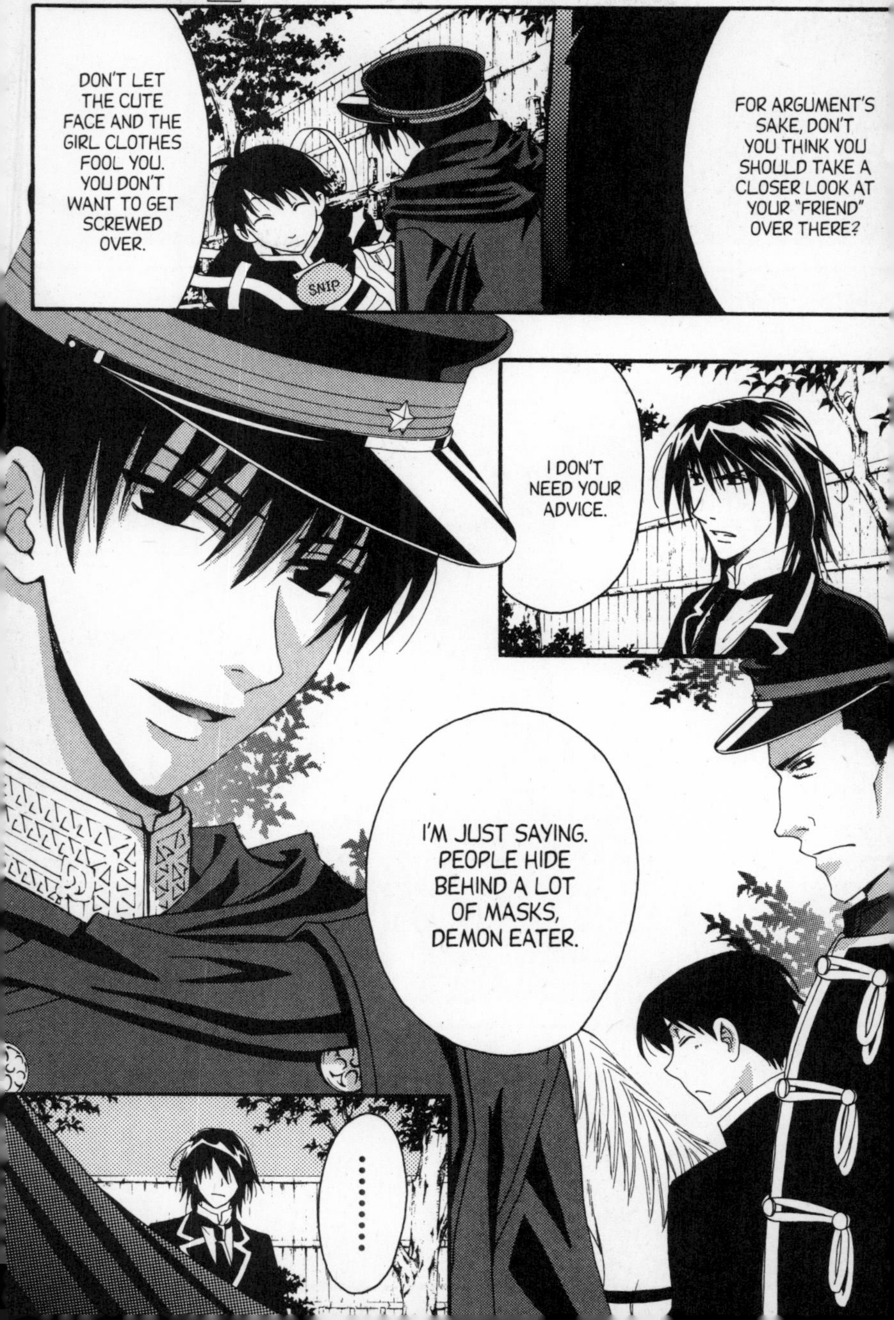
FOR ARGUMENT'S SAKE, DON'T YOU THINK YOU SHOULD TAKE A CLOSER LOOK AT YOUR "FRIEND" OVER THERE?
DON'T LET THE CUTE FACE AND THE GIRL CLOTHES FOOL YOU. YOU DON'T WANT TO GET SCREWED OVER.
SNIP
I DON'T NEED YOUR ADVICE.
I'M JUST SAYING. PEOPLE HIDE BEHIND A LOT OF MASKS, DEMON EATER.
....

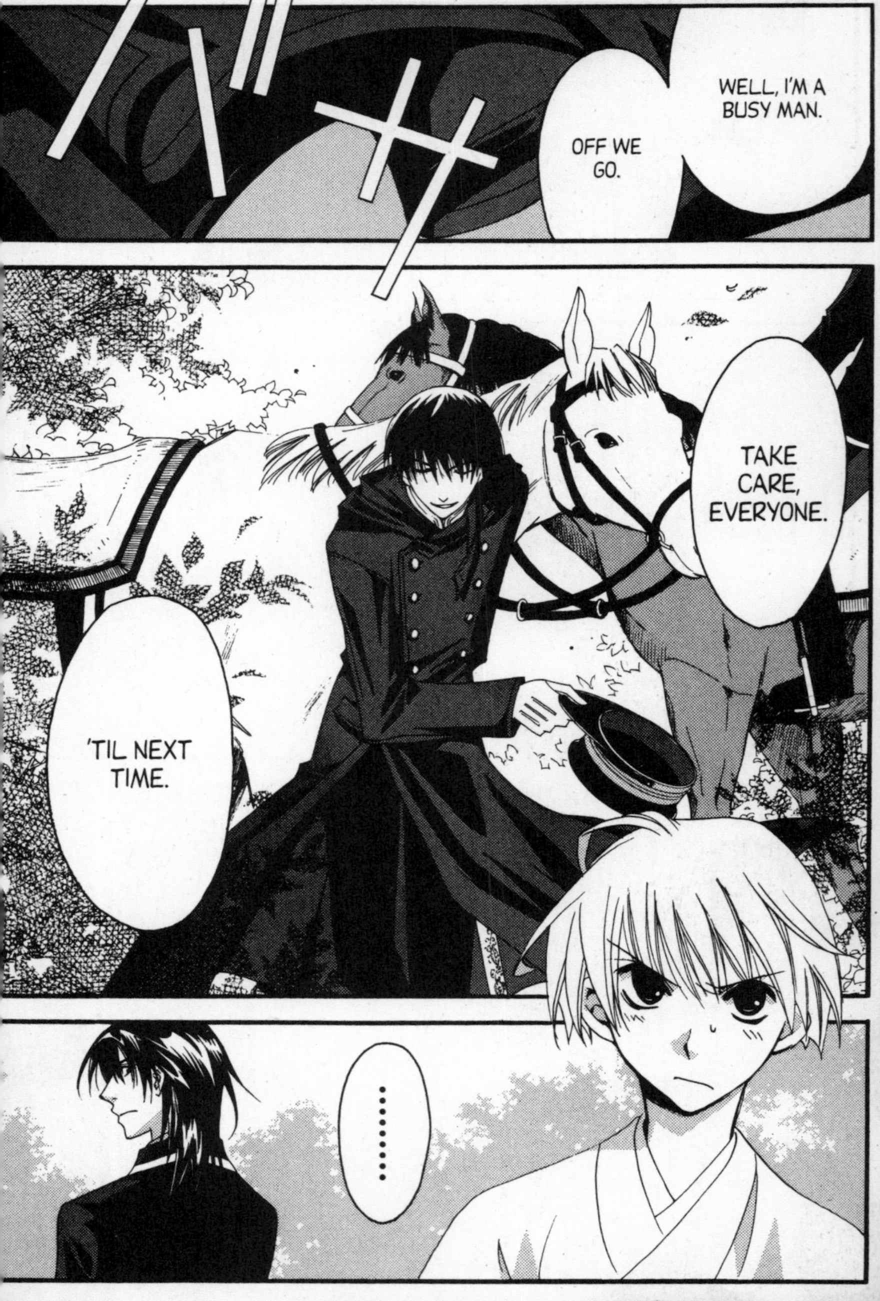
WELL, I'M A BUSY MAN.
OFF WE GO.
TAKE CARE, EVERYONE.
'TIL NEXT TIME.
....

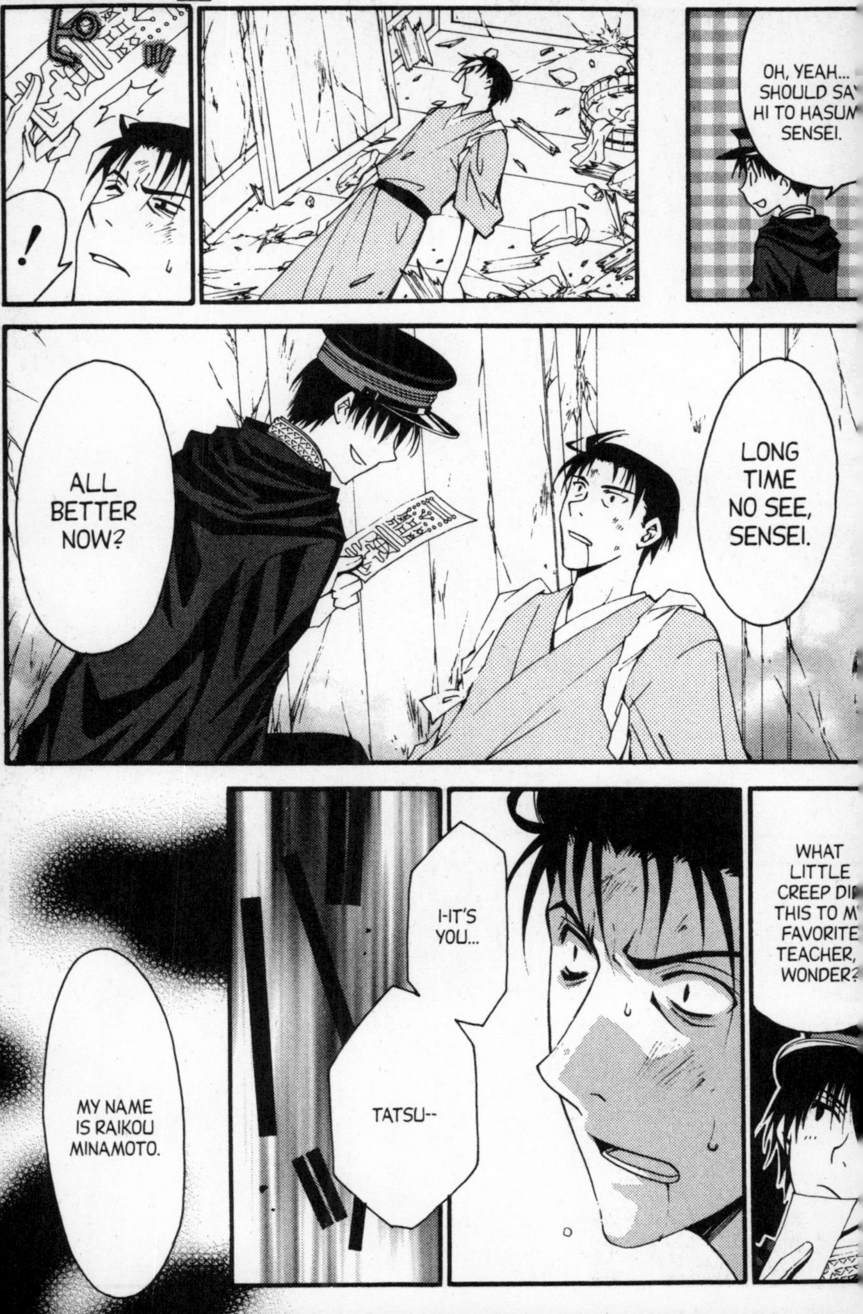
OH, YEAH... SHOULD SA HI TO HASUM SENSEI.
!
LONG TIME NO SEE, SENSEI.
ALL BETTER NOW?
WHAT LITTLE CREEP DI THIS TO M FAVORITE TEACHER, WONDER?
I-IT'S YOU...
TATSU--
MY NAME IS RAIKOU MINAMOTO.

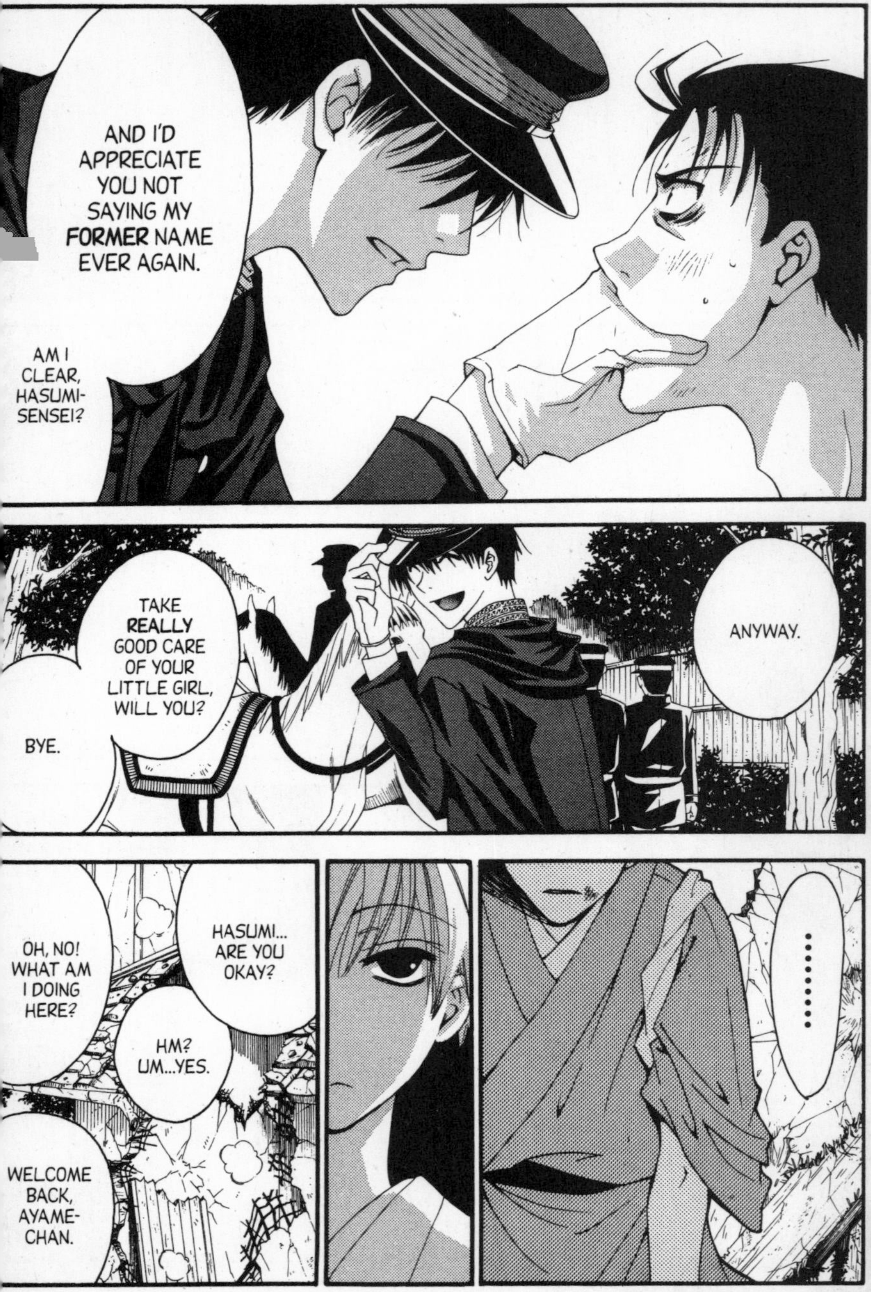
AND I'D APPRECIATE YOU NOT SAYING MY **FORMER** NAME EVER AGAIN.
AM I CLEAR, HASUMI-SENSEI?
ANYWAY.
TAKE **REALLY** GOOD CARE OF YOUR LITTLE GIRL, WILL YOU?
BYE.
......
HASUMI... ARE YOU OKAY?
OH, NO! WHAT AM I DOING HERE?
HM? UM...YES.
WELCOME BACK, AYAME-CHAN.

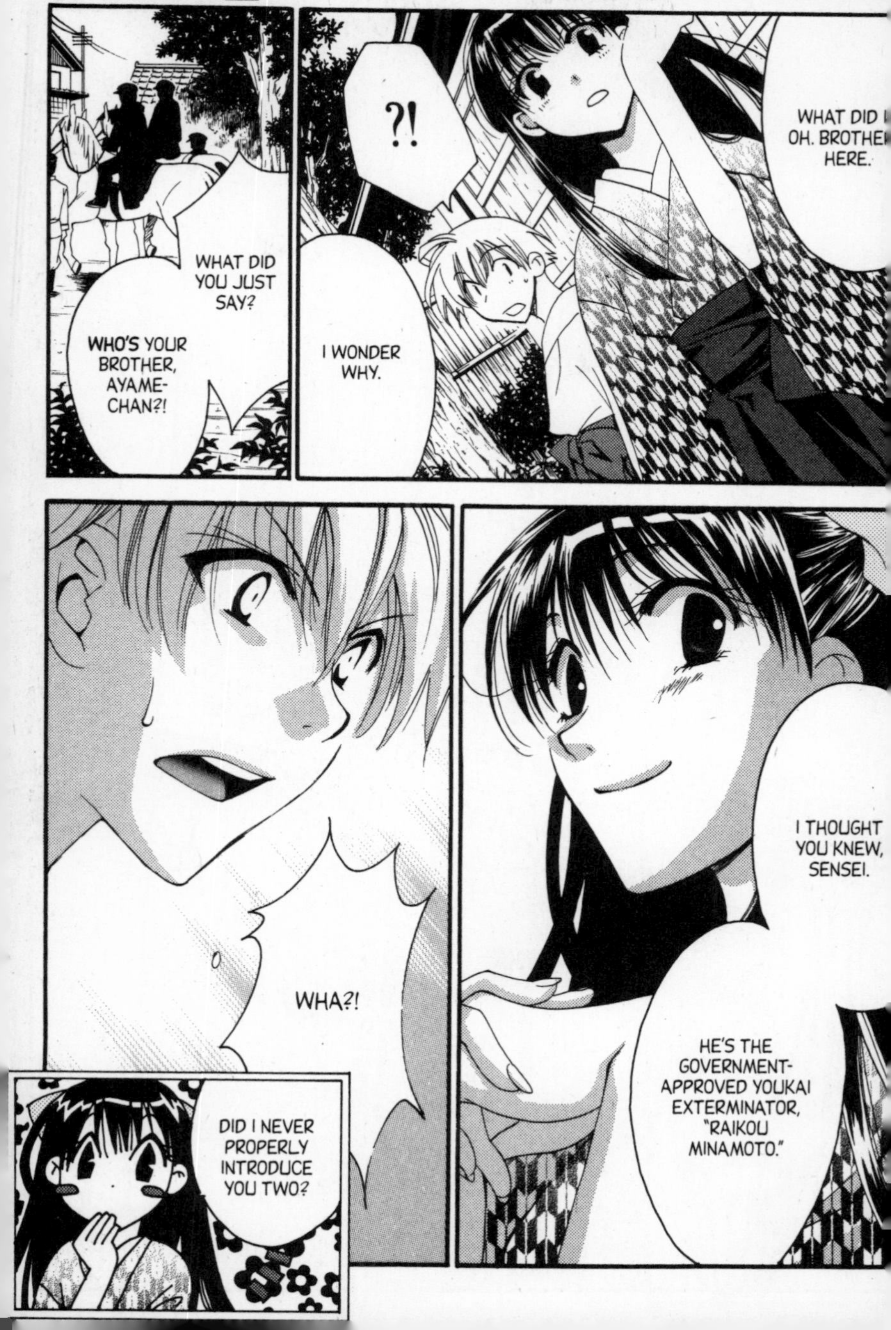
WHAT DID I OH. BROTHE HERE.
?!
I WONDER WHY.
WHAT DID YOU JUST SAY?
WHO'S YOUR BROTHER, AYAME-CHAN?!
I THOUGHT YOU KNEW, SENSEI.
HE'S THE GOVERNMENT-APPROVED YOUKAI EXTERMINATOR, "RAIKOU MINAMOTO."
WHA?!
DID I NEVER PROPERLY INTRODUCE YOU TWO?

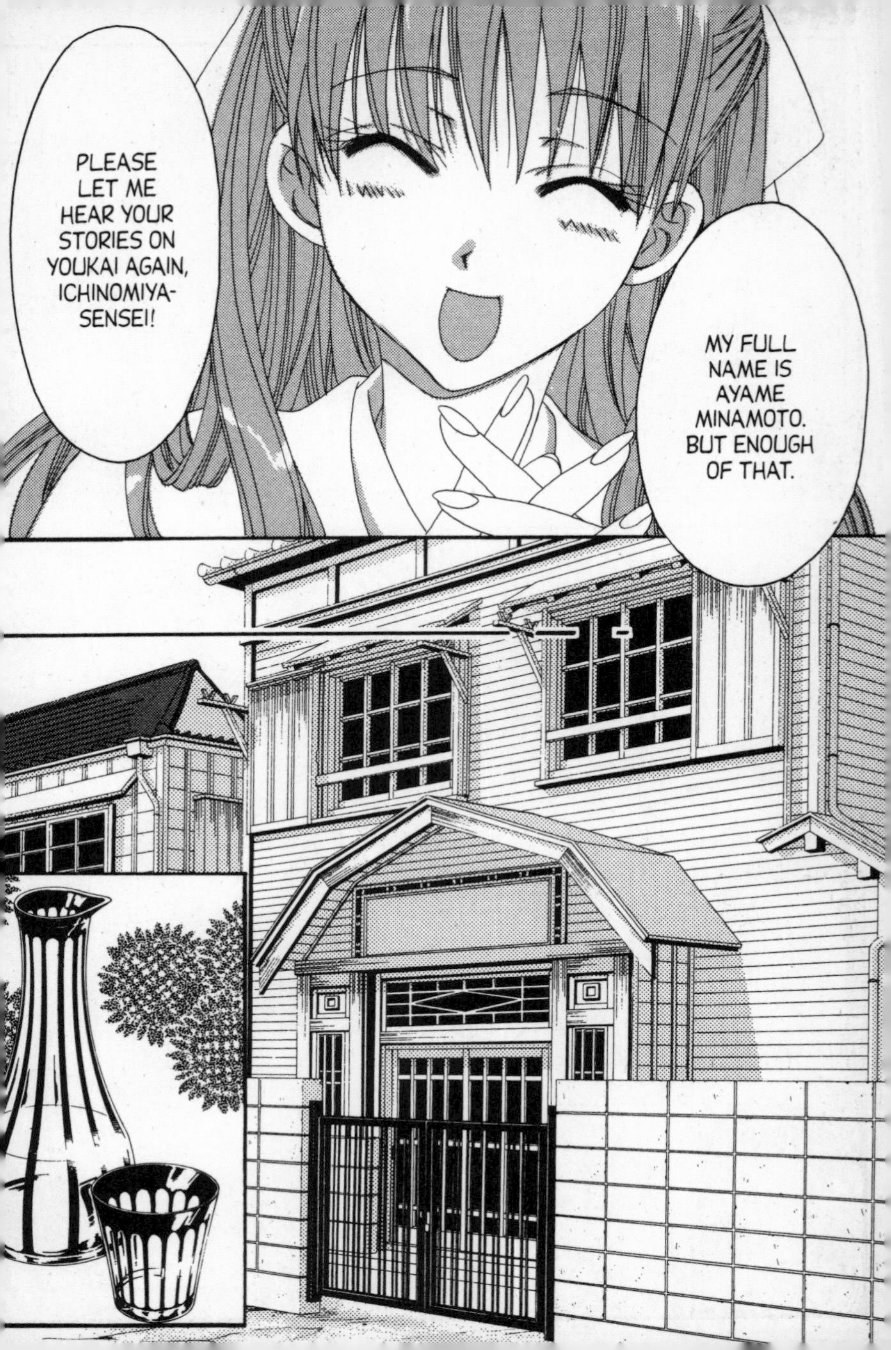
MY FULL NAME IS AYAME MINAMOTO. BUT ENOUGH OF THAT.
PLEASE LET ME HEAR YOUR STORIES ON YOUKAI AGAIN, ICHINOMIYA-SENSEI!

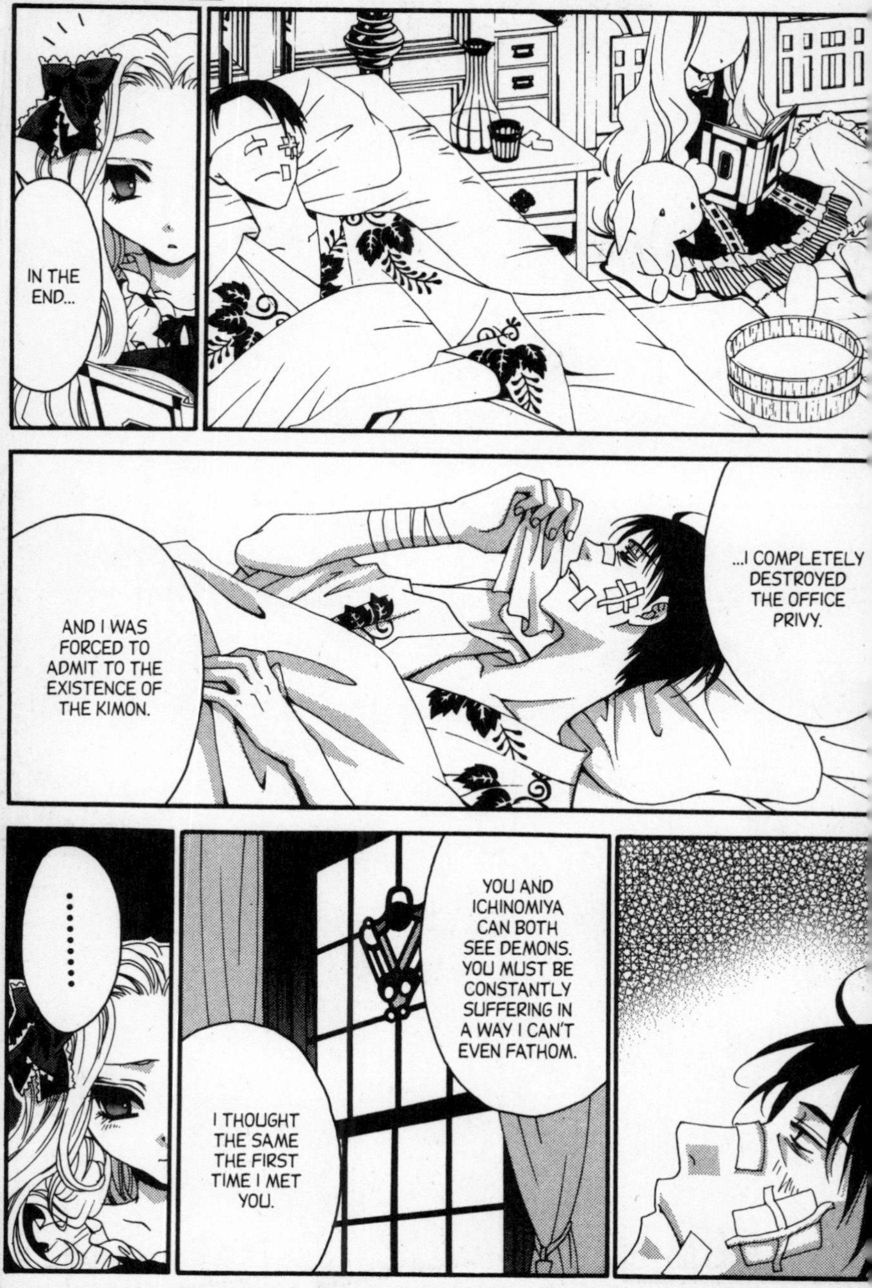
IN THE END...
...I COMPLETELY DESTROYED THE OFFICE PRIVY.
AND I WAS FORCED TO ADMIT TO THE EXISTENCE OF THE KIMON.
YOU AND ICHINOMIYA CAN BOTH SEE DEMONS. YOU MUST BE CONSTANTLY SUFFERING IN A WAY I CAN'T EVEN FATHOM.
I THOUGHT THE SAME THE FIRST TIME I MET YOU.
....

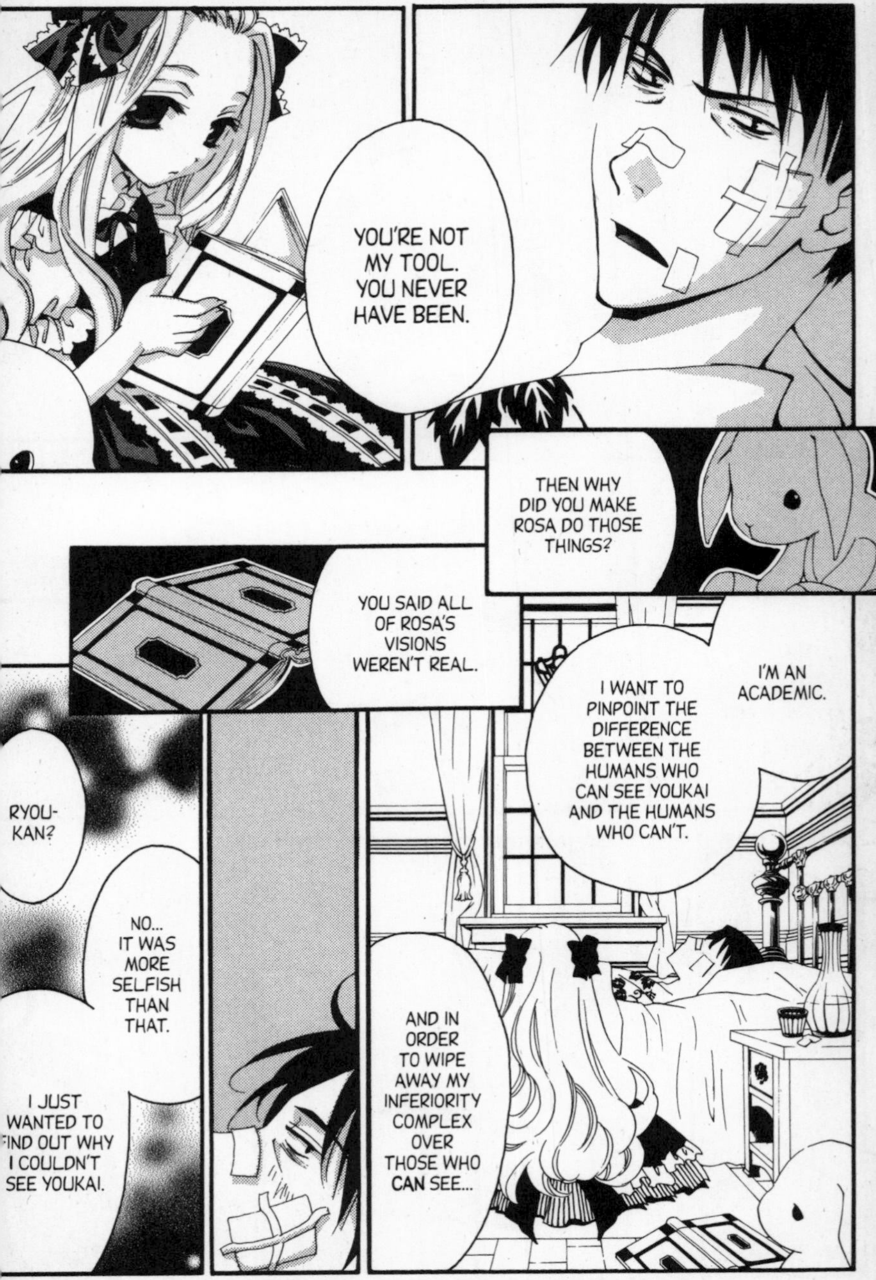
YOU'RE NOT MY TOOL. YOU NEVER HAVE BEEN.
THEN WHY DID YOU MAKE ROSA DO THOSE THINGS?
YOU SAID ALL OF ROSA'S VISIONS WEREN'T REAL.
I'M AN ACADEMIC.
I WANT TO PINPOINT THE DIFFERENCE BETWEEN THE HUMANS WHO CAN SEE YOUKAI AND THE HUMANS WHO CAN'T.
AND IN ORDER TO WIPE AWAY MY INFERIORITY COMPLEX OVER THOSE WHO CAN SEE...
RYOU-KAN?
NO... IT WAS MORE SELFISH THAN THAT.
I JUST WANTED TO FIND OUT WHY I COULDN'T SEE YOUKAI.

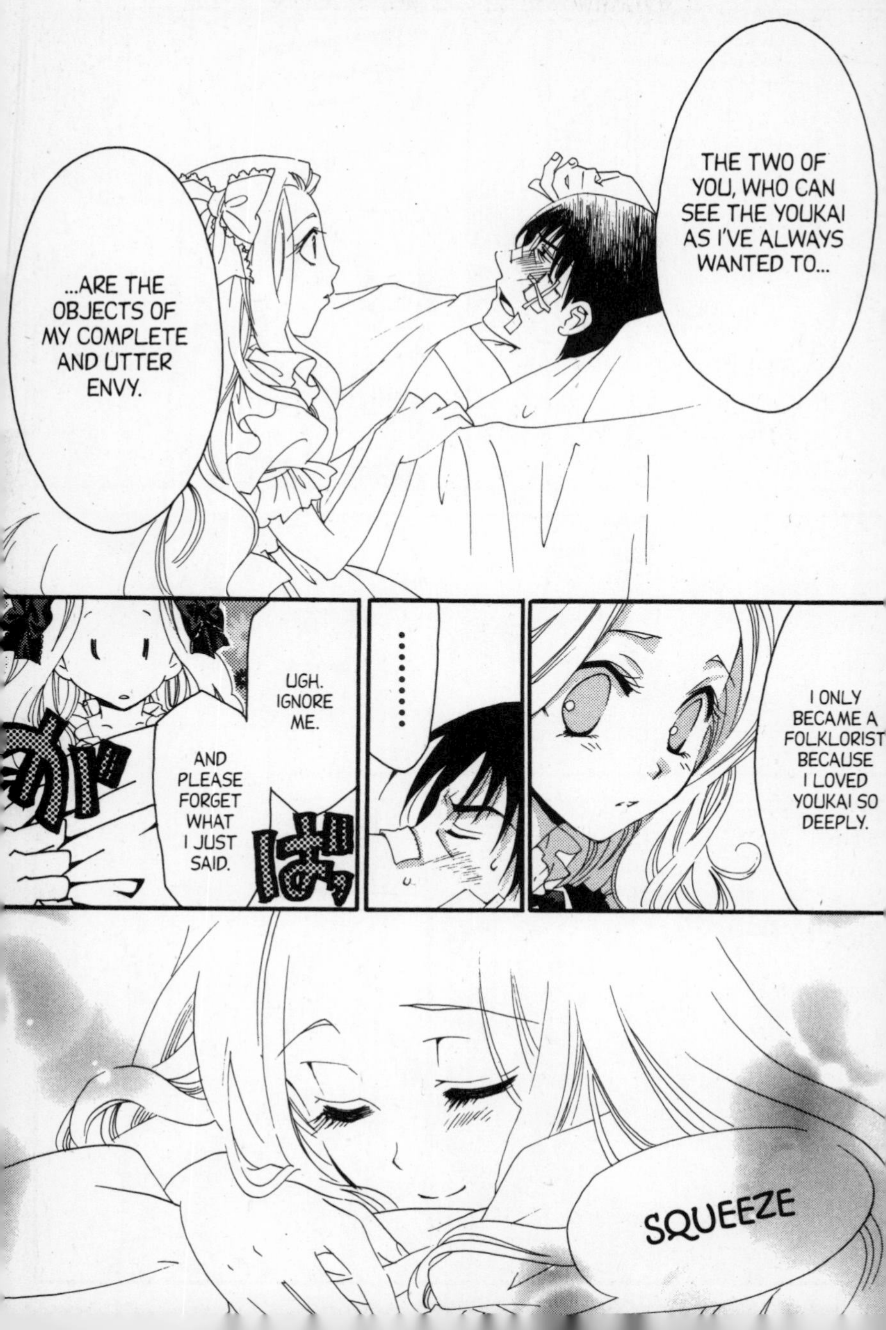
THE TWO OF YOU, WHO CAN SEE THE YOUKAI AS I'VE ALWAYS WANTED TO...
...ARE THE OBJECTS OF MY COMPLETE AND UTTER ENVY.
I ONLY BECAME A FOLKLORIST BECAUSE I LOVED YOUKAI SO DEEPLY.
....
UGH. IGNORE ME.
AND PLEASE FORGET WHAT I JUST SAID.
SQUEEZE

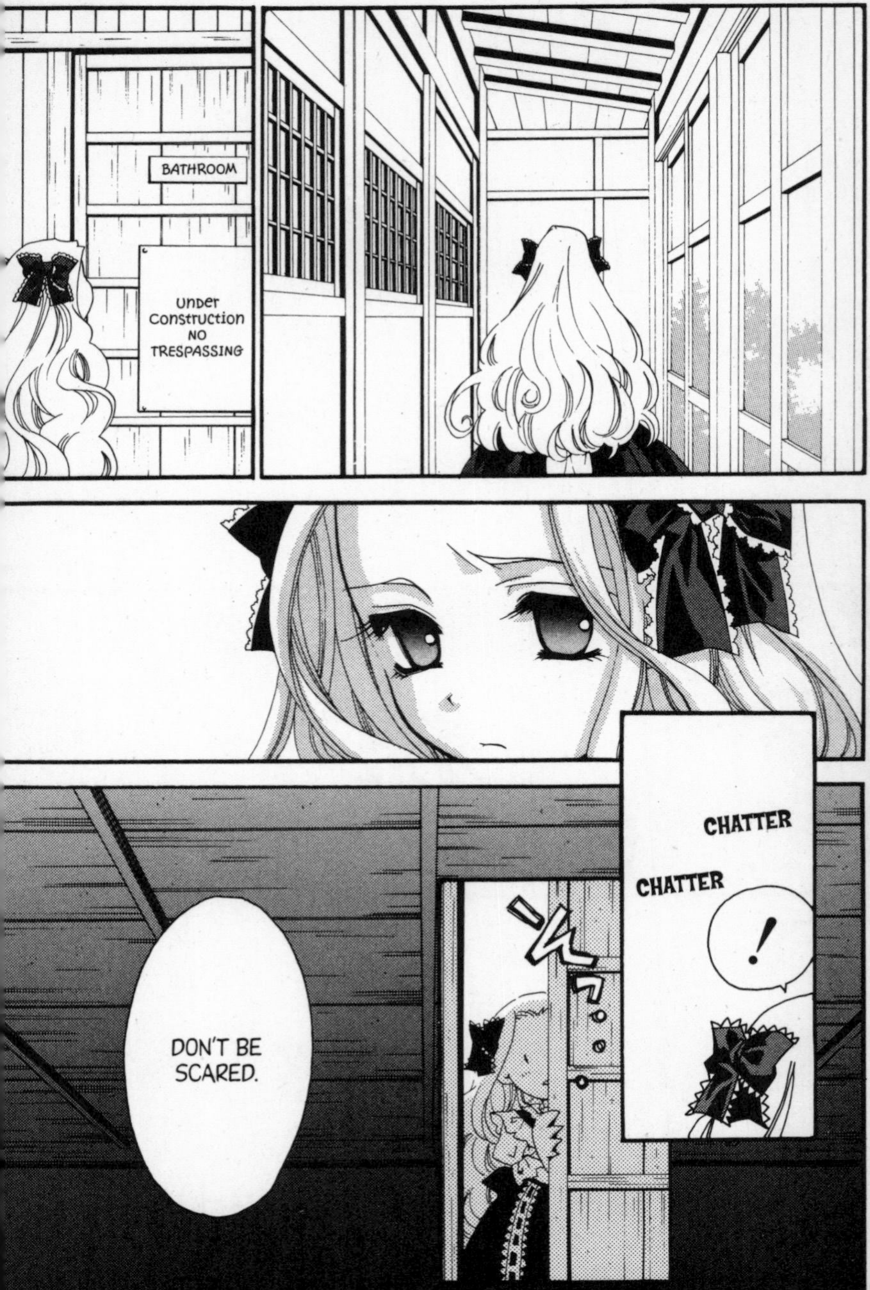
BATHROOM
Under Construction
NO
TRESPASSING
CHATTER
CHATTER
!
DON'T BE SCARED.

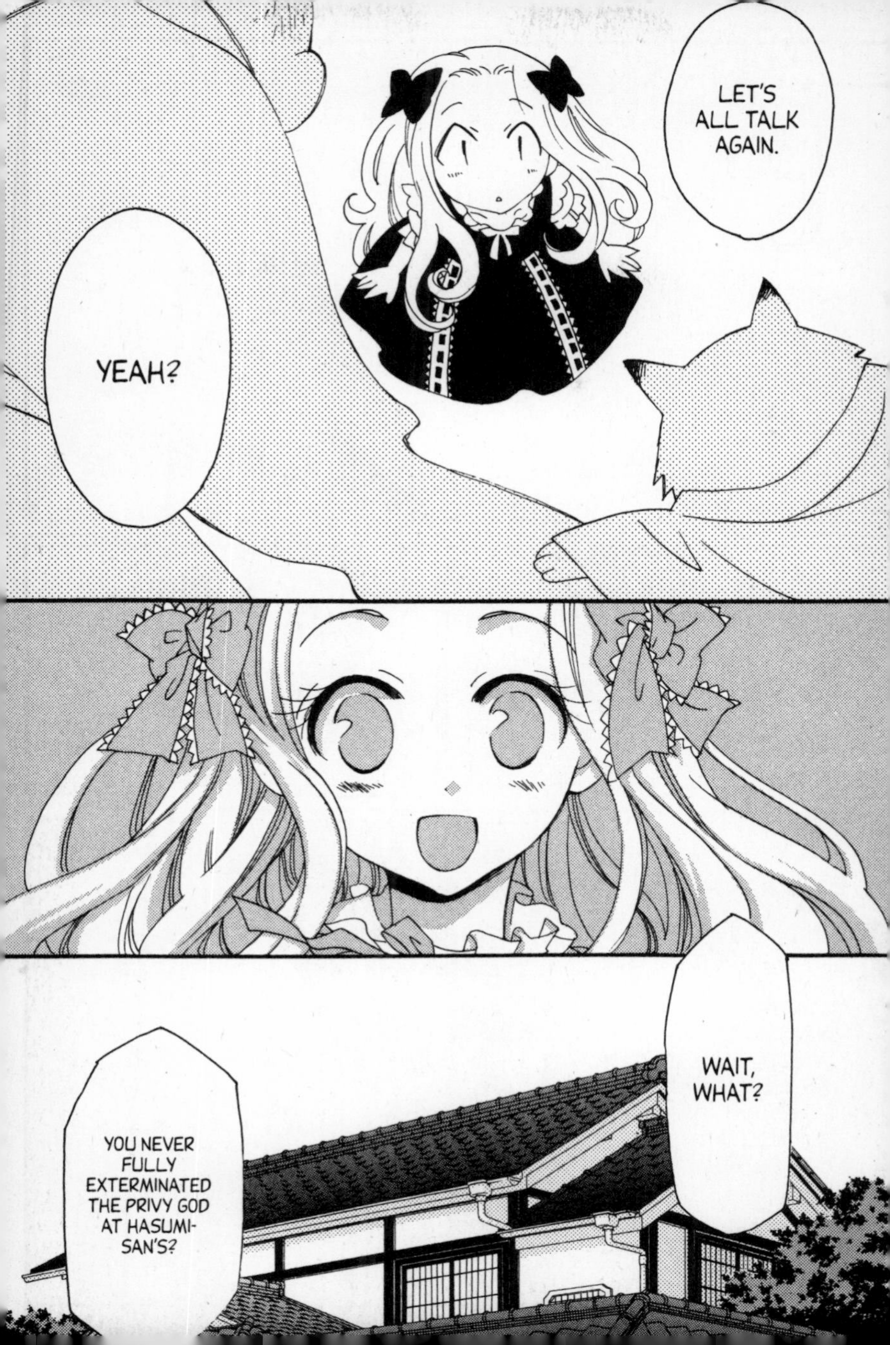
LET'S ALL TALK AGAIN.
YEAH?
WAIT, WHAT?
YOU NEVER FULLY EXTERMINATED THE PRIVY GOD AT HASUMI-SAN'S?

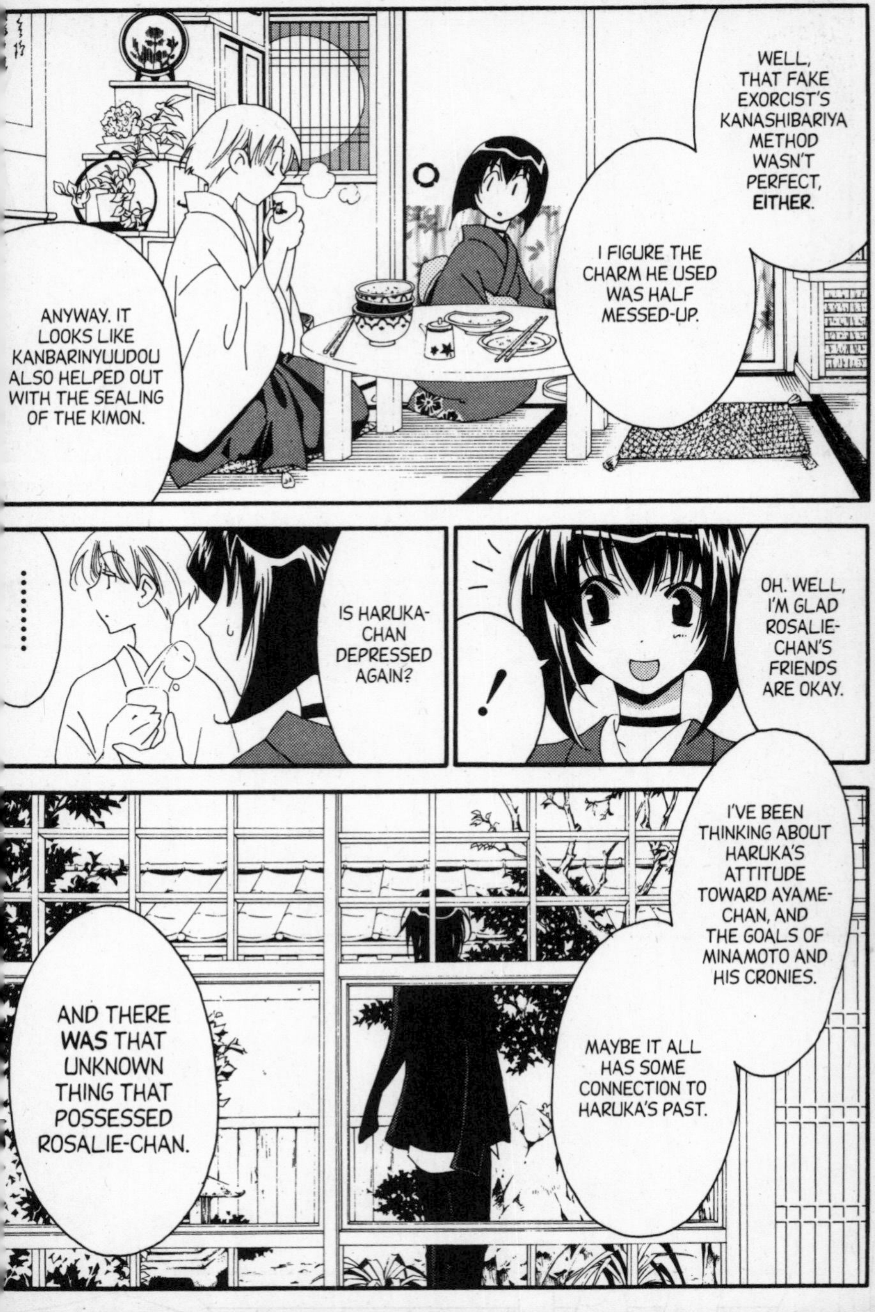
WELL, THAT FAKE EXORCIST'S KANASHIBARIYA METHOD WASN'T PERFECT, **EITHER**.
I FIGURE THE CHARM HE USED WAS HALF MESSED-UP.
ANYWAY. IT LOOKS LIKE KANBARINYUUDOU ALSO HELPED OUT WITH THE SEALING OF THE KIMON.
OH. WELL, I'M GLAD ROSALIE-CHAN'S FRIENDS ARE OKAY.
!
IS HARUKA-CHAN DEPRESSED AGAIN?
....
I'VE BEEN THINKING ABOUT HARUKA'S ATTITUDE TOWARD AYAME-CHAN, AND THE GOALS OF MINAMOTO AND HIS CRONIES.
MAYBE IT ALL HAS SOME CONNECTION TO HARUKA'S PAST.
AND THERE **WAS** THAT UNKNOWN THING THAT POSSESSED ROSALIE-CHAN.

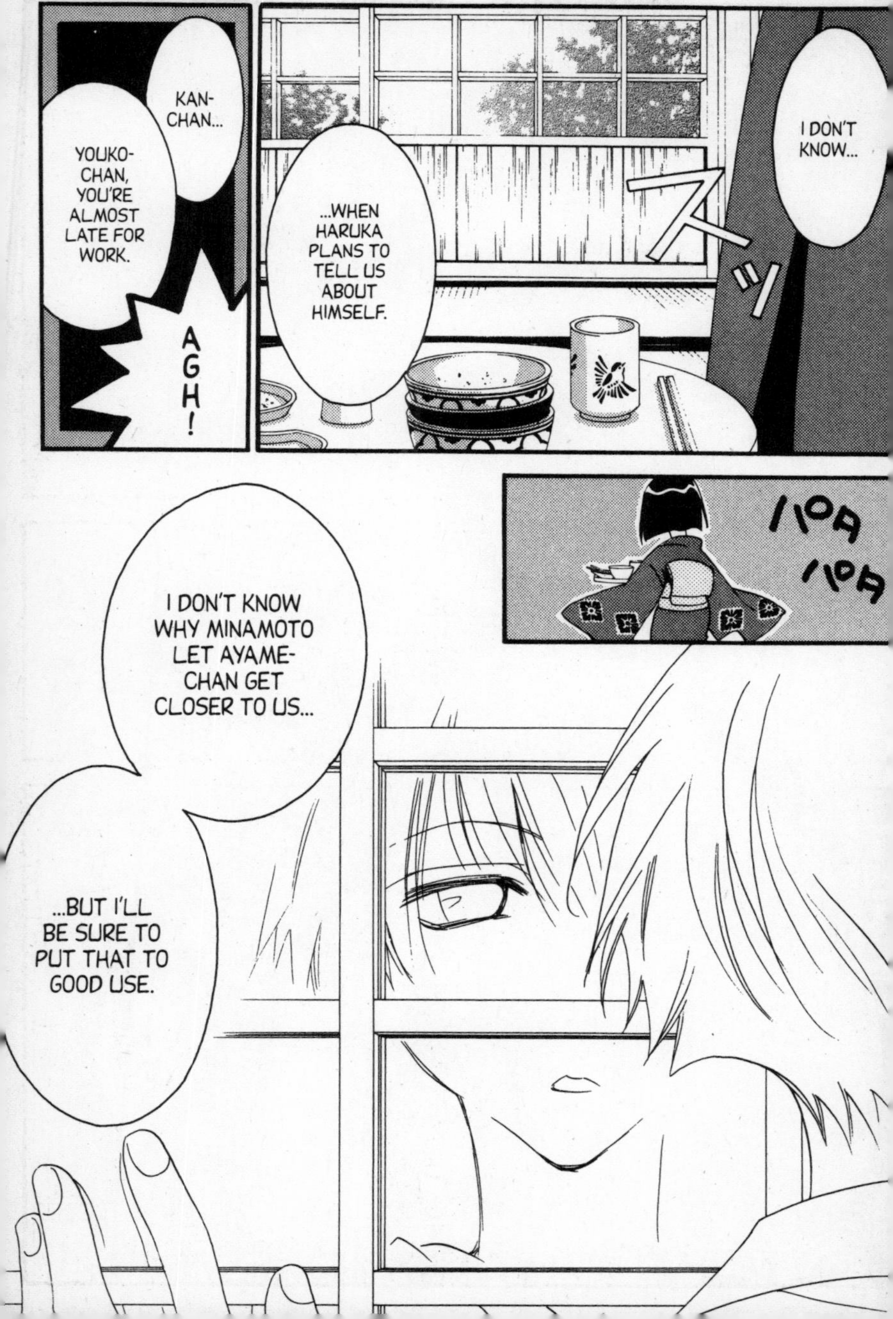
I DON'T KNOW...
...WHEN HARUKA PLANS TO TELL US ABOUT HIMSELF.
KAN-CHAN...
YOUKO-CHAN, YOU'RE ALMOST LATE FOR WORK.
AGH!
パタ パタ
I DON'T KNOW WHY MINAMOTO LET AYAME-CHAN GET CLOSER TO US...
...BUT I'LL BE SURE TO PUT THAT TO GOOD USE.

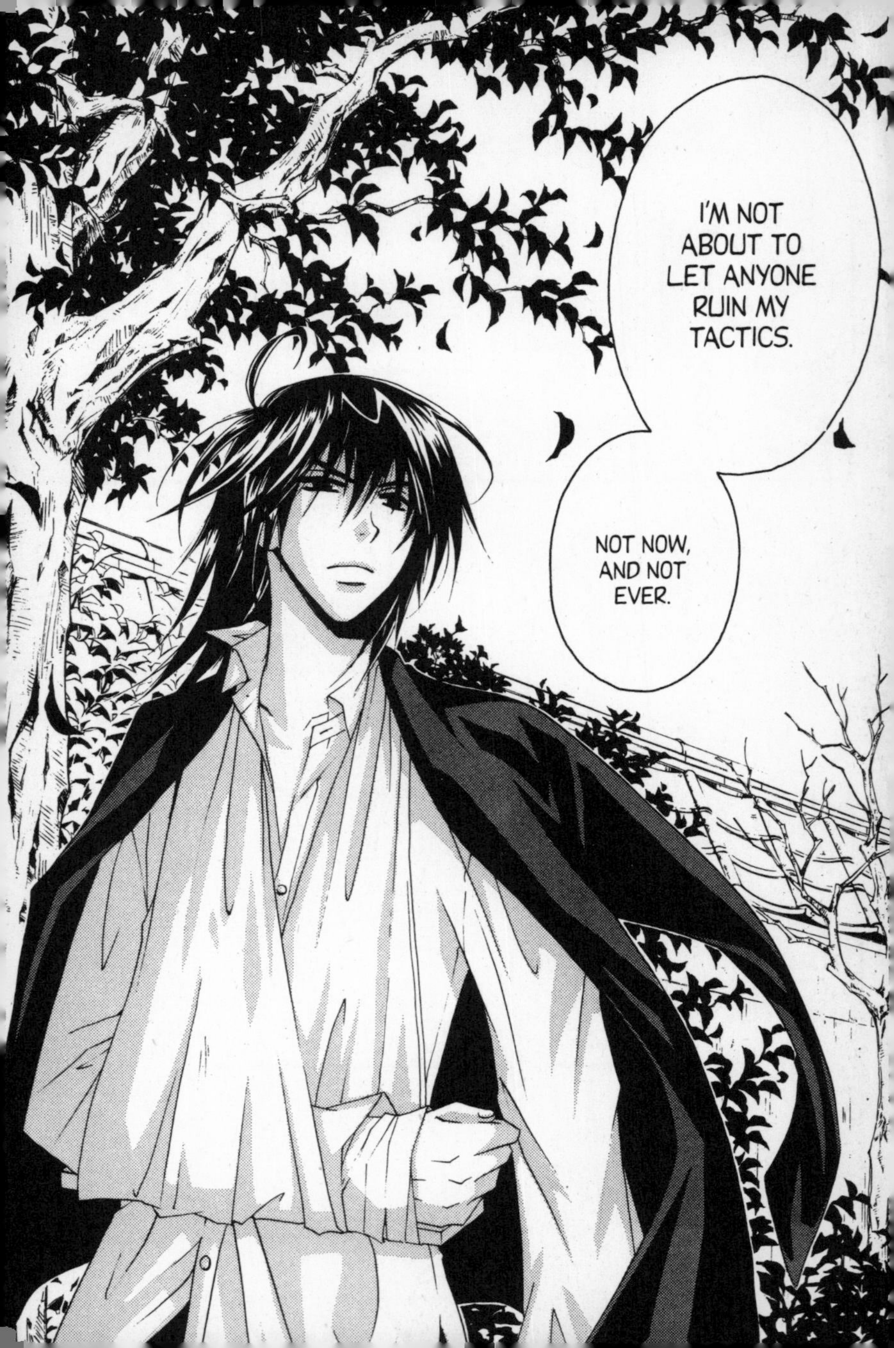
I'M NOT ABOUT TO LET ANYONE RUIN MY TACTICS.
NOT NOW, AND NOT EVER.

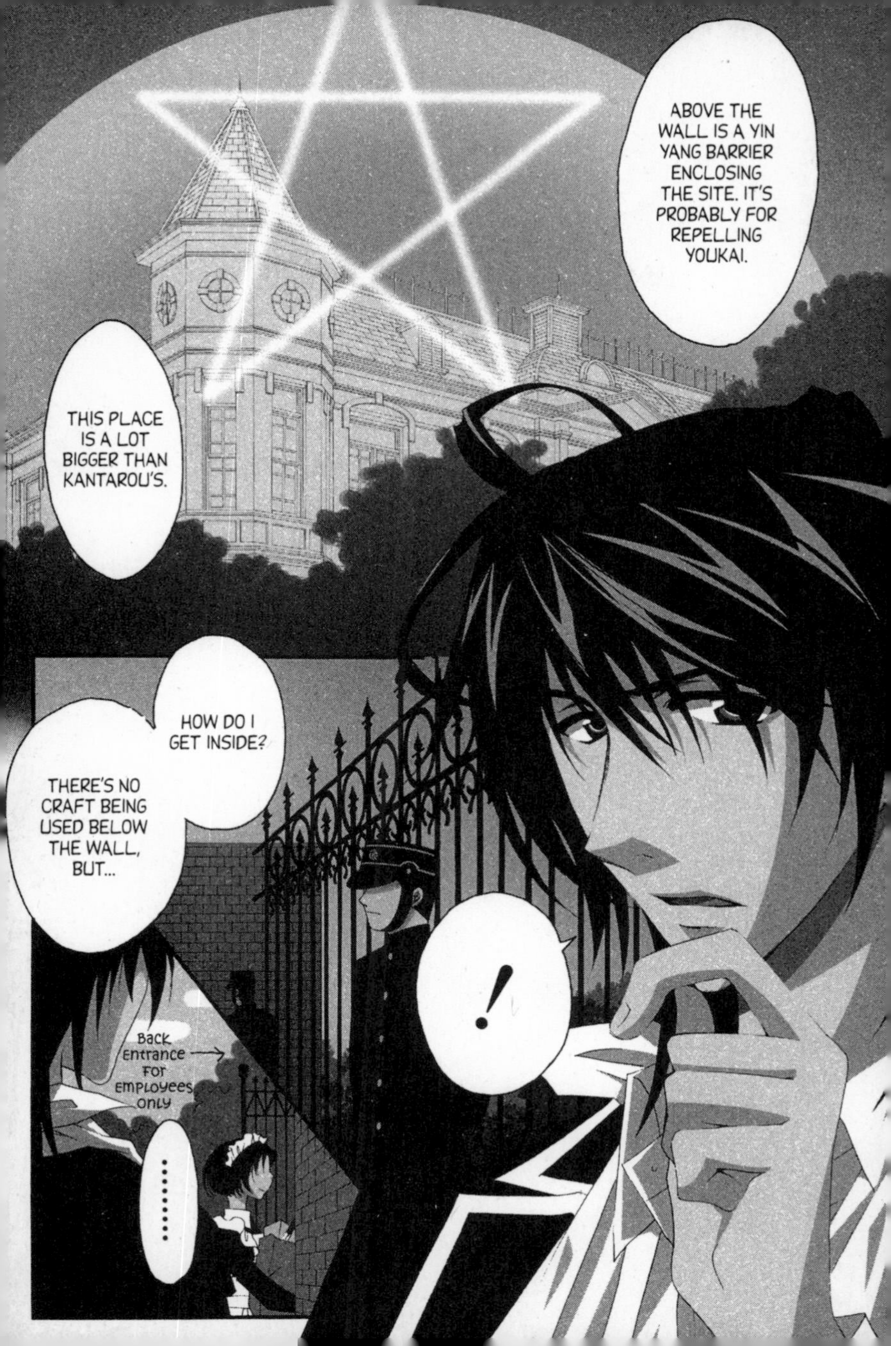
ABOVE THE WALL IS A YIN YANG BARRIER ENCLOSING THE SITE. IT'S PROBABLY FOR REPELLING YOUKAI.
THIS PLACE IS A LOT BIGGER THAN KANTAROU'S.
HOW DO I GET INSIDE?
THERE'S NO CRAFT BEING USED BELOW THE WALL, BUT...
!
Back entrance for employees only
......

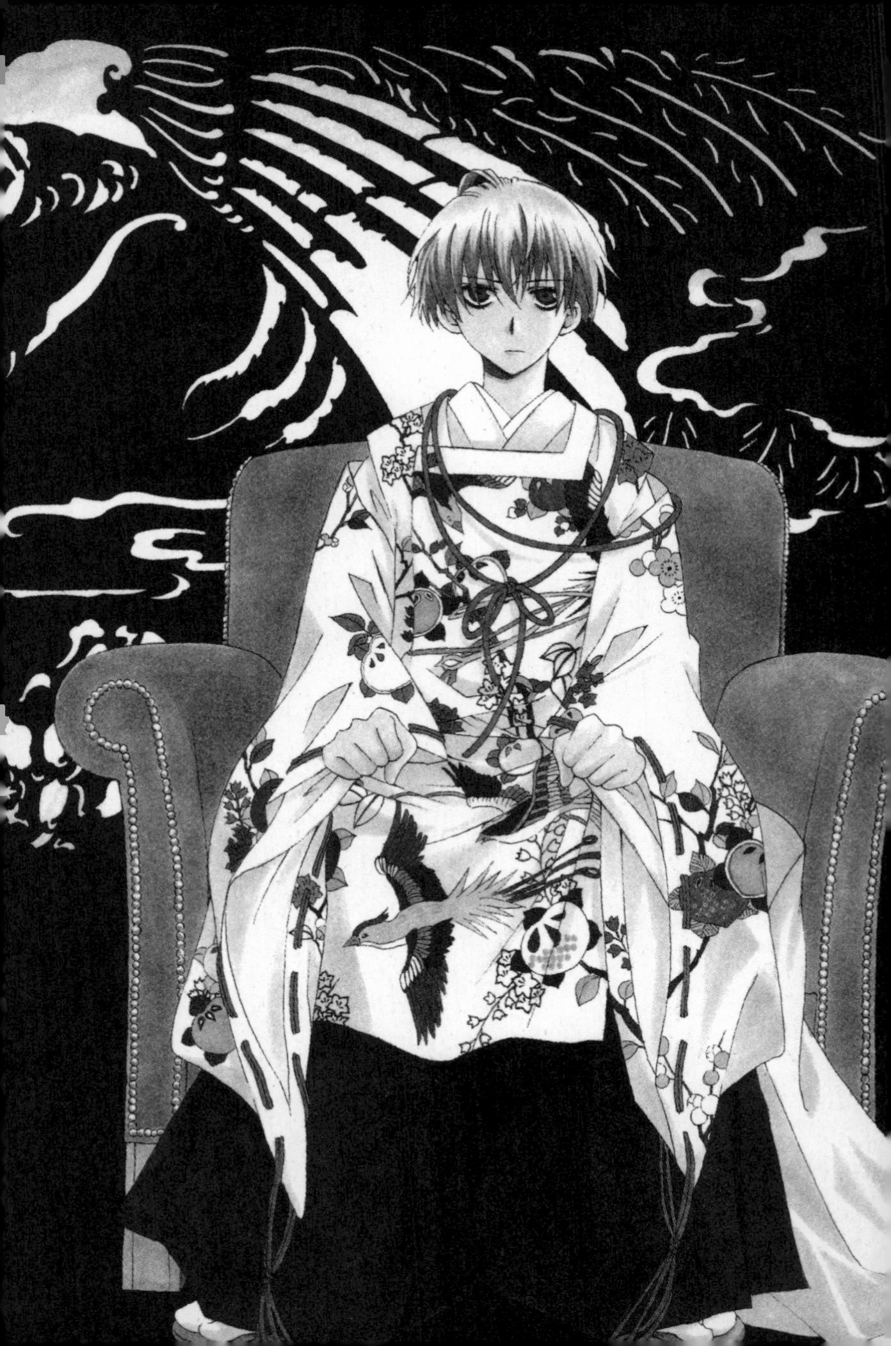

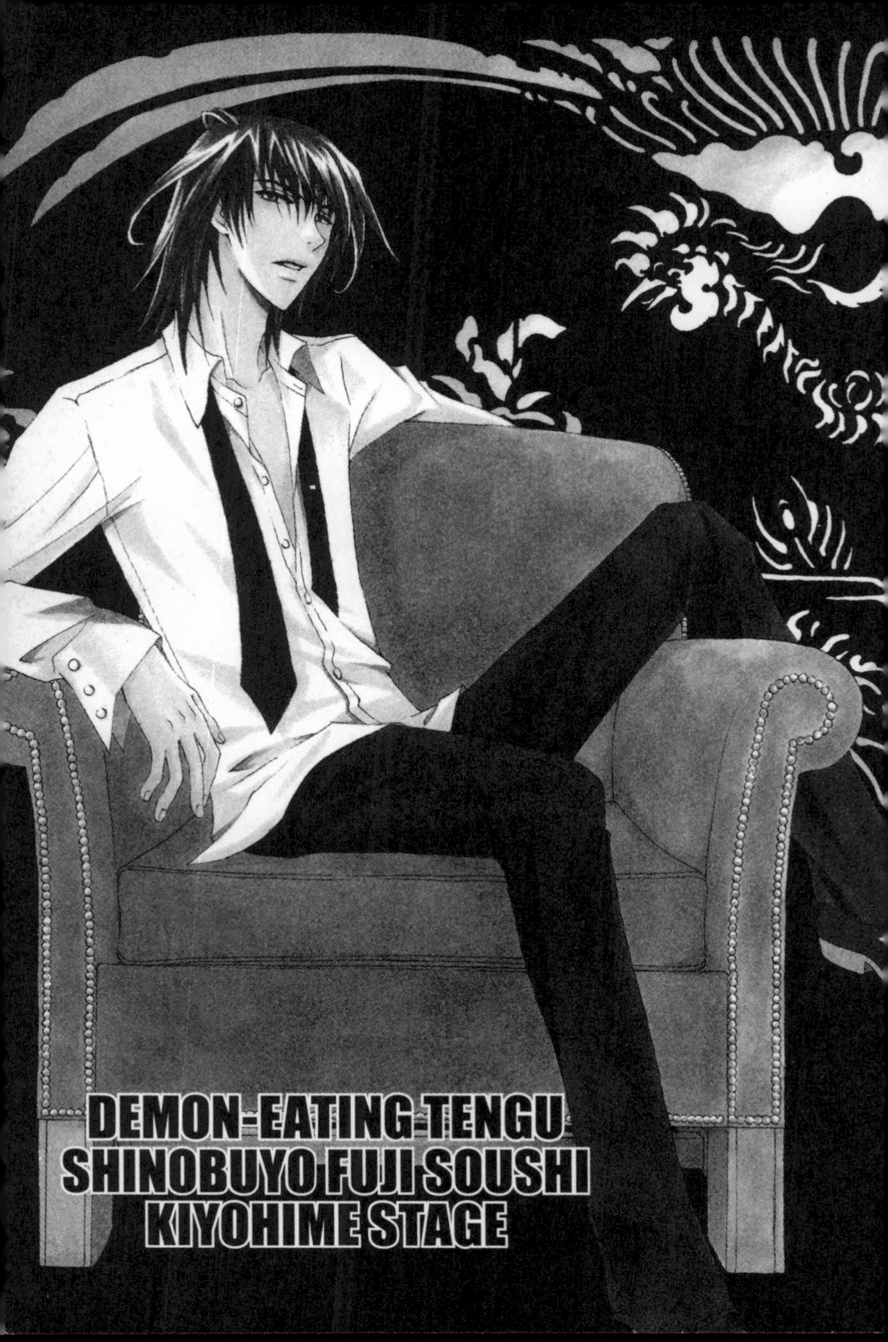
DEMON-EATING TENGU
SHINOBUYO FUJI SOUSHI
KIYOHIME STAGE

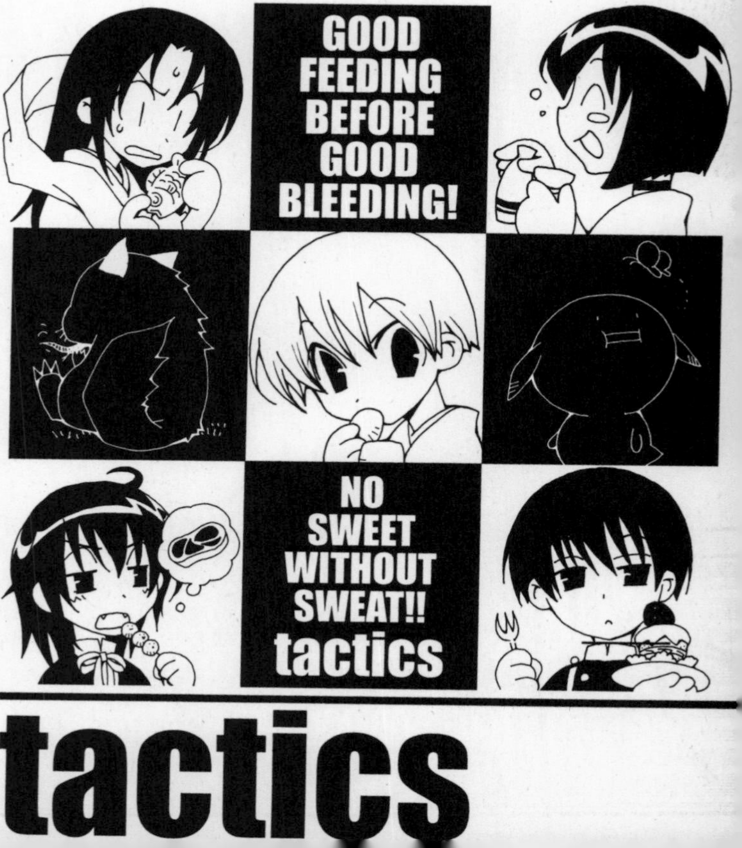
GOOD FEEDING BEFORE GOOD BLEEDING!
NO SWEET WITHOUT SWEAT!!
tactics

tactics

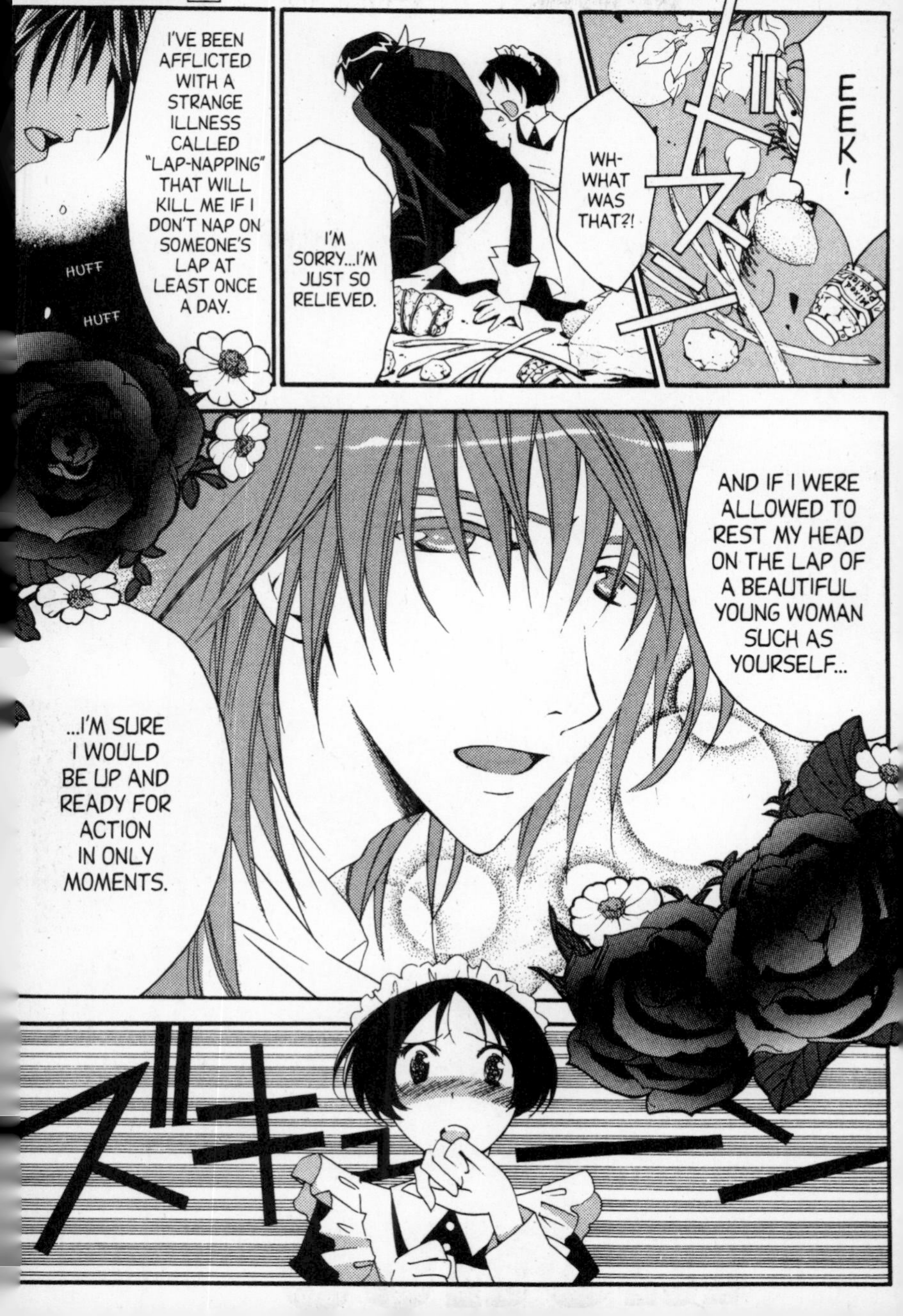
EEK!
WH- WHAT WAS THAT?!
I'M SORRY...I'M JUST SO RELIEVED.
I'VE BEEN AFFLICTED WITH A STRANGE ILLNESS CALLED "LAP-NAPPING" THAT WILL KILL ME IF I DON'T NAP ON SOMEONE'S LAP AT LEAST ONCE A DAY.
HUFF
HUFF
AND IF I WERE ALLOWED TO REST MY HEAD ON THE LAP OF A BEAUTIFUL YOUNG WOMAN SUCH AS YOURSELF...
...I'M SURE I WOULD BE UP AND READY FOR ACTION IN ONLY MOMENTS.

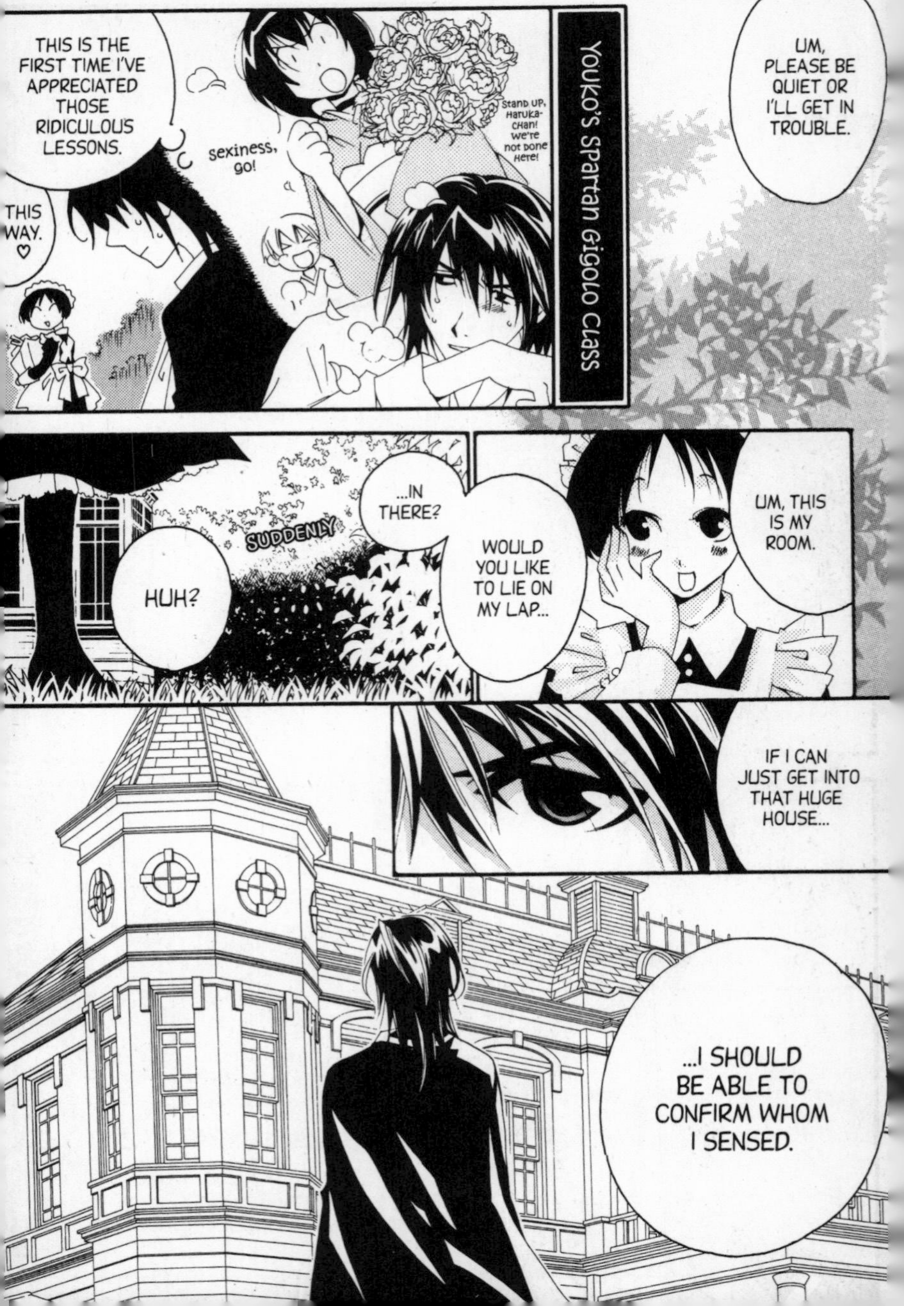
UM, PLEASE BE QUIET OR I'LL GET IN TROUBLE.
Youko's Spartan Gigolo Class
Stand up, Haruka-chan! We're not done here!
sexiness, go!
THIS IS THE FIRST TIME I'VE APPRECIATED THOSE RIDICULOUS LESSONS.
THIS WAY. ♡
UM, THIS IS MY ROOM.
WOULD YOU LIKE TO LIE ON MY LAP...
...IN THERE?
SUDDENLY
HUH?
IF I CAN JUST GET INTO THAT HUGE HOUSE...
...I SHOULD BE ABLE TO CONFIRM WHOM I SENSED.

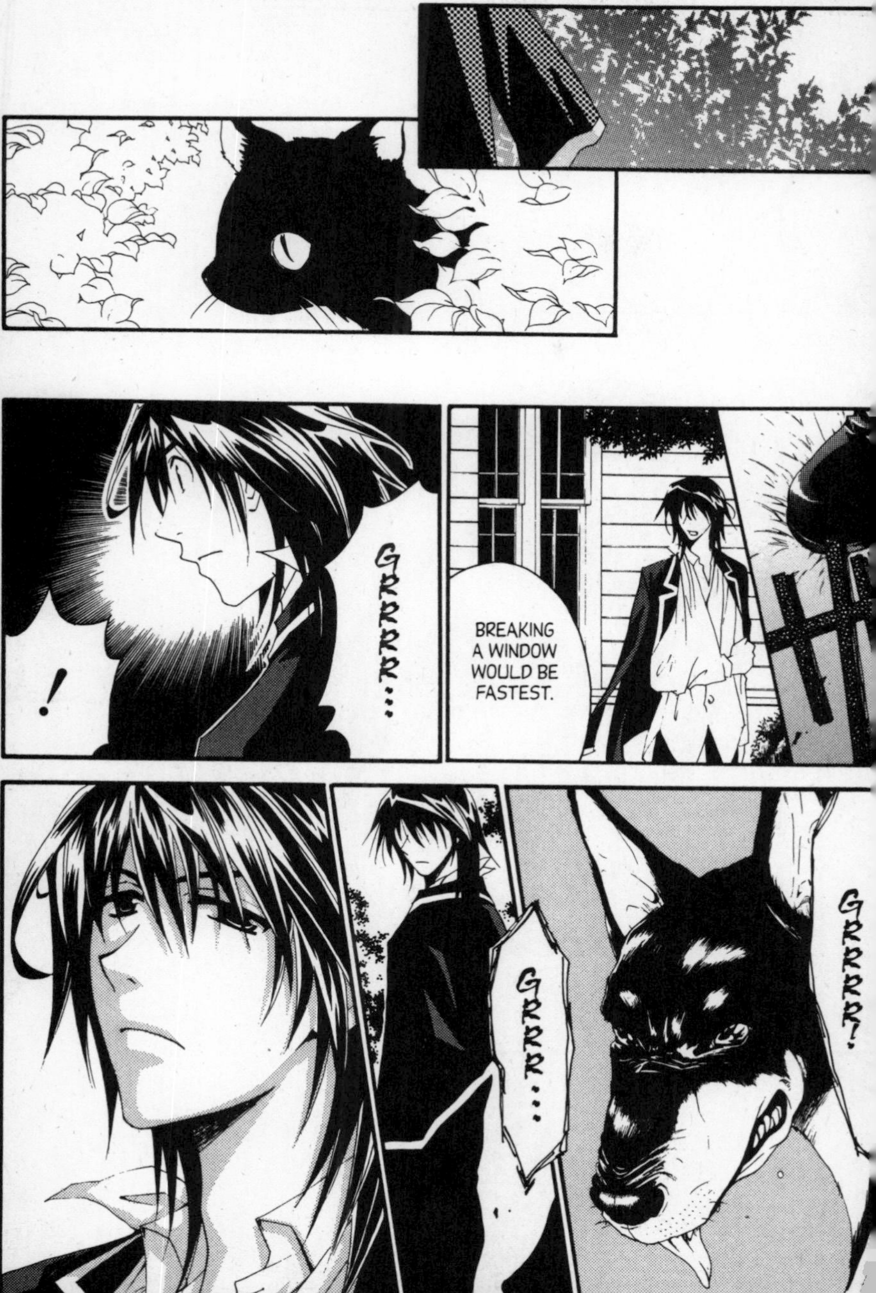
BREAKING A WINDOW WOULD BE FASTEST.
GRRRRR...
!
GRRRRR!
GRRRR...

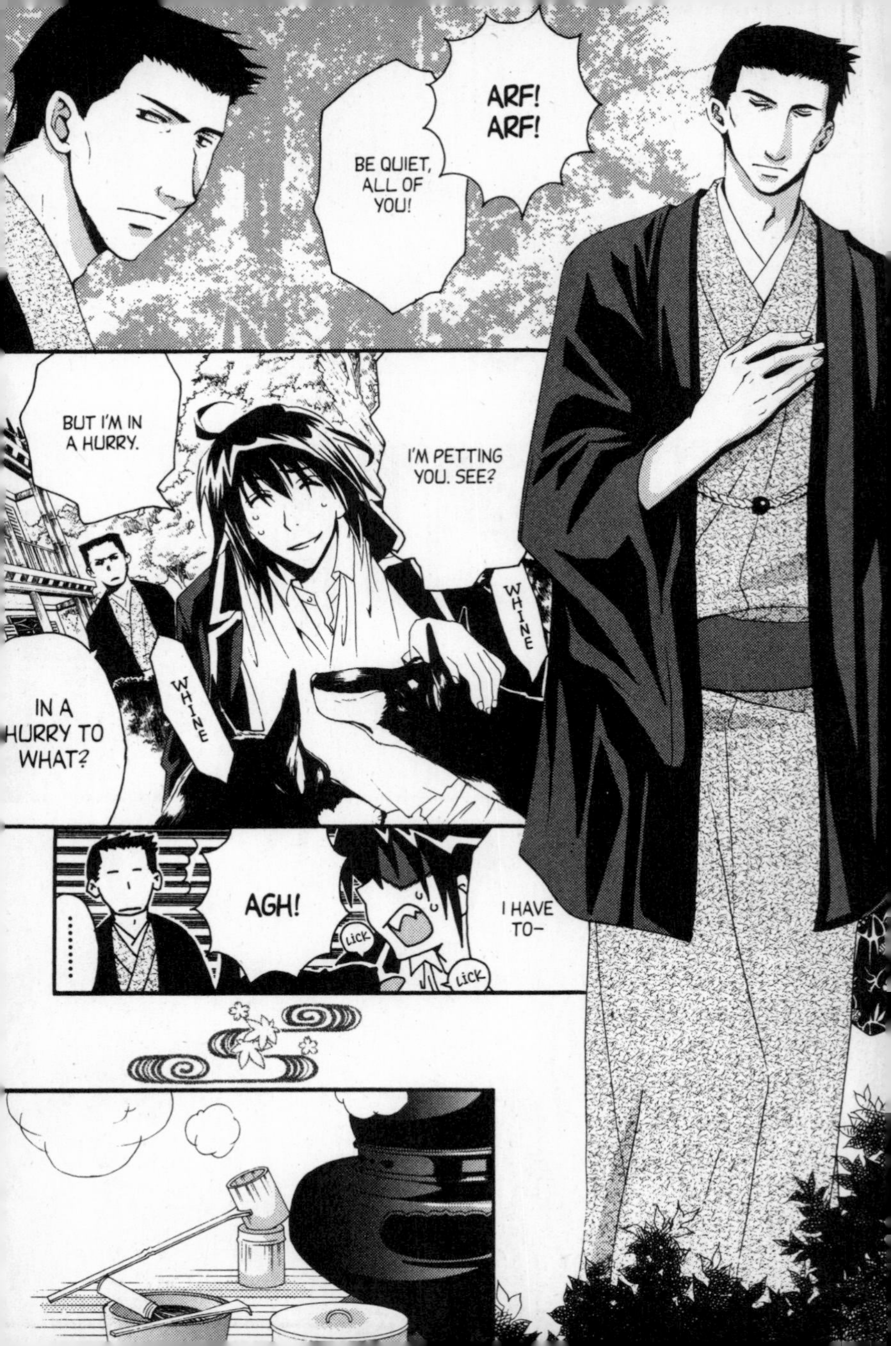
ARF! ARF!
BE QUIET, ALL OF YOU!
I'M PETTING YOU. SEE?
WHINE
BUT I'M IN A HURRY.
WHINE
IN A HURRY TO WHAT?
I HAVE TO—
LICK
LICK
AGH!
......

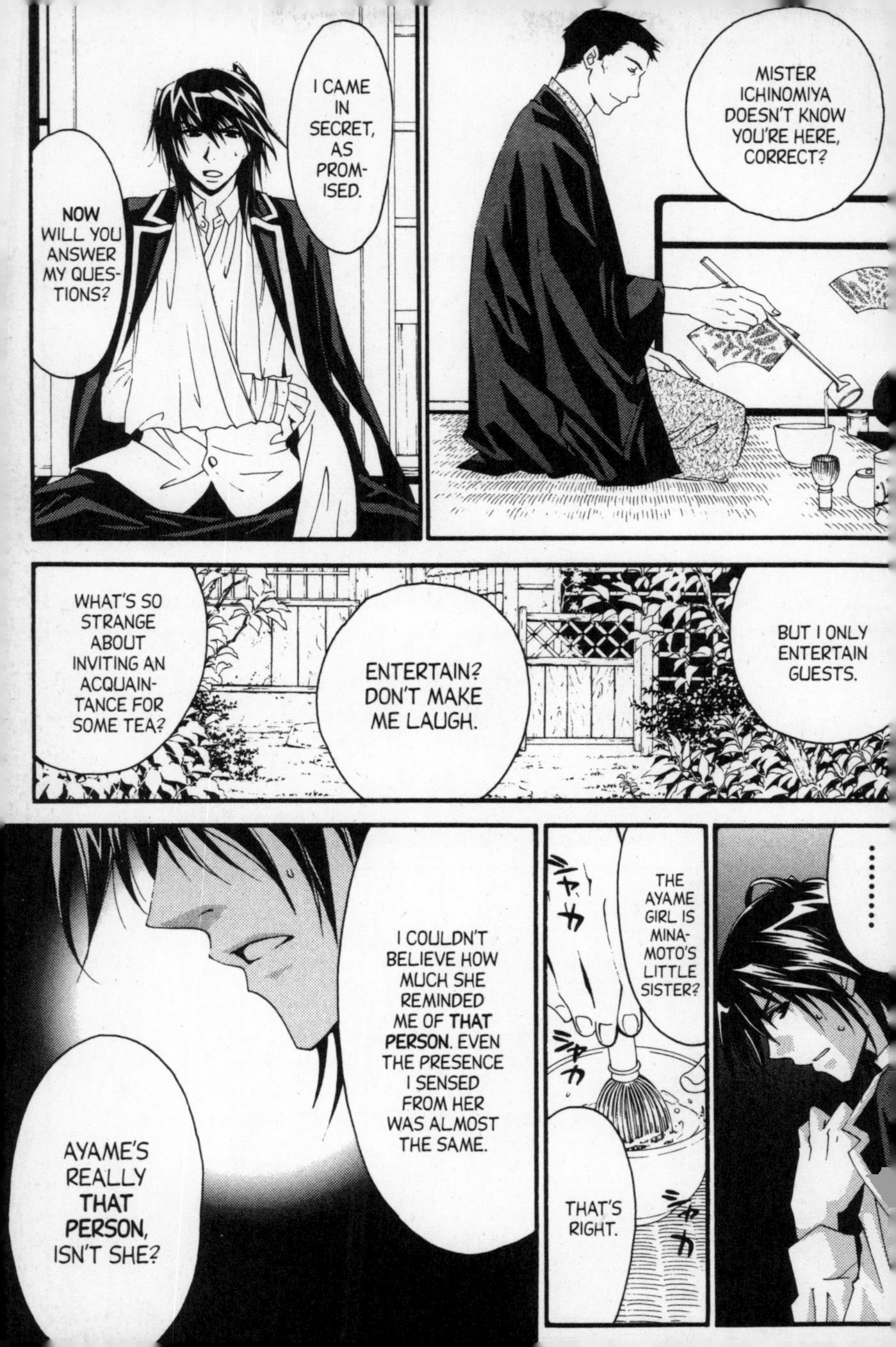
MISTER ICHINOMIYA DOESN'T KNOW YOU'RE HERE, CORRECT?
I CAME IN SECRET, AS PROM-ISED.
NOW WILL YOU ANSWER MY QUES-TIONS?
BUT I ONLY ENTERTAIN GUESTS.
ENTERTAIN? DON'T MAKE ME LAUGH.
WHAT'S SO STRANGE ABOUT INVITING AN ACQUAIN-TANCE FOR SOME TEA?
......
THE AYAME GIRL IS MINA-MOTO'S LITTLE SISTER?
シャカ
シャカ
THAT'S RIGHT.
シャカ
I COULDN'T BELIEVE HOW MUCH SHE REMINDED ME OF **THAT PERSON**. EVEN THE PRESENCE I SENSED FROM HER WAS ALMOST THE SAME.
AYAME'S REALLY **THAT PERSON**, ISN'T SHE?

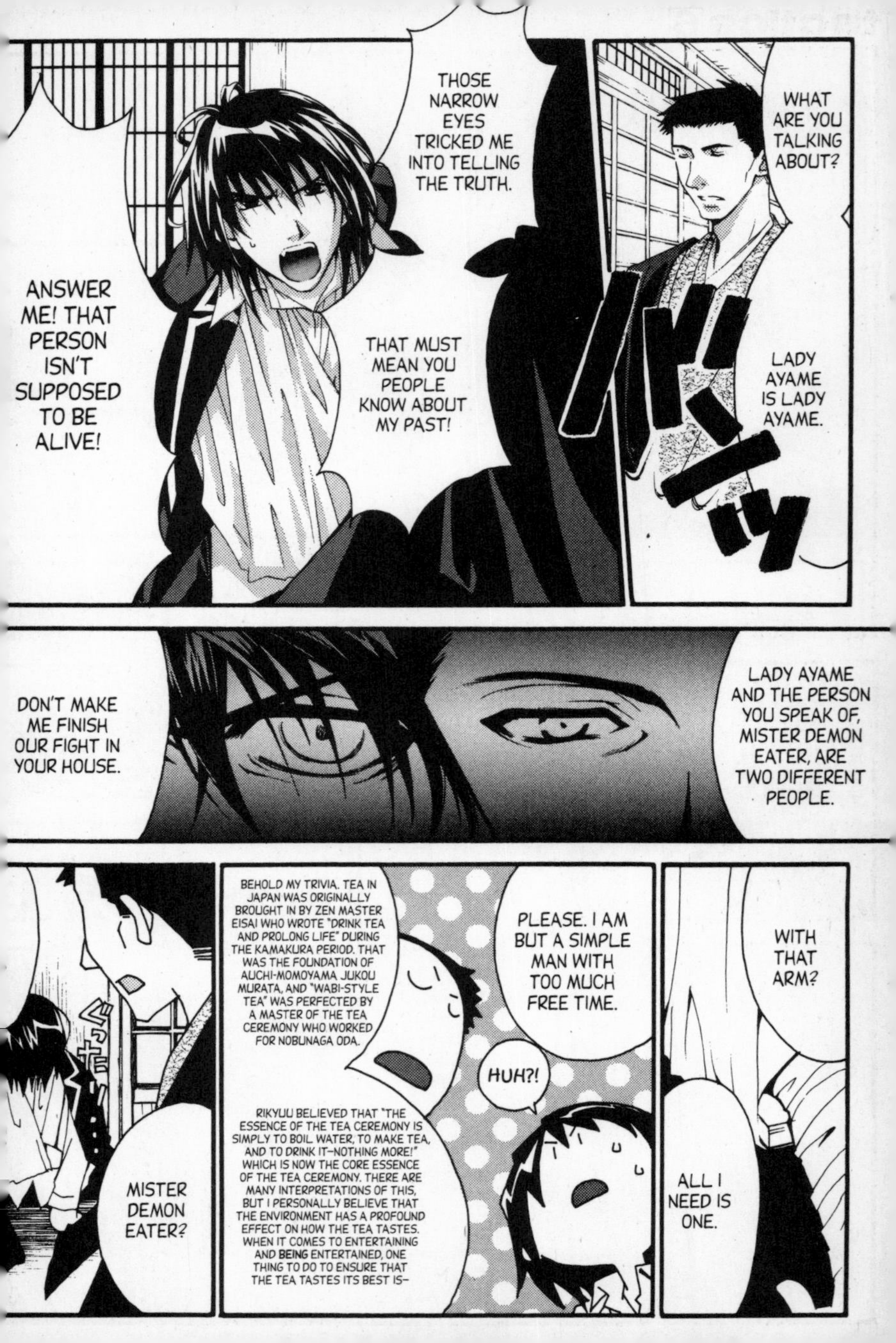
WHAT ARE YOU TALKING ABOUT?
LADY AYAME IS LADY AYAME.
THOSE NARROW EYES TRICKED ME INTO TELLING THE TRUTH.
THAT MUST MEAN YOU PEOPLE KNOW ABOUT MY PAST!
ANSWER ME! THAT PERSON ISN'T SUPPOSED TO BE ALIVE!
LADY AYAME AND THE PERSON YOU SPEAK OF, MISTER DEMON EATER, ARE TWO DIFFERENT PEOPLE.
DON'T MAKE ME FINISH OUR FIGHT IN YOUR HOUSE.
WITH THAT ARM?
ALL I NEED IS ONE.
PLEASE. I AM BUT A SIMPLE MAN WITH TOO MUCH FREE TIME.
BEHOLD MY TRIVIA. TEA IN JAPAN WAS ORIGINALLY BROUGHT IN BY ZEN MASTER EISAI WHO WROTE "DRINK TEA AND PROLONG LIFE" DURING THE KAMAKURA PERIOD. THAT WAS THE FOUNDATION OF AUCHI-MOMOYAMA JUKOU MURATA, AND "WABI-STYLE TEA" WAS PERFECTED BY A MASTER OF THE TEA CEREMONY WHO WORKED FOR NOBUNAGA ODA.
HUH?!
RIKYUU BELIEVED THAT "THE ESSENCE OF THE TEA CEREMONY IS SIMPLY TO BOIL WATER, TO MAKE TEA, AND TO DRINK IT—NOTHING MORE!" WHICH IS NOW THE CORE ESSENCE OF THE TEA CEREMONY. THERE ARE MANY INTERPRETATIONS OF THIS, BUT I PERSONALLY BELIEVE THAT THE ENVIRONMENT HAS A PROFOUND EFFECT ON HOW THE TEA TASTES. WHEN IT COMES TO ENTERTAINING AND BEING ENTERTAINED, ONE THING TO DO TO ENSURE THAT THE TEA TASTES ITS BEST IS—
MISTER DEMON EATER?

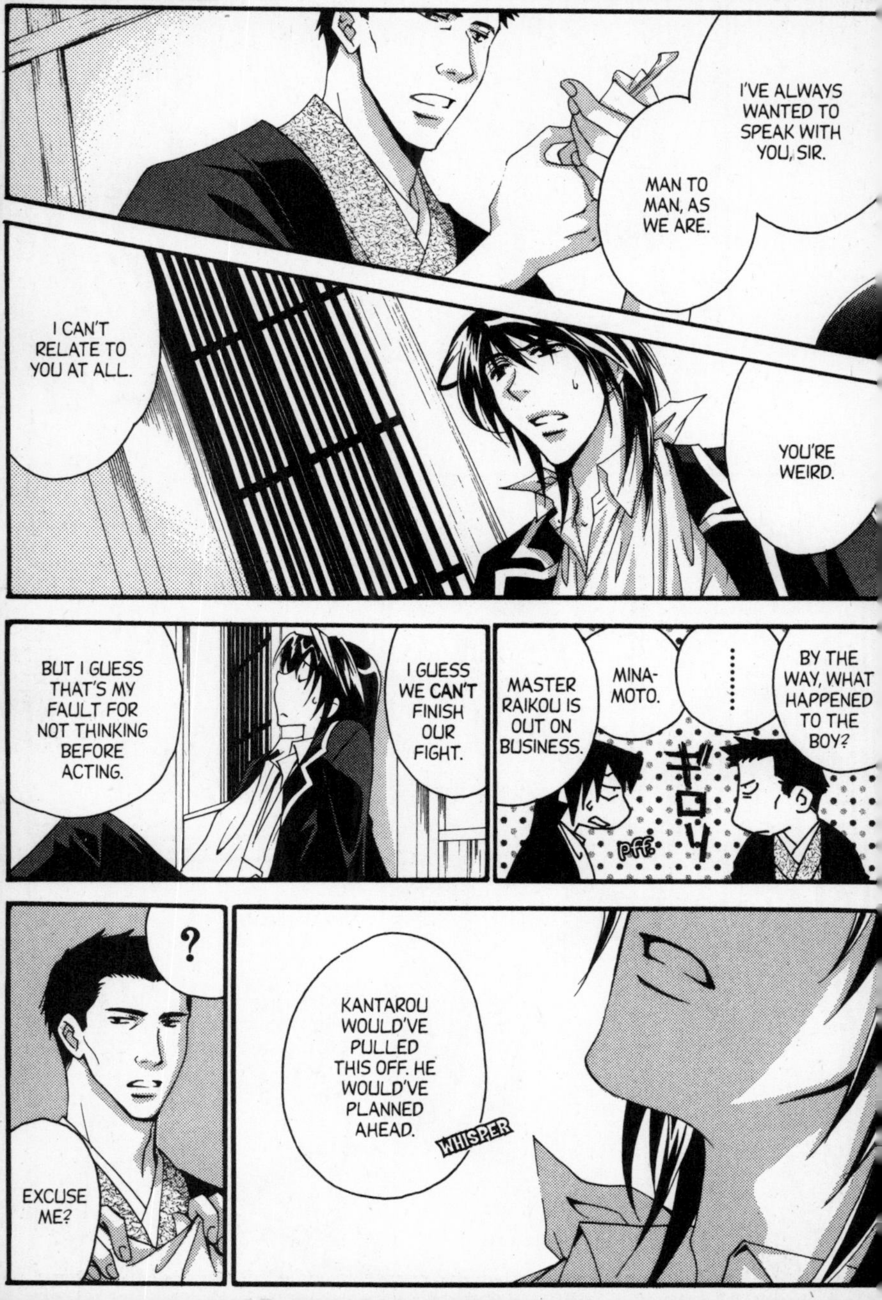
I'VE ALWAYS WANTED TO SPEAK WITH YOU, SIR.
MAN TO MAN, AS WE ARE.
YOU'RE WEIRD.
I CAN'T RELATE TO YOU AT ALL.
BY THE WAY, WHAT HAPPENED TO THE BOY?
......
MINA-MOTO.
MASTER RAIKOU IS OUT ON BUSINESS.
pff
I GUESS WE CAN'T FINISH OUR FIGHT.
BUT I GUESS THAT'S MY FAULT FOR NOT THINKING BEFORE ACTING.
KANTAROU WOULD'VE PULLED THIS OFF. HE WOULD'VE PLANNED AHEAD.
WHISPER
?
EXCUSE ME?

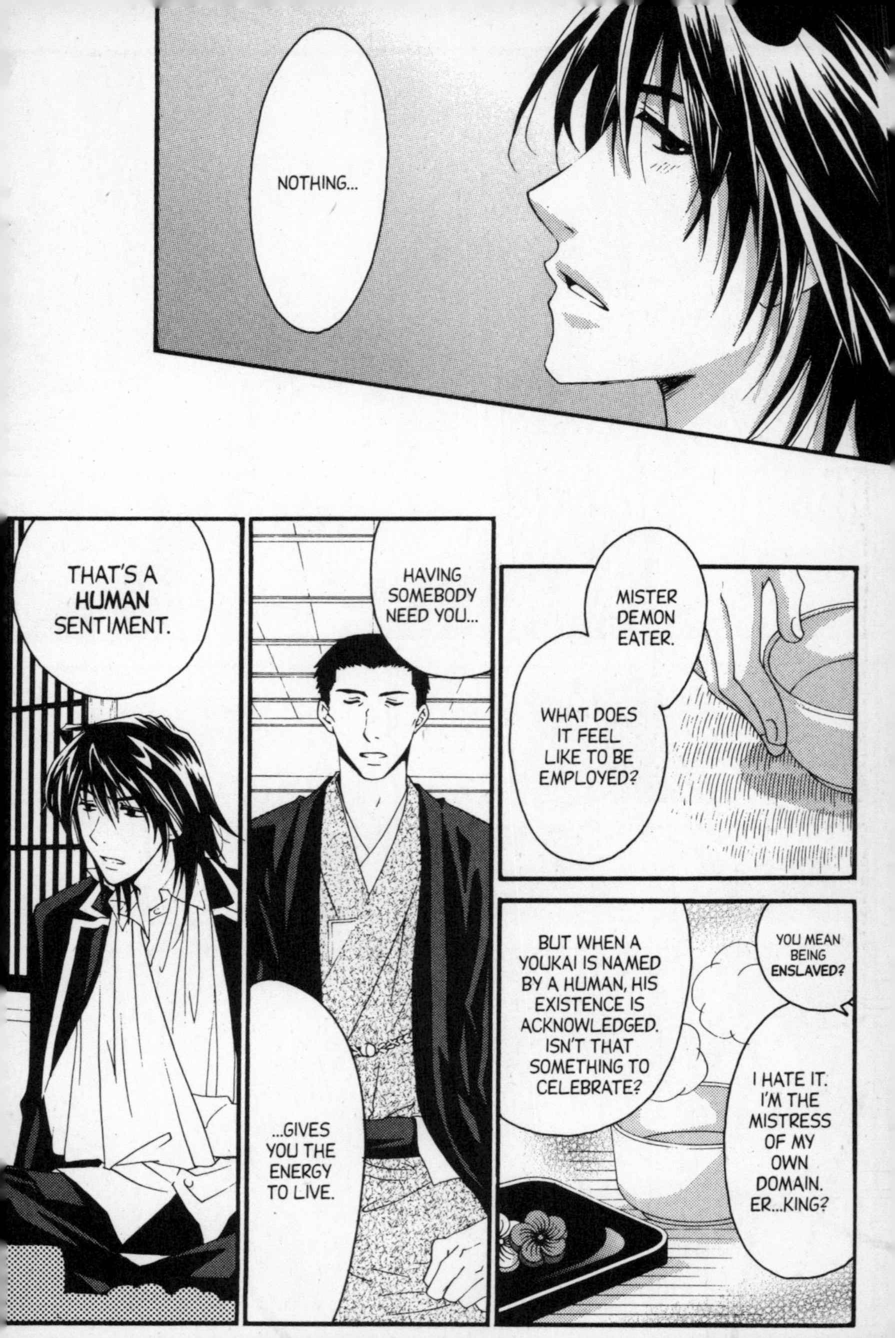
NOTHING...
MISTER DEMON EATER.
WHAT DOES IT FEEL LIKE TO BE EMPLOYED?
YOU MEAN BEING ENSLAVED?
I HATE IT. I'M THE MISTRESS OF MY OWN DOMAIN. ER...KING?
BUT WHEN A YOUKAI IS NAMED BY A HUMAN, HIS EXISTENCE IS ACKNOWLEDGED. ISN'T THAT SOMETHING TO CELEBRATE?
HAVING SOMEBODY NEED YOU...
...GIVES YOU THE ENERGY TO LIVE.
THAT'S A HUMAN SENTIMENT.

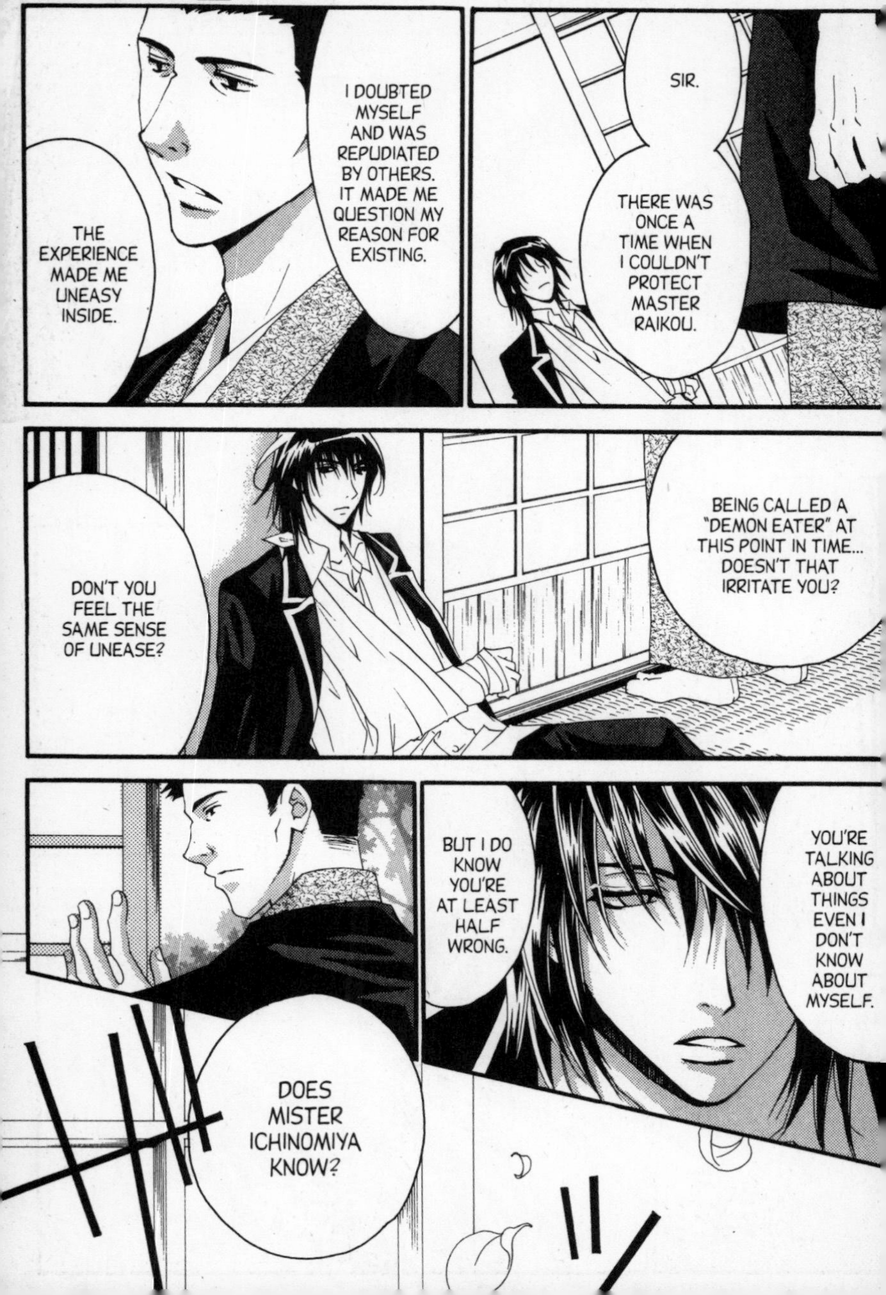
SIR.
THERE WAS ONCE A TIME WHEN I COULDN'T PROTECT MASTER RAIKOU.
I DOUBTED MYSELF AND WAS REPUDIATED BY OTHERS. IT MADE ME QUESTION MY REASON FOR EXISTING.
THE EXPERIENCE MADE ME UNEASY INSIDE.
BEING CALLED A "DEMON EATER" AT THIS POINT IN TIME... DOESN'T THAT IRRITATE YOU?
DON'T YOU FEEL THE SAME SENSE OF UNEASE?
YOU'RE TALKING ABOUT THINGS EVEN I DON'T KNOW ABOUT MYSELF.
BUT I DO KNOW YOU'RE AT LEAST HALF WRONG.
DOES MISTER ICHINOMIYA KNOW?

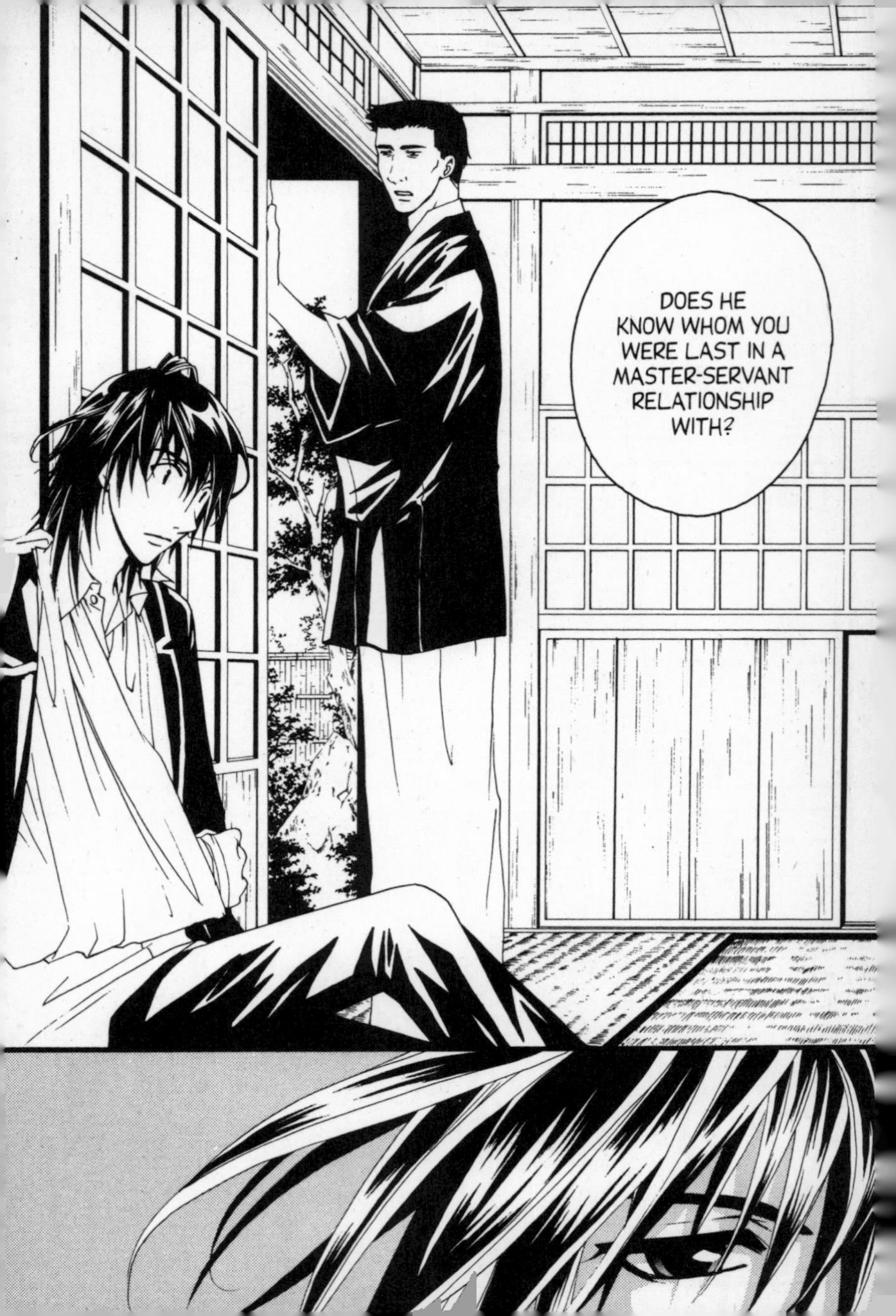
DOES HE KNOW WHOM YOU WERE LAST IN A MASTER-SERVANT RELATIONSHIP WITH?

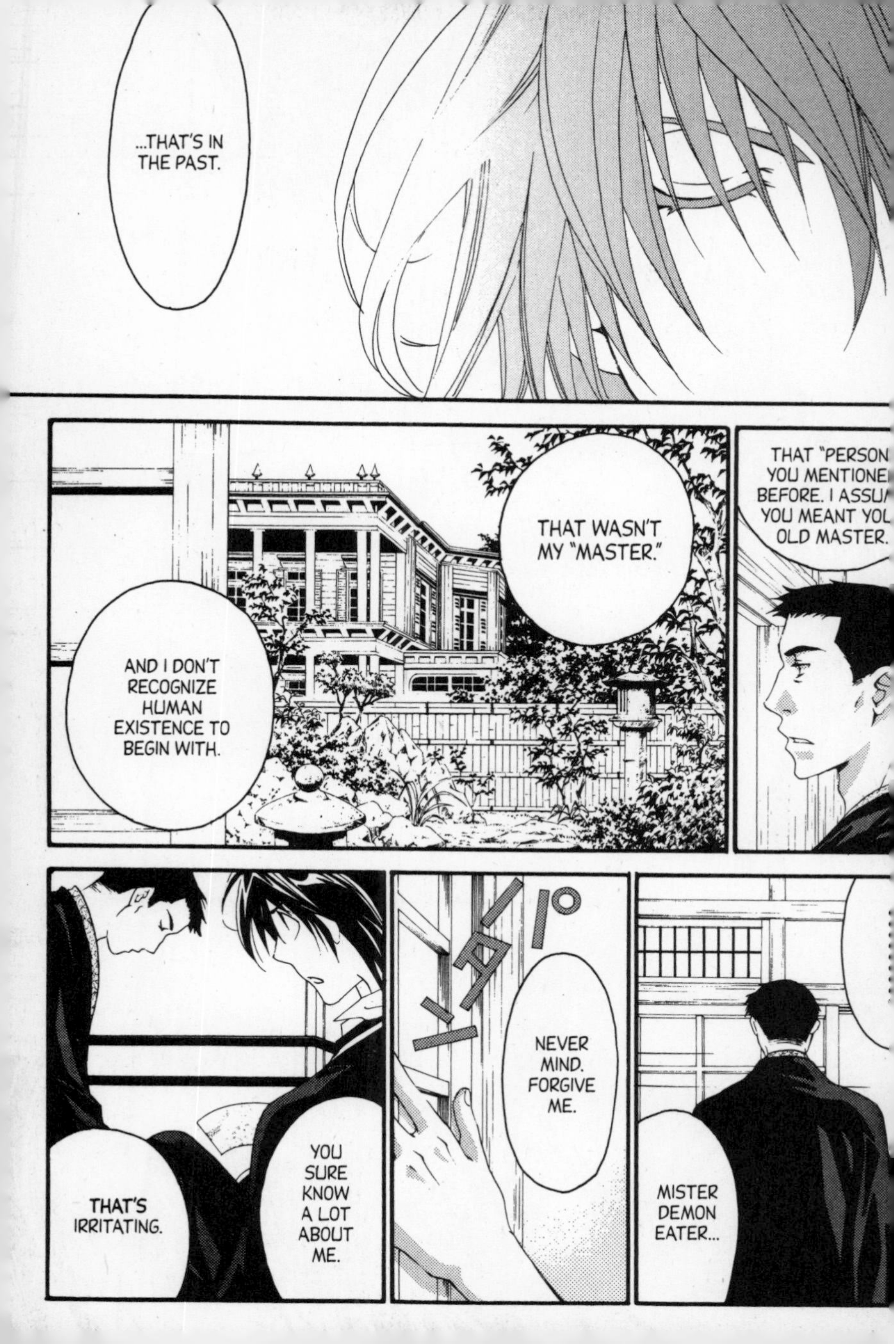
...THAT'S IN THE PAST.
THAT "PERSON YOU MENTIONE BEFORE. I ASSU YOU MEANT YO OLD MASTER.
THAT WASN'T MY "MASTER."
AND I DON'T RECOGNIZE HUMAN EXISTENCE TO BEGIN WITH.
MISTER DEMON EATER...
NEVER MIND. FORGIVE ME.
YOU SURE KNOW A LOT ABOUT ME.
THAT'S IRRITATING.

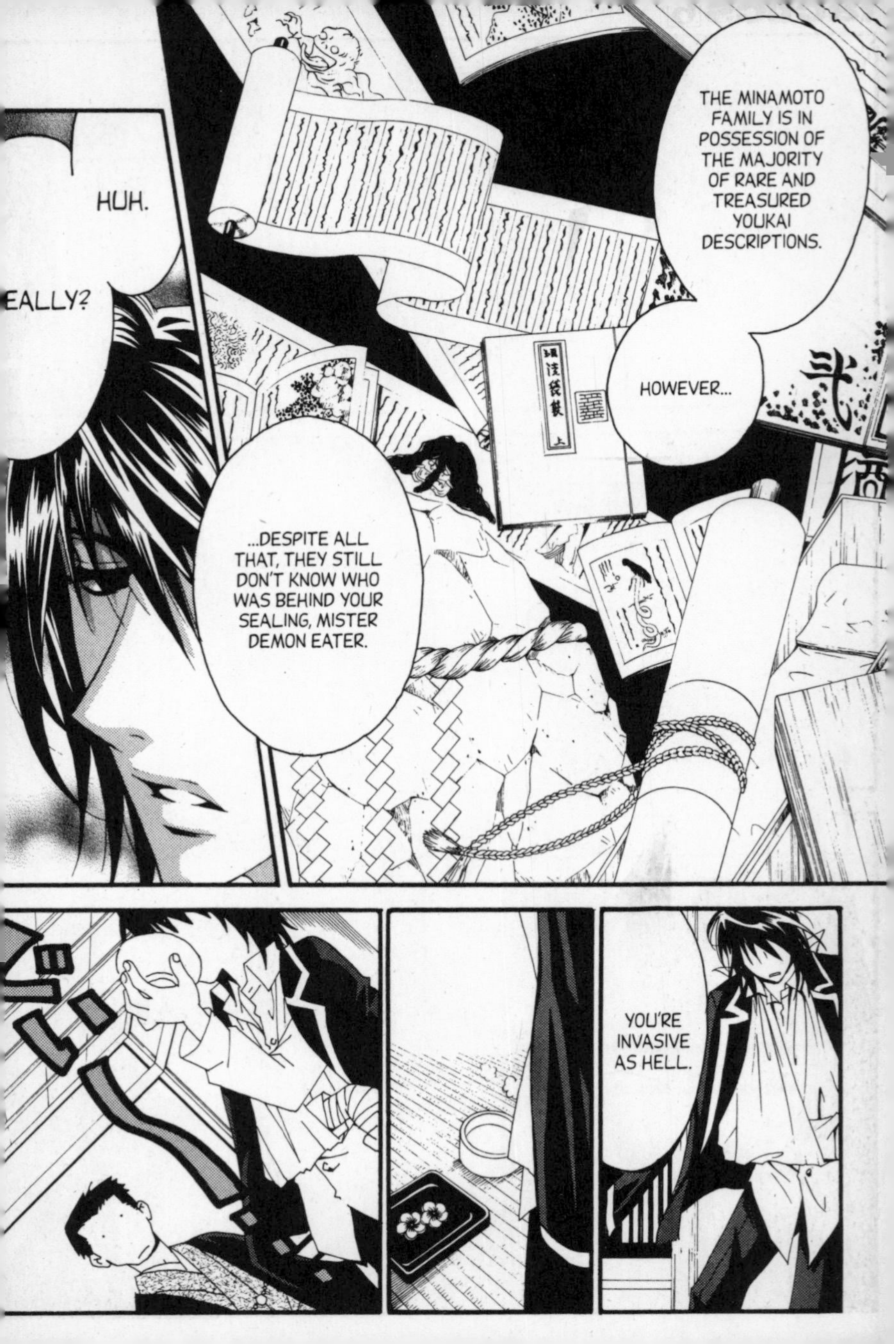
THE MINAMOTO FAMILY IS IN POSSESSION OF THE MAJORITY OF RARE AND TREASURED YOUKAI DESCRIPTIONS.
HOWEVER...
...DESPITE ALL THAT, THEY STILL DON'T KNOW WHO WAS BEHIND YOUR SEALING, MISTER DEMON EATER.
HUH.
EALLY?
YOU'RE INVASIVE AS HELL.

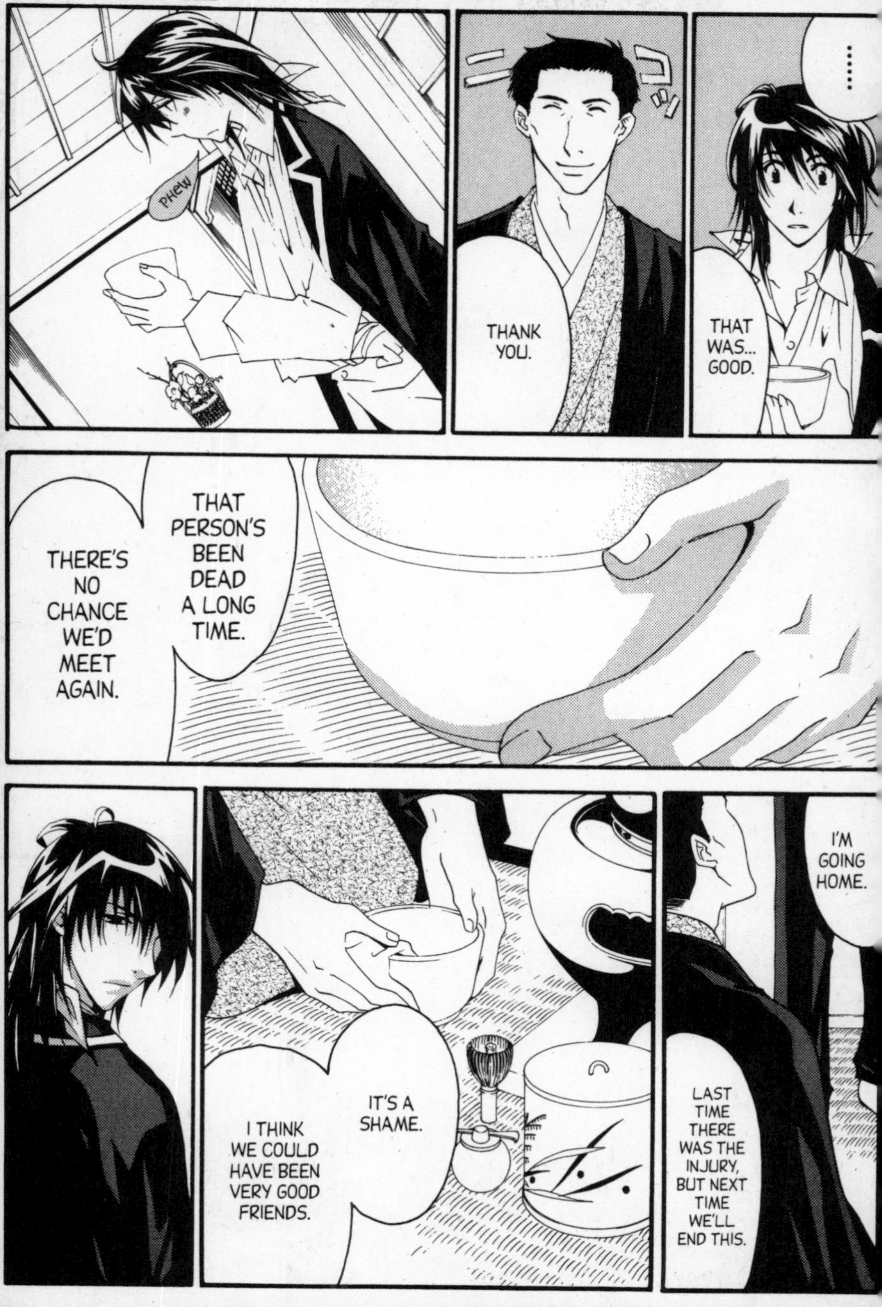
......
THAT WAS... GOOD.
THANK YOU.
PHEW
THAT PERSON'S BEEN DEAD A LONG TIME.
THERE'S NO CHANCE WE'D MEET AGAIN.
I'M GOING HOME.
LAST TIME THERE WAS THE INJURY, BUT NEXT TIME WE'LL END THIS.
IT'S A SHAME.
I THINK WE COULD HAVE BEEN VERY GOOD FRIENDS.

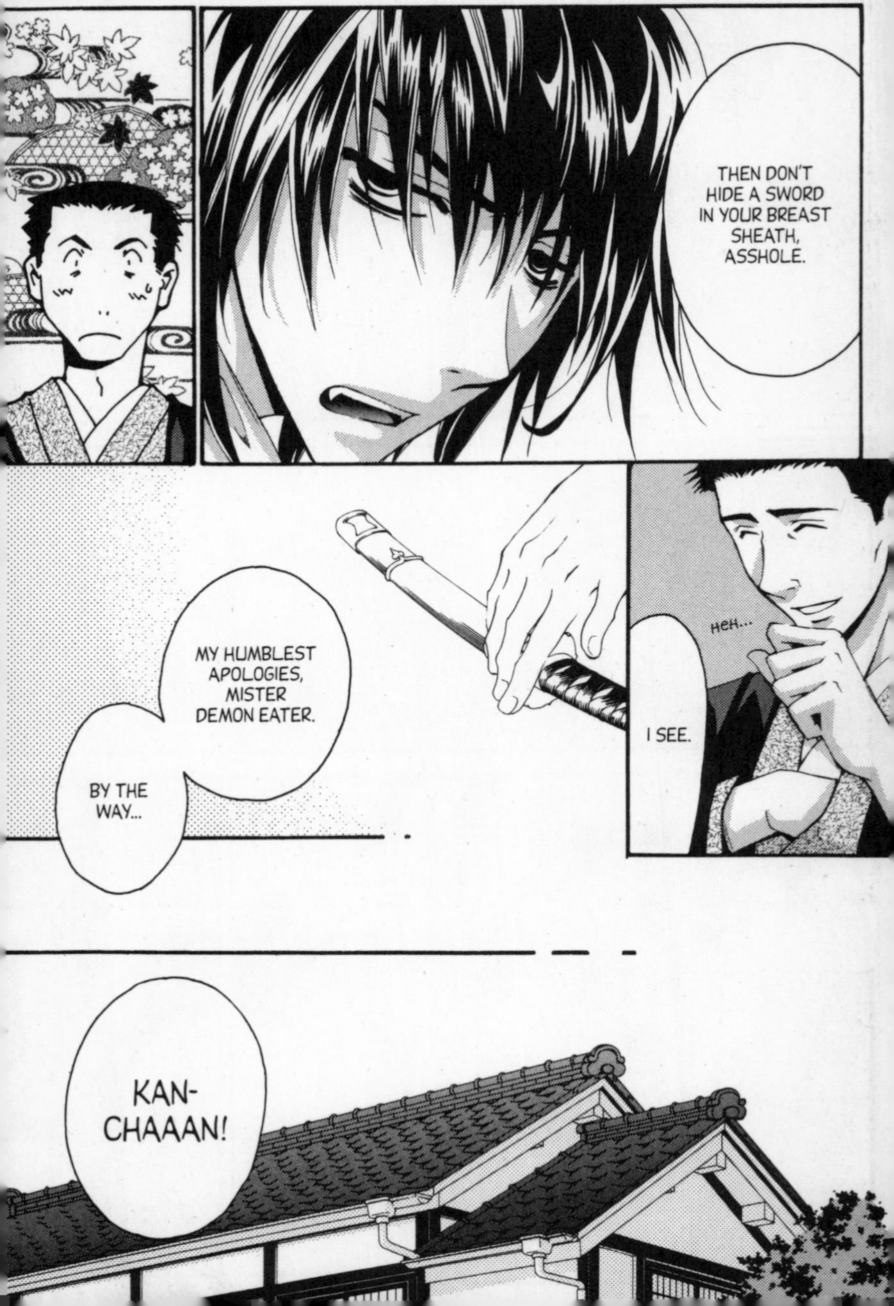
THEN DON'T HIDE A SWORD IN YOUR BREAST SHEATH, ASSHOLE.
HEH...
I SEE.
MY HUMBLEST APOLOGIES, MISTER DEMON EATER.
BY THE WAY...
KAN-CHAAAN!

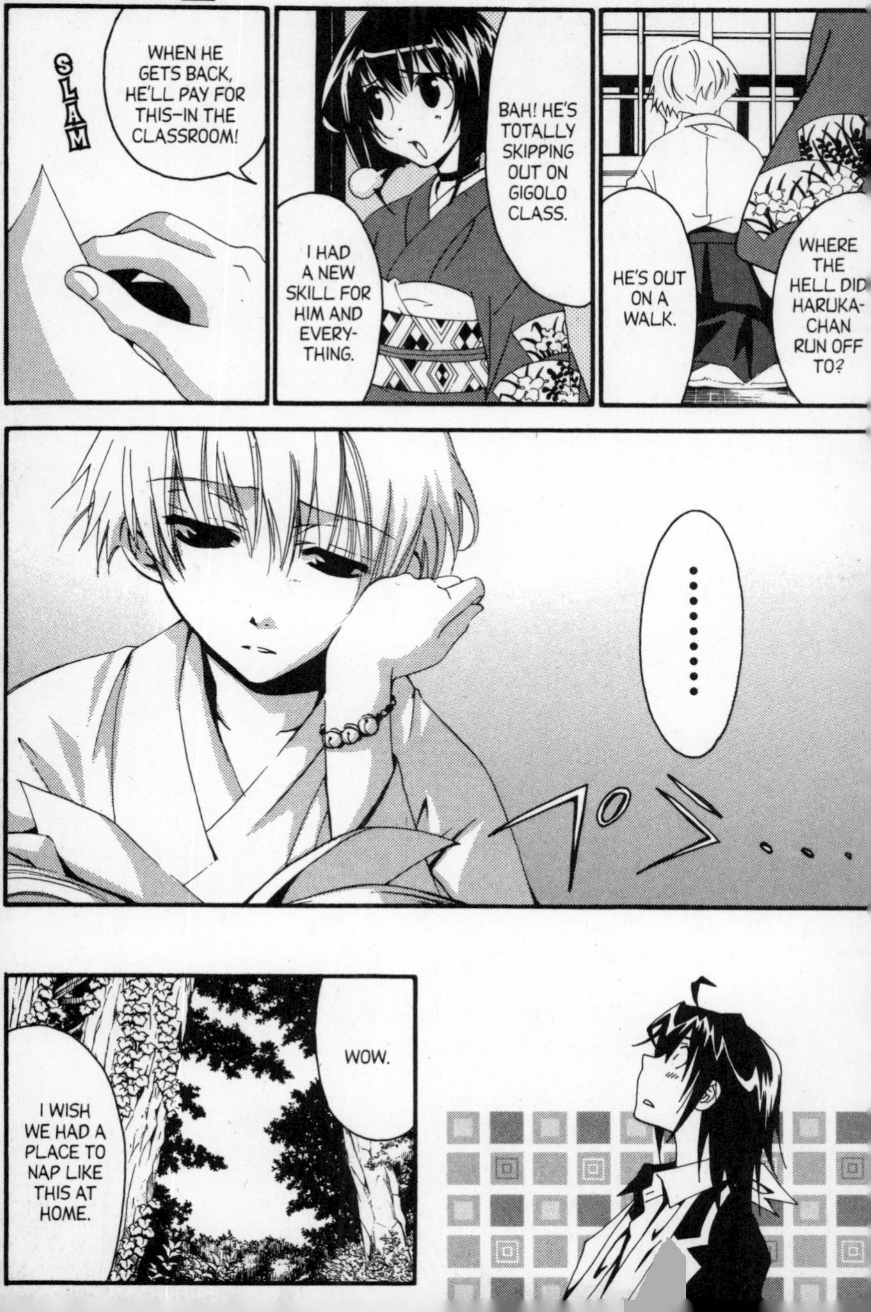
WHERE THE HELL DID HARUKA-CHAN RUN OFF TO?
HE'S OUT ON A WALK.
BAH! HE'S TOTALLY SKIPPING OUT ON GIGOLO CLASS.
I HAD A NEW SKILL FOR HIM AND EVERYTHING.
WHEN HE GETS BACK, HE'LL PAY FOR THIS—IN THE CLASSROOM!
SLAM
....
WOW.
I WISH WE HAD A PLACE TO NAP LIKE THIS AT HOME.

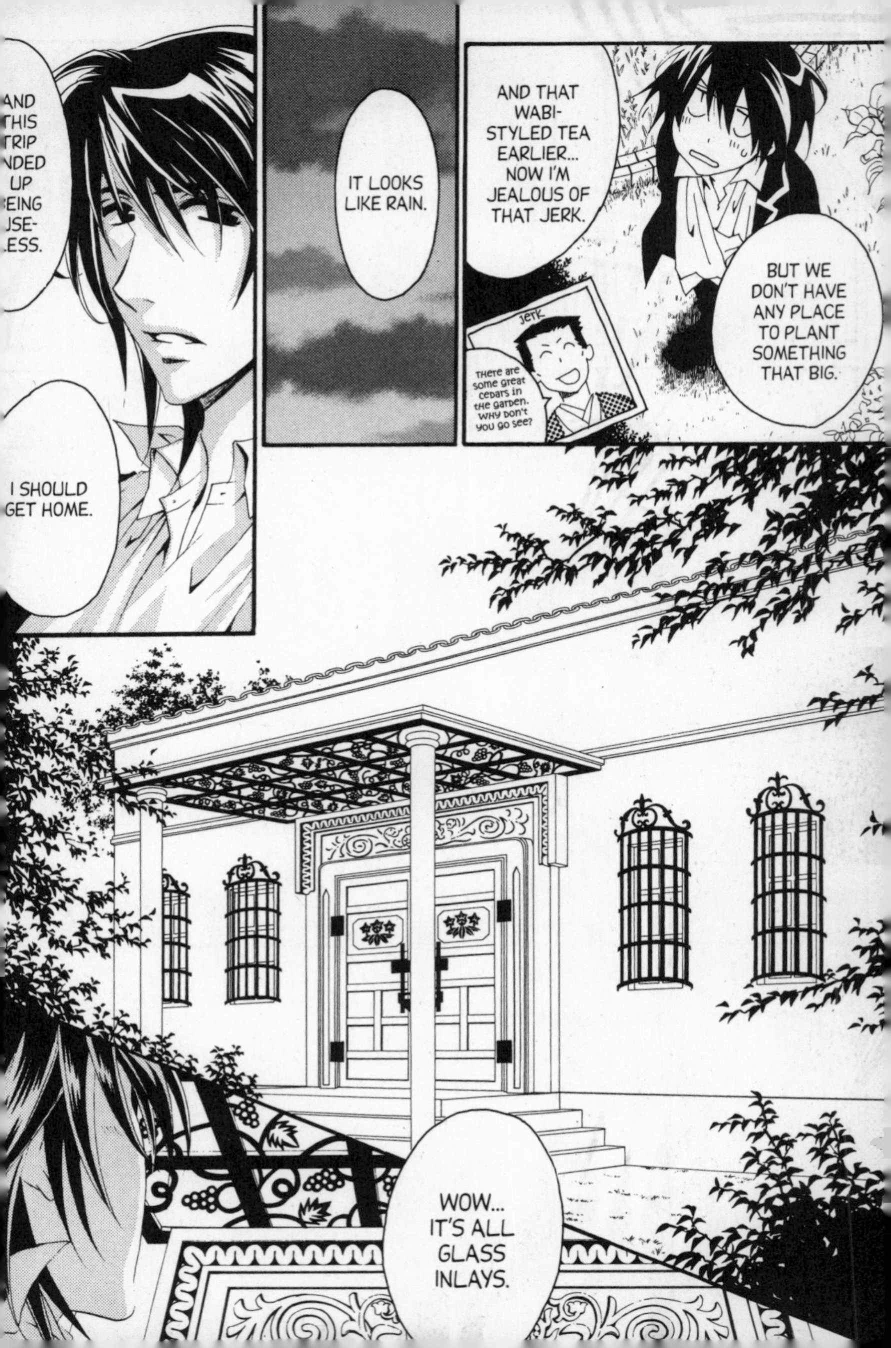
AND THAT WABI-STYLED TEA EARLIER... NOW I'M JEALOUS OF THAT JERK.
JERK
There are some great cedars in the garden. Why don't you go see?
BUT WE DON'T HAVE ANY PLACE TO PLANT SOMETHING THAT BIG.
IT LOOKS LIKE RAIN.
AND THIS TRIP NDED UP EING USE- LESS.
I SHOULD GET HOME.
WOW... IT'S ALL GLASS INLAYS.

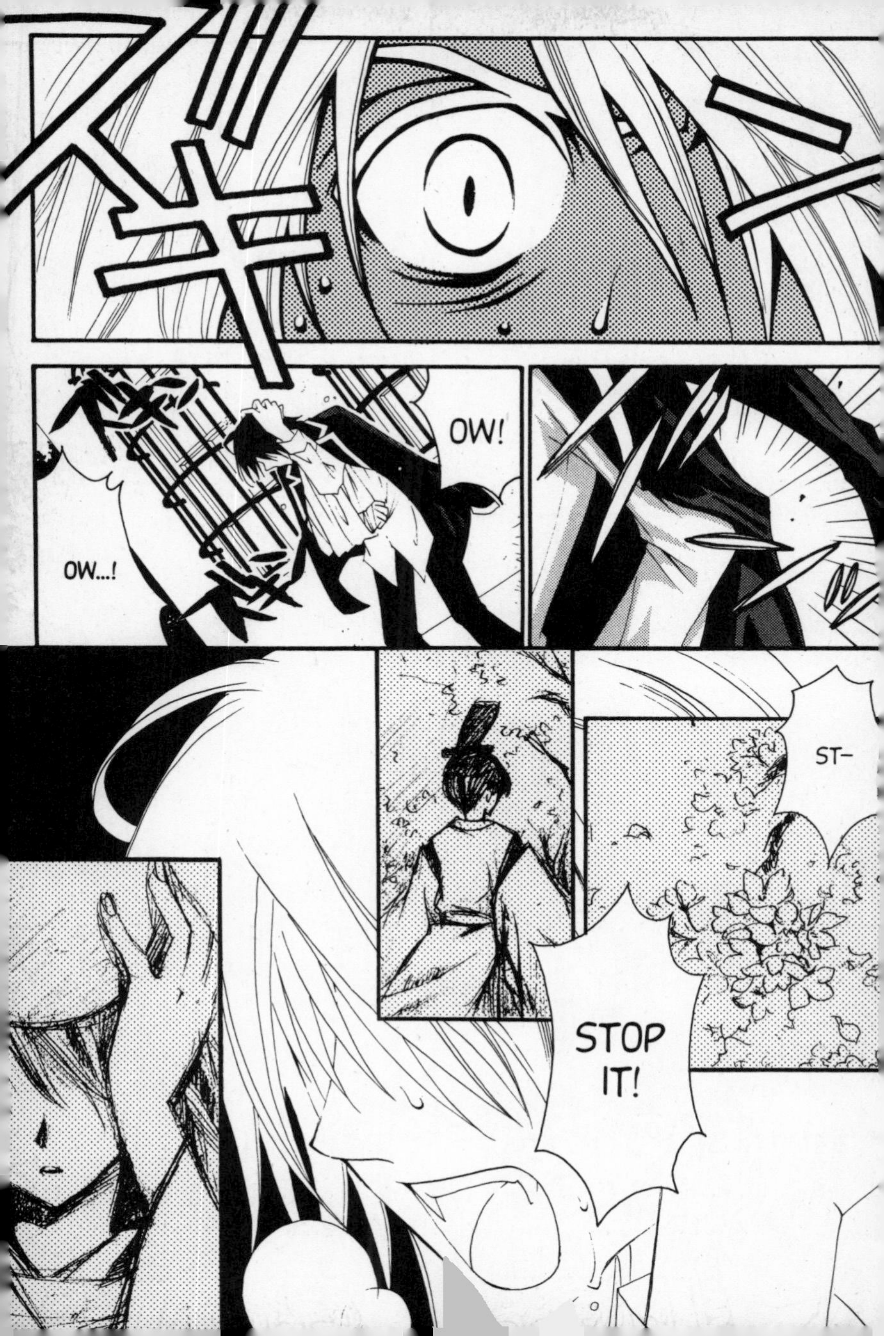
OW!
OW...!
ST–
STOP IT!

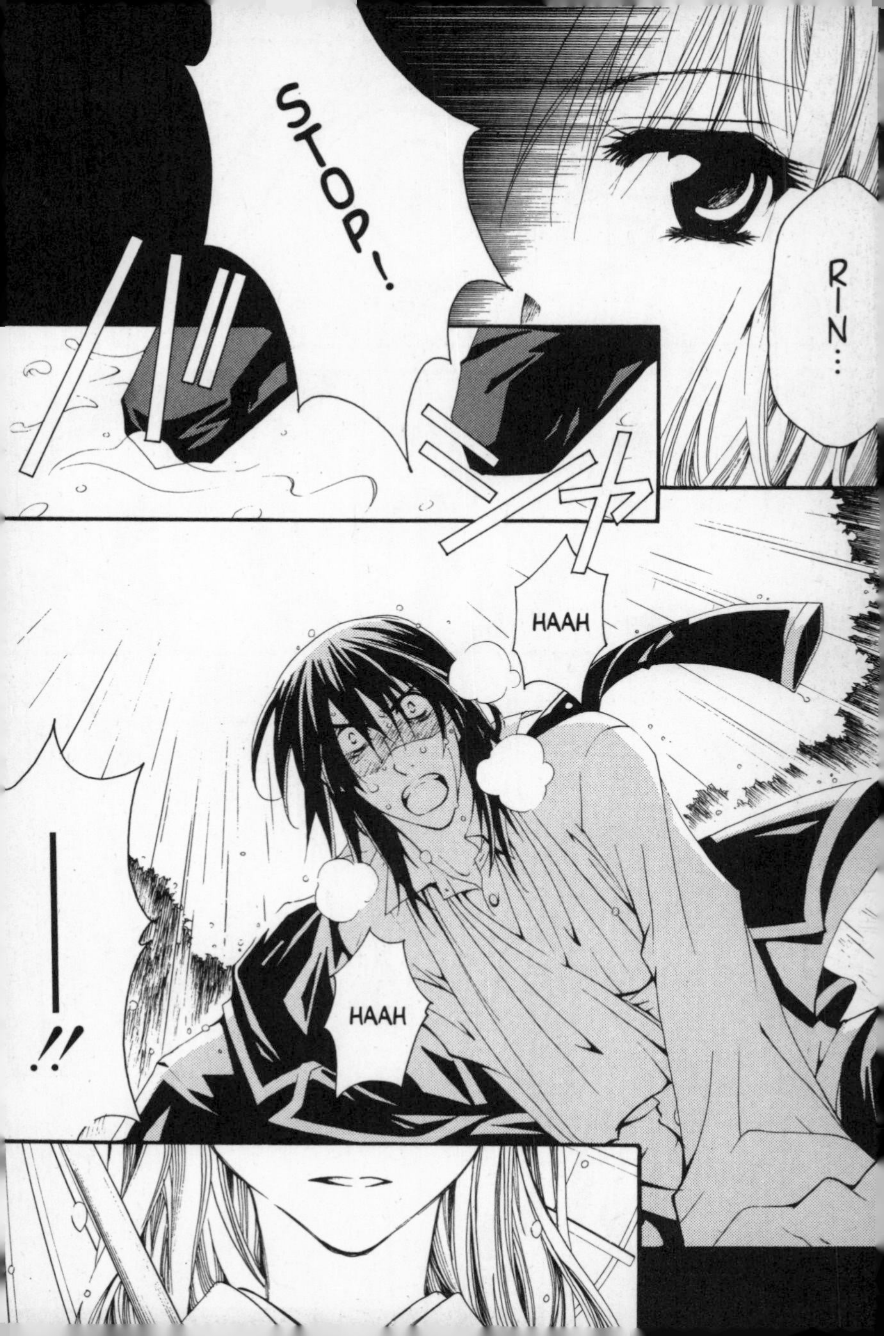

RIN...
STOP!
HAAH
HAAH
—!!

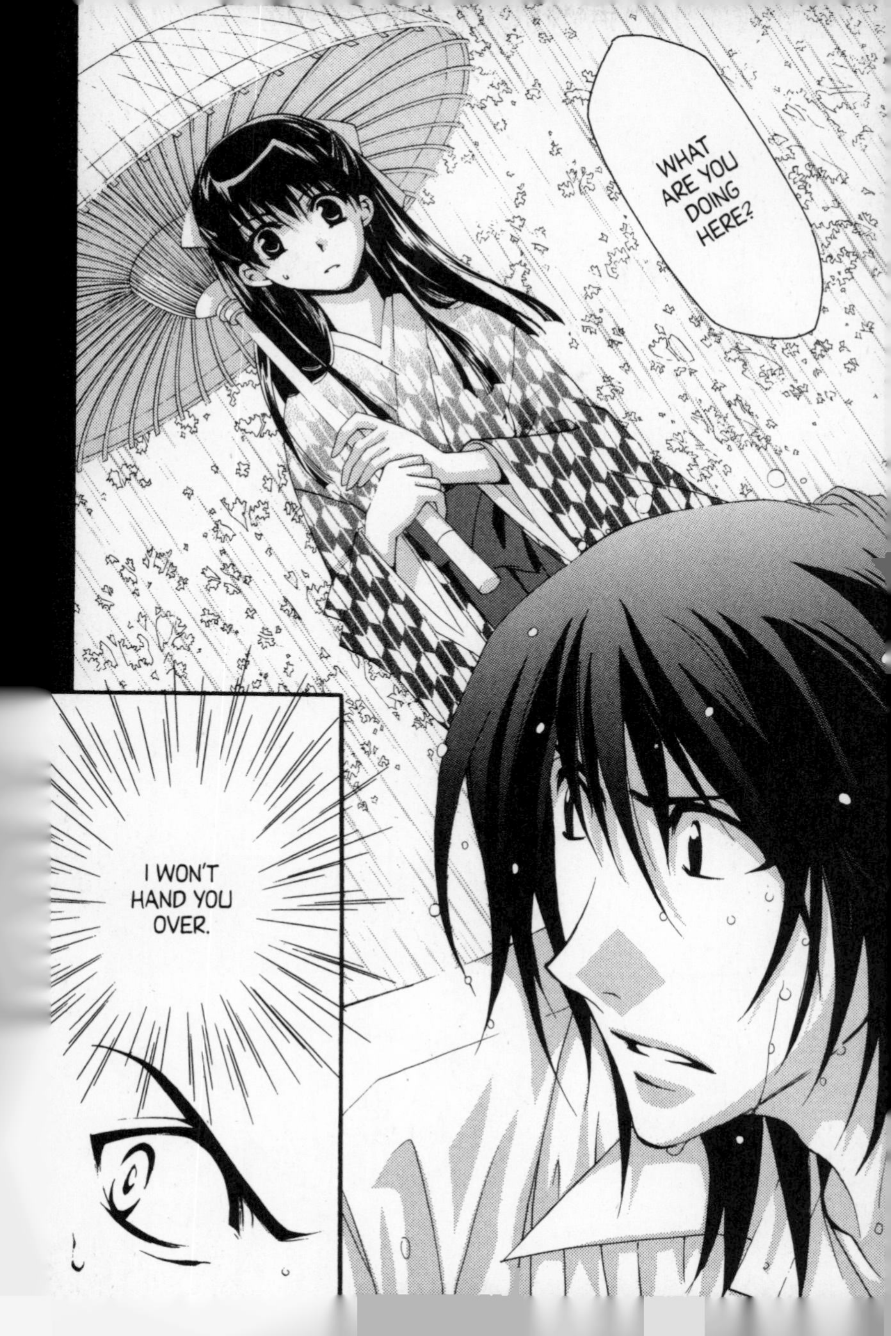
WHAT ARE YOU DOING HERE?
I WON'T HAND YOU OVER.

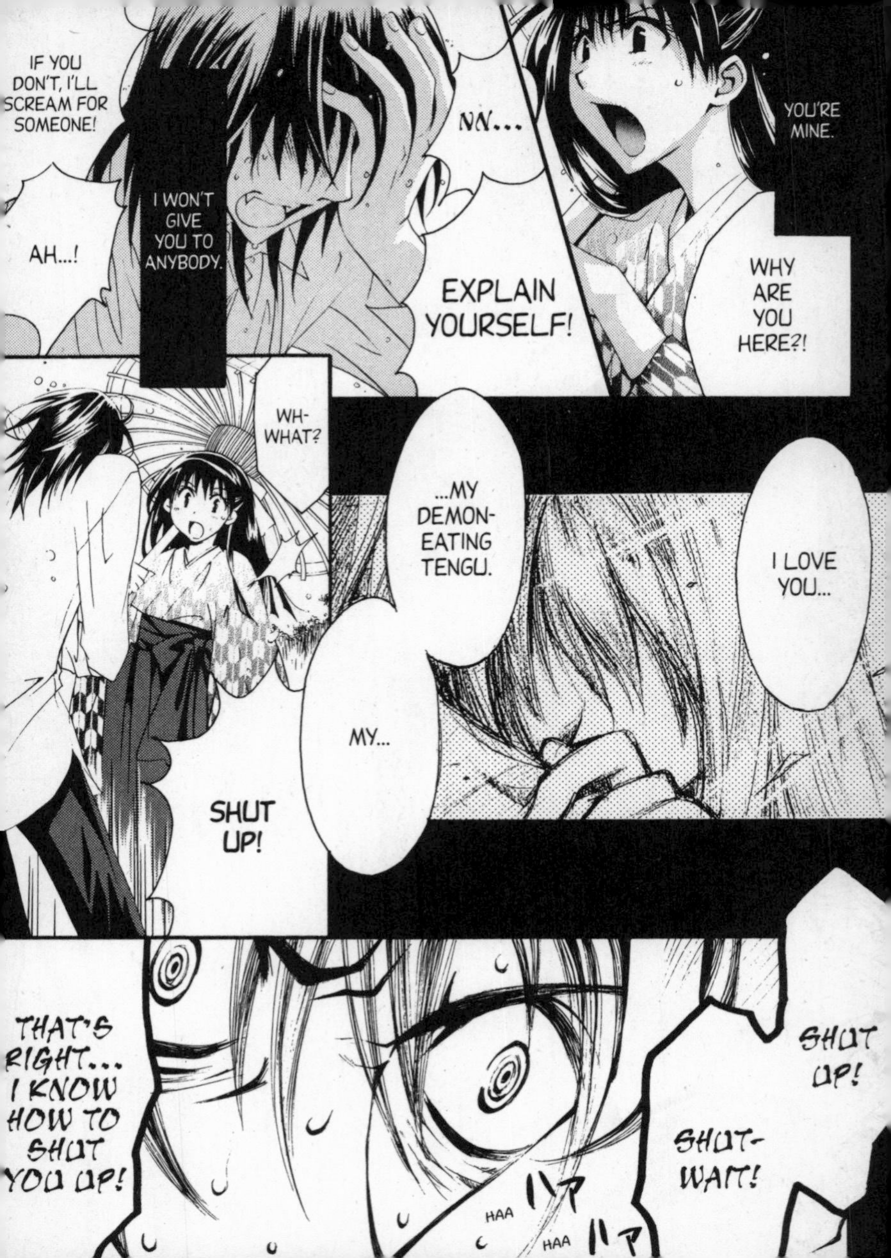
YOU'RE MINE.
WHY ARE YOU HERE?!
EXPLAIN YOURSELF!
NN...
I WON'T GIVE YOU TO ANYBODY.
IF YOU DON'T, I'LL SCREAM FOR SOMEONE!
AH...!
I LOVE YOU...
...MY DEMON-EATING TENGU.
MY...
WH-WHAT?
SHUT UP!
SHUT UP!
SHUT-WAIT!
ハア HAA
ハア HAA
THAT'S RIGHT... I KNOW HOW TO SHUT YOU UP!

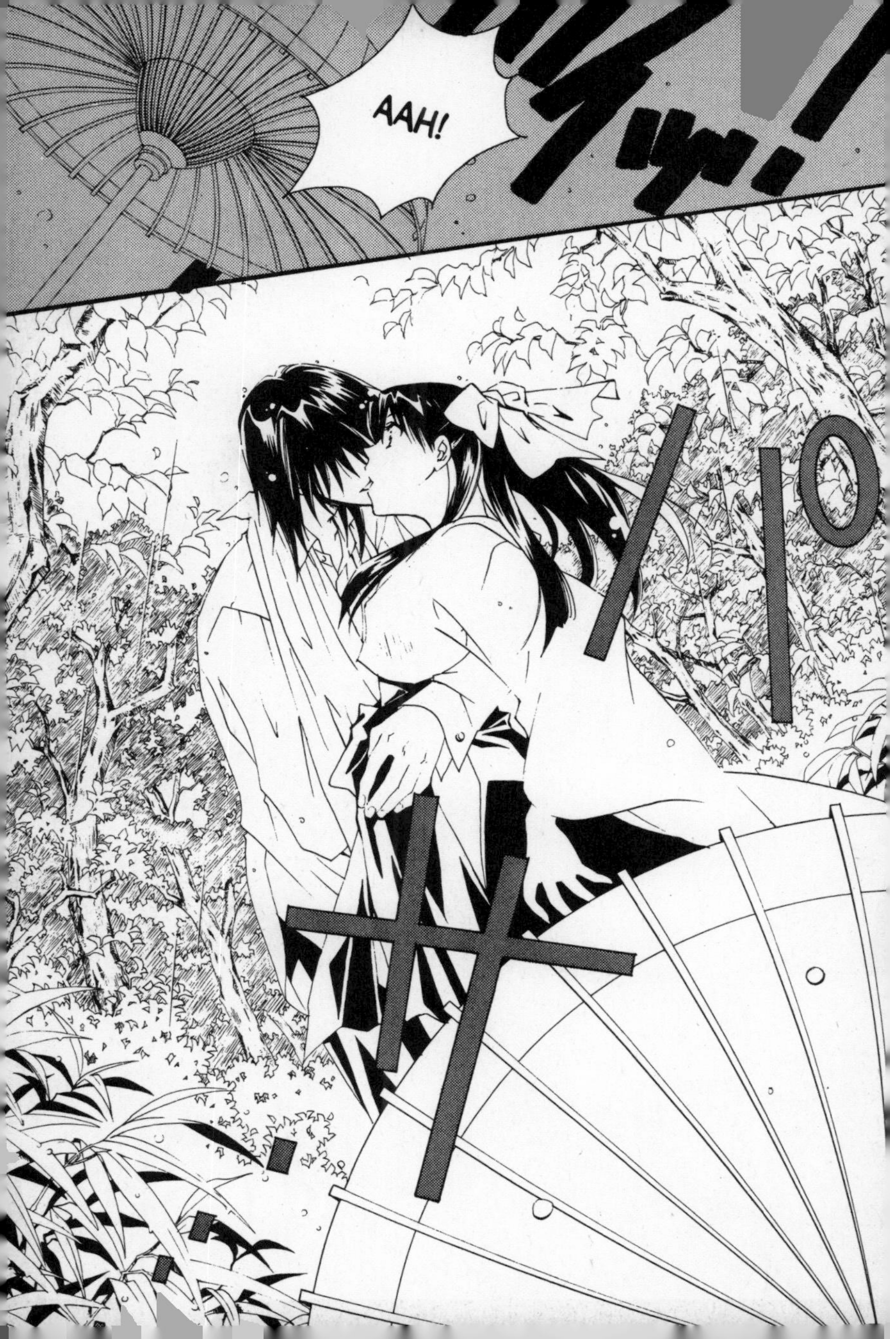
AAH!

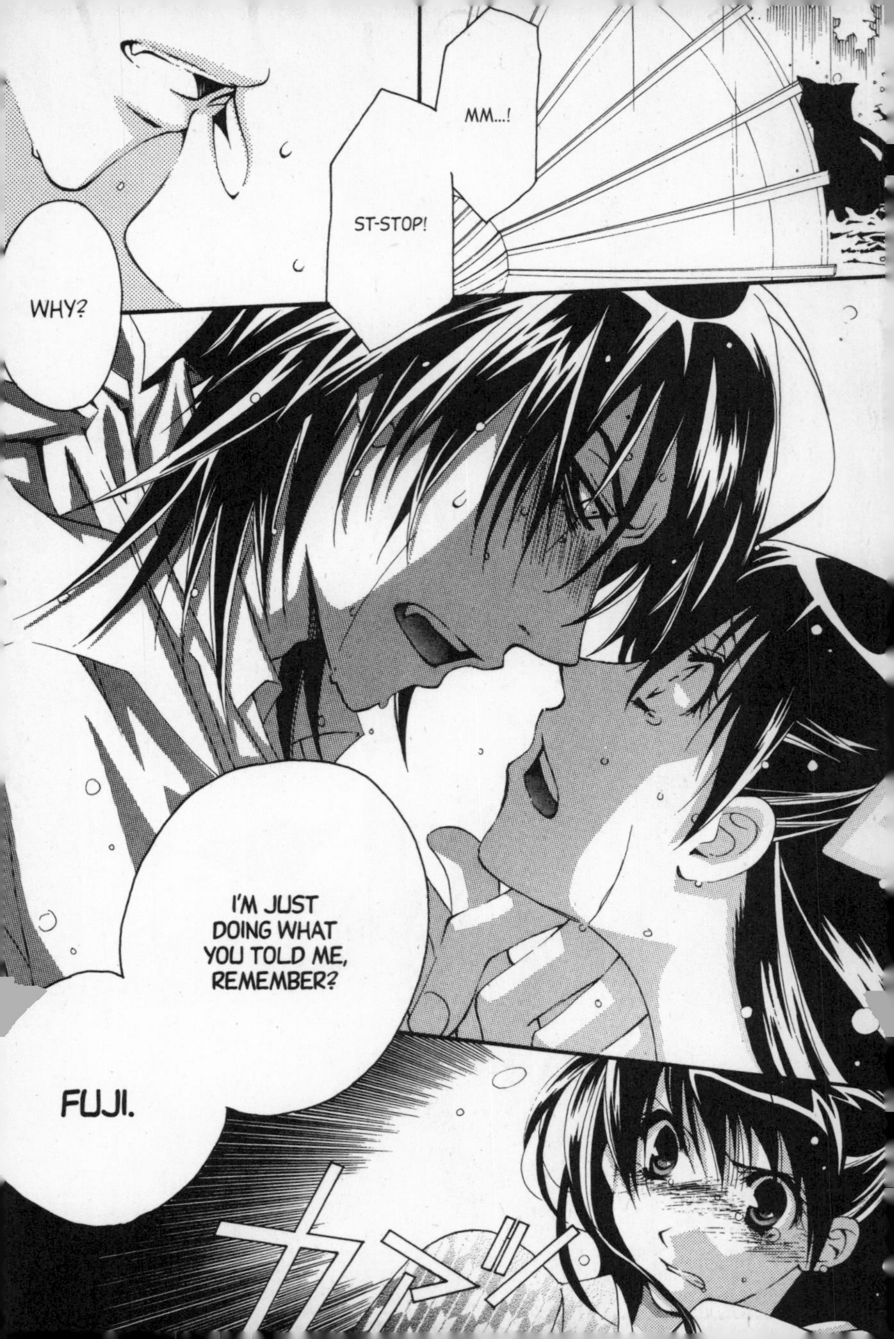
MM...!
ST-STOP!
WHY?
I'M JUST DOING WHAT YOU TOLD ME, REMEMBER?
FUJI.

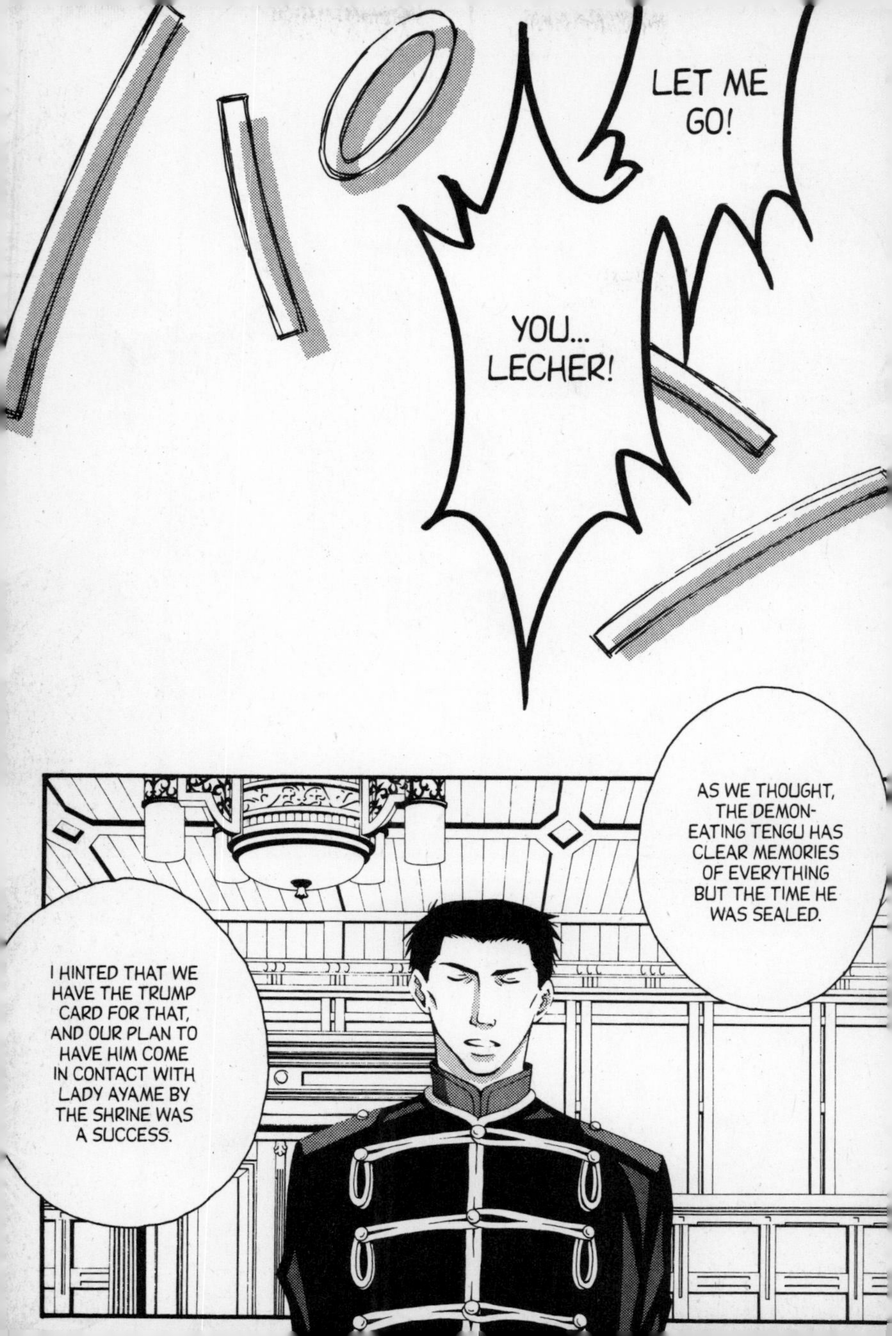
LET ME GO!
YOU... LECHER!
AS WE THOUGHT, THE DEMON-EATING TENGU HAS CLEAR MEMORIES OF EVERYTHING BUT THE TIME HE WAS SEALED.
I HINTED THAT WE HAVE THE TRUMP CARD FOR THAT, AND OUR PLAN TO HAVE HIM COME IN CONTACT WITH LADY AYAME BY THE SHRINE WAS A SUCCESS.

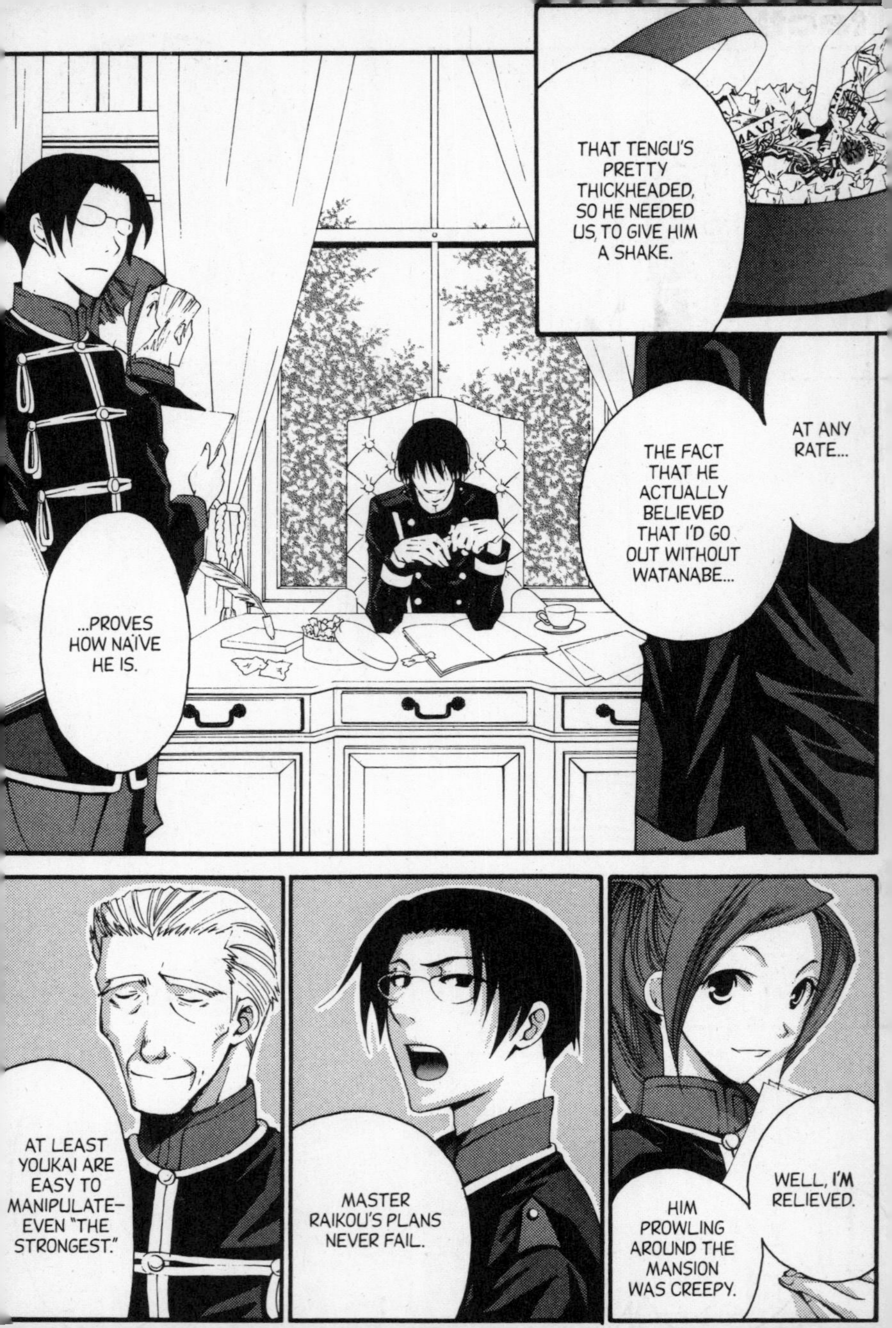
THAT TENGU'S PRETTY THICKHEADED, SO HE NEEDED US TO GIVE HIM A SHAKE.
AT ANY RATE...
THE FACT THAT HE ACTUALLY BELIEVED THAT I'D GO OUT WITHOUT WATANABE...
...PROVES HOW NAÏVE HE IS.
WELL, I'M RELIEVED.
HIM PROWLING AROUND THE MANSION WAS CREEPY.
MASTER RAIKOU'S PLANS NEVER FAIL.
AT LEAST YOUKAI ARE EASY TO MANIPULATE—EVEN "THE STRONGEST."

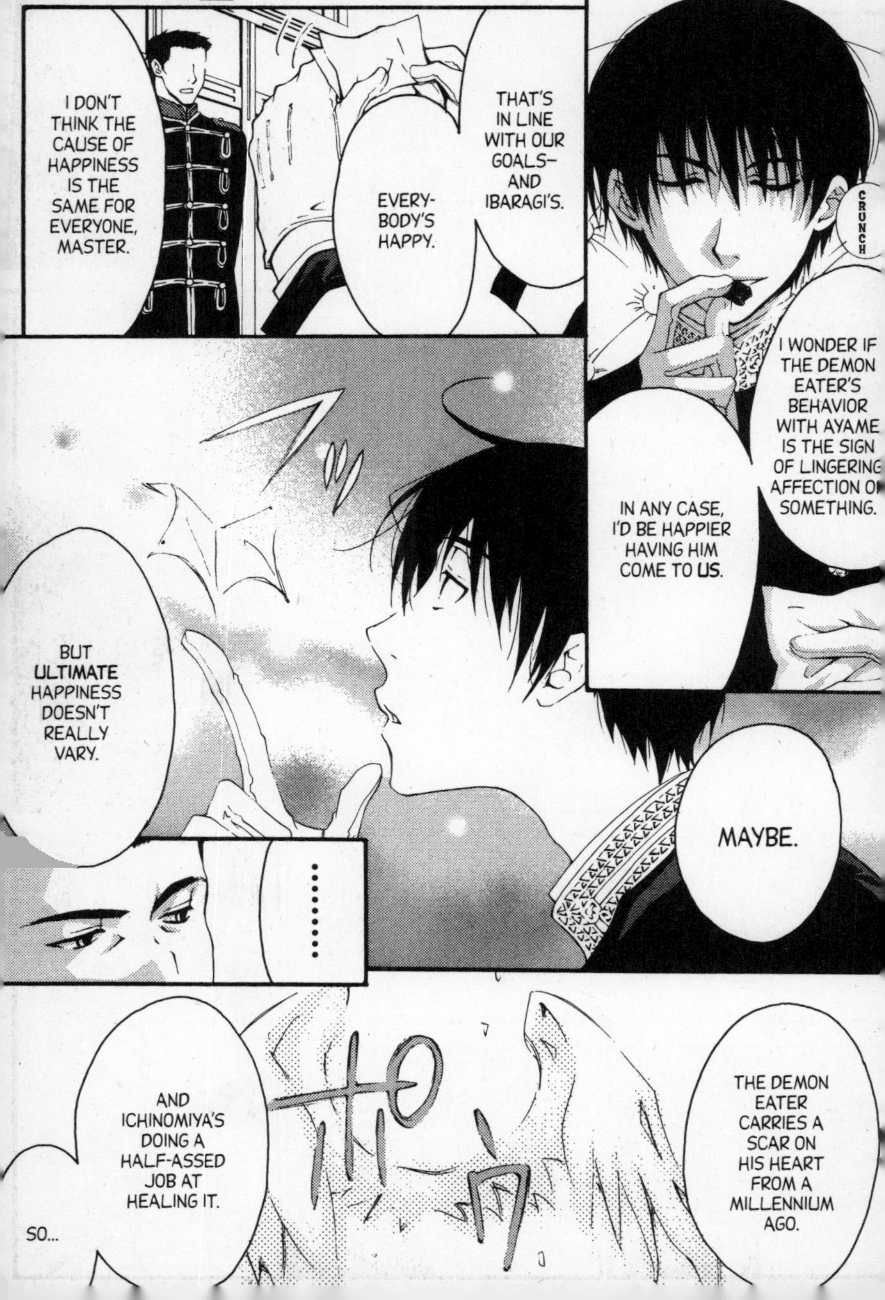
CRUNCH
I WONDER IF THE DEMON EATER'S BEHAVIOR WITH AYAME IS THE SIGN OF LINGERING AFFECTION OR SOMETHING.
IN ANY CASE, I'D BE HAPPIER HAVING HIM COME TO **US**.
THAT'S IN LINE WITH OUR GOALS— AND IBARAGI'S.
EVERY-BODY'S HAPPY.
I DON'T THINK THE CAUSE OF HAPPINESS IS THE SAME FOR EVERYONE, MASTER.
MAYBE.
BUT **ULTIMATE** HAPPINESS DOESN'T REALLY VARY.
....
THE DEMON EATER CARRIES A SCAR ON HIS HEART FROM A MILLENNIUM AGO.
AND ICHINOMIYA'S DOING A HALF-ASSED JOB AT HEALING IT.
SO...

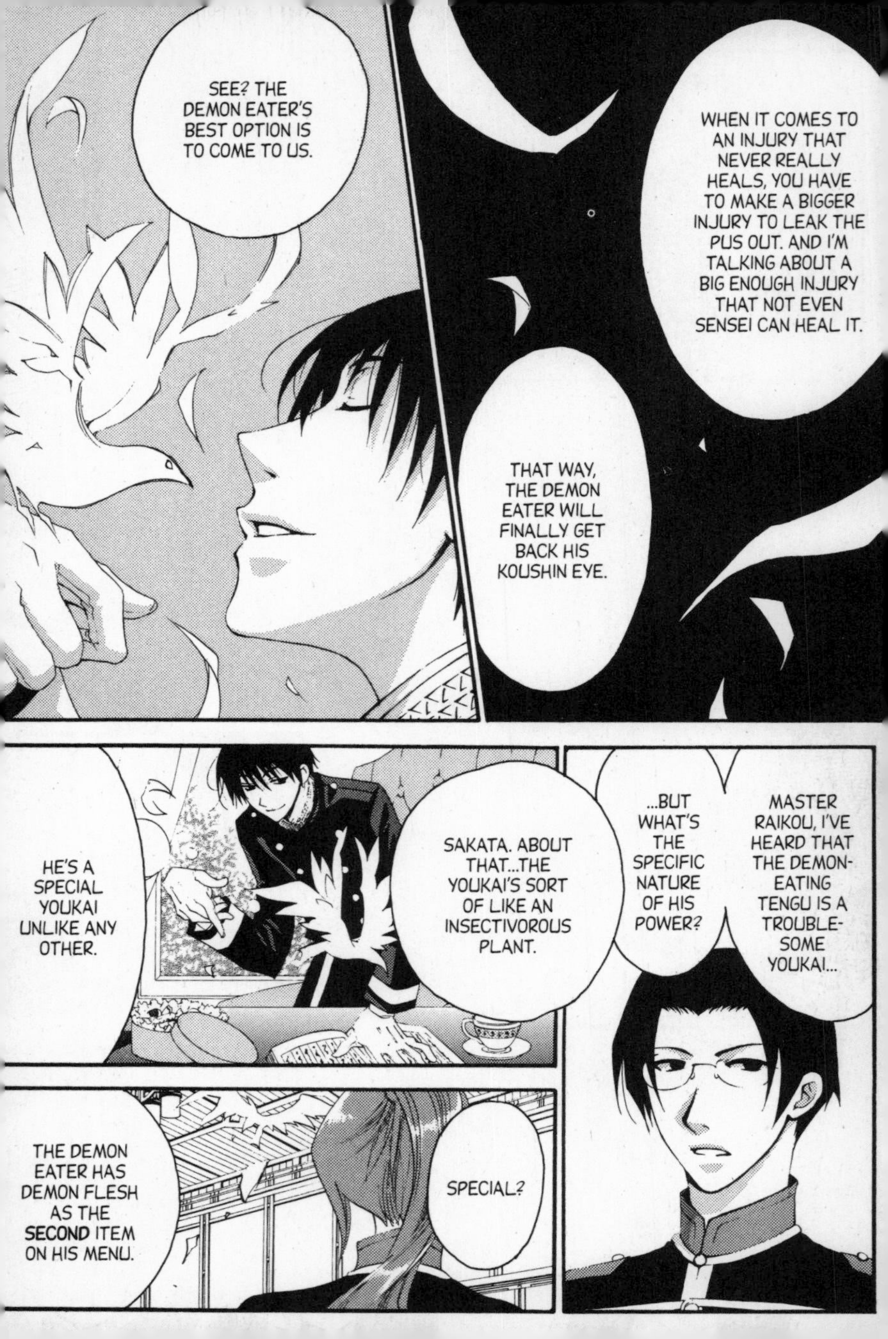
WHEN IT COMES TO AN INJURY THAT NEVER REALLY HEALS, YOU HAVE TO MAKE A BIGGER INJURY TO LEAK THE PUS OUT. AND I'M TALKING ABOUT A BIG ENOUGH INJURY THAT NOT EVEN SENSEI CAN HEAL IT.
THAT WAY, THE DEMON EATER WILL FINALLY GET BACK HIS KOUSHIN EYE.
SEE? THE DEMON EATER'S BEST OPTION IS TO COME TO US.
MASTER RAIKOU, I'VE HEARD THAT THE DEMON-EATING TENGU IS A TROUBLE-SOME YOUKAI...
...BUT WHAT'S THE SPECIFIC NATURE OF HIS POWER?
SAKATA. ABOUT THAT...THE YOUKAI'S SORT OF LIKE AN INSECTIVOROUS PLANT.
HE'S A SPECIAL YOUKAI UNLIKE ANY OTHER.
SPECIAL?
THE DEMON EATER HAS DEMON FLESH AS THE **SECOND** ITEM ON HIS MENU.

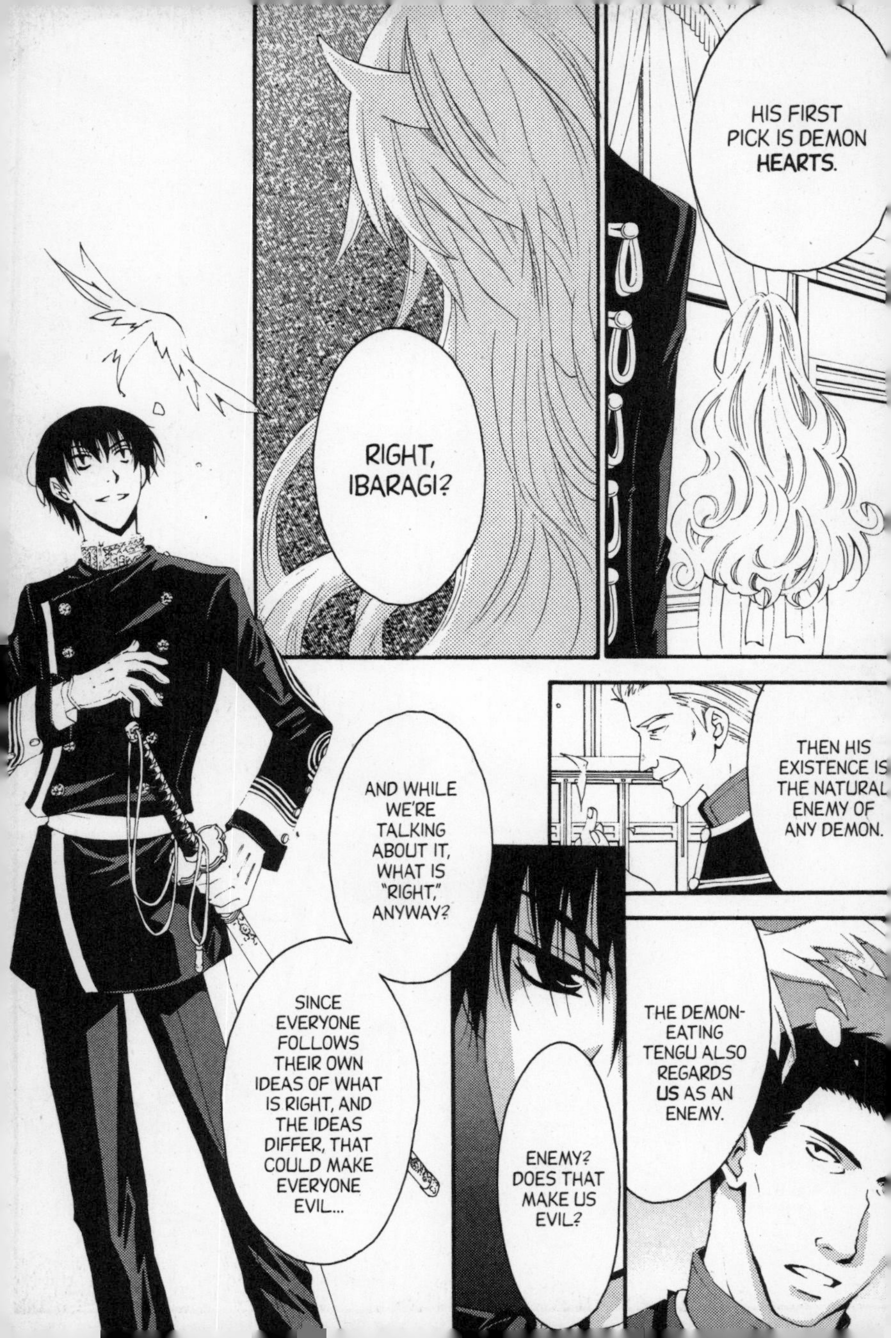
HIS FIRST PICK IS DEMON HEARTS.
RIGHT, IBARAGI?
THEN HIS EXISTENCE IS THE NATURAL ENEMY OF ANY DEMON.
THE DEMON-EATING TENGU ALSO REGARDS US AS AN ENEMY.
ENEMY? DOES THAT MAKE US EVIL?
AND WHILE WE'RE TALKING ABOUT IT, WHAT IS "RIGHT," ANYWAY?
SINCE EVERYONE FOLLOWS THEIR OWN IDEAS OF WHAT IS RIGHT, AND THE IDEAS DIFFER, THAT COULD MAKE EVERYONE EVIL...

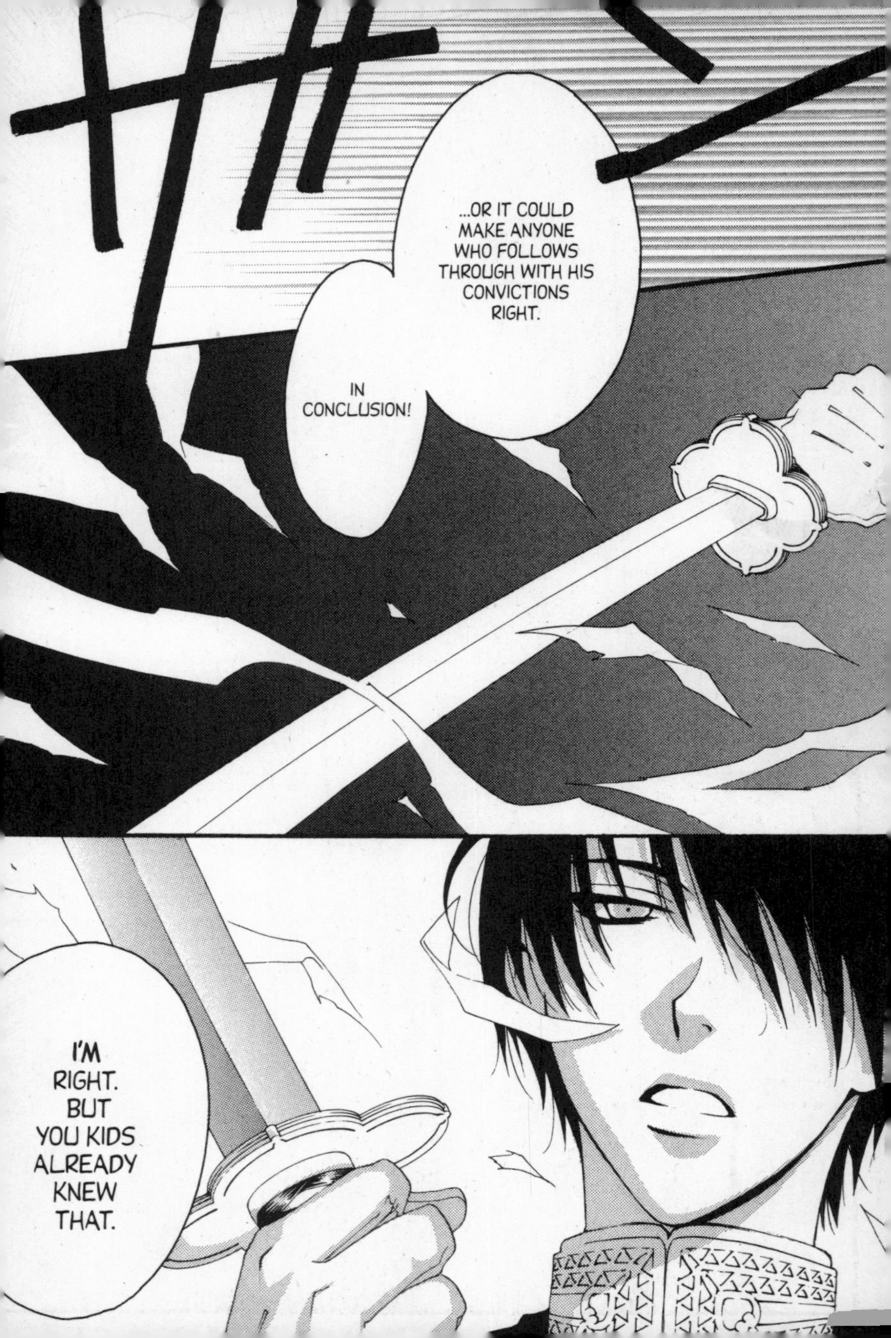
...OR IT COULD MAKE ANYONE WHO FOLLOWS THROUGH WITH HIS CONVICTIONS RIGHT.
IN CONCLUSION!
I'M RIGHT. BUT YOU KIDS ALREADY KNEW THAT.

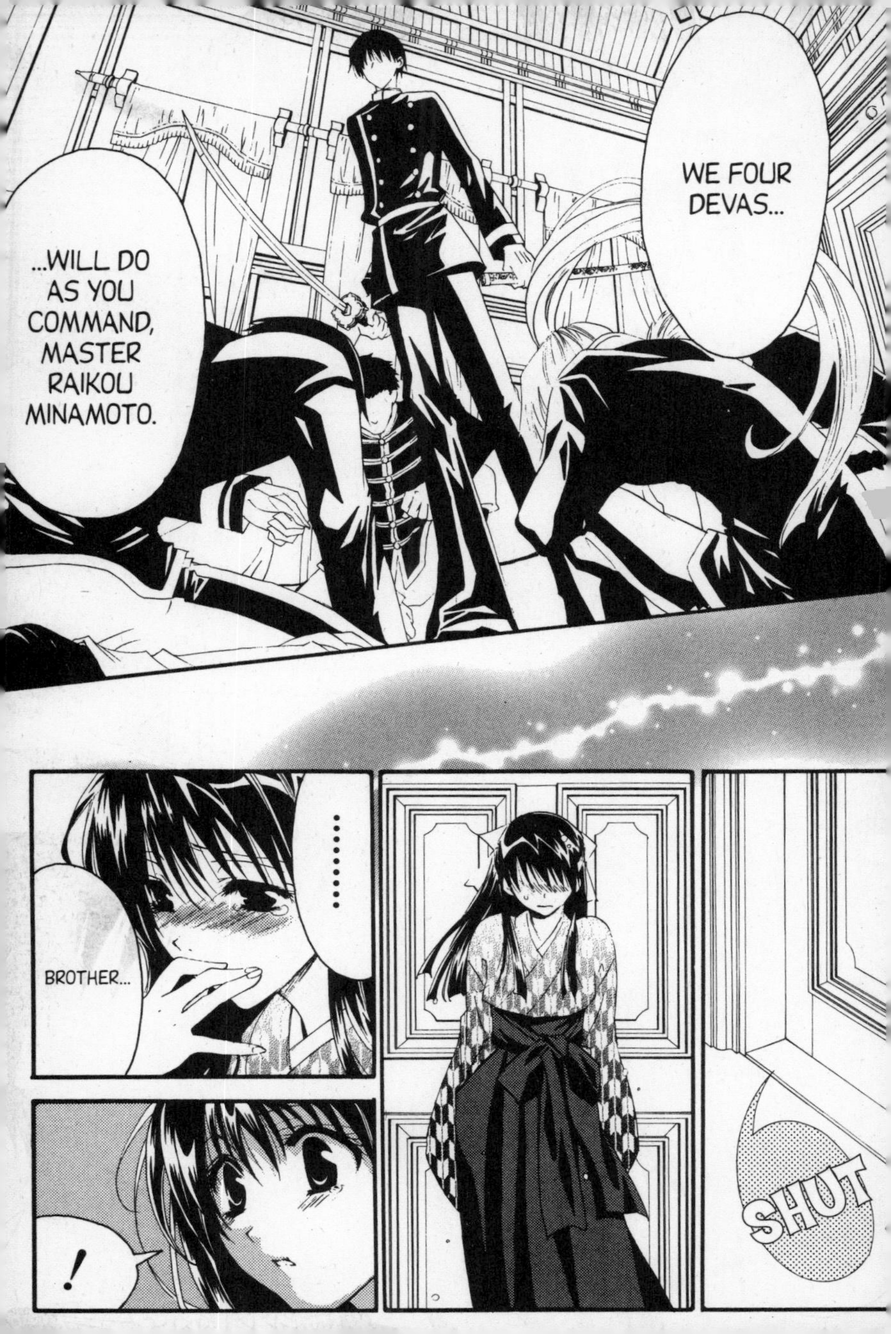
WE FOUR DEVAS...
...WILL DO AS YOU COMMAND, MASTER RAIKOU MINAMOTO.
SHUT
....
BROTHER...
!

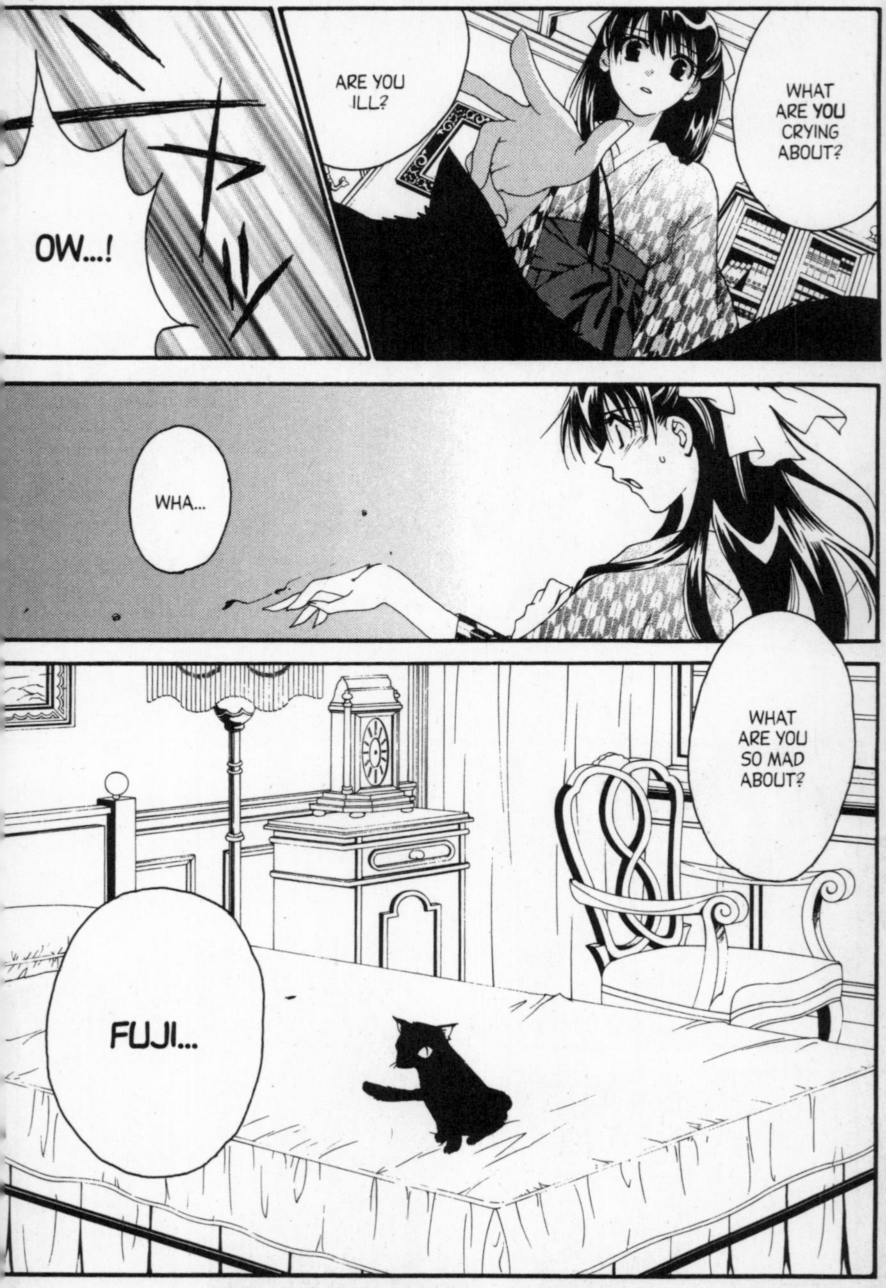
WHAT ARE YOU CRYING ABOUT?
ARE YOU ILL?
OW...!
WHA...
WHAT ARE YOU SO MAD ABOUT?
FUJI...

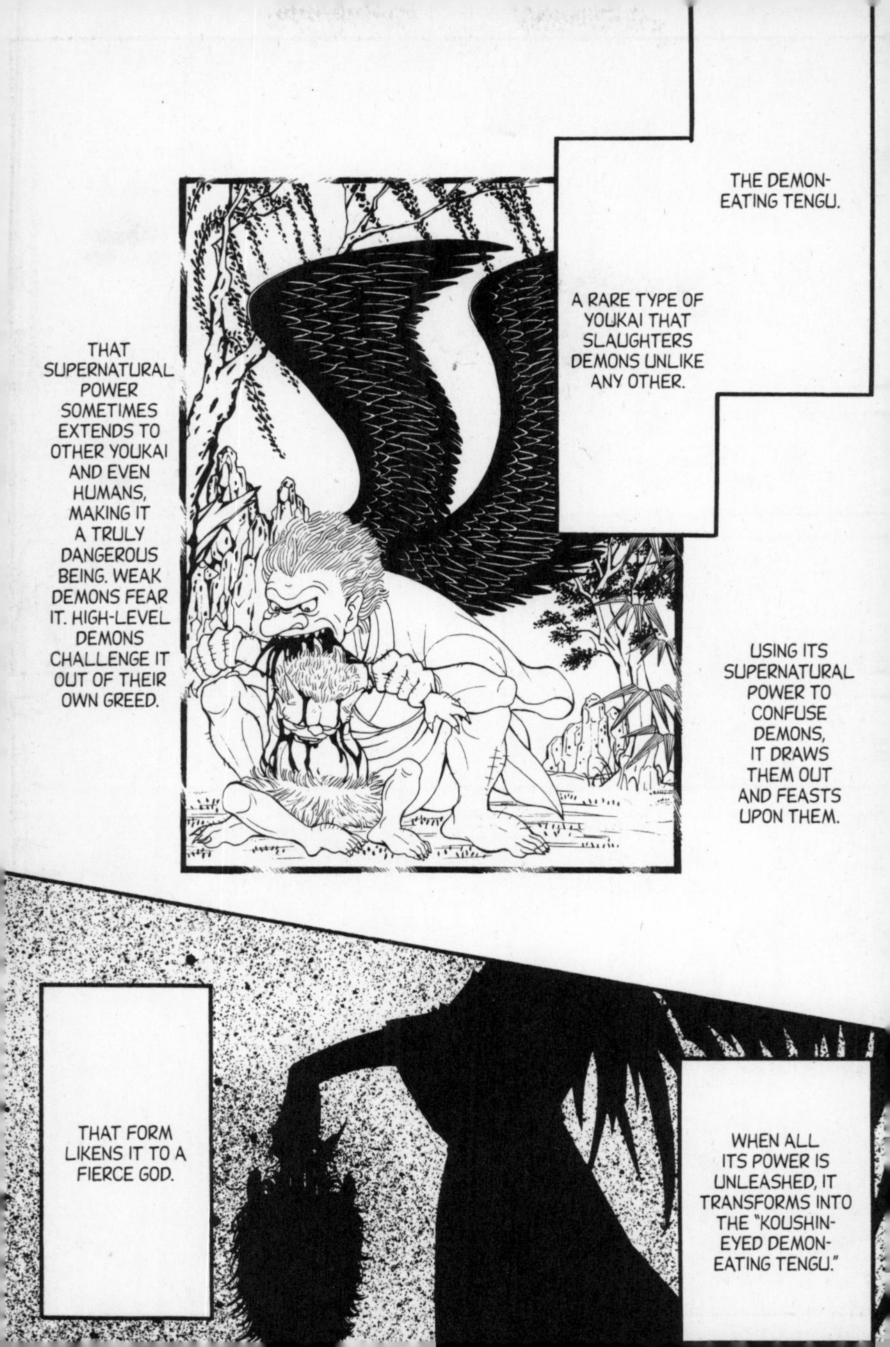
THE DEMON-EATING TENGU.
A RARE TYPE OF YOUKAI THAT SLAUGHTERS DEMONS UNLIKE ANY OTHER.
USING ITS SUPERNATURAL POWER TO CONFUSE DEMONS, IT DRAWS THEM OUT AND FEASTS UPON THEM.
THAT SUPERNATURAL POWER SOMETIMES EXTENDS TO OTHER YOUKAI AND EVEN HUMANS, MAKING IT A TRULY DANGEROUS BEING. WEAK DEMONS FEAR IT. HIGH-LEVEL DEMONS CHALLENGE IT OUT OF THEIR OWN GREED.
WHEN ALL ITS POWER IS UNLEASHED, IT TRANSFORMS INTO THE "KOUSHIN-EYED DEMON-EATING TENGU."
THAT FORM LIKENS IT TO A FIERCE GOD.

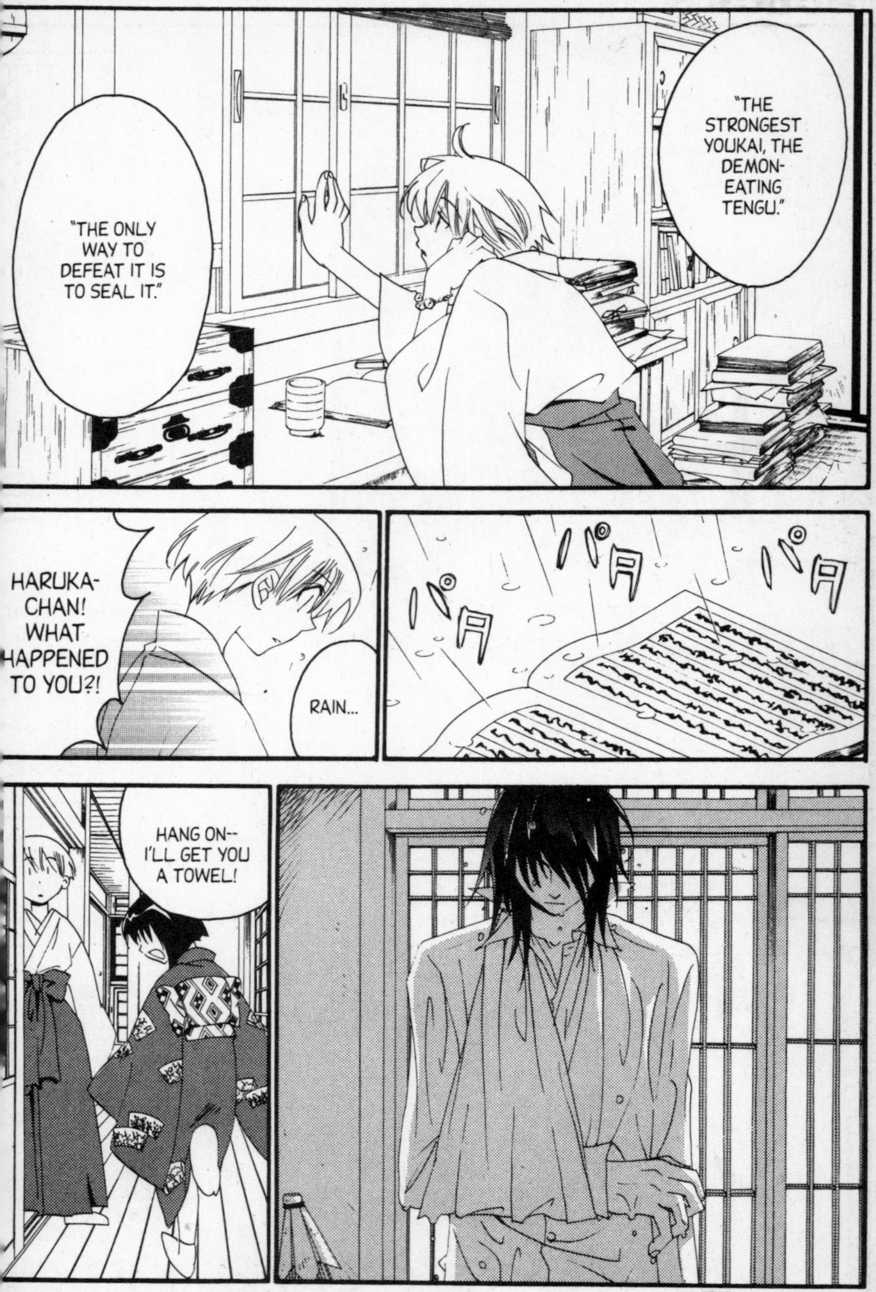
"THE STRONGEST YOUKAI, THE DEMON-EATING TENGU."
"THE ONLY WAY TO DEFEAT IT IS TO SEAL IT."
パタ
パタ
パタ
RAIN...
HARUKA-CHAN! WHAT HAPPENED TO YOU?!
HANG ON-- I'LL GET YOU A TOWEL!

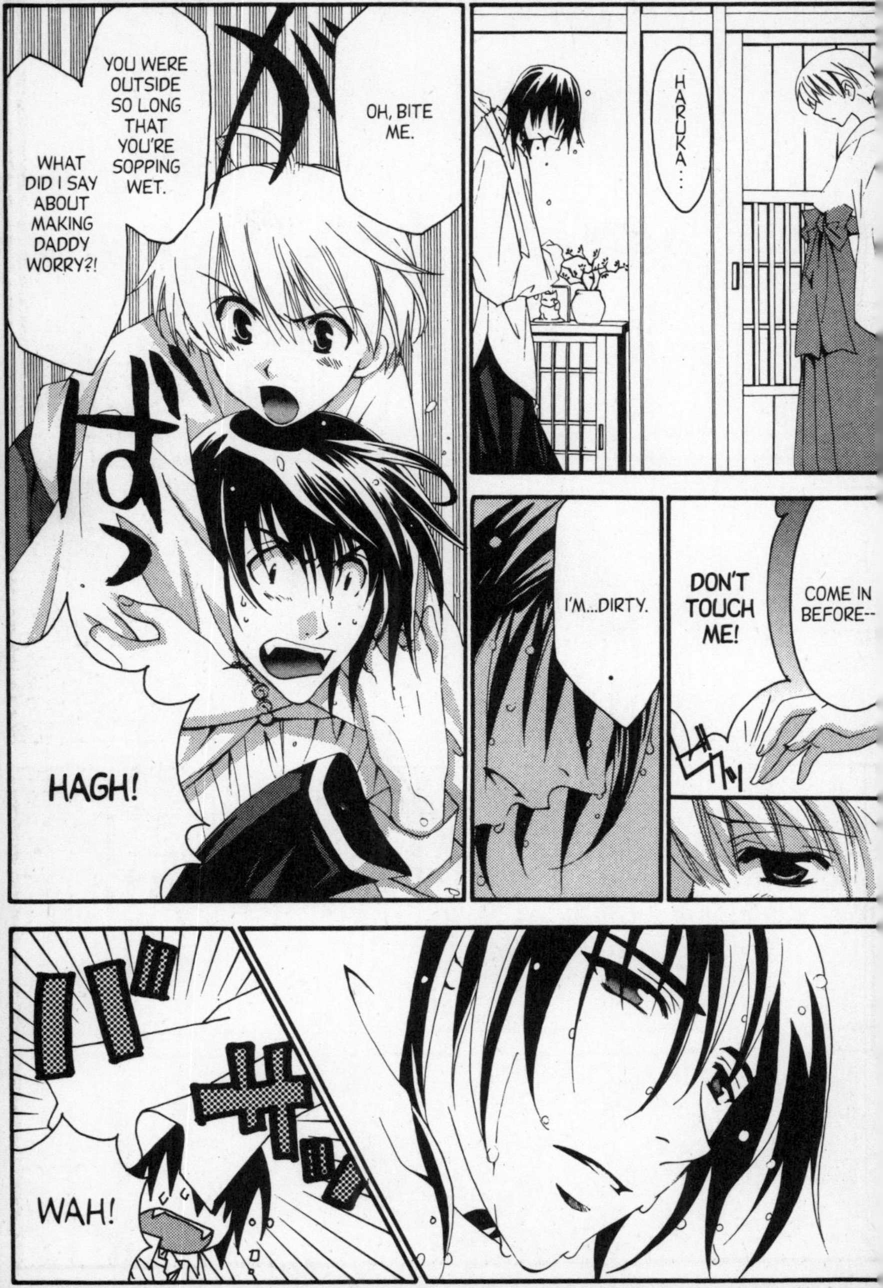
HARUKA...
COME IN BEFORE--
DON'T TOUCH ME!
I'M...DIRTY.
OH, BITE ME.
YOU WERE OUTSIDE SO LONG THAT YOU'RE SOPPING WET.
WHAT DID I SAY ABOUT MAKING DADDY WORRY?!
HAGH!
WAH!

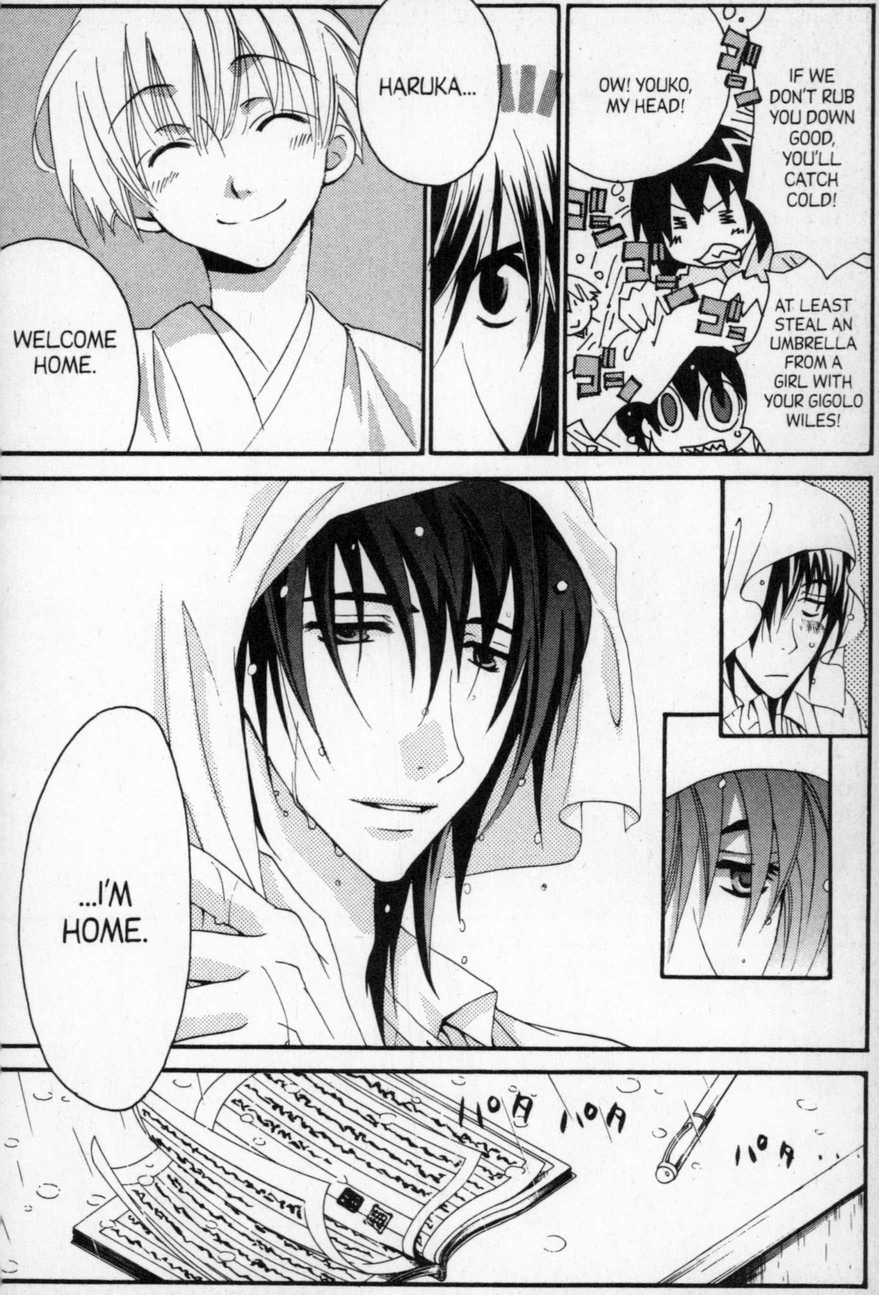
IF WE DON'T RUB YOU DOWN GOOD, YOU'LL CATCH COLD!
OW! YOUKO, MY HEAD!
AT LEAST STEAL AN UMBRELLA FROM A GIRL WITH YOUR GIGOLO WILES!
HARUKA...
WELCOME HOME.
...I'M HOME.

YOU WERE ASSIGNED AS MY DUTY FROM THE MOMENT OF YOUR BIRTH. I WAS DRILLED SEVERELY FOR THINGS I COULDN'T EVEN SEE.

BUT EVEN THOUGH I WAS TOLD TO "RISK MY LIFE TO FULFILL MY DUTY" TO THOSE UNSEEN THINGS, I WASN'T SKILLED ENOUGH FOR THAT— THAT TALK WAS AS LOFTY AS A DREAM.

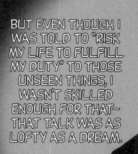

THAT ALL CHANGED AS OF THAT VERY INSTANT.

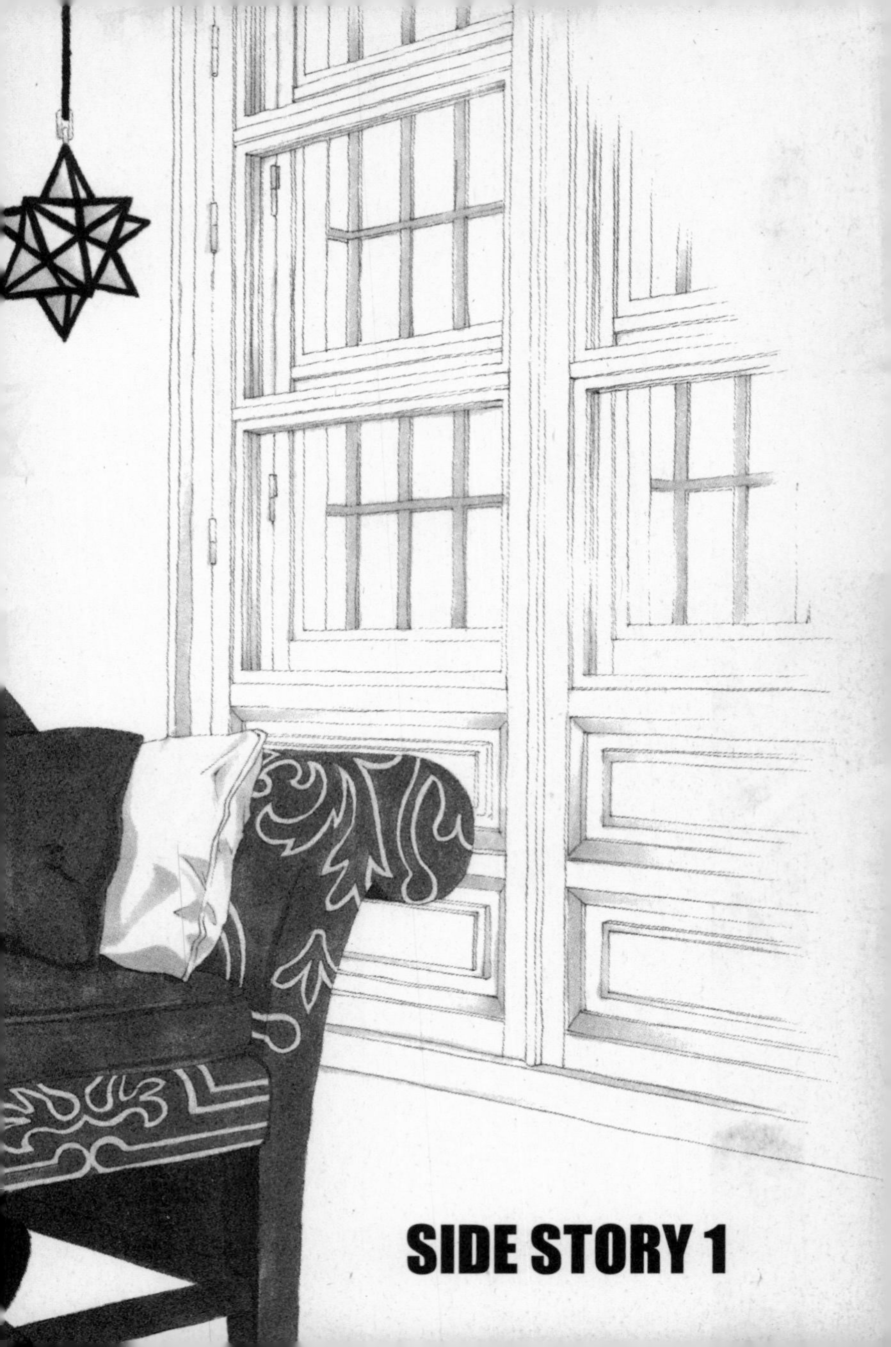

SIDE STORY 1

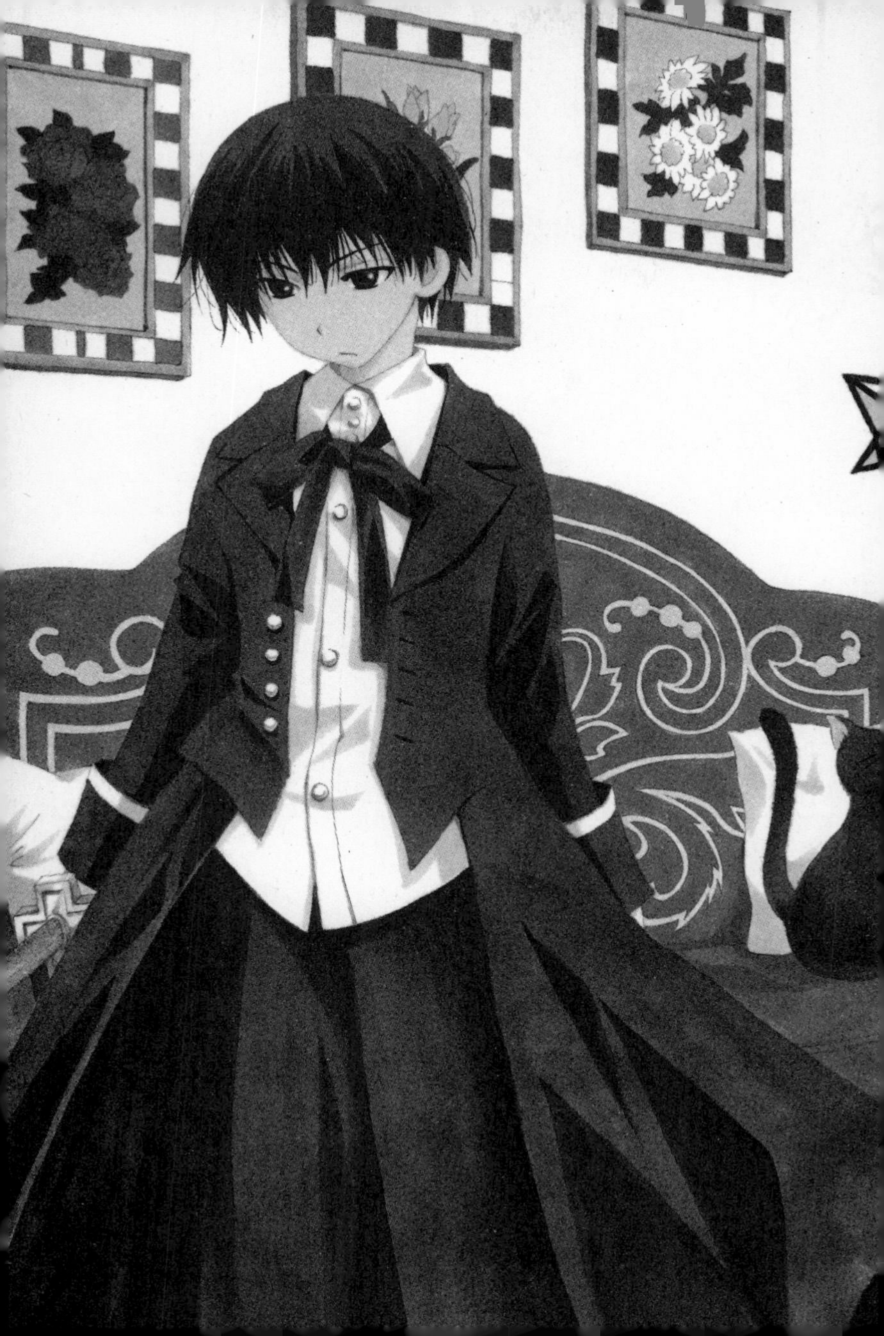

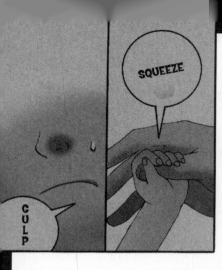

SQUEEZE

GULP

I WAITED TWELVE LONG YEARS TO MEET YOU.

HOW LONG I THIRSTED FOR IT; AT LAST MY EXISTENCE HAD BEEN GIVEN VALUE.

IT FELT LIKE MY LEGS WERE FINALLY PLANTED ON THE GROUND.

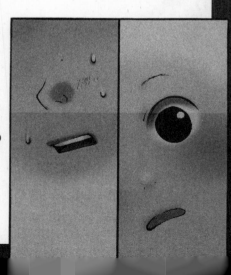

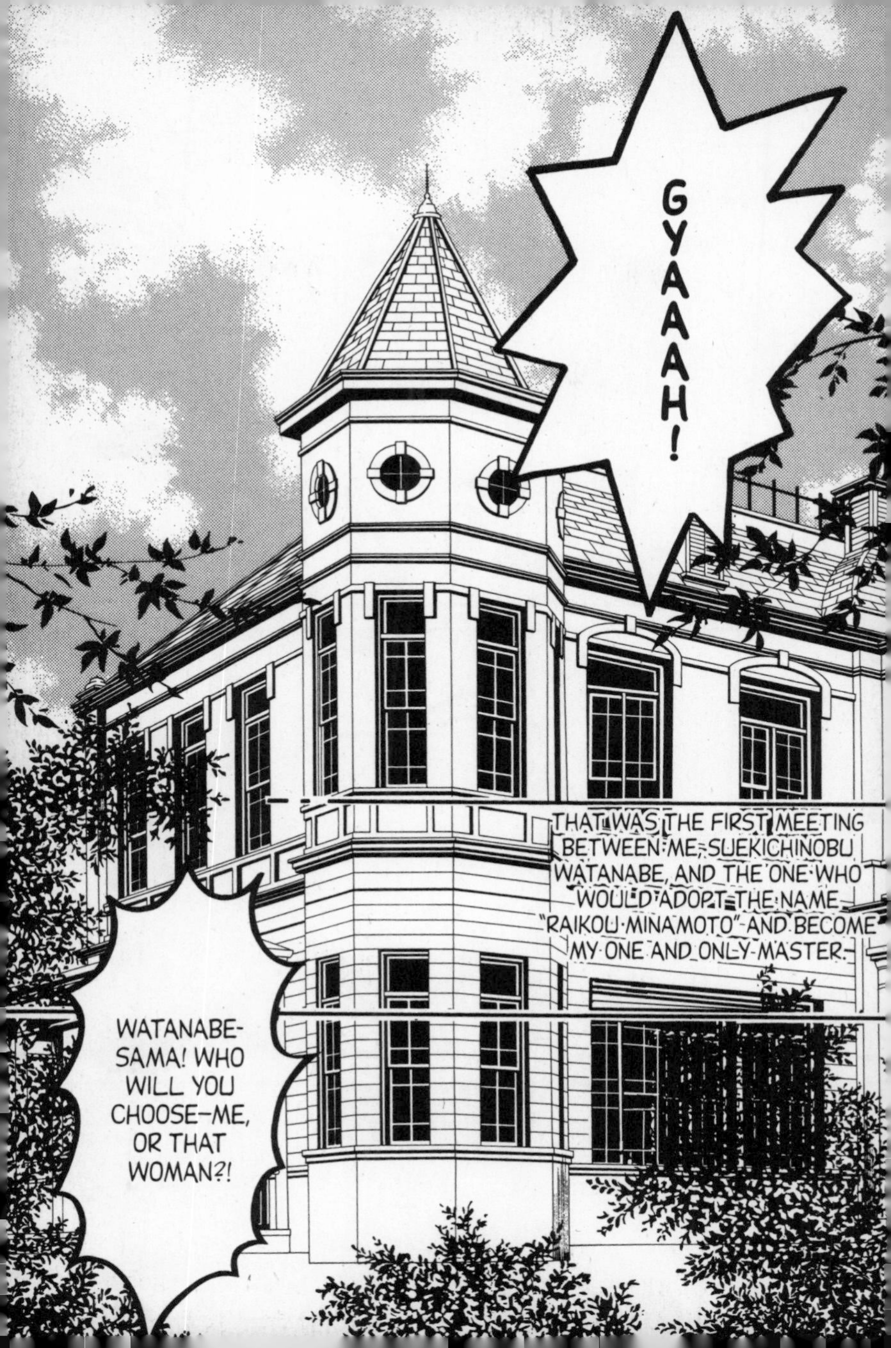
GYAAAH!
THAT WAS THE FIRST MEETING BETWEEN ME, SUEKICHINOBU WATANABE, AND THE ONE WHO WOULD ADOPT THE NAME "RAIKOU MINAMOTO" AND BECOME MY ONE AND ONLY MASTER.
WATANABE-SAMA! WHO WILL YOU CHOOSE—ME, OR THAT WOMAN?!

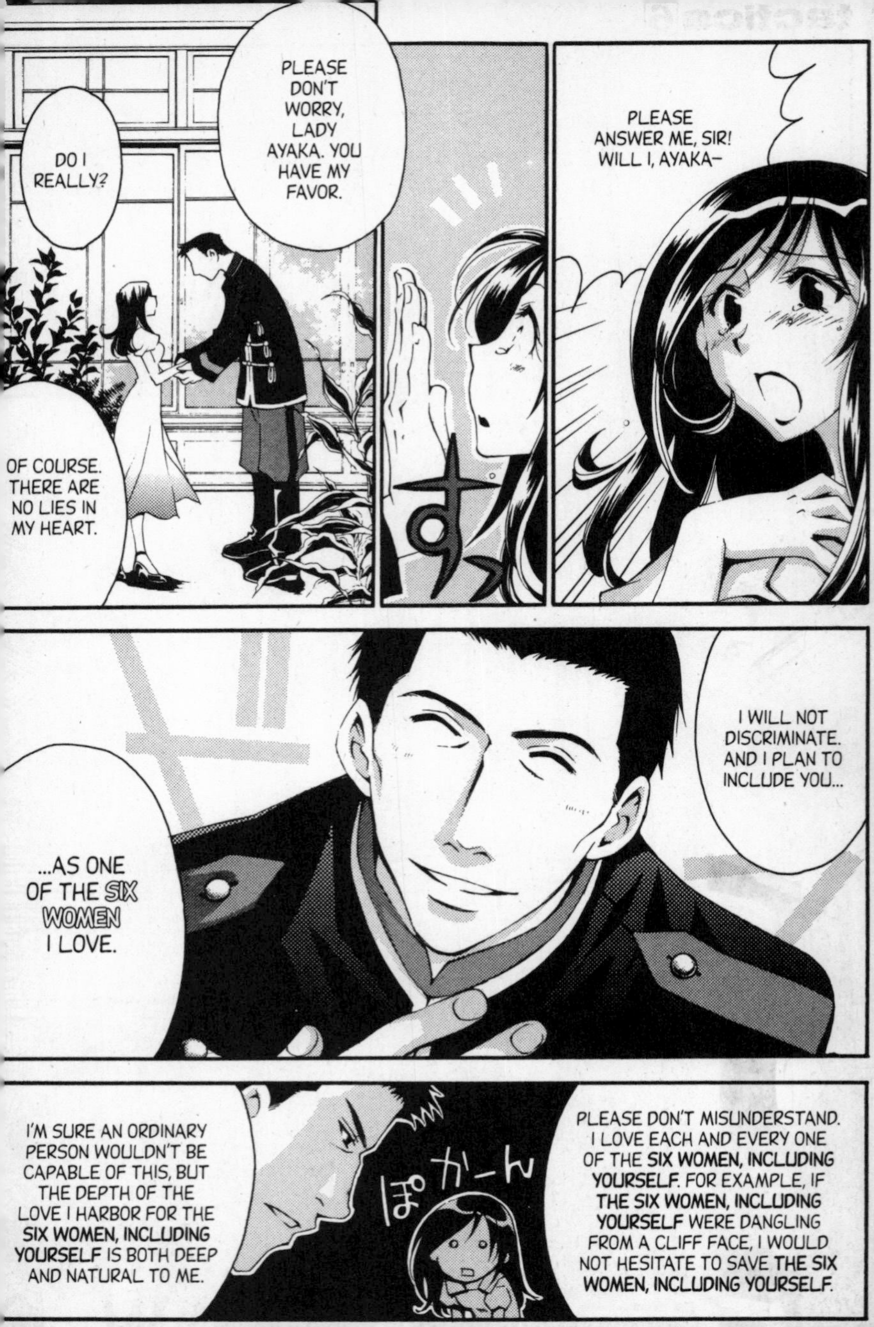
PLEASE ANSWER ME, SIR! WILL I, AYAKA–
す
PLEASE DON'T WORRY, LADY AYAKA. YOU HAVE MY FAVOR.
DO I REALLY?
OF COURSE. THERE ARE NO LIES IN MY HEART.
I WILL NOT DISCRIMINATE. AND I PLAN TO INCLUDE YOU...
...AS ONE OF THE SIX WOMEN I LOVE.
PLEASE DON'T MISUNDERSTAND. I LOVE EACH AND EVERY ONE OF THE SIX WOMEN, INCLUDING YOURSELF. FOR EXAMPLE, IF THE SIX WOMEN, INCLUDING YOURSELF WERE DANGLING FROM A CLIFF FACE, I WOULD NOT HESITATE TO SAVE THE SIX WOMEN, INCLUDING YOURSELF.
ぽかーん
I'M SURE AN ORDINARY PERSON WOULDN'T BE CAPABLE OF THIS, BUT THE DEPTH OF THE LOVE I HARBOR FOR THE SIX WOMEN, INCLUDING YOURSELF IS BOTH DEEP AND NATURAL TO ME.

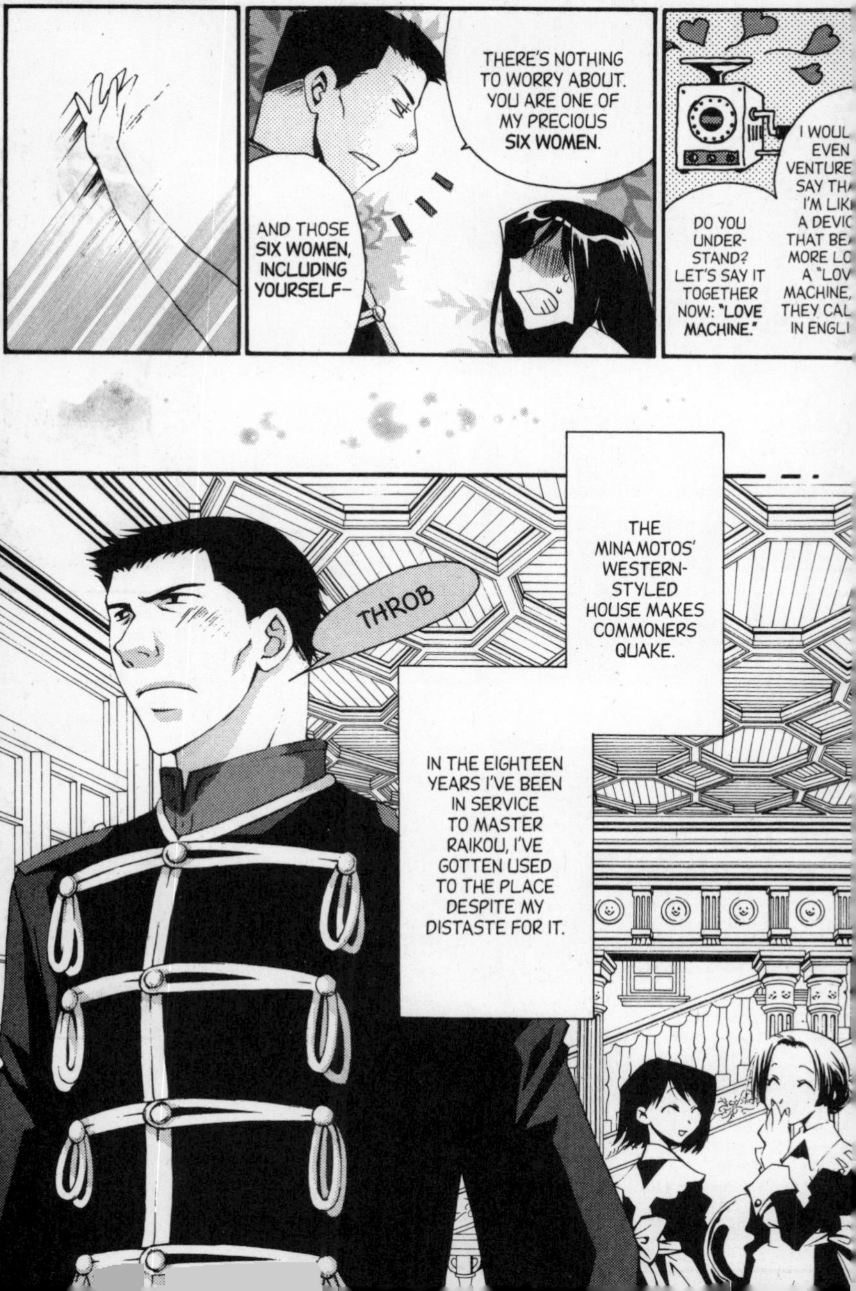
I WOUL
EVEN
VENTURE
SAY THA
I'M LIK
A DEVIC
THAT BEA
MORE LO
A "LOV
MACHINE,
THEY CAL
IN ENGLI
DO YOU UNDERSTAND? LET'S SAY IT TOGETHER NOW: "LOVE MACHINE."
THERE'S NOTHING TO WORRY ABOUT. YOU ARE ONE OF MY PRECIOUS SIX WOMEN.
AND THOSE SIX WOMEN, INCLUDING YOURSELF—
THE MINAMOTOS' WESTERN-STYLED HOUSE MAKES COMMONERS QUAKE.
THROB
IN THE EIGHTEEN YEARS I'VE BEEN IN SERVICE TO MASTER RAIKOU, I'VE GOTTEN USED TO THE PLACE DESPITE MY DISTASTE FOR IT.

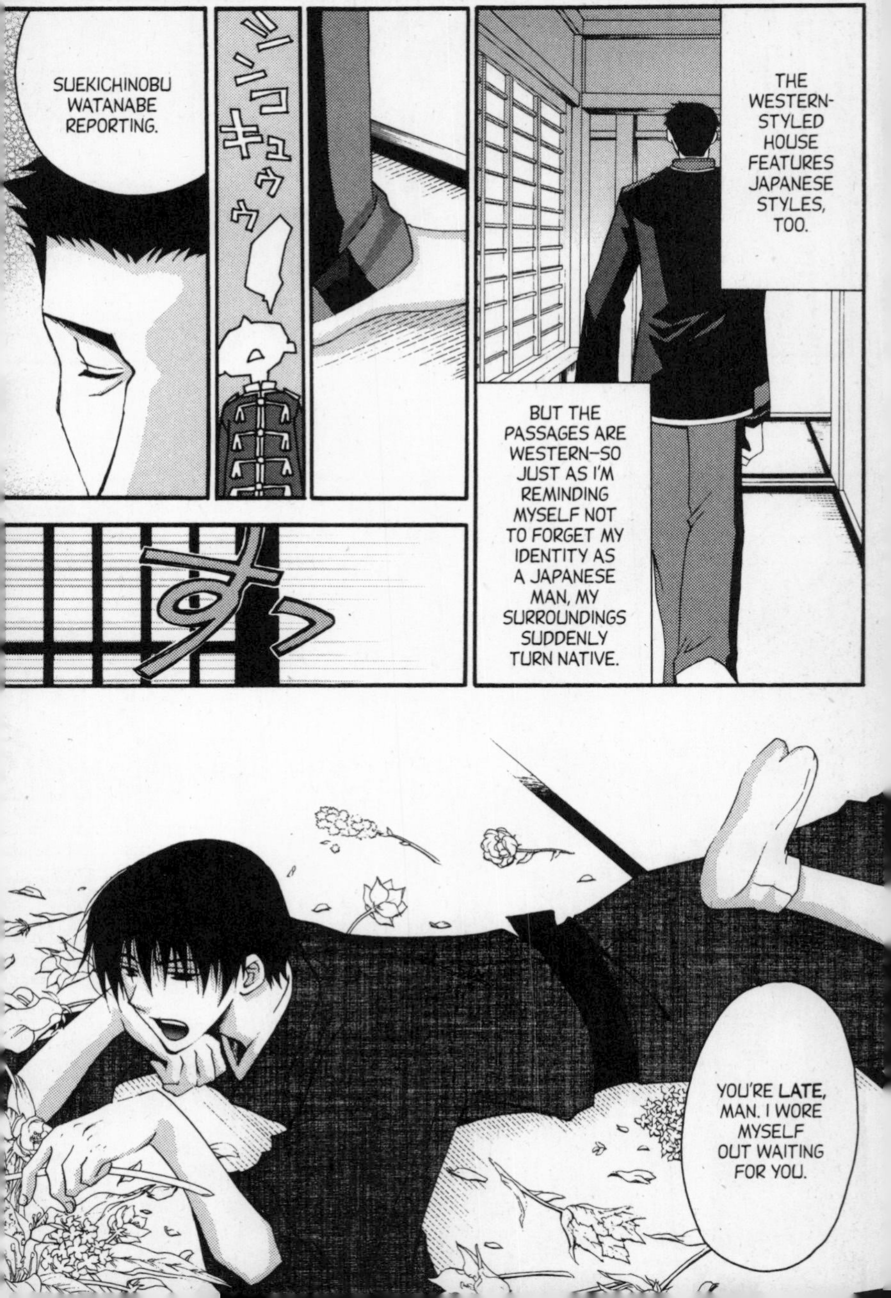
THE WESTERN-STYLED HOUSE FEATURES JAPANESE STYLES, TOO.
BUT THE PASSAGES ARE WESTERN—SO JUST AS I'M REMINDING MYSELF NOT TO FORGET MY IDENTITY AS A JAPANESE MAN, MY SURROUNDINGS SUDDENLY TURN NATIVE.
SUEKICHINOBU WATANABE REPORTING.
すっ
YOU'RE LATE, MAN. I WORE MYSELF OUT WAITING FOR YOU.

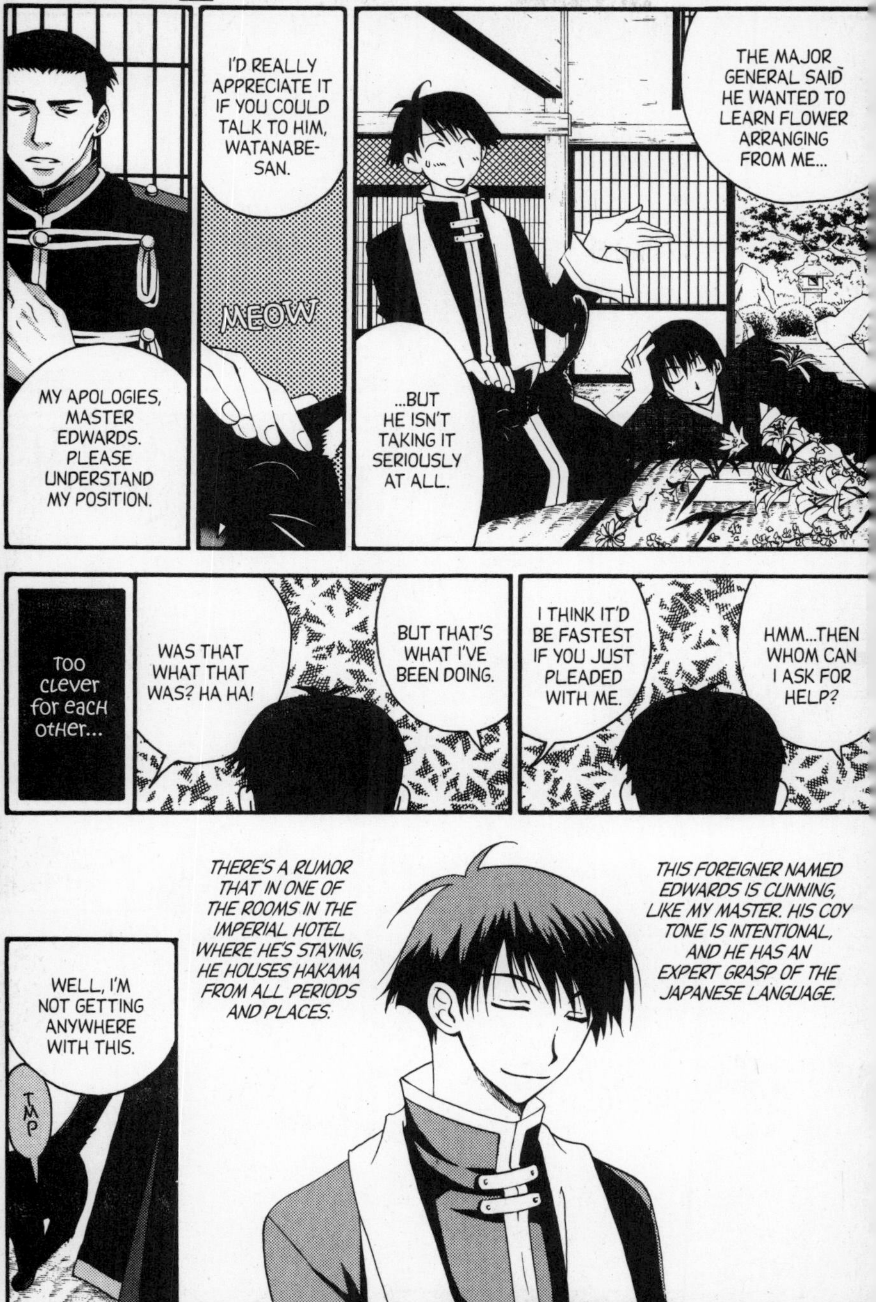
THE MAJOR GENERAL SAID HE WANTED TO LEARN FLOWER ARRANGING FROM ME...
...BUT HE ISN'T TAKING IT SERIOUSLY AT ALL.
I'D REALLY APPRECIATE IT IF YOU COULD TALK TO HIM, WATANABE-SAN.
MEOW
MY APOLOGIES, MASTER EDWARDS. PLEASE UNDERSTAND MY POSITION.
HMM...THEN WHOM CAN I ASK FOR HELP?
I THINK IT'D BE FASTEST IF YOU JUST PLEADED WITH ME.
BUT THAT'S WHAT I'VE BEEN DOING.
WAS THAT WHAT THAT WAS? HA HA!
Too clever for each other...
THIS FOREIGNER NAMED EDWARDS IS CUNNING, LIKE MY MASTER. HIS COY TONE IS INTENTIONAL, AND HE HAS AN EXPERT GRASP OF THE JAPANESE LANGUAGE.
THERE'S A RUMOR THAT IN ONE OF THE ROOMS IN THE IMPERIAL HOTEL WHERE HE'S STAYING, HE HOUSES HAKAMA FROM ALL PERIODS AND PLACES.
WELL, I'M NOT GETTING ANYWHERE WITH THIS.
TMP

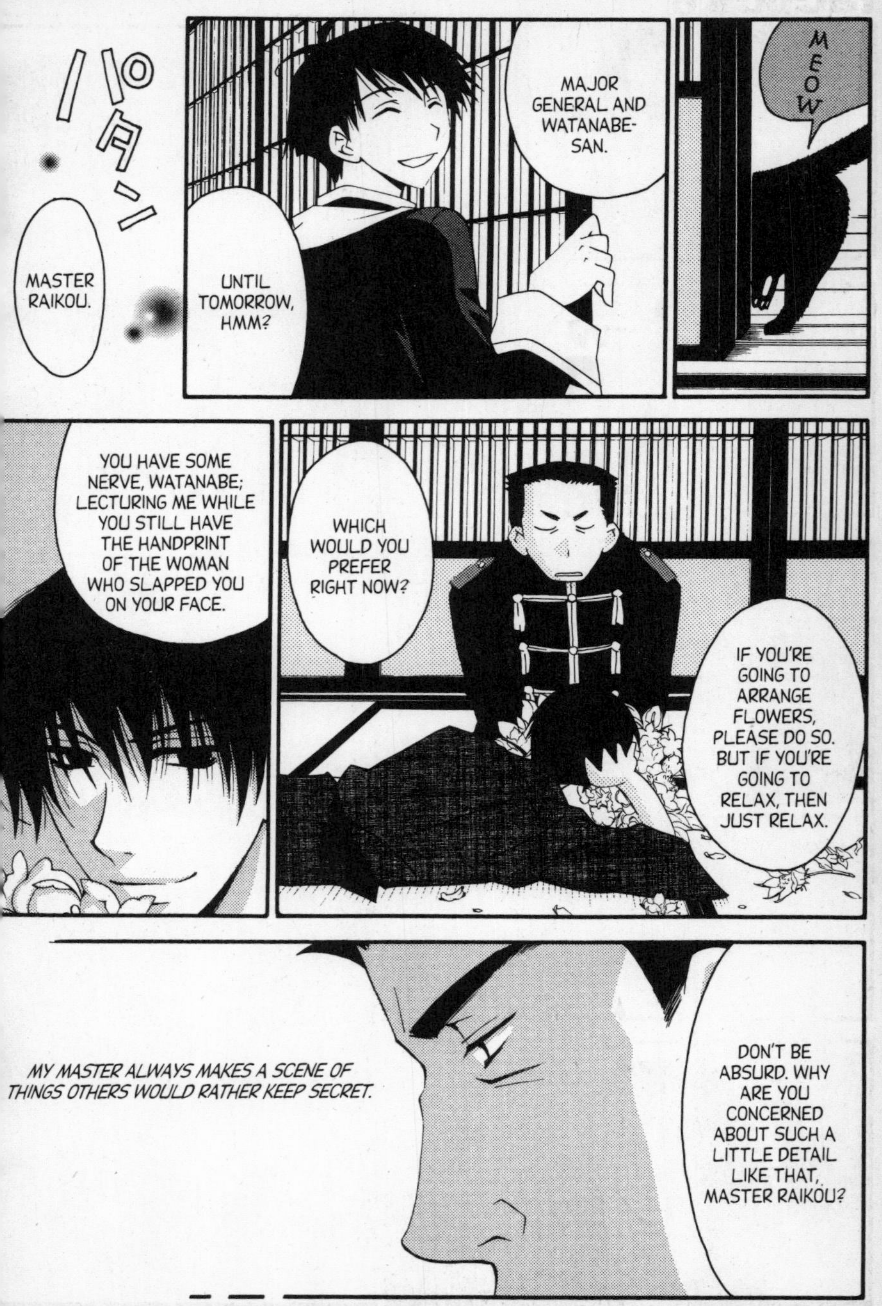
MEOW
MAJOR GENERAL AND WATANABE-SAN.
UNTIL TOMORROW, HMM?
パタン
MASTER RAIKOU.
WHICH WOULD YOU PREFER RIGHT NOW?
IF YOU'RE GOING TO ARRANGE FLOWERS, PLEASE DO SO. BUT IF YOU'RE GOING TO RELAX, THEN JUST RELAX.
YOU HAVE SOME NERVE, WATANABE; LECTURING ME WHILE YOU STILL HAVE THE HANDPRINT OF THE WOMAN WHO SLAPPED YOU ON YOUR FACE.
DON'T BE ABSURD. WHY ARE YOU CONCERNED ABOUT SUCH A LITTLE DETAIL LIKE THAT, MASTER RAIKOU?
MY MASTER ALWAYS MAKES A SCENE OF THINGS OTHERS WOULD RATHER KEEP SECRET.

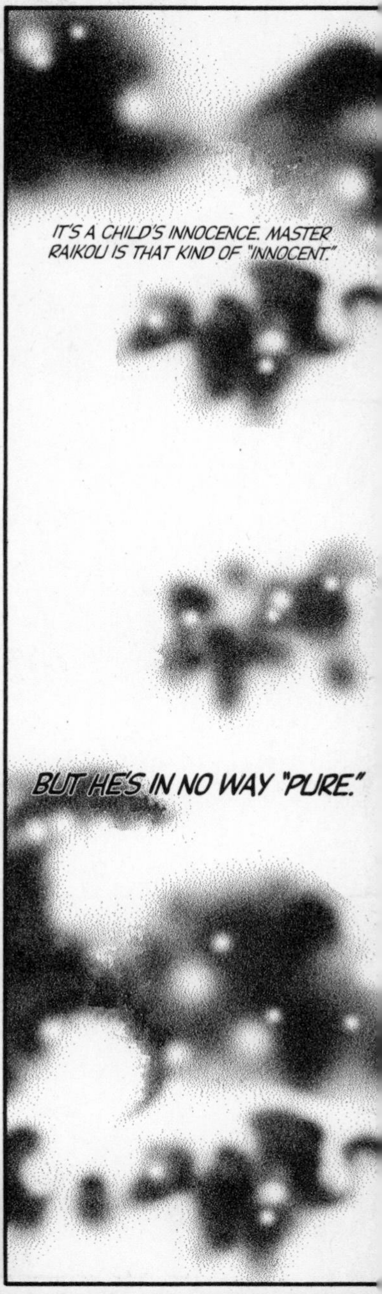
IT'S A CHILD'S INNOCENCE. MASTER RAIKOU IS THAT KIND OF "INNOCENT."
BUT HE'S IN NO WAY "PURE."

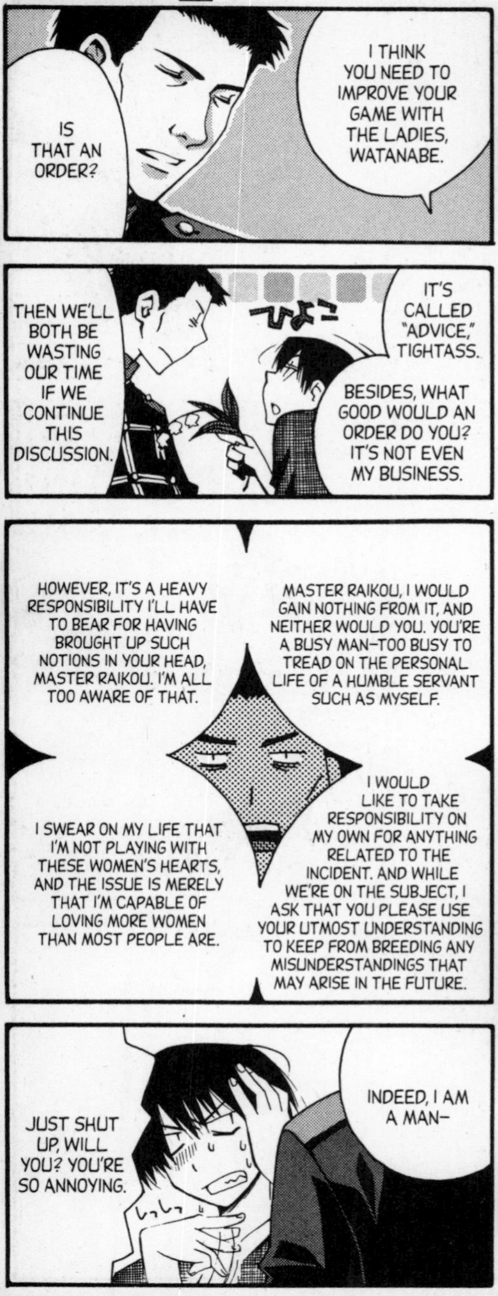
I THINK YOU NEED TO IMPROVE YOUR GAME WITH THE LADIES, WATANABE.
IS THAT AN ORDER?
IT'S CALLED "ADVICE," TIGHTASS.
BESIDES, WHAT GOOD WOULD AN ORDER DO YOU? IT'S NOT EVEN MY BUSINESS.
THEN WE'LL BOTH BE WASTING OUR TIME IF WE CONTINUE THIS DISCUSSION.
MASTER RAIKOU, I WOULD GAIN NOTHING FROM IT, AND NEITHER WOULD YOU. YOU'RE A BUSY MAN—TOO BUSY TO TREAD ON THE PERSONAL LIFE OF A HUMBLE SERVANT SUCH AS MYSELF.
HOWEVER, IT'S A HEAVY RESPONSIBILITY I'LL HAVE TO BEAR FOR HAVING BROUGHT UP SUCH NOTIONS IN YOUR HEAD, MASTER RAIKOU. I'M ALL TOO AWARE OF THAT.
I WOULD LIKE TO TAKE RESPONSIBILITY ON MY OWN FOR ANYTHING RELATED TO THE INCIDENT. AND WHILE WE'RE ON THE SUBJECT, I ASK THAT YOU PLEASE USE YOUR UTMOST UNDERSTANDING TO KEEP FROM BREEDING ANY MISUNDERSTANDINGS THAT MAY ARISE IN THE FUTURE.
I SWEAR ON MY LIFE THAT I'M NOT PLAYING WITH THESE WOMEN'S HEARTS, AND THE ISSUE IS MERELY THAT I'M CAPABLE OF LOVING MORE WOMEN THAN MOST PEOPLE ARE.
INDEED, I AM A MAN—
JUST SHUT UP, WILL YOU? YOU'RE SO ANNOYING.

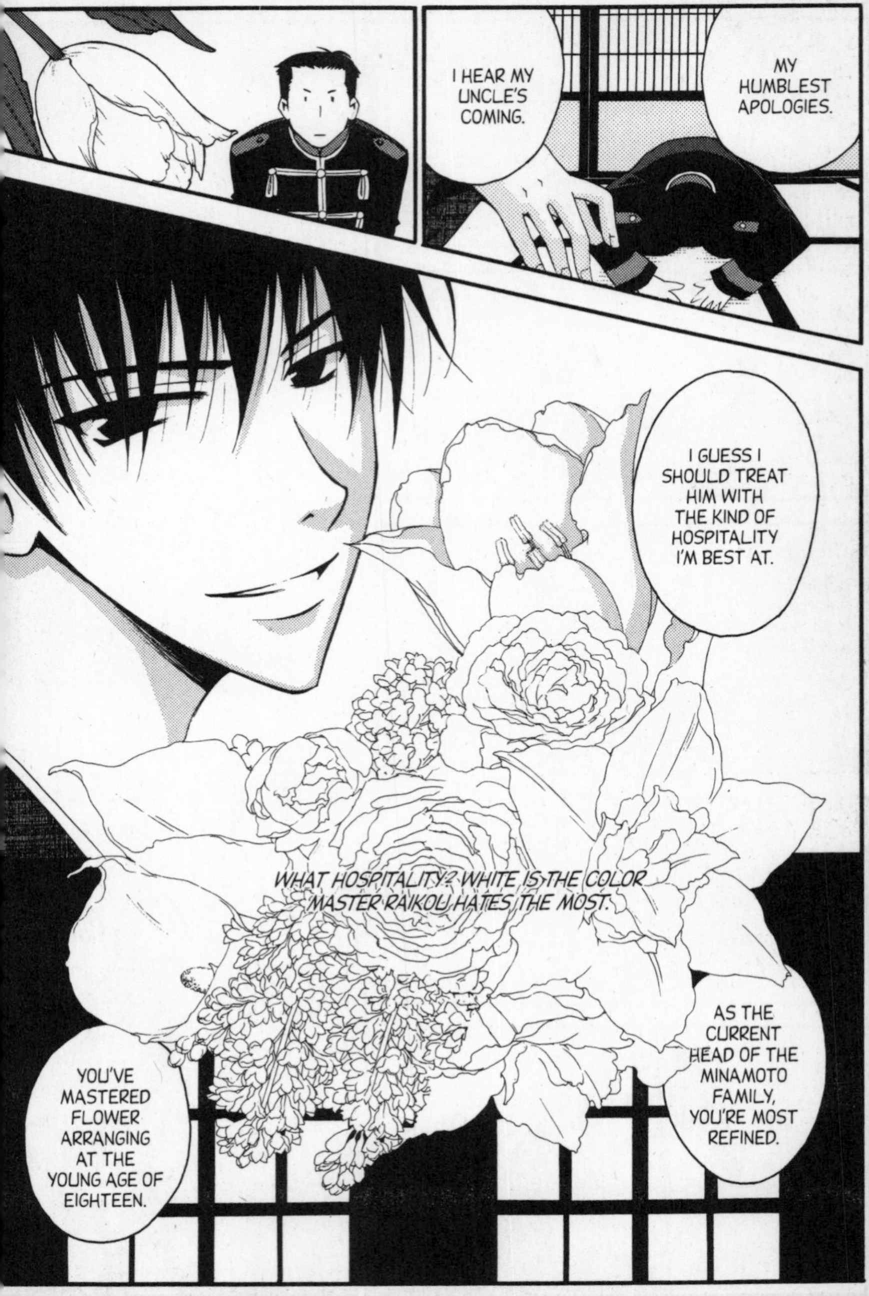
MY HUMBLEST APOLOGIES.
I HEAR MY UNCLE'S COMING.
I GUESS I SHOULD TREAT HIM WITH THE KIND OF HOSPITALITY I'M BEST AT.
WHAT HOSPITALITY? WHITE IS THE COLOR MASTER RAIKOU HATES THE MOST.
AS THE CURRENT HEAD OF THE MINAMOTO FAMILY, YOU'RE MOST REFINED.
YOU'VE MASTERED FLOWER ARRANGING AT THE YOUNG AGE OF EIGHTEEN.

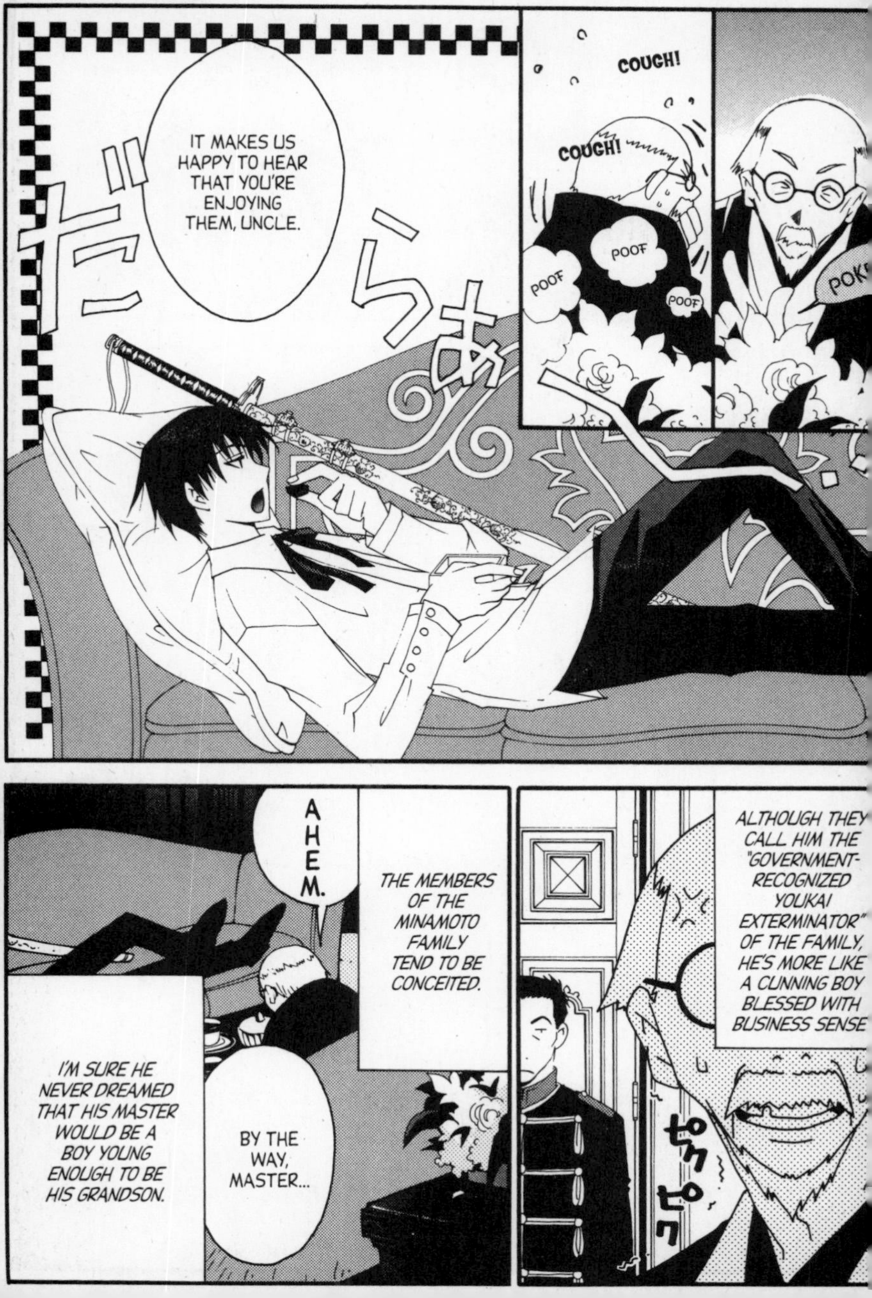
POK
COUGH!
COUGH!
POOF
POOF
POOF
IT MAKES US HAPPY TO HEAR THAT YOU'RE ENJOYING THEM, UNCLE.
だらぁ
ALTHOUGH THEY CALL HIM THE "GOVERNMENT-RECOGNIZED YOUKAI EXTERMINATOR" OF THE FAMILY, HE'S MORE LIKE A CUNNING BOY BLESSED WITH BUSINESS SENSE
ぴくぴく
THE MEMBERS OF THE MINAMOTO FAMILY TEND TO BE CONCEITED.
AHEM.
BY THE WAY, MASTER...
I'M SURE HE NEVER DREAMED THAT HIS MASTER WOULD BE A BOY YOUNG ENOUGH TO BE HIS GRANDSON.

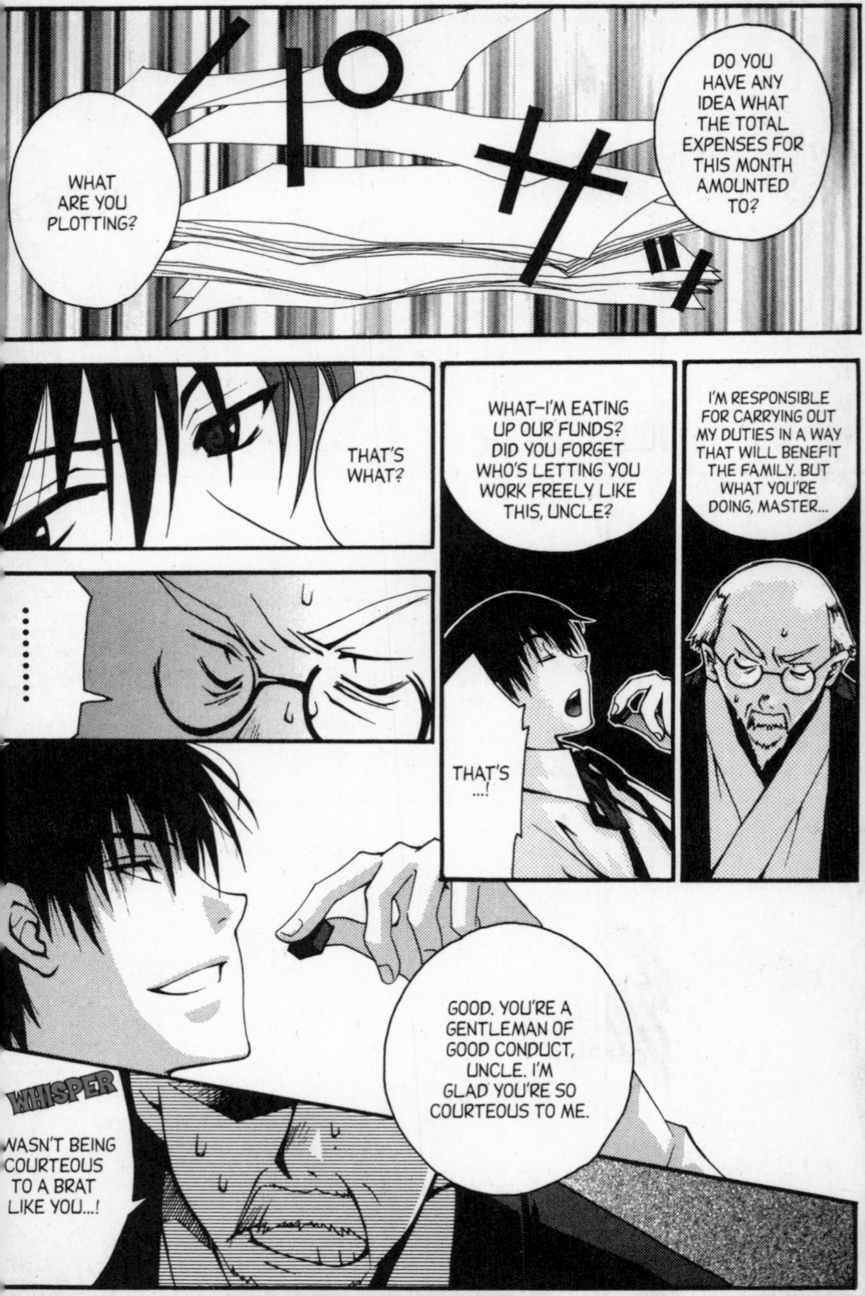

DO YOU HAVE ANY IDEA WHAT THE TOTAL EXPENSES FOR THIS MONTH AMOUNTED TO?
WHAT ARE YOU PLOTTING?
I'M RESPONSIBLE FOR CARRYING OUT MY DUTIES IN A WAY THAT WILL BENEFIT THE FAMILY. BUT WHAT YOU'RE DOING, MASTER...
WHAT—I'M EATING UP OUR FUNDS? DID YOU FORGET WHO'S LETTING YOU WORK FREELY LIKE THIS, UNCLE?
THAT'S ...!
THAT'S WHAT?
....
GOOD. YOU'RE A GENTLEMAN OF GOOD CONDUCT, UNCLE. I'M GLAD YOU'RE SO COURTEOUS TO ME.
WHISPER
WASN'T BEING COURTEOUS TO A BRAT LIKE YOU...!

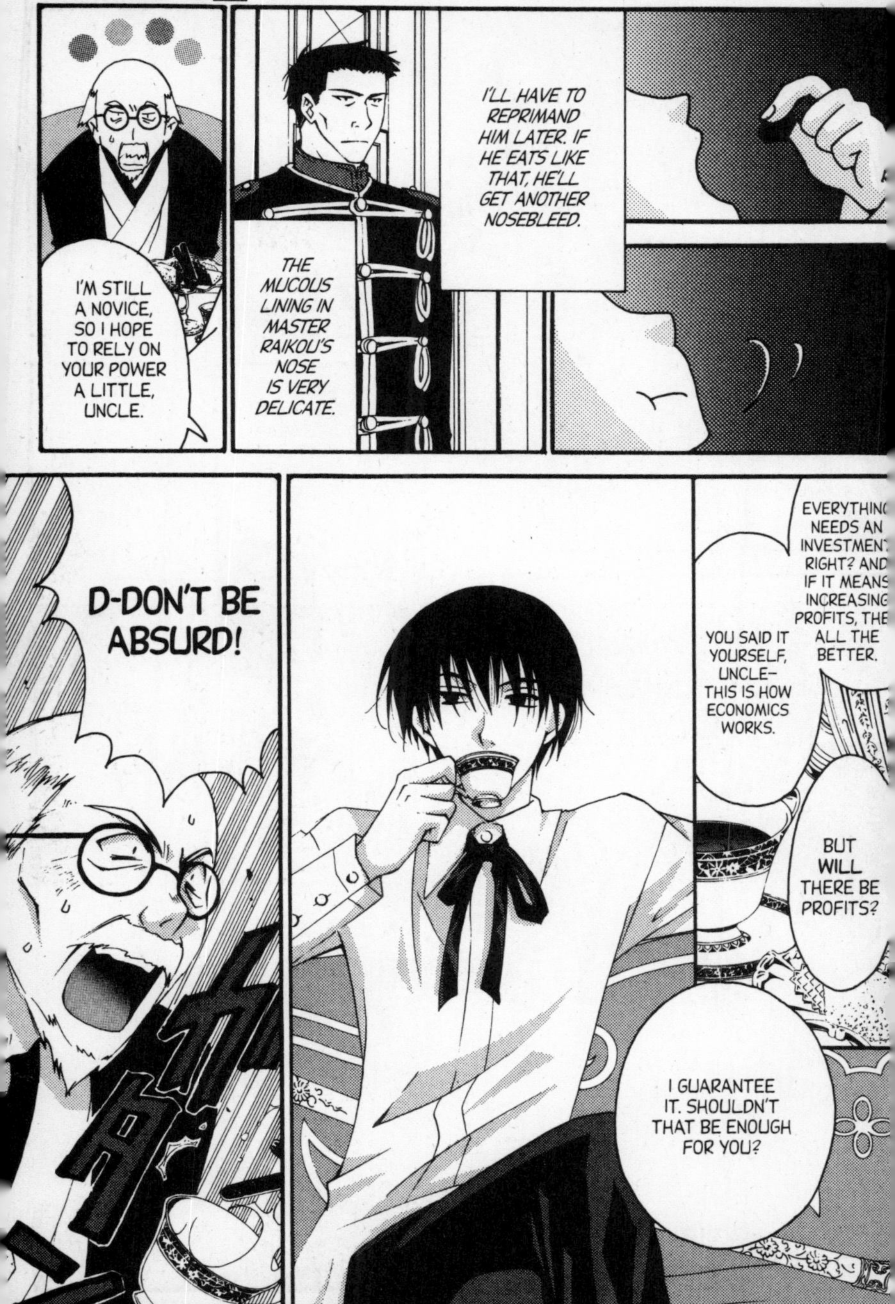
I'LL HAVE TO REPRIMAND HIM LATER. IF HE EATS LIKE THAT, HE'LL GET ANOTHER NOSEBLEED.
THE MUCOUS LINING IN MASTER RAIKOU'S NOSE IS VERY DELICATE.
I'M STILL A NOVICE, SO I HOPE TO RELY ON YOUR POWER A LITTLE, UNCLE.
EVERYTHIN NEEDS AN INVESTMEN RIGHT? AND IF IT MEANS INCREASING PROFITS, THE ALL THE BETTER.
YOU SAID IT YOURSELF, UNCLE– THIS IS HOW ECONOMICS WORKS.
BUT WILL THERE BE PROFITS?
I GUARANTEE IT. SHOULDN'T THAT BE ENOUGH FOR YOU?
D-DON'T BE ABSURD!

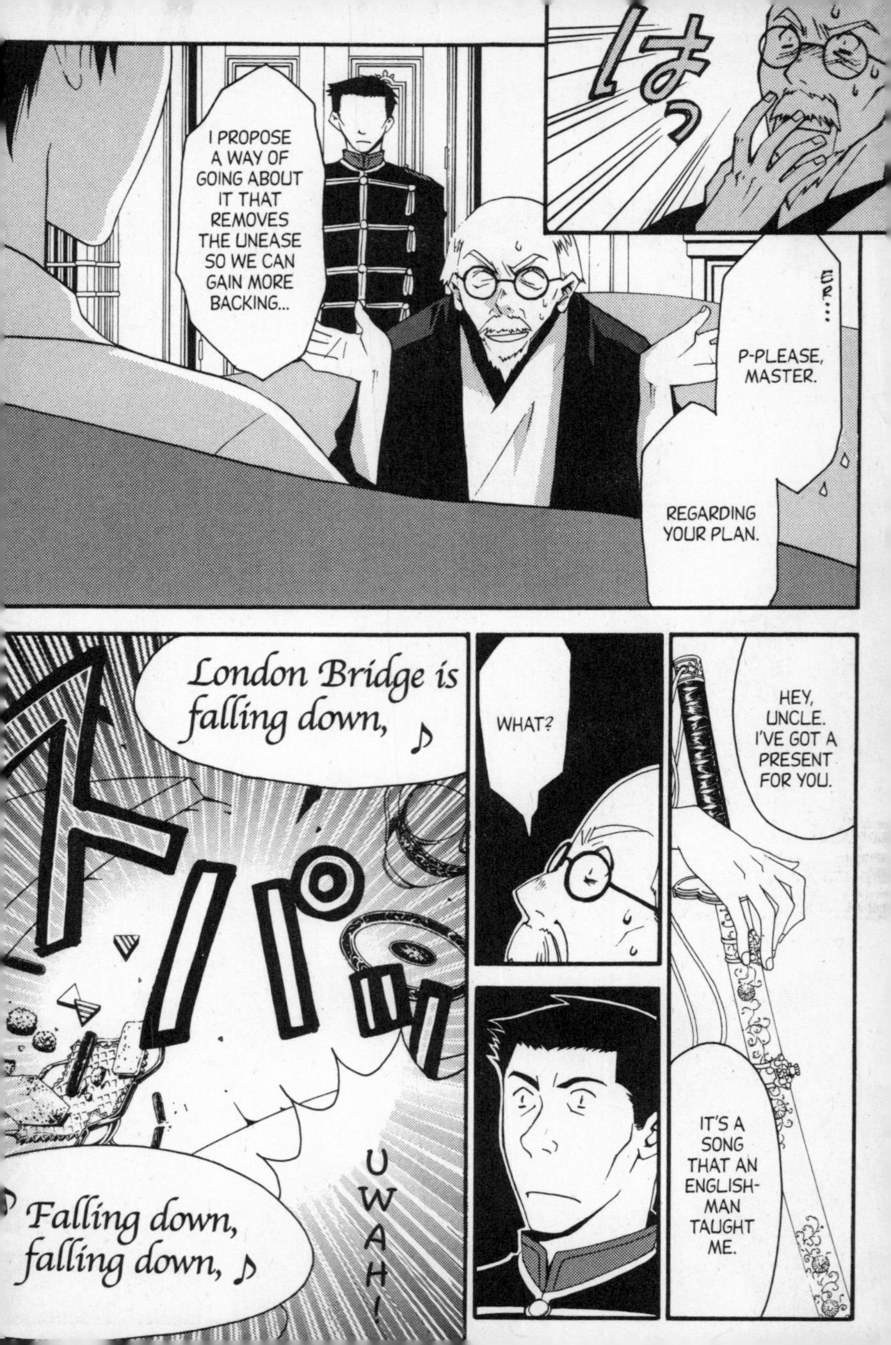
はっ
ER...
P-PLEASE, MASTER.
REGARDING YOUR PLAN.
I PROPOSE A WAY OF GOING ABOUT IT THAT REMOVES THE UNEASE SO WE CAN GAIN MORE BACKING...
HEY, UNCLE. I'VE GOT A PRESENT FOR YOU.
IT'S A SONG THAT AN ENGLISH-MAN TAUGHT ME.
WHAT?
London Bridge is falling down, ♪
ドパーン
UWAH!
♪ Falling down, falling down, ♪

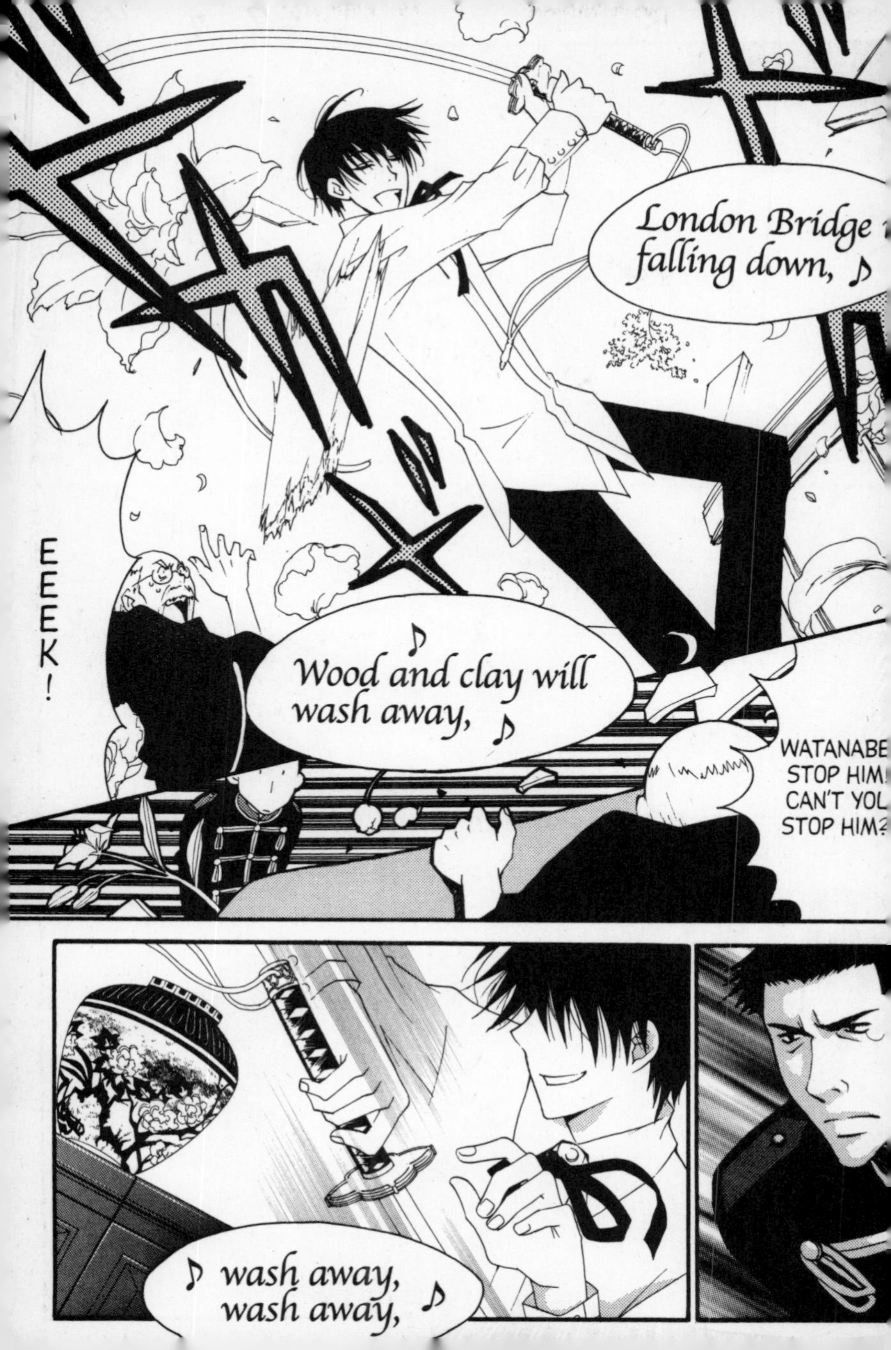
London Bridge falling down, ♪
EEEK!
♪ Wood and clay will wash away, ♪
WATANABE STOP HIM! CAN'T YOU STOP HIM?
♪ wash away, wash away, ♪

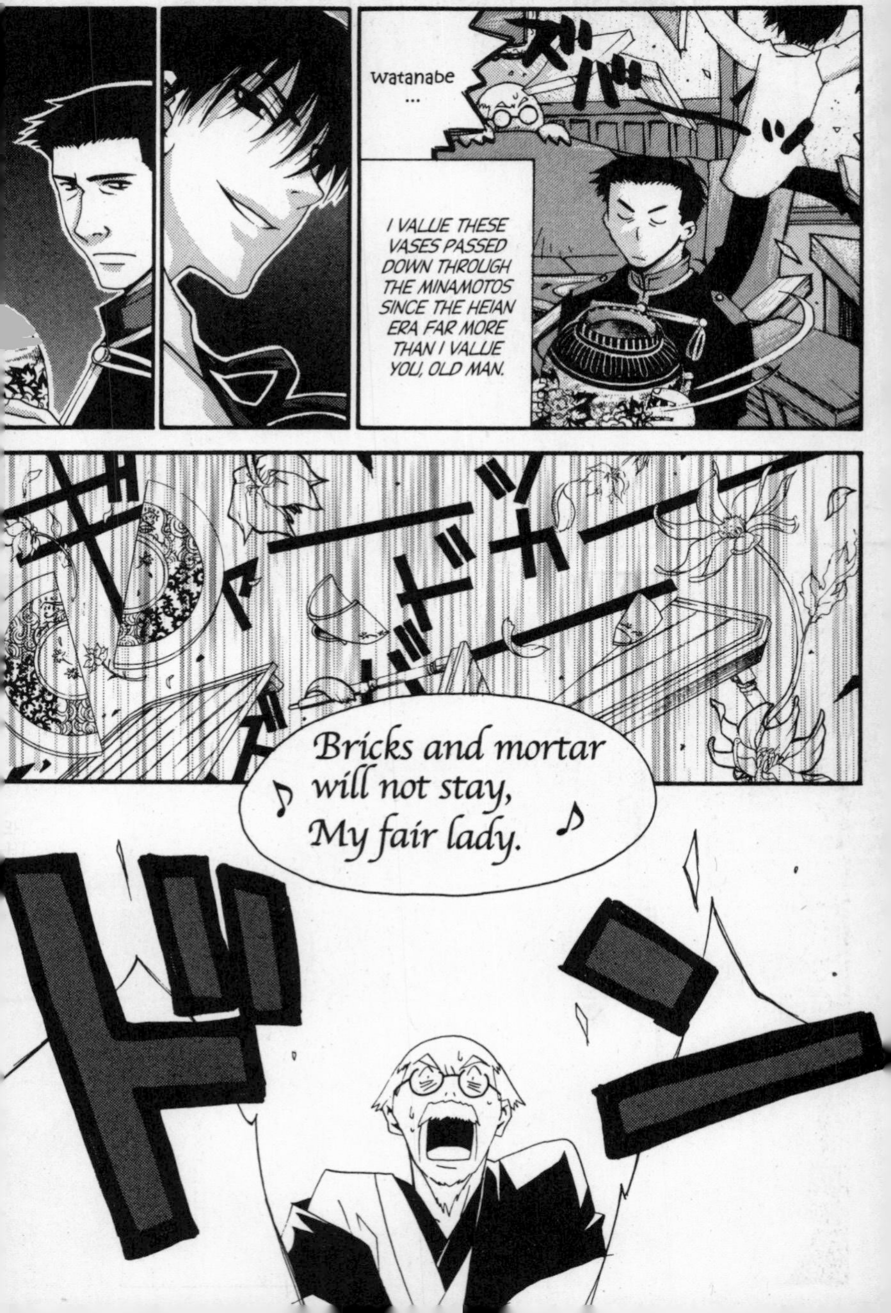
Watanabe ...
I VALUE THESE VASES PASSED DOWN THROUGH THE MINAMOTOS SINCE THE HEIAN ERA FAR MORE THAN I VALUE YOU, OLD MAN.
♪ Bricks and mortar will not stay, My fair lady. ♪

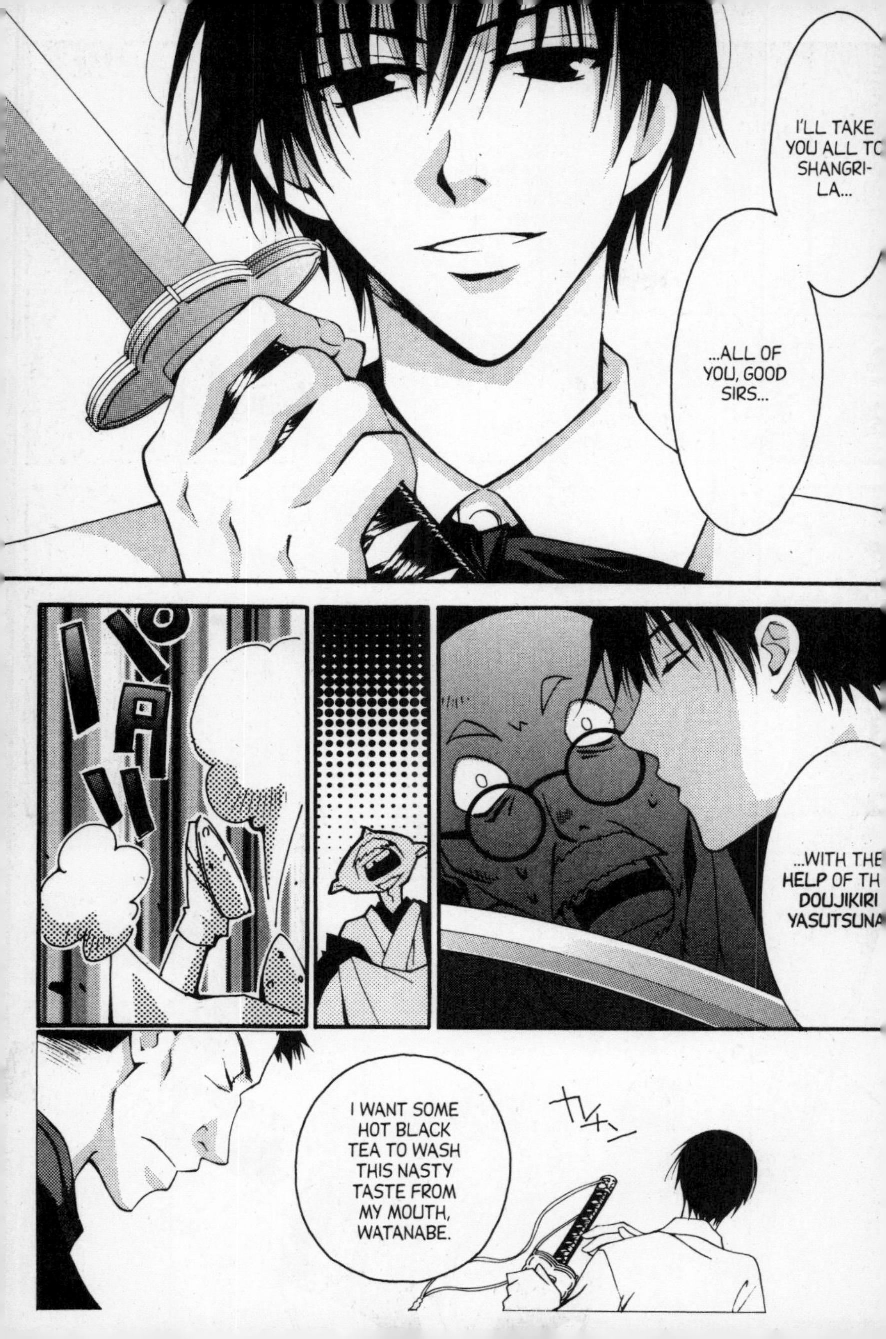
I'LL TAKE YOU ALL TO SHANGRI-LA...
...ALL OF YOU, GOOD SIRS...
...WITH THE HELP OF TH DOUJIKIRI YASUTSUNA
I WANT SOME HOT BLACK TEA TO WASH THIS NASTY TASTE FROM MY MOUTH, WATANABE.

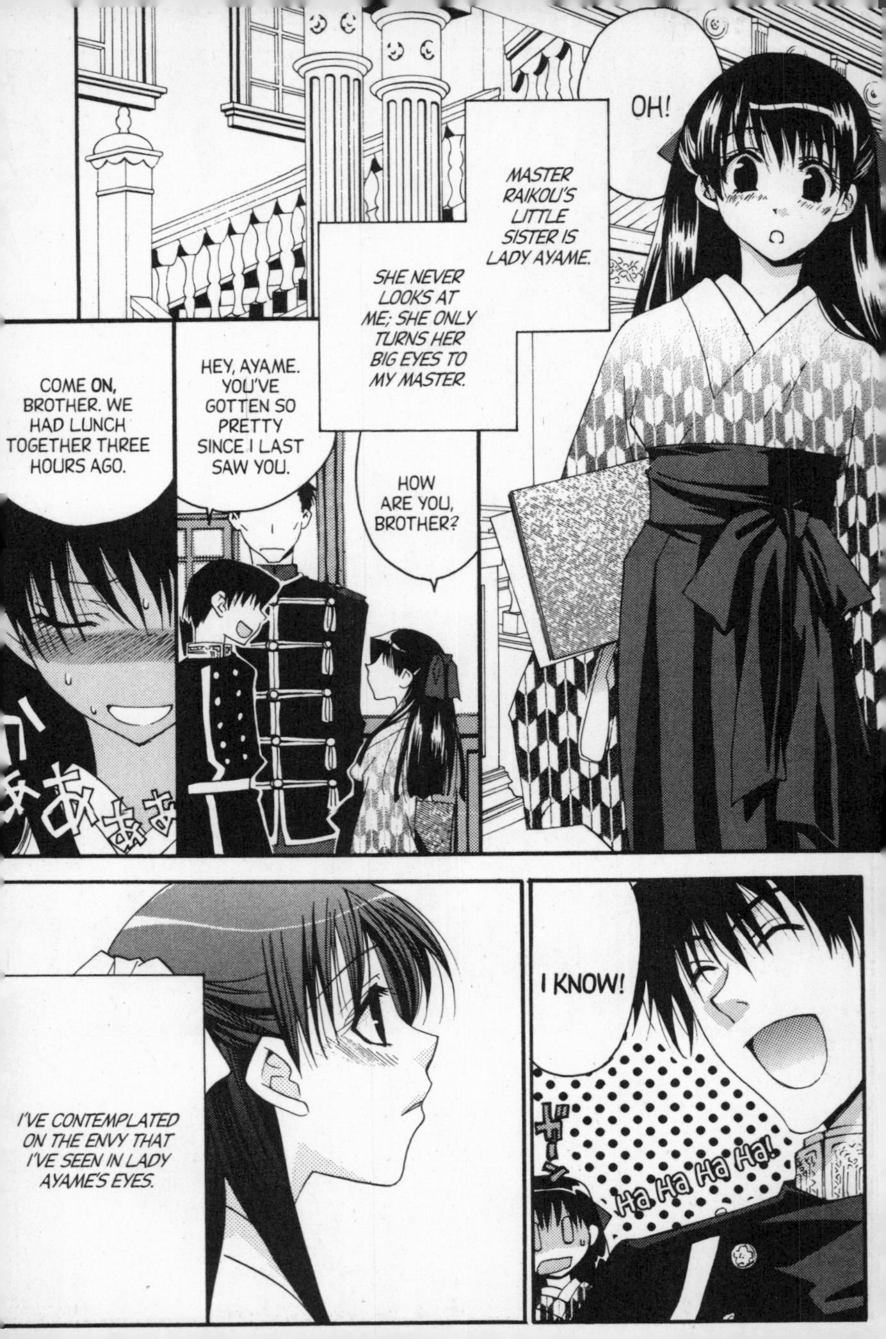
OH!
MASTER RAIKOU'S LITTLE SISTER IS LADY AYAME.
SHE NEVER LOOKS AT ME; SHE ONLY TURNS HER BIG EYES TO MY MASTER.
HOW ARE YOU, BROTHER?
HEY, AYAME. YOU'VE GOTTEN SO PRETTY SINCE I LAST SAW YOU.
COME ON, BROTHER. WE HAD LUNCH TOGETHER THREE HOURS AGO.
I KNOW!
Ha Ha Ha Ha Ha!
I'VE CONTEMPLATED ON THE ENVY THAT I'VE SEEN IN LADY AYAME'S EYES.

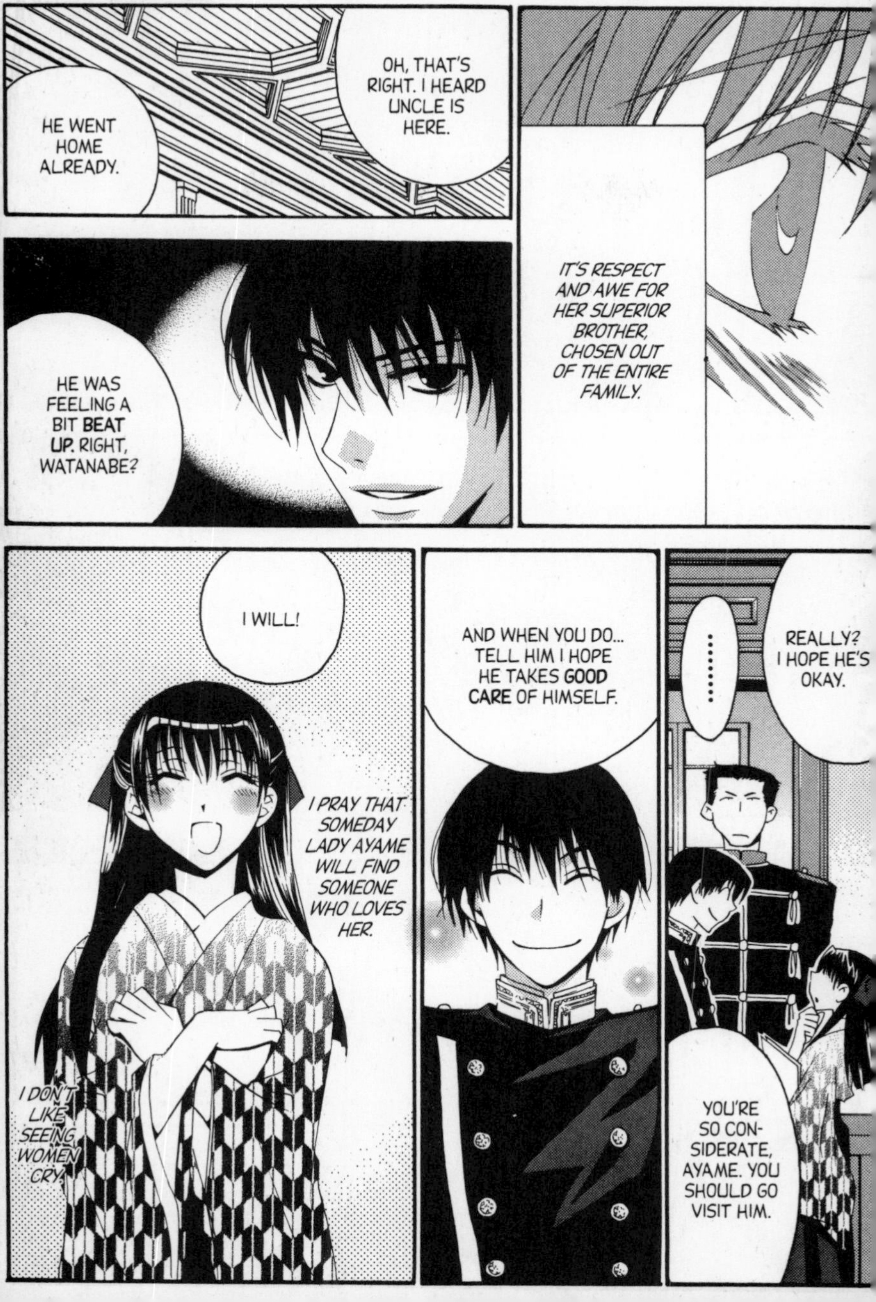
IT'S RESPECT AND AWE FOR HER SUPERIOR BROTHER, CHOSEN OUT OF THE ENTIRE FAMILY.
OH, THAT'S RIGHT. I HEARD UNCLE IS HERE.
HE WENT HOME ALREADY.
HE WAS FEELING A BIT BEAT UP. RIGHT, WATANABE?
REALLY? I HOPE HE'S OKAY.
......
YOU'RE SO CONSIDERATE, AYAME. YOU SHOULD GO VISIT HIM.
AND WHEN YOU DO... TELL HIM I HOPE HE TAKES GOOD CARE OF HIMSELF.
I WILL!
I PRAY THAT SOMEDAY LADY AYAME WILL FIND SOMEONE WHO LOVES HER.
I DON'T LIKE SEEING WOMEN CRY.

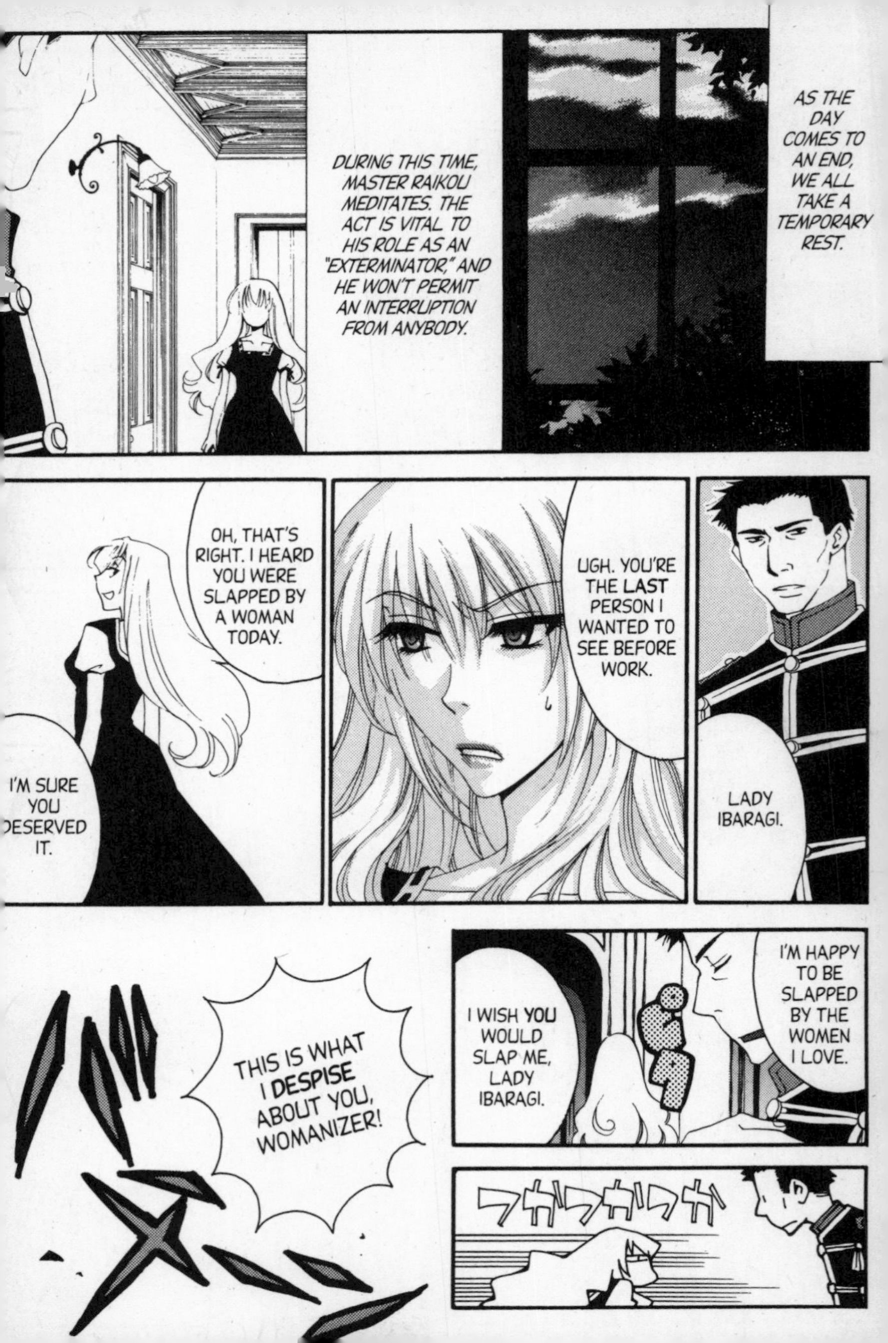
AS THE DAY COMES TO AN END, WE ALL TAKE A TEMPORARY REST.
DURING THIS TIME, MASTER RAIKOU MEDITATES. THE ACT IS VITAL TO HIS ROLE AS AN "EXTERMINATOR," AND HE WON'T PERMIT AN INTERRUPTION FROM ANYBODY.
LADY IBARAGI.
UGH. YOU'RE THE LAST PERSON I WANTED TO SEE BEFORE WORK.
OH, THAT'S RIGHT. I HEARD YOU WERE SLAPPED BY A WOMAN TODAY.
I'M SURE YOU DESERVED IT.
I'M HAPPY TO BE SLAPPED BY THE WOMEN I LOVE.
I WISH YOU WOULD SLAP ME, LADY IBARAGI.
THIS IS WHAT I DESPISE ABOUT YOU, WOMANIZER!

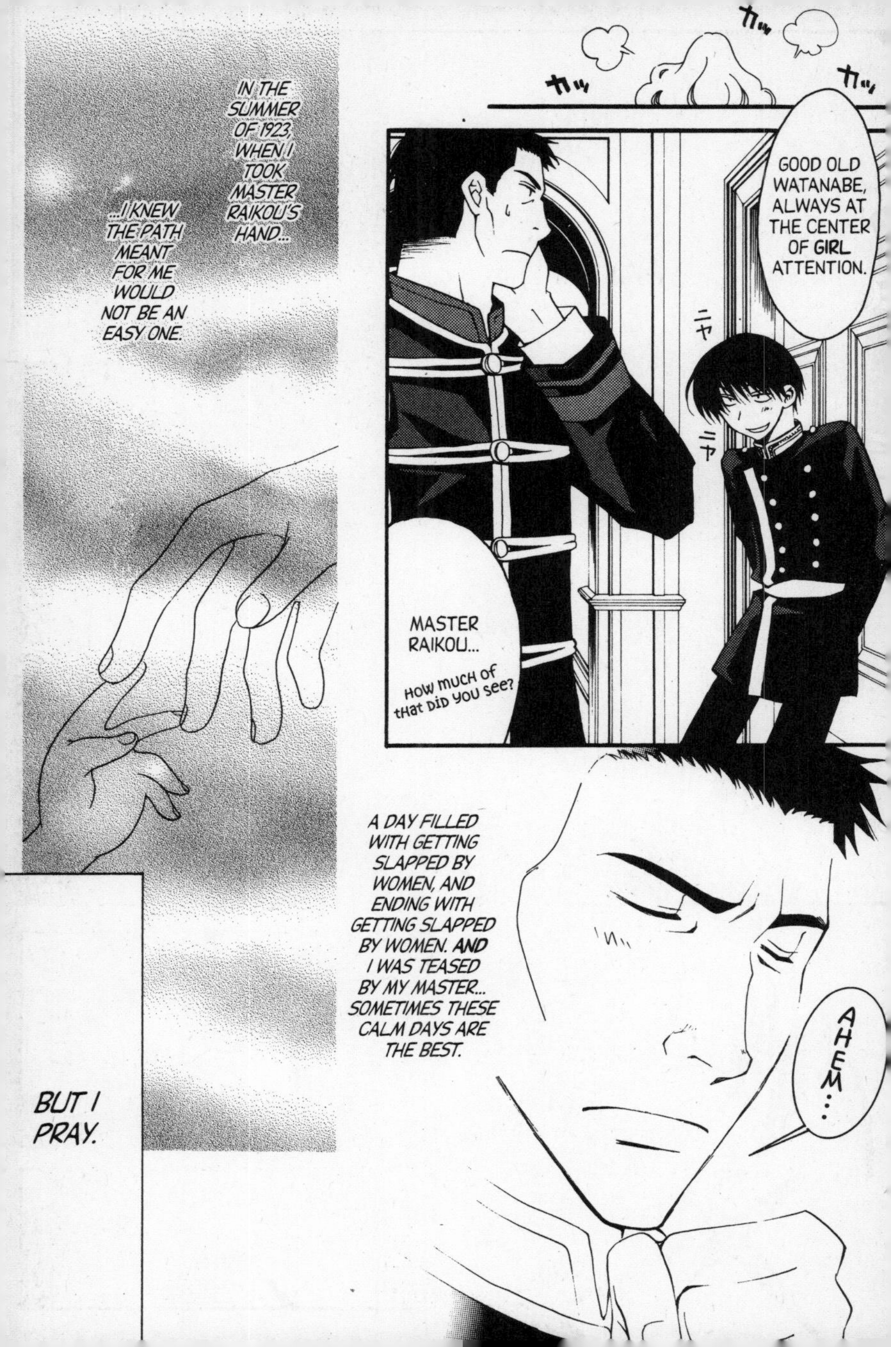
カッ
カッ
カッ
GOOD OLD WATANABE, ALWAYS AT THE CENTER OF GIRL ATTENTION.
ニヤ
ニヤ
MASTER RAIKOU...
HOW MUCH OF THAT DID YOU SEE?
AHEM...
A DAY FILLED WITH GETTING SLAPPED BY WOMEN, AND ENDING WITH GETTING SLAPPED BY WOMEN. AND I WAS TEASED BY MY MASTER... SOMETIMES THESE CALM DAYS ARE THE BEST.
IN THE SUMMER OF 1923, WHEN I TOOK MASTER RAIKOU'S HAND...
...I KNEW THE PATH MEANT FOR ME WOULD NOT BE AN EASY ONE.
BUT I PRAY.

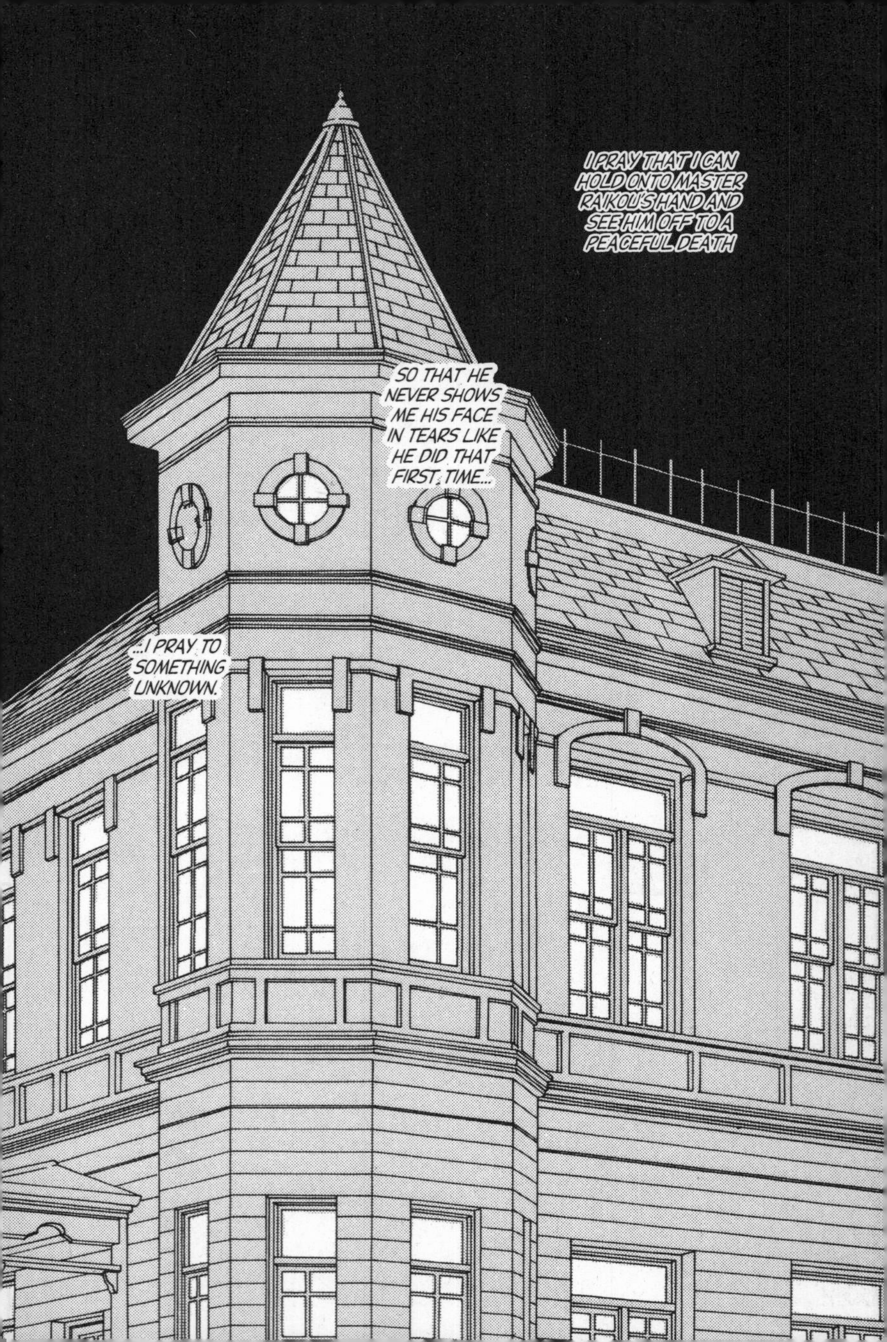
I PRAY THAT I CAN HOLD ONTO MASTER RAIKOU'S HAND AND SEE HIM OFF TO A PEACEFUL DEATH
SO THAT HE NEVER SHOWS ME HIS FACE IN TEARS LIKE HE DID THAT FIRST TIME...
...I PRAY TO SOMETHING UNKNOWN.

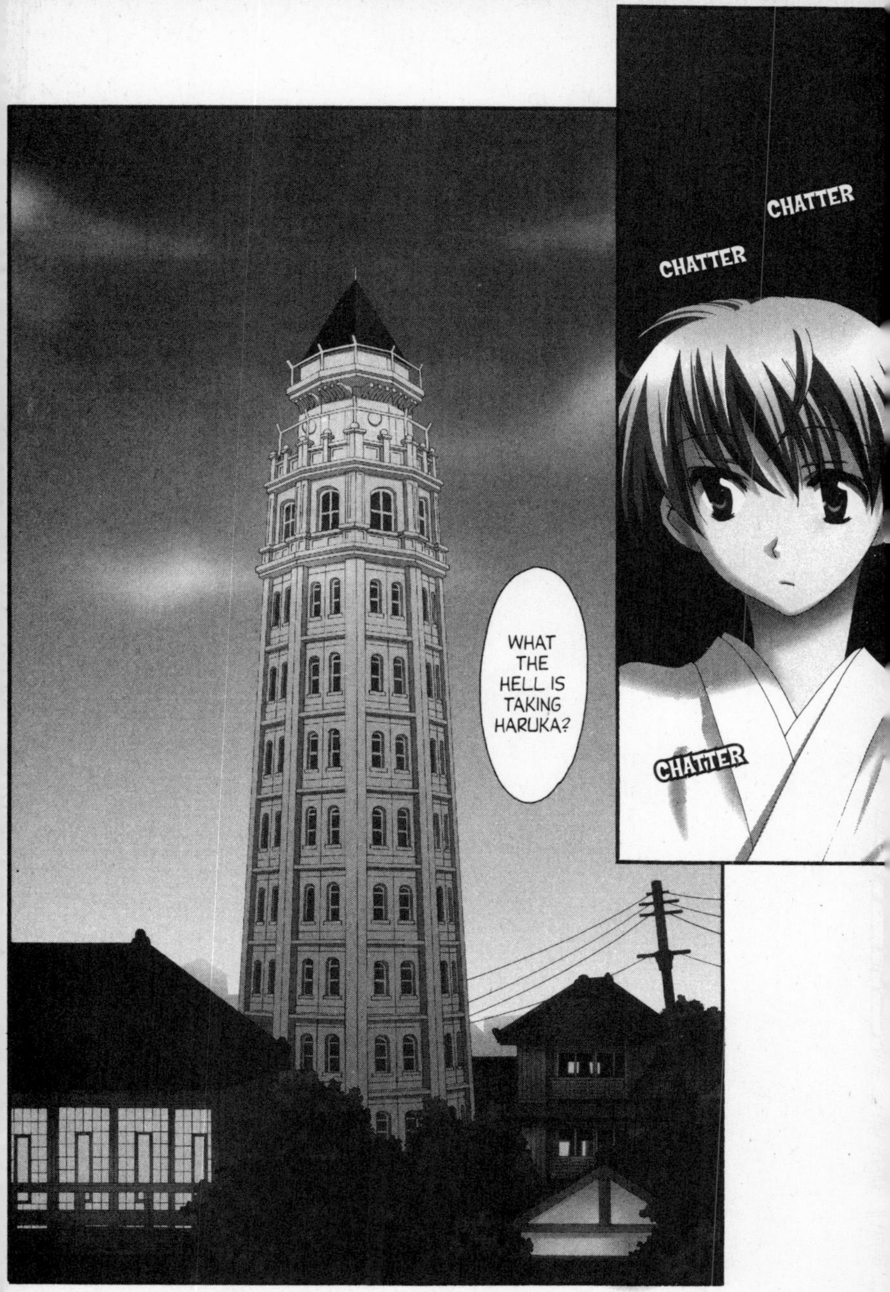
CHATTER
CHATTER
CHATTER
WHAT THE HELL IS TAKING HARUKA?

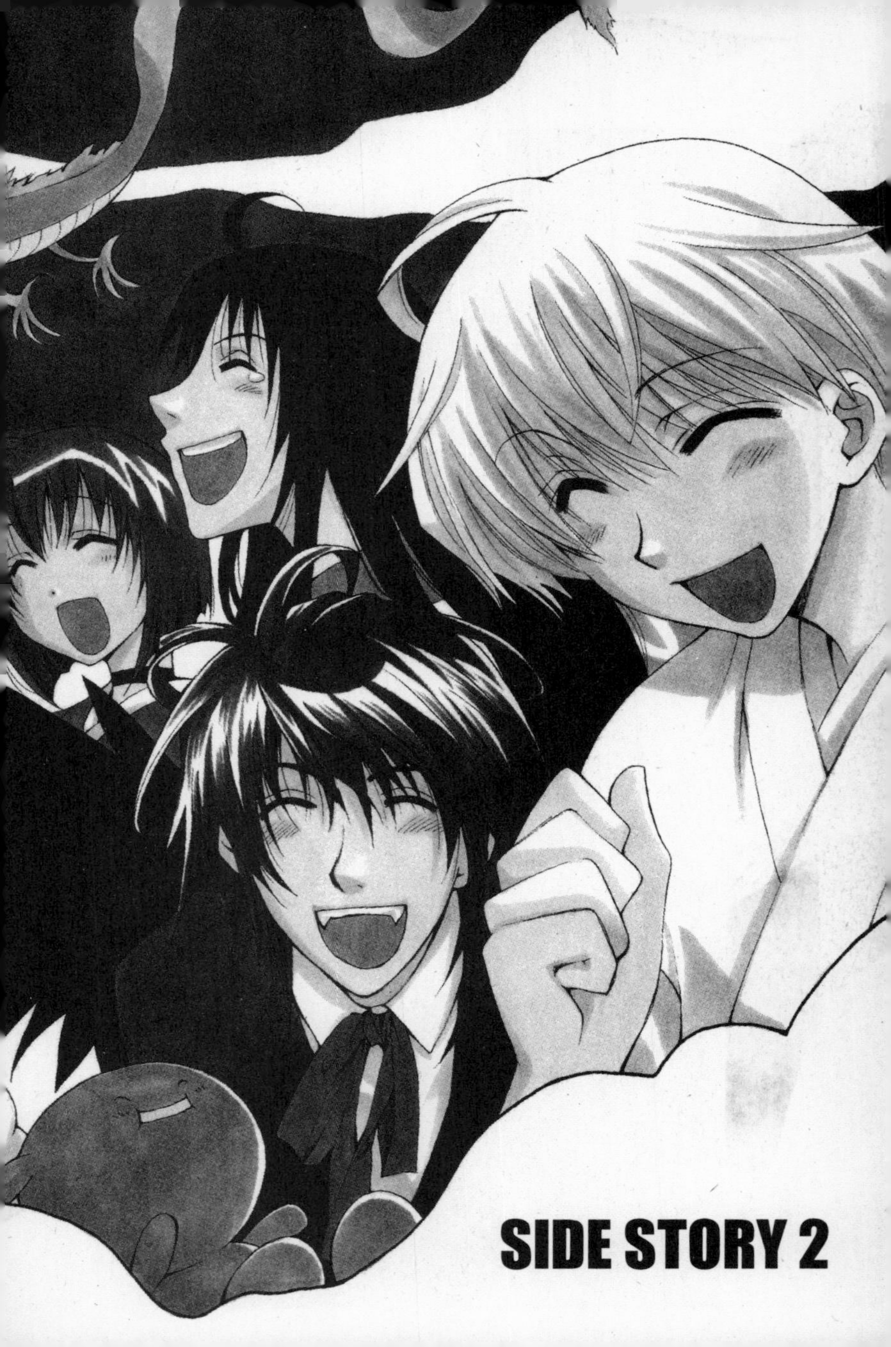

SIDE STORY 2

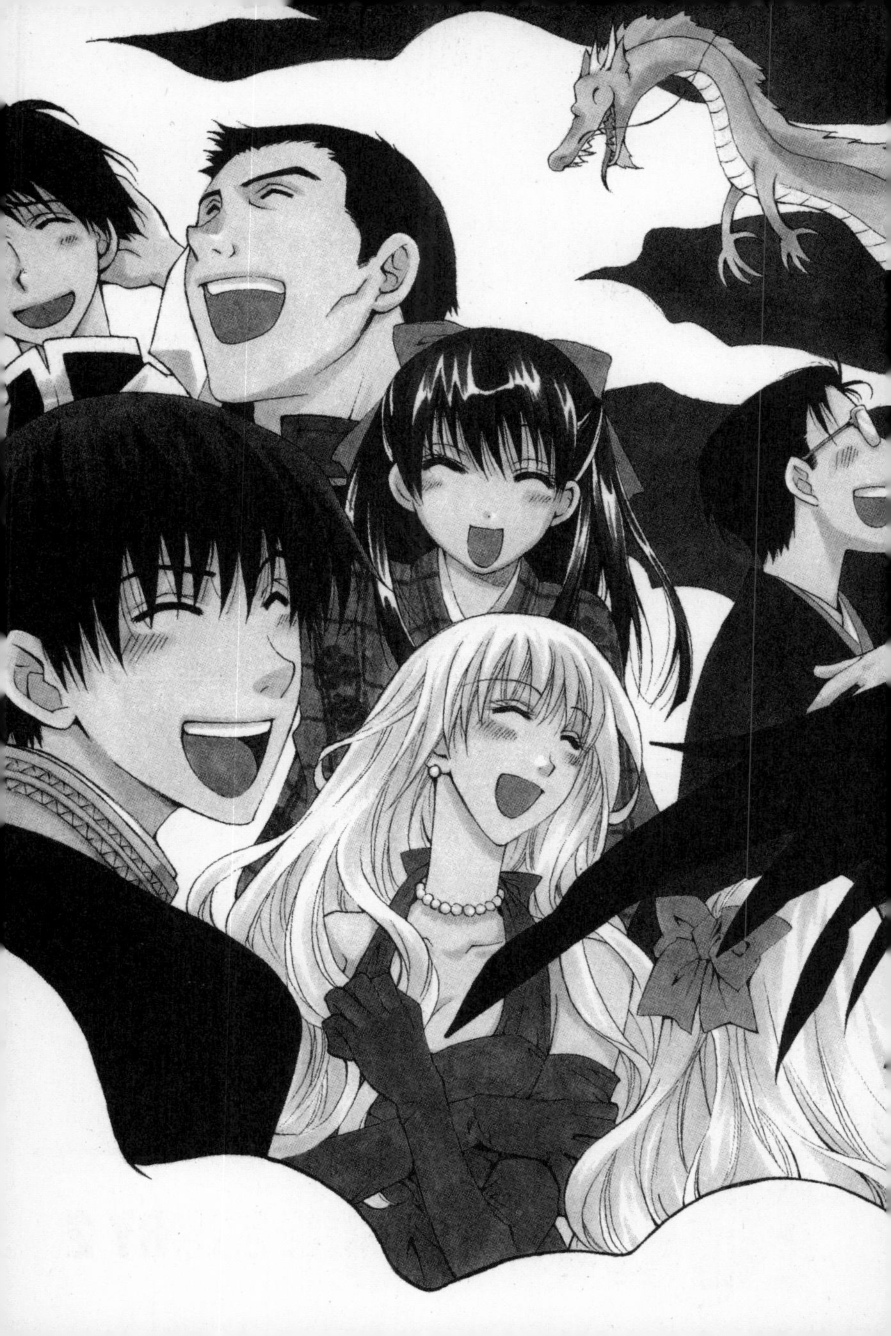

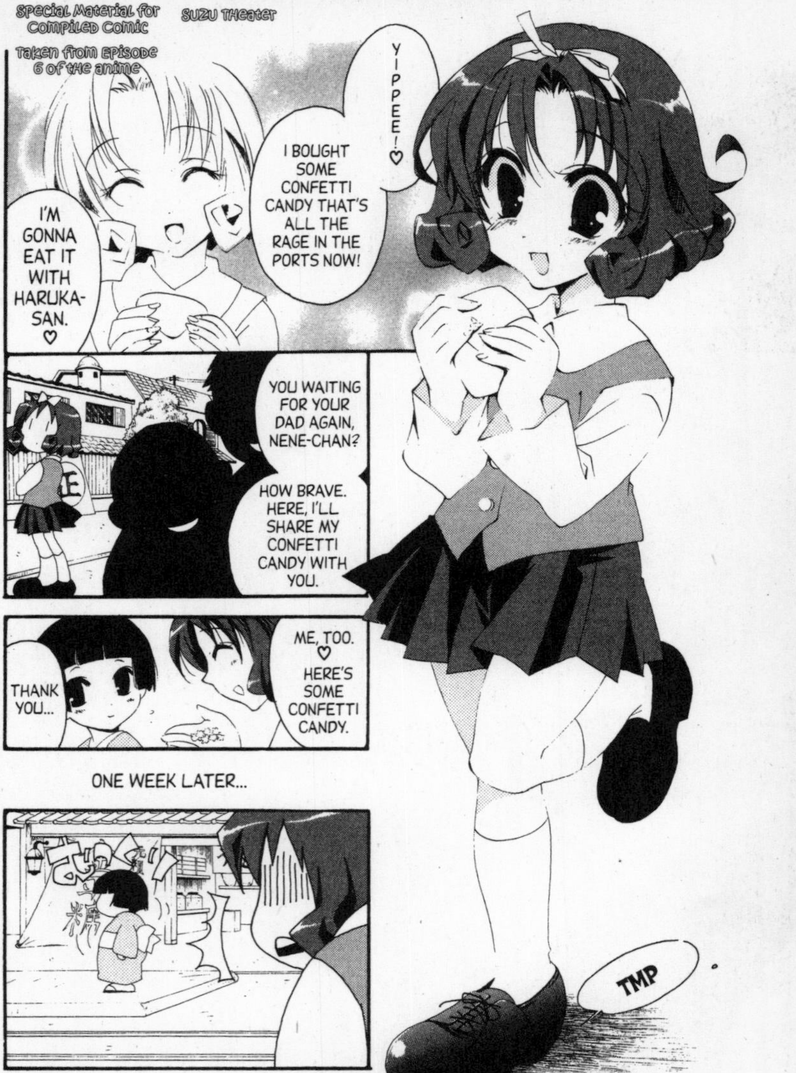
Special Material for Compiled Comic
SUZU Theater
Taken from Episode 6 of the anime
YIPPEE!♡
I BOUGHT SOME CONFETTI CANDY THAT'S ALL THE RAGE IN THE PORTS NOW!
I'M GONNA EAT IT WITH HARUKA-SAN. ♡
YOU WAITING FOR YOUR DAD AGAIN, NENE-CHAN?
HOW BRAVE. HERE, I'LL SHARE MY CONFETTI CANDY WITH YOU.
ME, TOO. ♡ HERE'S SOME CONFETTI CANDY.
THANK YOU...
ONE WEEK LATER...
TMP

THE END

tactics

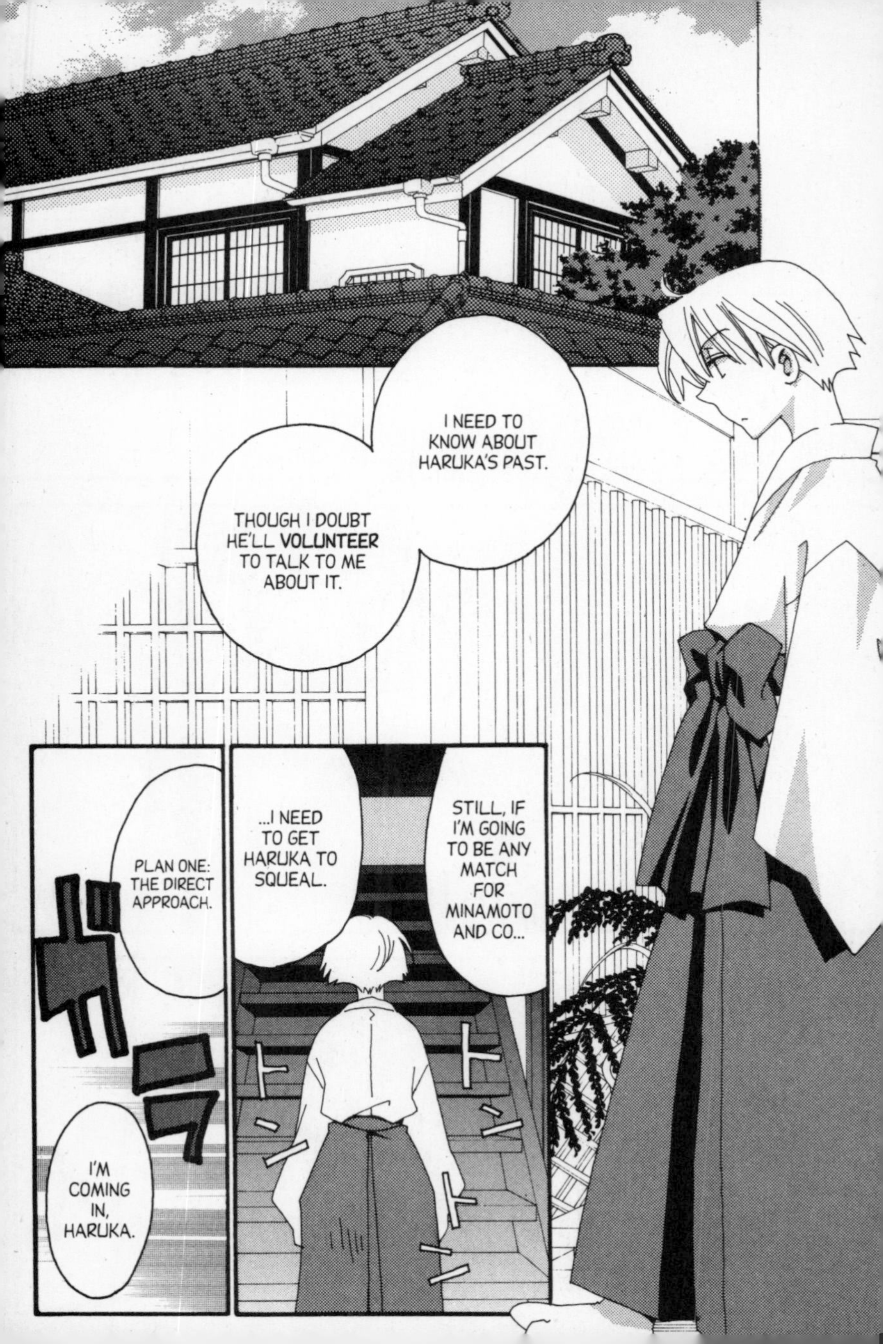
I NEED TO KNOW ABOUT HARUKA'S PAST.
THOUGH I DOUBT HE'LL **VOLUNTEER** TO TALK TO ME ABOUT IT.
STILL, IF I'M GOING TO BE ANY MATCH FOR MINAMOTO AND CO...
...I NEED TO GET HARUKA TO SQUEAL.
PLAN ONE: THE DIRECT APPROACH.
I'M COMING IN, HARUKA.

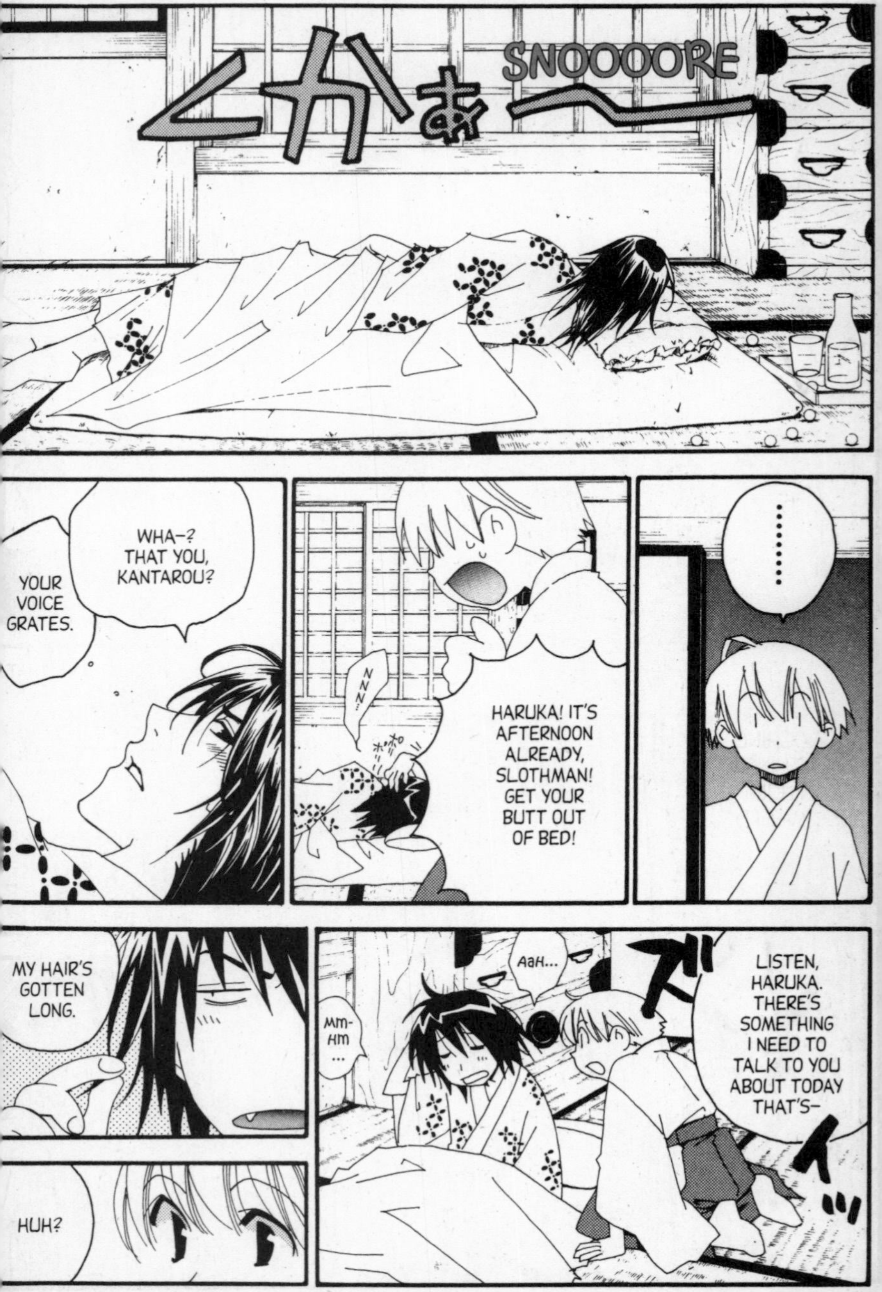

くかぁ〜
SNOOOORE
......
HARUKA! IT'S AFTERNOON ALREADY, SLOTHMAN! GET YOUR BUTT OUT OF BED!
NNN...
WHA-? THAT YOU, KANTAROU?
YOUR VOICE GRATES.
LISTEN, HARUKA. THERE'S SOMETHING I NEED TO TALK TO YOU ABOUT TODAY THAT'S–
AaH...
MM-HM ...
MY HAIR'S GOTTEN LONG.
HUH?

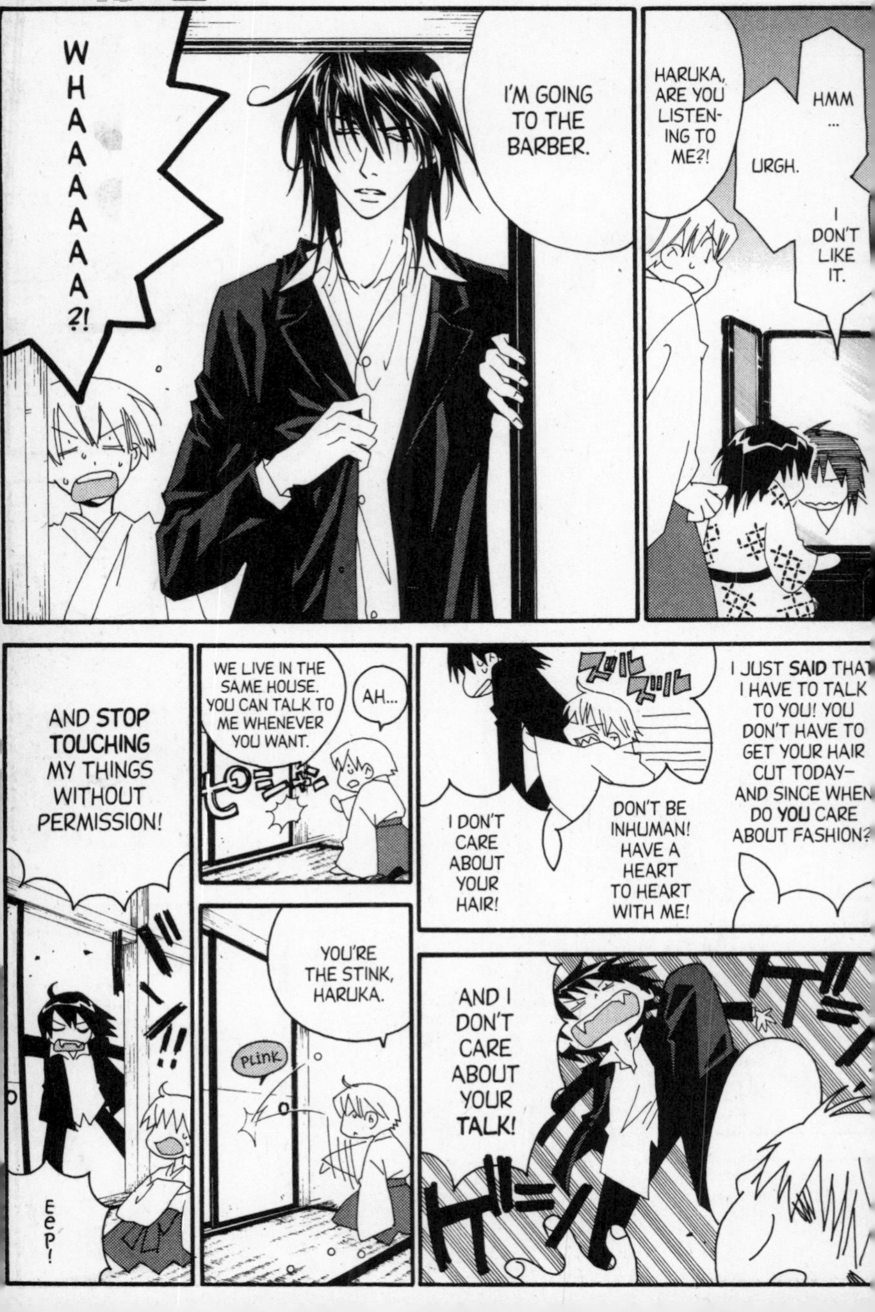
HMM ...
HARUKA, ARE YOU LISTEN-ING TO ME?!
URGH.
I DON'T LIKE IT.
I'M GOING TO THE BARBER.
WHAAAAAAAA?!
I JUST SAID THAT I HAVE TO TALK TO YOU! YOU DON'T HAVE TO GET YOUR HAIR CUT TODAY— AND SINCE WHEN DO YOU CARE ABOUT FASHION?
DON'T BE INHUMAN! HAVE A HEART TO HEART WITH ME!
I DON'T CARE ABOUT YOUR HAIR!
AND I DON'T CARE ABOUT YOUR TALK!
WE LIVE IN THE SAME HOUSE. YOU CAN TALK TO ME WHENEVER YOU WANT.
AH...
YOU'RE THE STINK, HARUKA.
PLINK
AND STOP TOUCHING MY THINGS WITHOUT PERMISSION!
EEP!

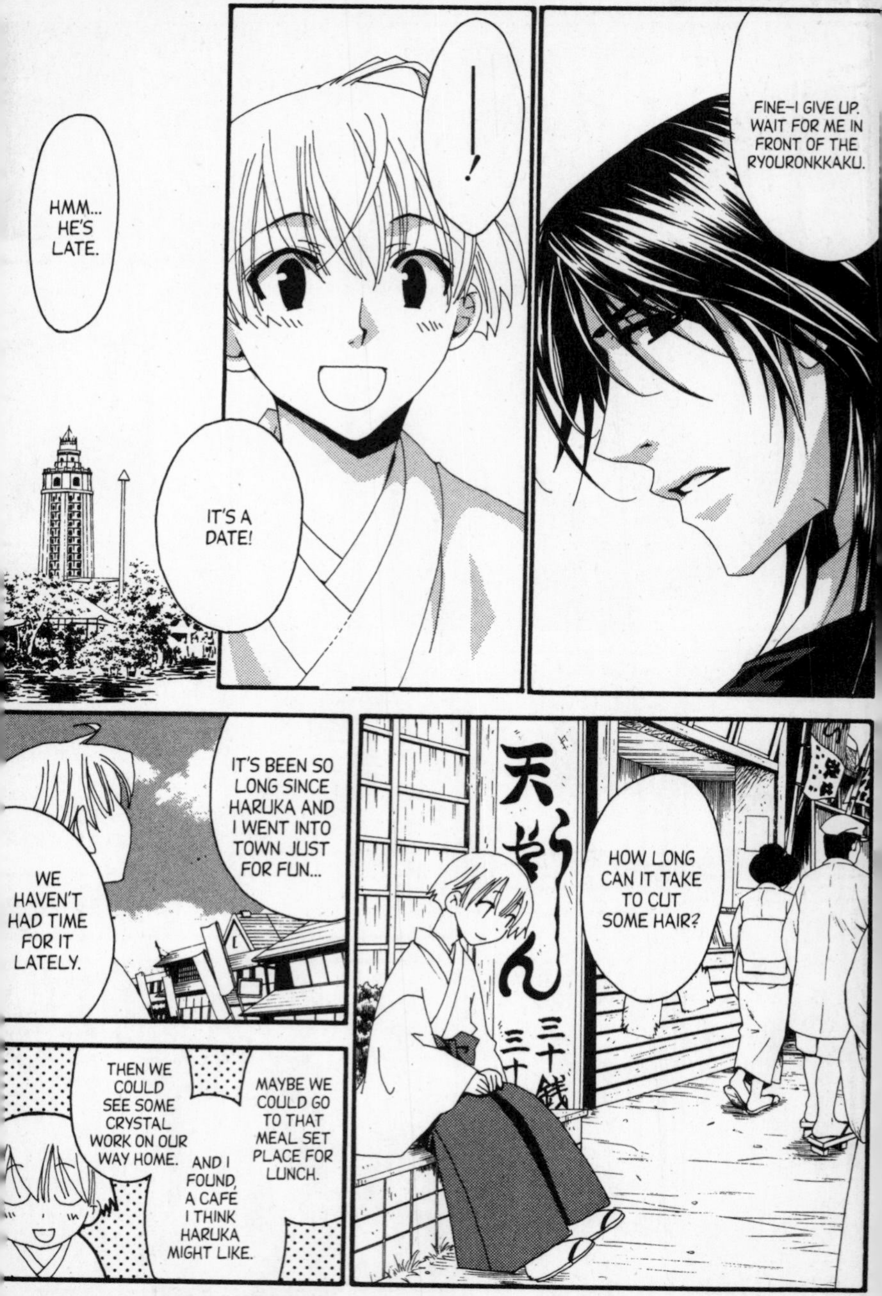
FINE—I GIVE UP. WAIT FOR ME IN FRONT OF THE RYOURONKKAKU.
—!
IT'S A DATE!
HMM... HE'S LATE.
HOW LONG CAN IT TAKE TO CUT SOME HAIR?
三十銭
IT'S BEEN SO LONG SINCE HARUKA AND I WENT INTO TOWN JUST FOR FUN...
WE HAVEN'T HAD TIME FOR IT LATELY.
MAYBE WE COULD GO TO THAT MEAL SET PLACE FOR LUNCH.
AND I FOUND, A CAFE I THINK HARUKA MIGHT LIKE.
THEN WE COULD SEE SOME CRYSTAL WORK ON OUR WAY HOME.

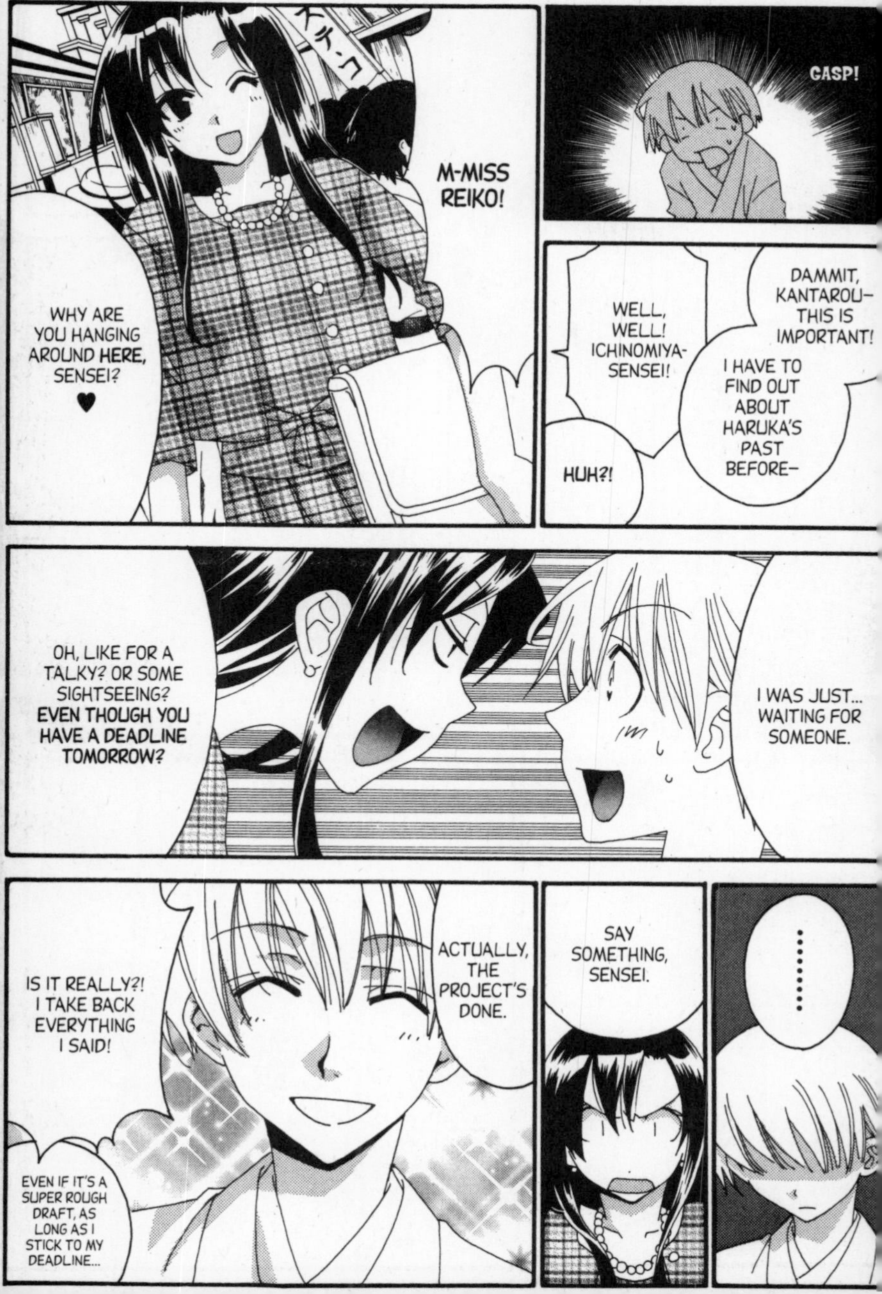
GASP!
DAMMIT, KANTAROU— THIS IS IMPORTANT!
I HAVE TO FIND OUT ABOUT HARUKA'S PAST BEFORE—
WELL, WELL! ICHINOMIYA-SENSEI!
HUH?!
M-MISS REIKO!
WHY ARE YOU HANGING AROUND HERE, SENSEI? ♥
I WAS JUST... WAITING FOR SOMEONE.
OH, LIKE FOR A TALKY? OR SOME SIGHTSEEING? EVEN THOUGH YOU HAVE A DEADLINE TOMORROW?
……
SAY SOMETHING, SENSEI.
ACTUALLY, THE PROJECT'S DONE.
IS IT REALLY?! I TAKE BACK EVERYTHING I SAID!
EVEN IF IT'S A SUPER ROUGH DRAFT, AS LONG AS I STICK TO MY DEADLINE...

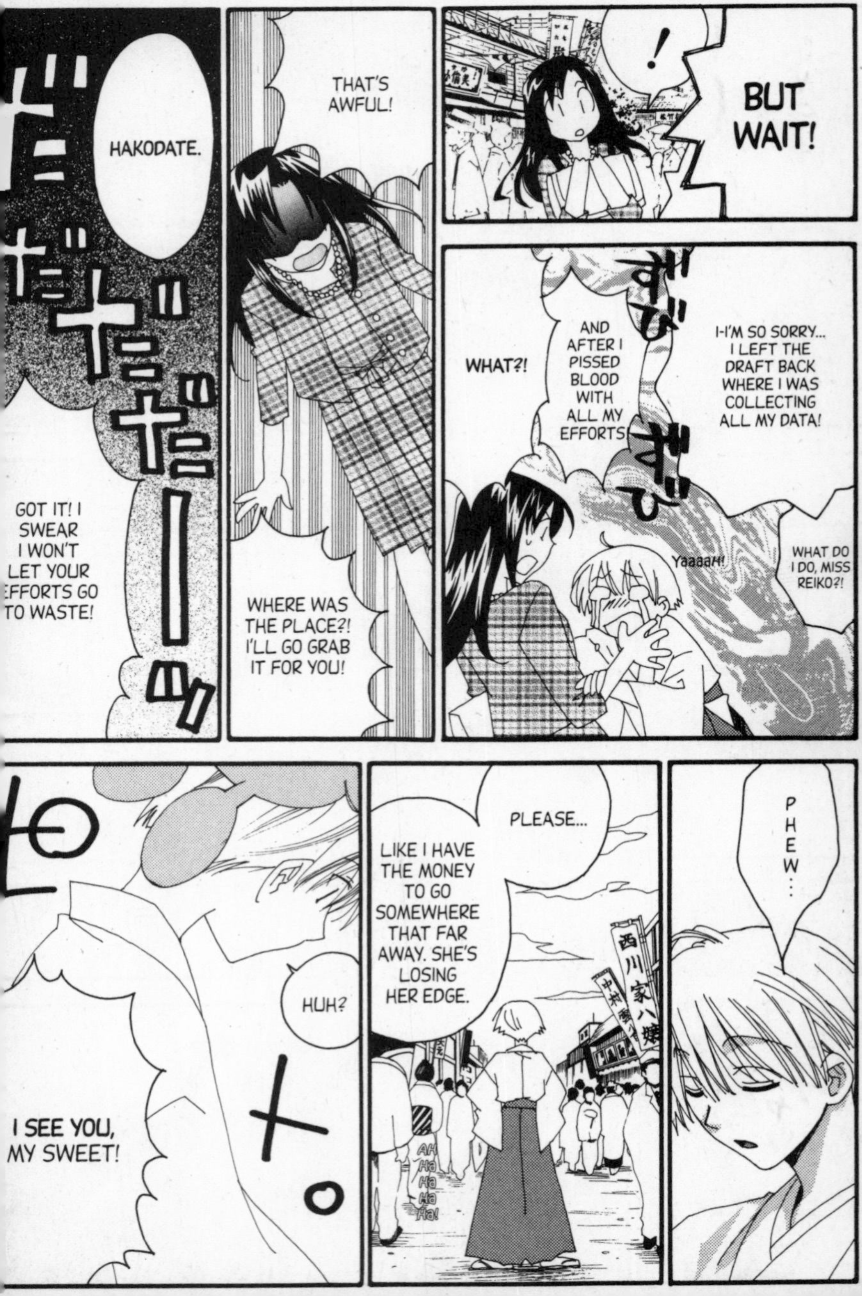
!
BUT WAIT!
I-I'M SO SORRY... I LEFT THE DRAFT BACK WHERE I WAS COLLECTING ALL MY DATA!
AND AFTER I PISSED BLOOD WITH ALL MY EFFORTS
WHAT?!
WHAT DO I DO, MISS REIKO?!
YaaaaH!
THAT'S AWFUL!
WHERE WAS THE PLACE?! I'LL GO GRAB IT FOR YOU!
HAKODATE.
GOT IT! I SWEAR I WON'T LET YOUR EFFORTS GO TO WASTE!
PHEW...
PLEASE...
LIKE I HAVE THE MONEY TO GO SOMEWHERE THAT FAR AWAY. SHE'S LOSING HER EDGE.
HUH?
AH HA HA HA HA!
I SEE YOU, MY SWEET!

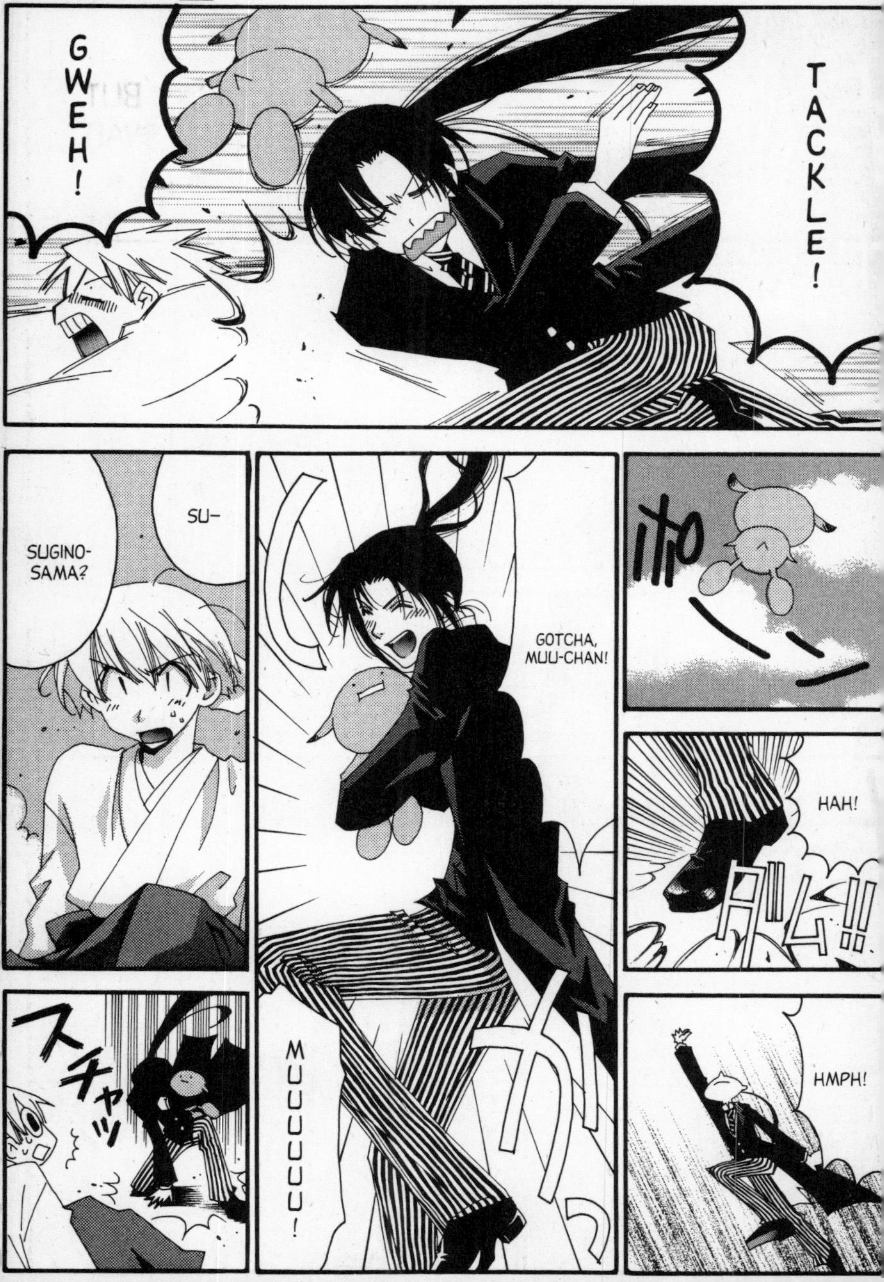
TACKLE!
GWEH!
HAH!
HMPH!
GOTCHA, MUU-CHAN!
MUUUUUUU!
SU-
SUGINO-SAMA?
スチャッ

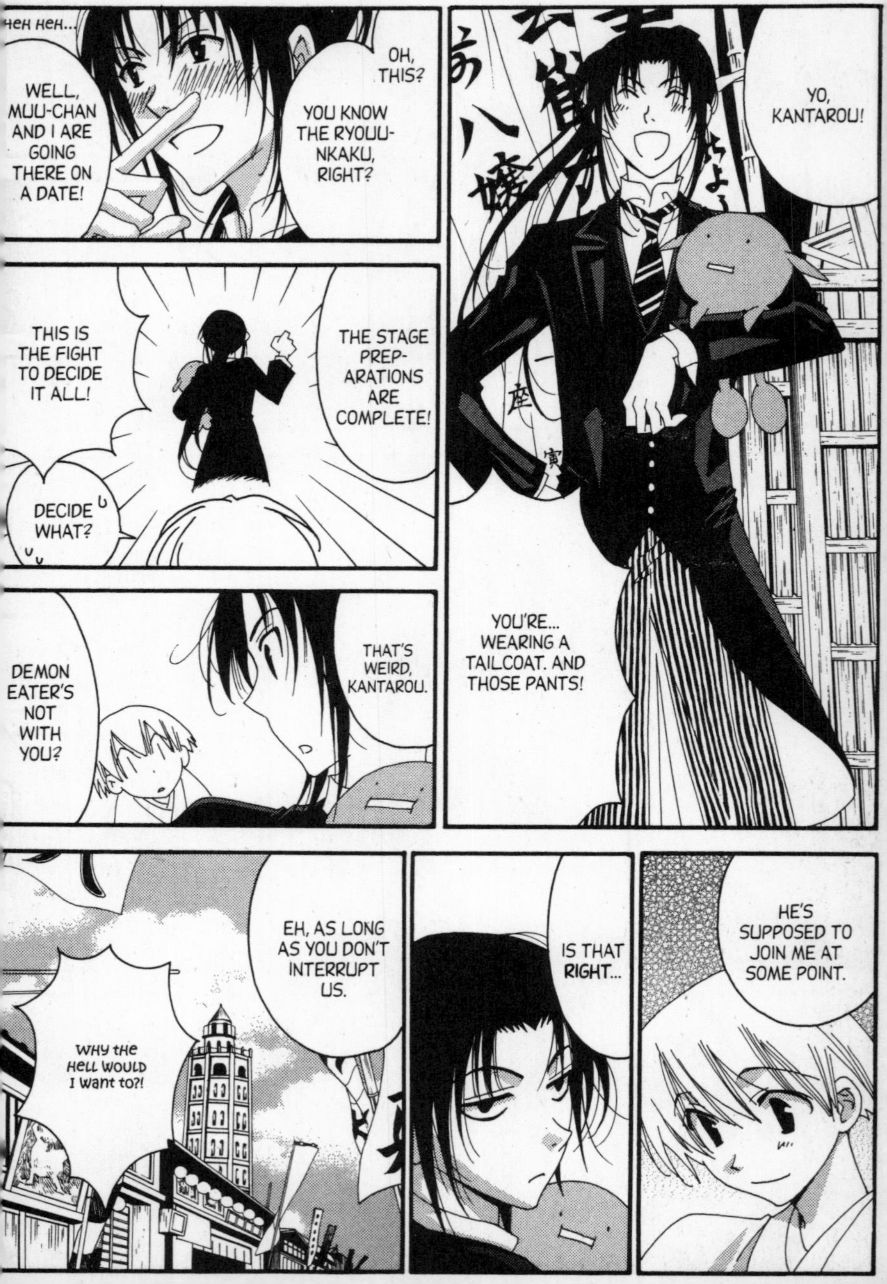
YO, KANTAROU!
YOU'RE... WEARING A TAILCOAT. AND THOSE PANTS!
OH, THIS?
YOU KNOW THE RYOUU-NKAKU, RIGHT?
HEH HEH...
WELL, MUU-CHAN AND I ARE GOING THERE ON A DATE!
THE STAGE PREP-ARATIONS ARE COMPLETE!
THIS IS THE FIGHT TO DECIDE IT ALL!
DECIDE WHAT?
THAT'S WEIRD, KANTAROU.
DEMON EATER'S NOT WITH YOU?
HE'S SUPPOSED TO JOIN ME AT SOME POINT.
IS THAT RIGHT...
EH, AS LONG AS YOU DON'T INTERRUPT US.
WHY THE HELL WOULD I WANT TO?!

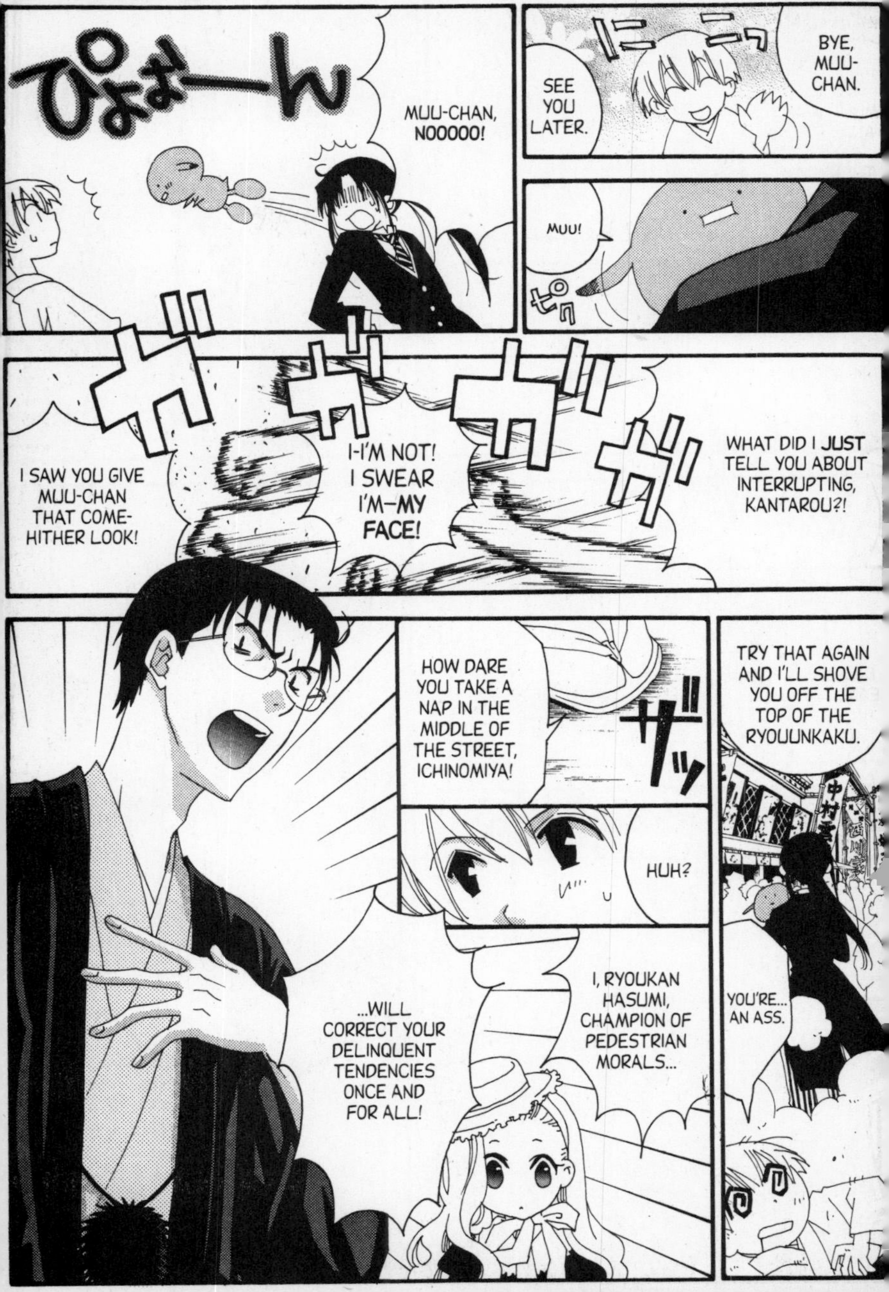
BYE, MUU-CHAN.
SEE YOU LATER.
MUU!
MUU-CHAN, NOOOOO!
WHAT DID I JUST TELL YOU ABOUT INTERRUPTING, KANTAROU?!
I-I'M NOT! I SWEAR I'M—MY FACE!
I SAW YOU GIVE MUU-CHAN THAT COME-HITHER LOOK!
TRY THAT AGAIN AND I'LL SHOVE YOU OFF THE TOP OF THE RYOUUNKAKU.
YOU'RE... AN ASS.
HOW DARE YOU TAKE A NAP IN THE MIDDLE OF THE STREET, ICHINOMIYA!
HUH?
I, RYOUKAN HASUMI, CHAMPION OF PEDESTRIAN MORALS...
...WILL CORRECT YOUR DELINQUENT TENDENCIES ONCE AND FOR ALL!

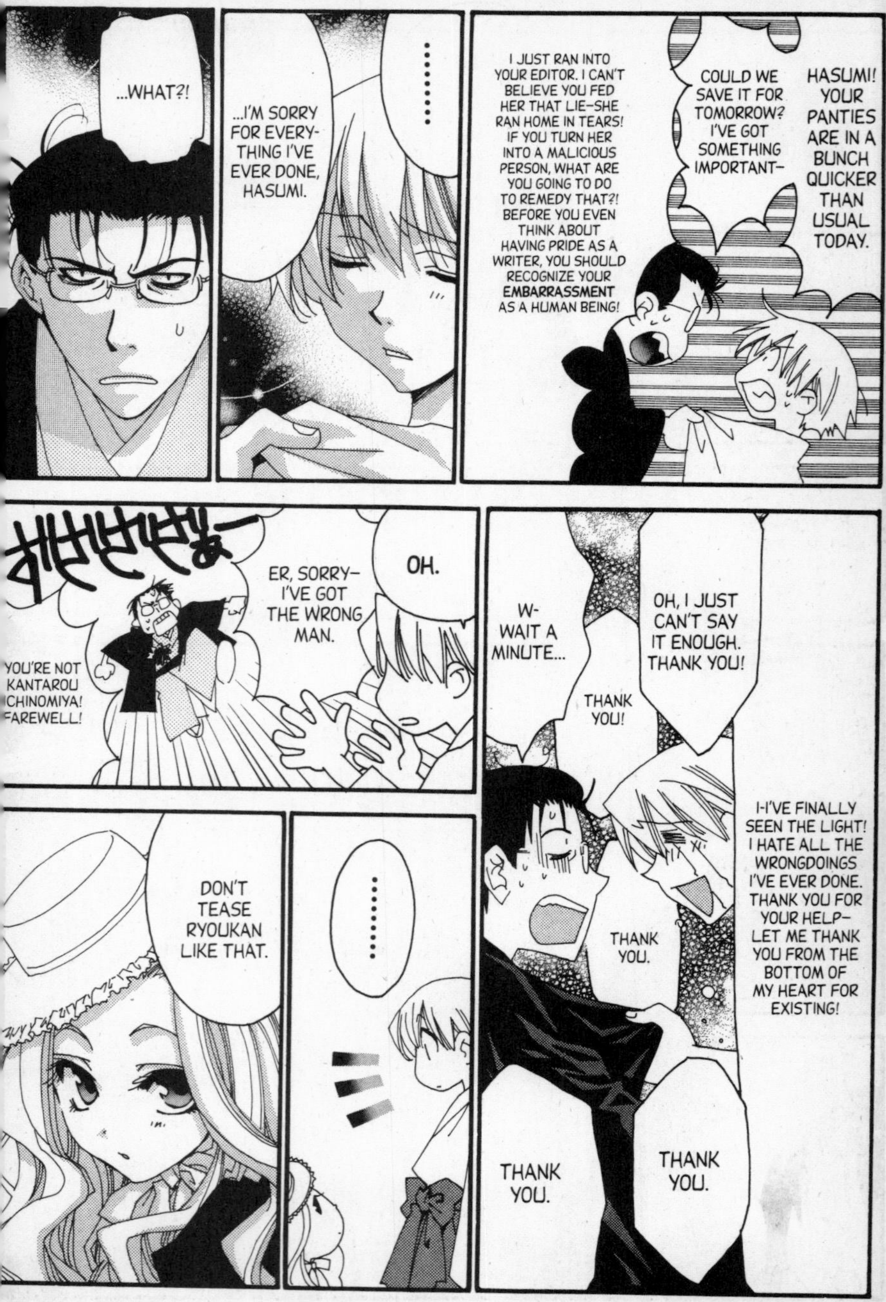
HASUMI! YOUR PANTIES ARE IN A BUNCH QUICKER THAN USUAL TODAY.
COULD WE SAVE IT FOR TOMORROW? I'VE GOT SOMETHING IMPORTANT–
I JUST RAN INTO YOUR EDITOR. I CAN'T BELIEVE YOU FED HER THAT LIE–SHE RAN HOME IN TEARS! IF YOU TURN HER INTO A MALICIOUS PERSON, WHAT ARE YOU GOING TO DO TO REMEDY THAT?! BEFORE YOU EVEN THINK ABOUT HAVING PRIDE AS A WRITER, YOU SHOULD RECOGNIZE YOUR **EMBARRASSMENT** AS A HUMAN BEING!
....
...I'M SORRY FOR EVERY-THING I'VE EVER DONE, HASUMI.
...WHAT?!
OH, I JUST CAN'T SAY IT ENOUGH. THANK YOU!
W-WAIT A MINUTE...
THANK YOU!
I-I'VE FINALLY SEEN THE LIGHT! I HATE ALL THE WRONGDOINGS I'VE EVER DONE. THANK YOU FOR YOUR HELP– LET ME THANK YOU FROM THE BOTTOM OF MY HEART FOR EXISTING!
THANK YOU.
THANK YOU.
THANK YOU.
OH.
ER, SORRY– I'VE GOT THE WRONG MAN.
YOU'RE NOT KANTAROU ICHINOMIYA! FAREWELL!
....
DON'T TEASE RYOUKAN LIKE THAT.

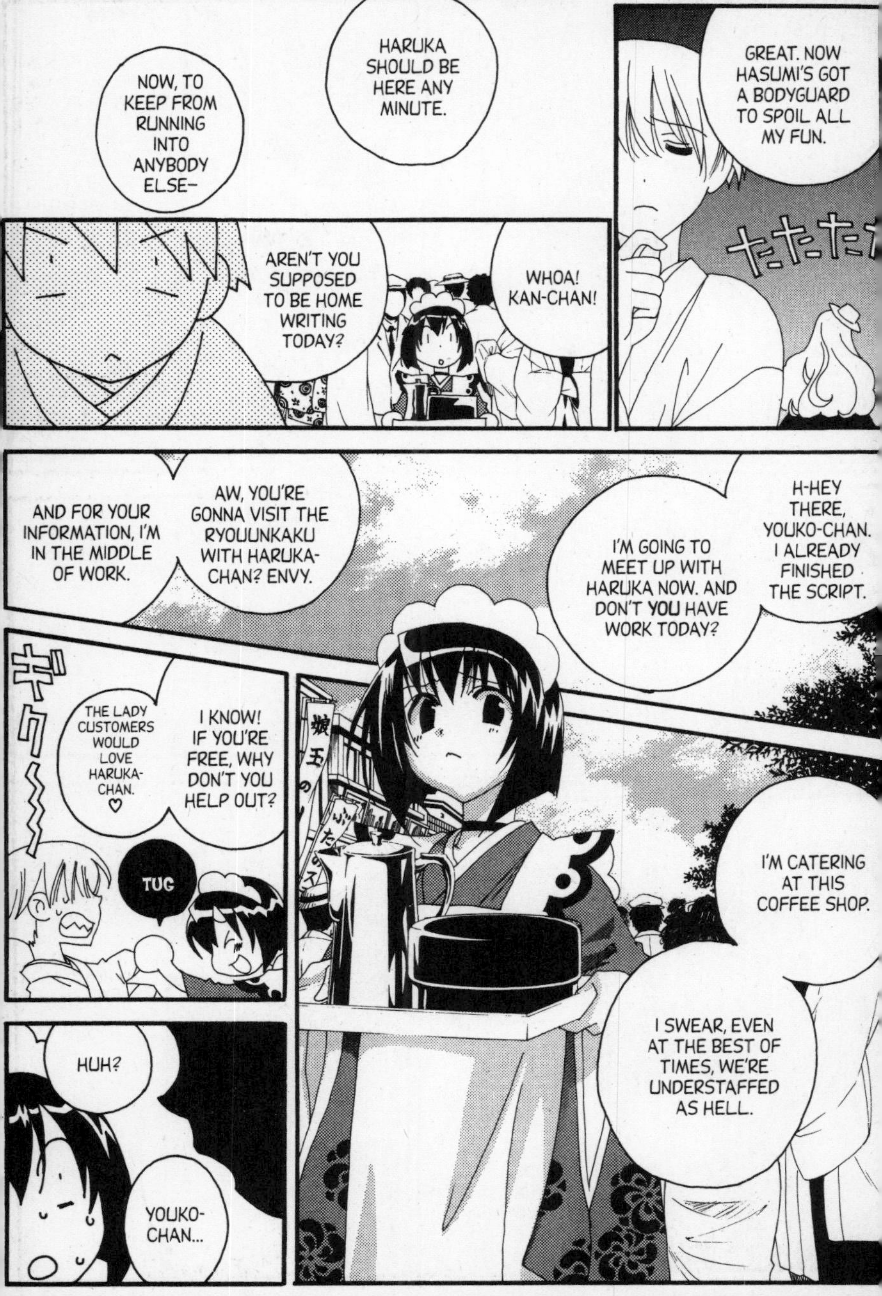
GREAT. NOW HASUMI'S GOT A BODYGUARD TO SPOIL ALL MY FUN.
HARUKA SHOULD BE HERE ANY MINUTE.
NOW, TO KEEP FROM RUNNING INTO ANYBODY ELSE–
WHOA! KAN-CHAN!
AREN'T YOU SUPPOSED TO BE HOME WRITING TODAY?
H-HEY THERE, YOUKO-CHAN. I ALREADY FINISHED THE SCRIPT.
I'M GOING TO MEET UP WITH HARUKA NOW. AND DON'T YOU HAVE WORK TODAY?
AW, YOU'RE GONNA VISIT THE RYOUUNKAKU WITH HARUKA-CHAN? ENVY.
AND FOR YOUR INFORMATION, I'M IN THE MIDDLE OF WORK.
I'M CATERING AT THIS COFFEE SHOP.
I SWEAR, EVEN AT THE BEST OF TIMES, WE'RE UNDERSTAFFED AS HELL.
I KNOW! IF YOU'RE FREE, WHY DON'T YOU HELP OUT?
THE LADY CUSTOMERS WOULD LOVE HARUKA-CHAN. ♡
TUG
HUH?
YOUKO-CHAN...

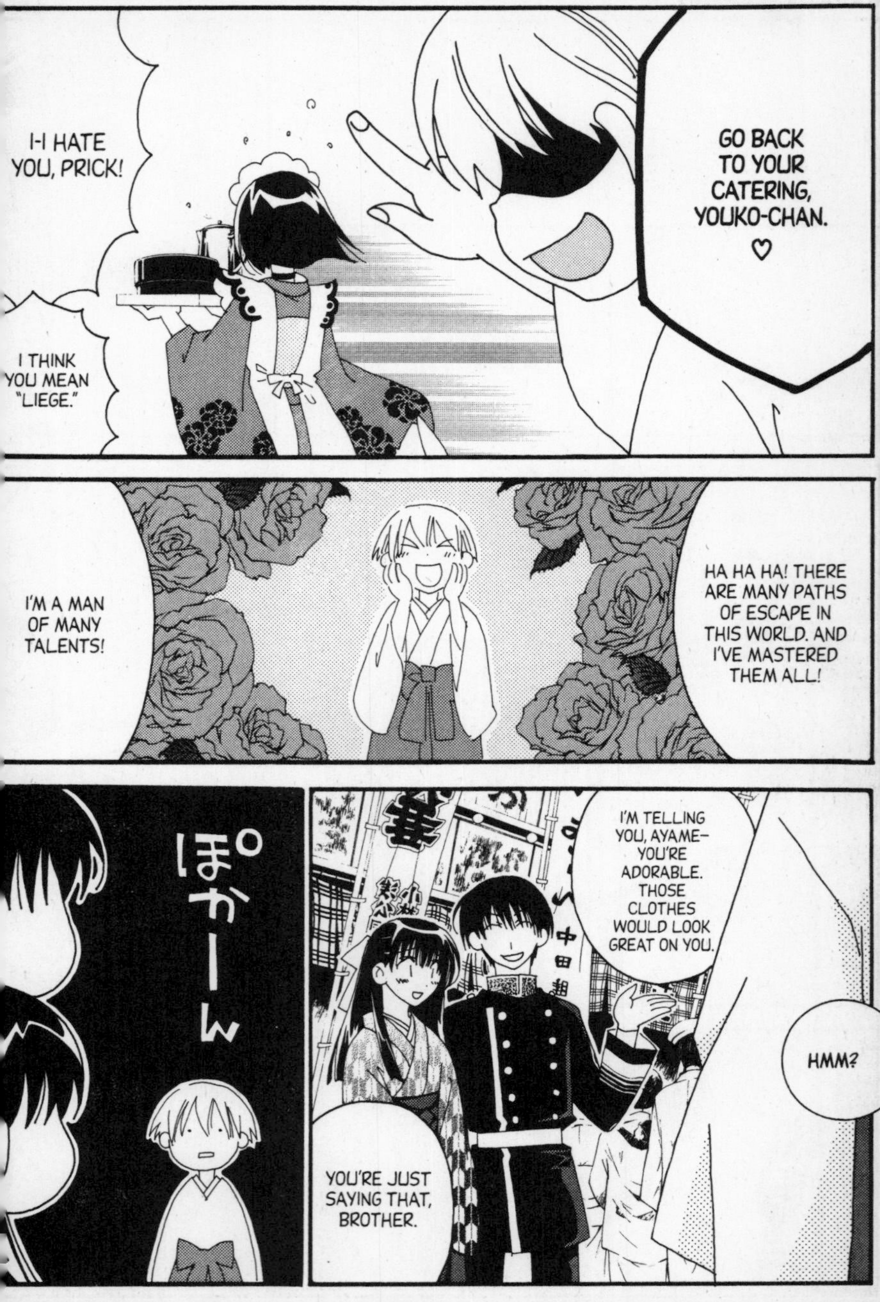
GO BACK TO YOUR CATERING, YOUKO-CHAN. ♡
I-I HATE YOU, PRICK!
I THINK YOU MEAN "LIEGE."
HA HA HA! THERE ARE MANY PATHS OF ESCAPE IN THIS WORLD. AND I'VE MASTERED THEM ALL!
I'M A MAN OF MANY TALENTS!
I'M TELLING YOU, AYAME— YOU'RE ADORABLE. THOSE CLOTHES WOULD LOOK GREAT ON YOU.
YOU'RE JUST SAYING THAT, BROTHER.
HMM?
ぽかーん

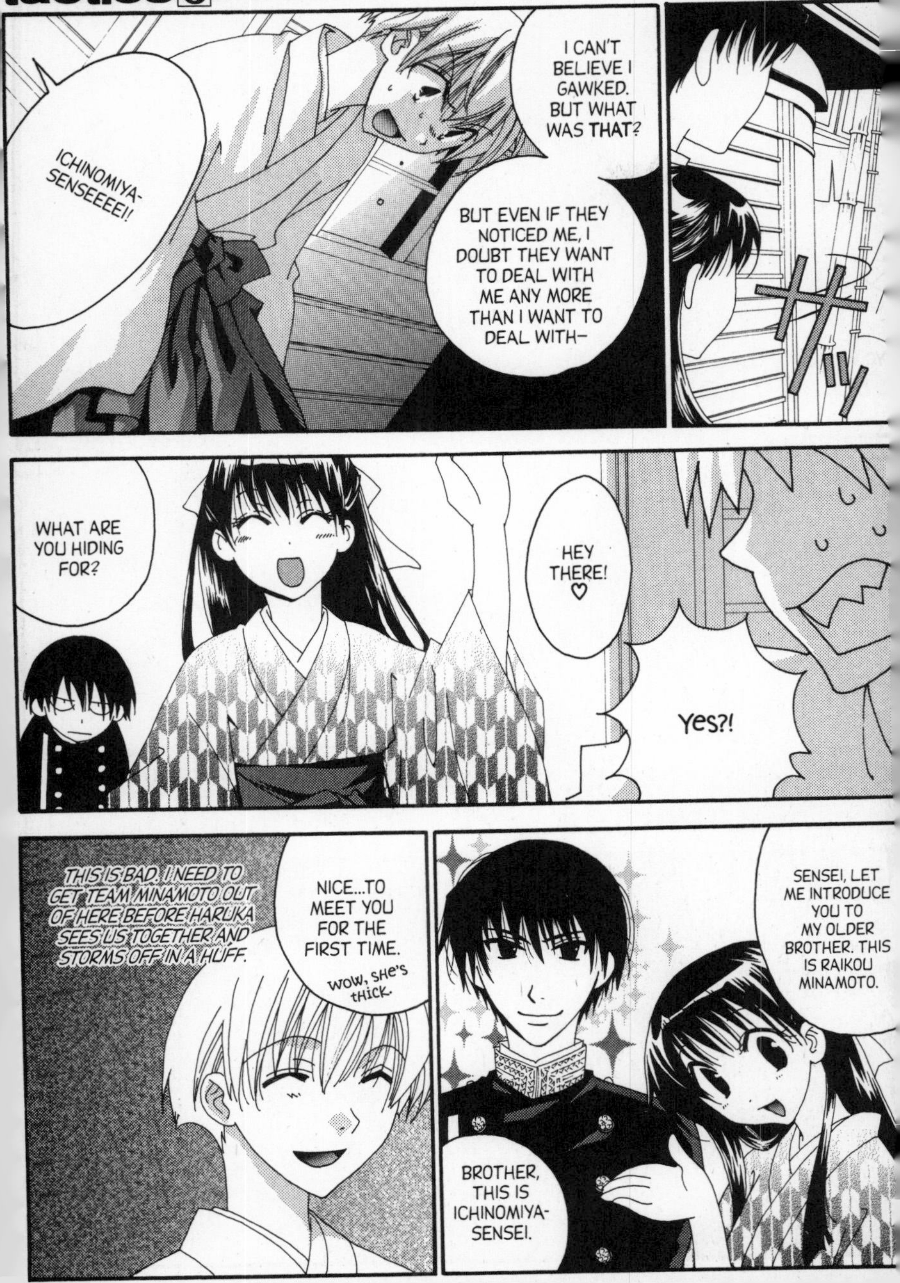
I CAN'T BELIEVE I GAWKED. BUT WHAT WAS THAT?
BUT EVEN IF THEY NOTICED ME, I DOUBT THEY WANT TO DEAL WITH ME ANY MORE THAN I WANT TO DEAL WITH—
ICHINOMIYA-SENSEEEEI!
Yes?!
HEY THERE! ♡
WHAT ARE YOU HIDING FOR?
SENSEI, LET ME INTRODUCE YOU TO MY OLDER BROTHER. THIS IS RAIKOU MINAMOTO.
BROTHER, THIS IS ICHINOMIYA-SENSEI.
NICE...TO MEET YOU FOR THE FIRST TIME.
Wow, she's thick.
THIS IS BAD. I NEED TO GET TEAM MINAMOTO OUT OF HERE BEFORE HARUKA SEES US TOGETHER AND STORMS OFF IN A HUFF.

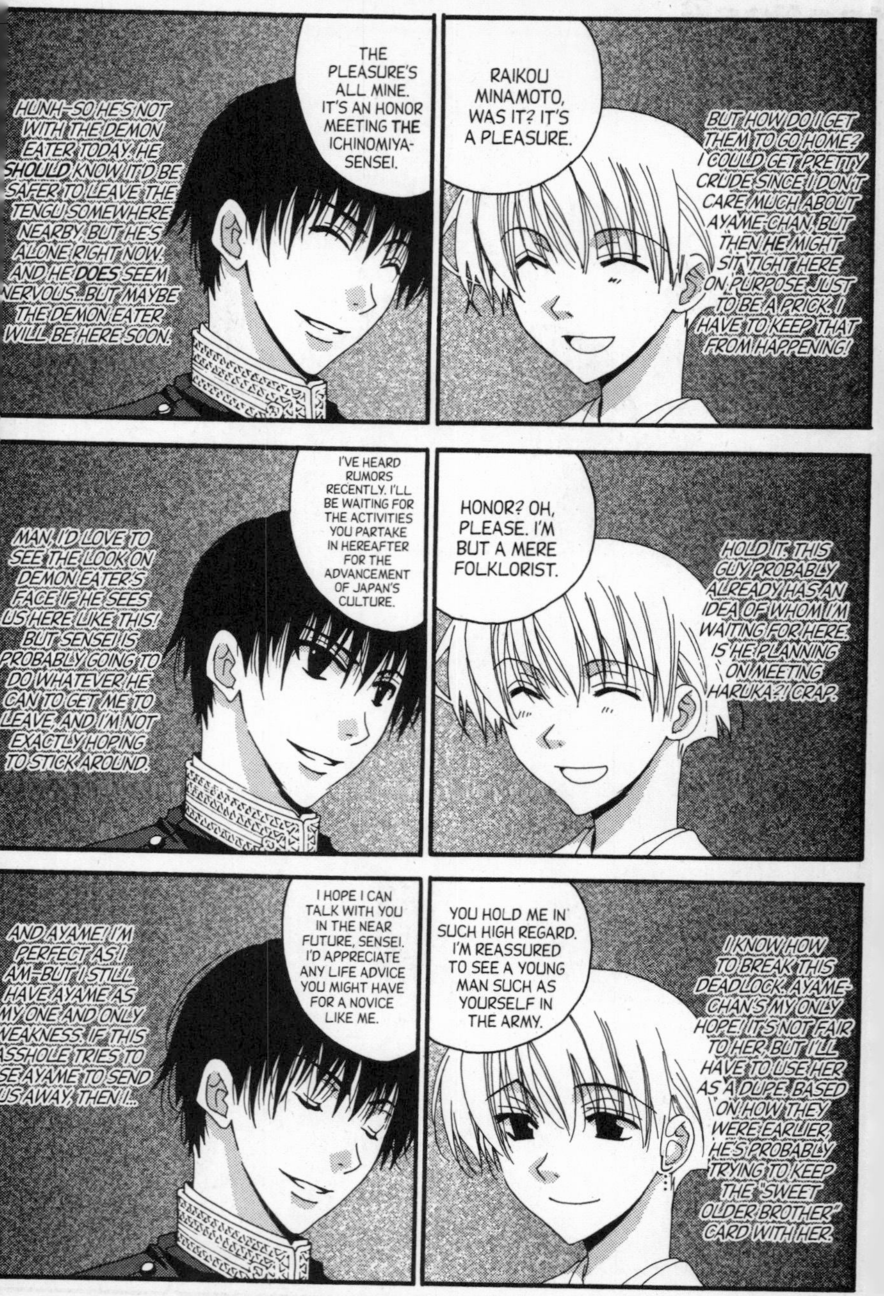
RAIKOU MINAMOTO, WAS IT? IT'S A PLEASURE.
BUT HOW DO I GET THEM TO GO HOME? I COULD GET PRETTY CRUDE SINCE I DON'T CARE MUCH ABOUT AYAME-CHAN, BUT THEN HE MIGHT SIT TIGHT HERE ON PURPOSE JUST TO BE A PRICK. I HAVE TO KEEP THAT FROM HAPPENING!
THE PLEASURE'S ALL MINE. IT'S AN HONOR MEETING THE ICHINOMIYA-SENSEI.
HUNH—SO HE'S NOT WITH THE DEMON EATER TODAY. HE SHOULD KNOW IT'D BE SAFER TO LEAVE THE TENGU SOMEWHERE NEARBY, BUT HE'S ALONE RIGHT NOW. AND HE DOES SEEM NERVOUS... BUT MAYBE THE DEMON EATER WILL BE HERE SOON.
HONOR? OH, PLEASE. I'M BUT A MERE FOLKLORIST.
HOLD IT. THIS GUY PROBABLY ALREADY HAS AN IDEA OF WHOM I'M WAITING FOR HERE. IS HE PLANNING ON MEETING HARUKA?! CRAP.
I'VE HEARD RUMORS RECENTLY. I'LL BE WAITING FOR THE ACTIVITIES YOU PARTAKE IN HEREAFTER FOR THE ADVANCEMENT OF JAPAN'S CULTURE.
MAN, I'D LOVE TO SEE THE LOOK ON DEMON EATER'S FACE IF HE SEES US HERE LIKE THIS! BUT SENSEI IS PROBABLY GOING TO DO WHATEVER HE CAN TO GET ME TO LEAVE, AND I'M NOT EXACTLY HOPING TO STICK AROUND.
YOU HOLD ME IN SUCH HIGH REGARD. I'M REASSURED TO SEE A YOUNG MAN SUCH AS YOURSELF IN THE ARMY.
I KNOW HOW TO BREAK THIS DEADLOCK. AYAME-CHAN'S MY ONLY HOPE! IT'S NOT FAIR TO HER, BUT I'LL HAVE TO USE HER AS A DUPE. BASED ON HOW THEY WERE EARLIER, HE'S PROBABLY TRYING TO KEEP THE "SWEET OLDER BROTHER" CARD WITH HER.
I HOPE I CAN TALK WITH YOU IN THE NEAR FUTURE, SENSEI. I'D APPRECIATE ANY LIFE ADVICE YOU MIGHT HAVE FOR A NOVICE LIKE ME.
AND AYAME! I'M PERFECT AS I AM—BUT I STILL HAVE AYAME AS MY ONE AND ONLY WEAKNESS. IF THIS ASSHOLE TRIES TO USE AYAME TO SEND US AWAY, THEN I...

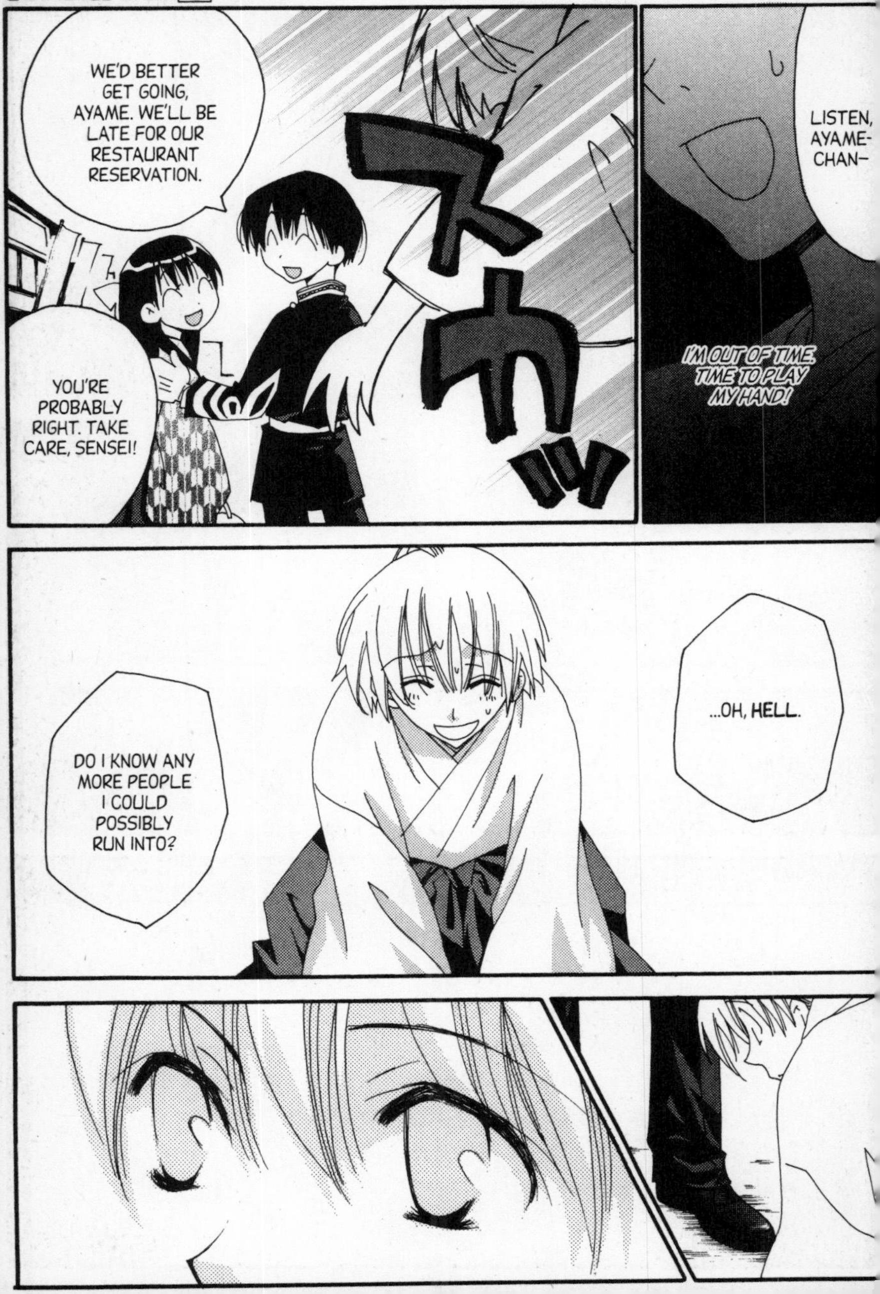
LISTEN, AYAME-CHAN—
I'M OUT OF TIME. TIME TO PLAY MY HAND!
WE'D BETTER GET GOING, AYAME. WE'LL BE LATE FOR OUR RESTAURANT RESERVATION.
YOU'RE PROBABLY RIGHT. TAKE CARE, SENSEI!
...OH, HELL.
DO I KNOW ANY MORE PEOPLE I COULD POSSIBLY RUN INTO?

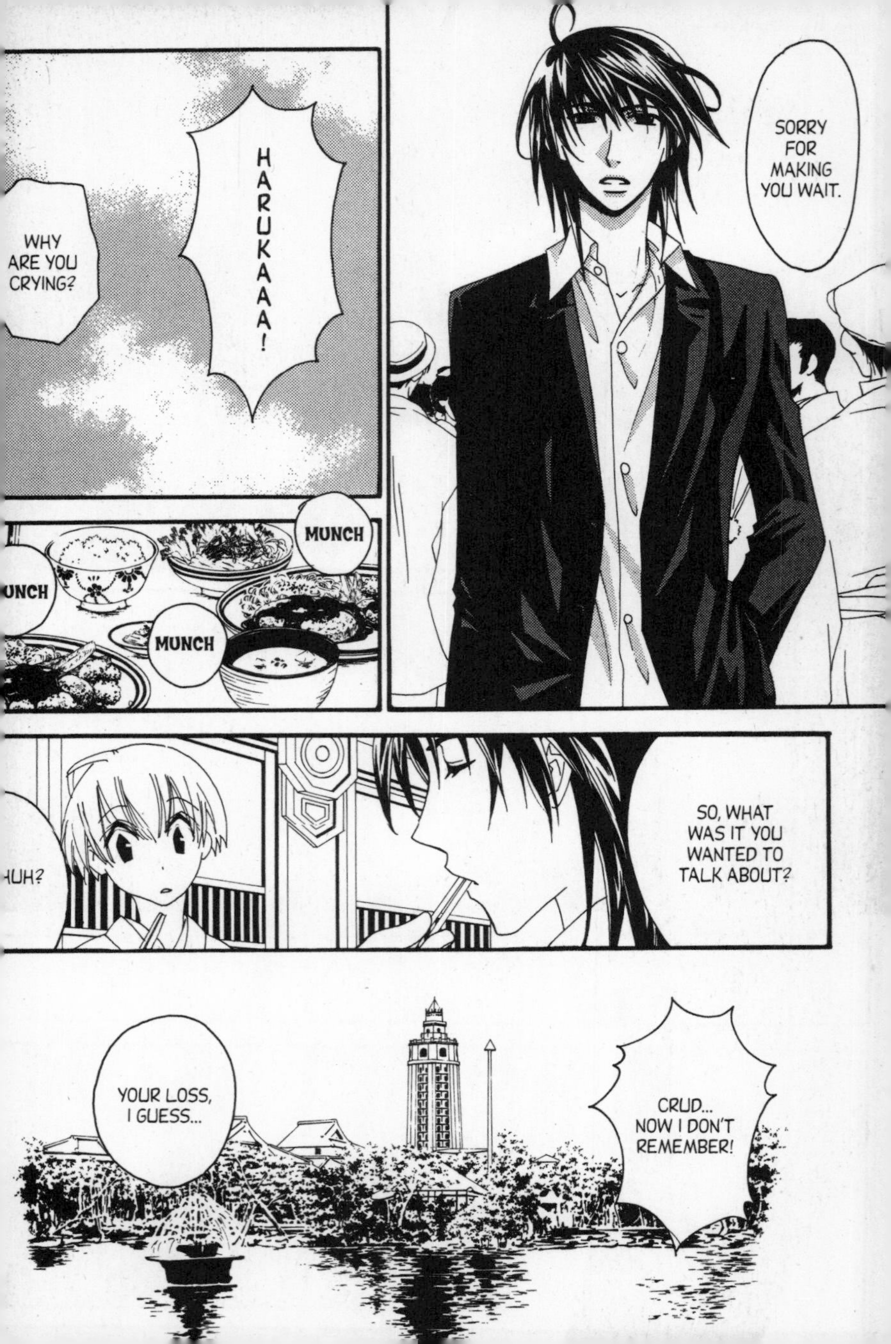
SORRY FOR MAKING YOU WAIT.
HARUKAAAA!
WHY ARE YOU CRYING?
MUNCH
UNCH
MUNCH
SO, WHAT WAS IT YOU WANTED TO TALK ABOUT?
HUH?
CRUD... NOW I DON'T REMEMBER!
YOUR LOSS, I GUESS...

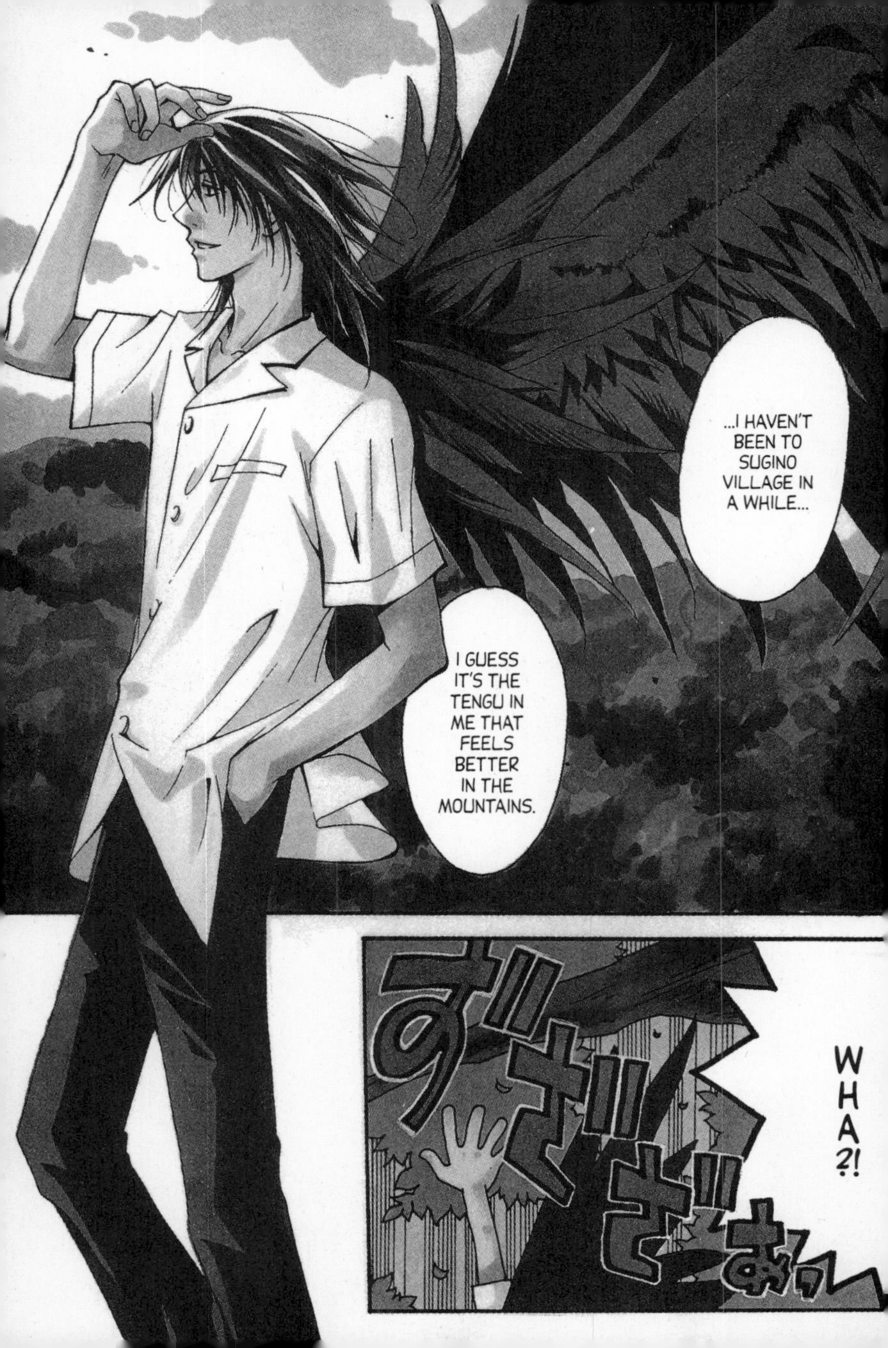
...I HAVEN'T BEEN TO SUGINO VILLAGE IN A WHILE...
I GUESS IT'S THE TENGU IN ME THAT FEELS BETTER IN THE MOUNTAINS.
WHA?!

SIDE STORY 3

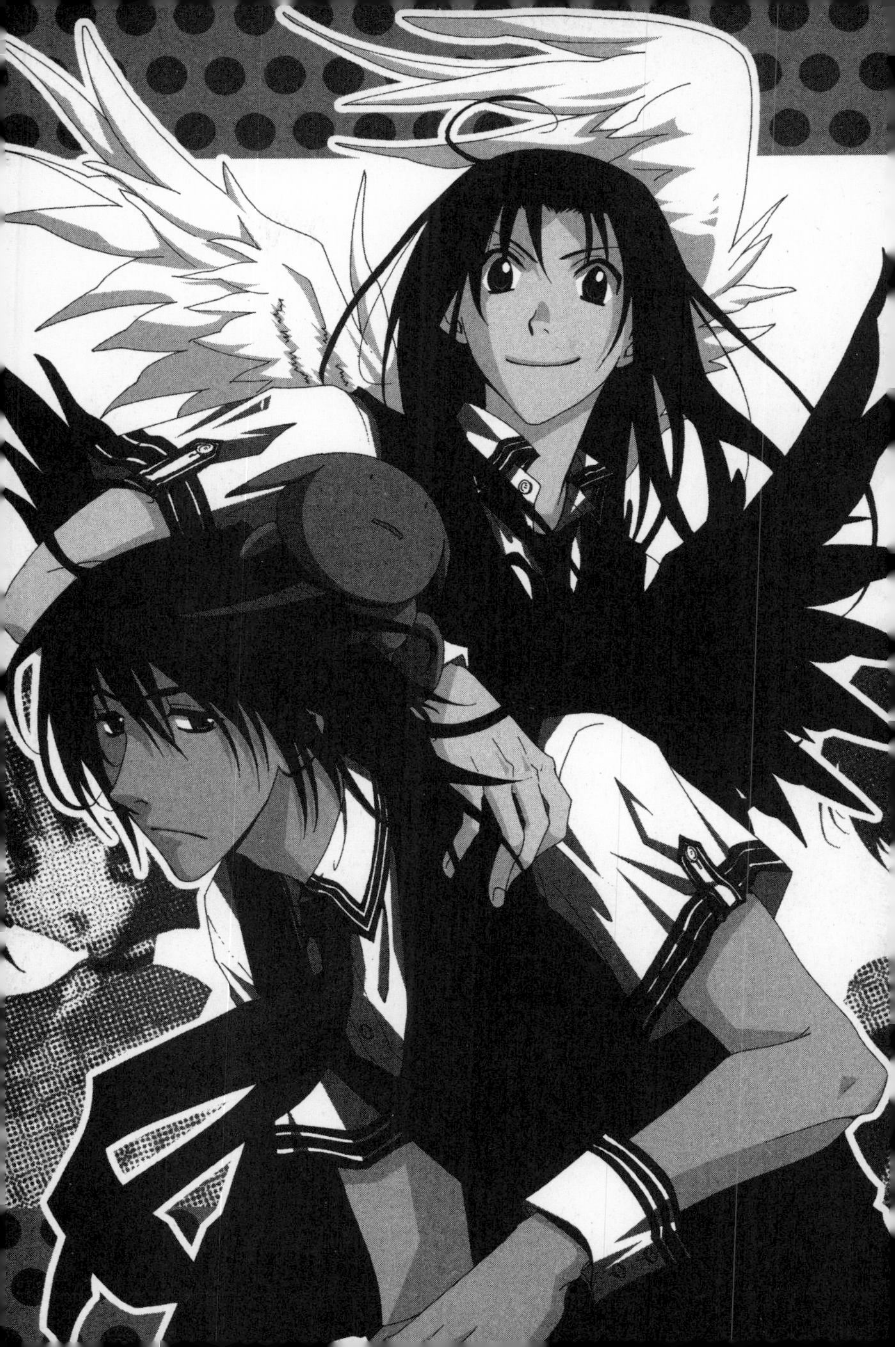

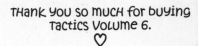

THANK YOU SO MUCH FOR BUYING
TACTICS VOLUME 6.
♡

I MUST SAY, THE MAIN STORY'S
TURNING OUT QUITE WELL.
HARUKA, HANG IN THERE!

WITH THE STORY HAVING GOTTEN SO
FAR, IT MAKES ME WANT TO WRITE
WHAT'S GOING TO HAPPEN NEXT RIGHT
AWAY! I WANT TO WRITE SO BAD, I
CAN'T TAKE IT ANYMORE! BUT MY
PHYSICAL STRENGTH CAN'T KEEP UP
WITH THAT DESIRE FOR PRODUCTIVITY!

YAAARGH!

THE DEMON-EATING TENGU
SHINOBUYO FUJI SOUSHI
ARC STILL HAS A WAYS TO GO.
THERE'S A LOT I WANT TO WRITE.
AND I'M GONNA DO MY BEST!

WELL, LET'S SEE EACH OTHER
AGAIN IN VOLUME 7!

2005.3
木下さくら
SAKURA KINOSHITA

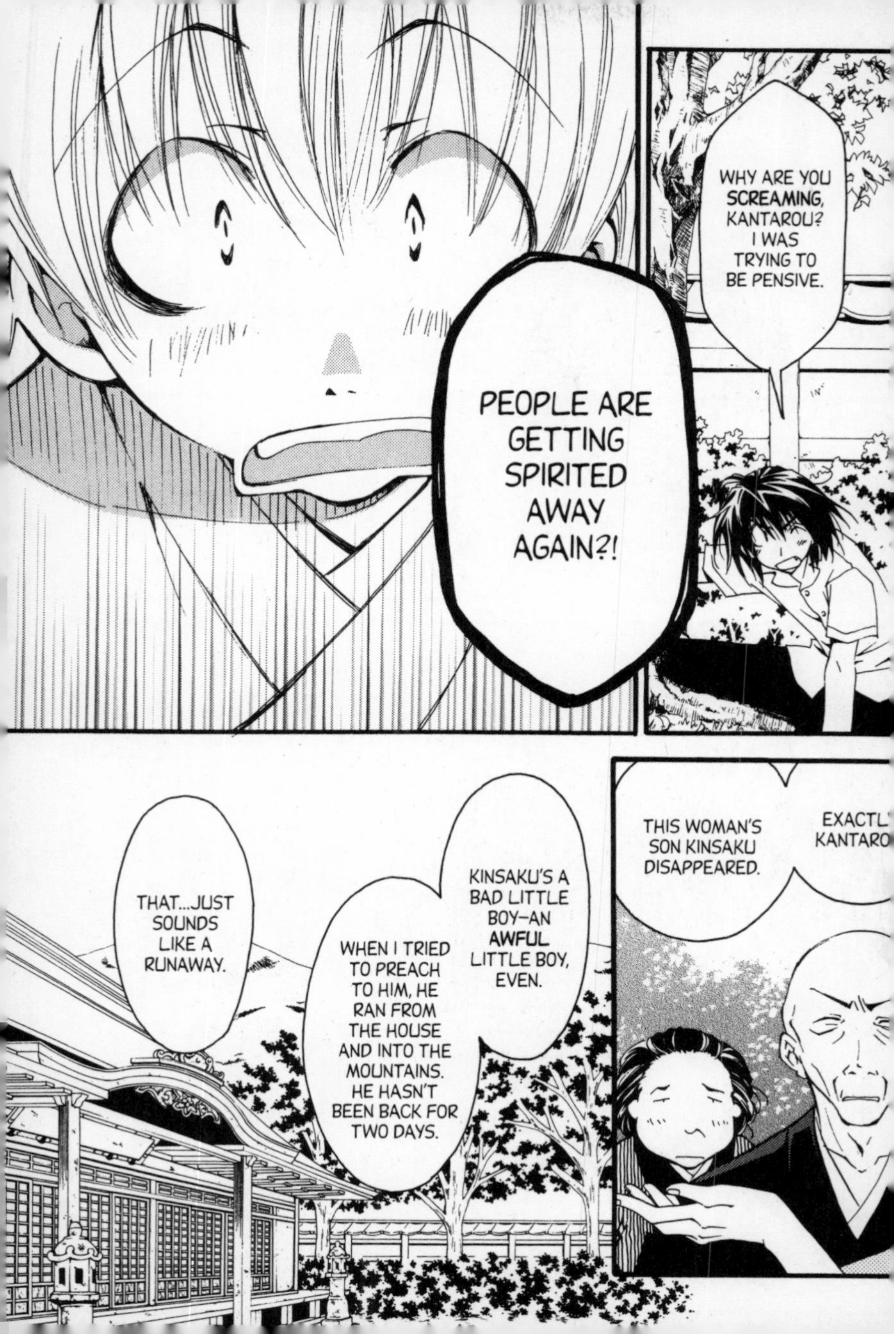
WHY ARE YOU SCREAMING, KANTAROU? I WAS TRYING TO BE PENSIVE.
PEOPLE ARE GETTING SPIRITED AWAY AGAIN?!
EXACTL KANTARO
THIS WOMAN'S SON KINSAKU DISAPPEARED.
KINSAKU'S A BAD LITTLE BOY—AN AWFUL LITTLE BOY, EVEN.
WHEN I TRIED TO PREACH TO HIM, HE RAN FROM THE HOUSE AND INTO THE MOUNTAINS. HE HASN'T BEEN BACK FOR TWO DAYS.
THAT...JUST SOUNDS LIKE A RUNAWAY.

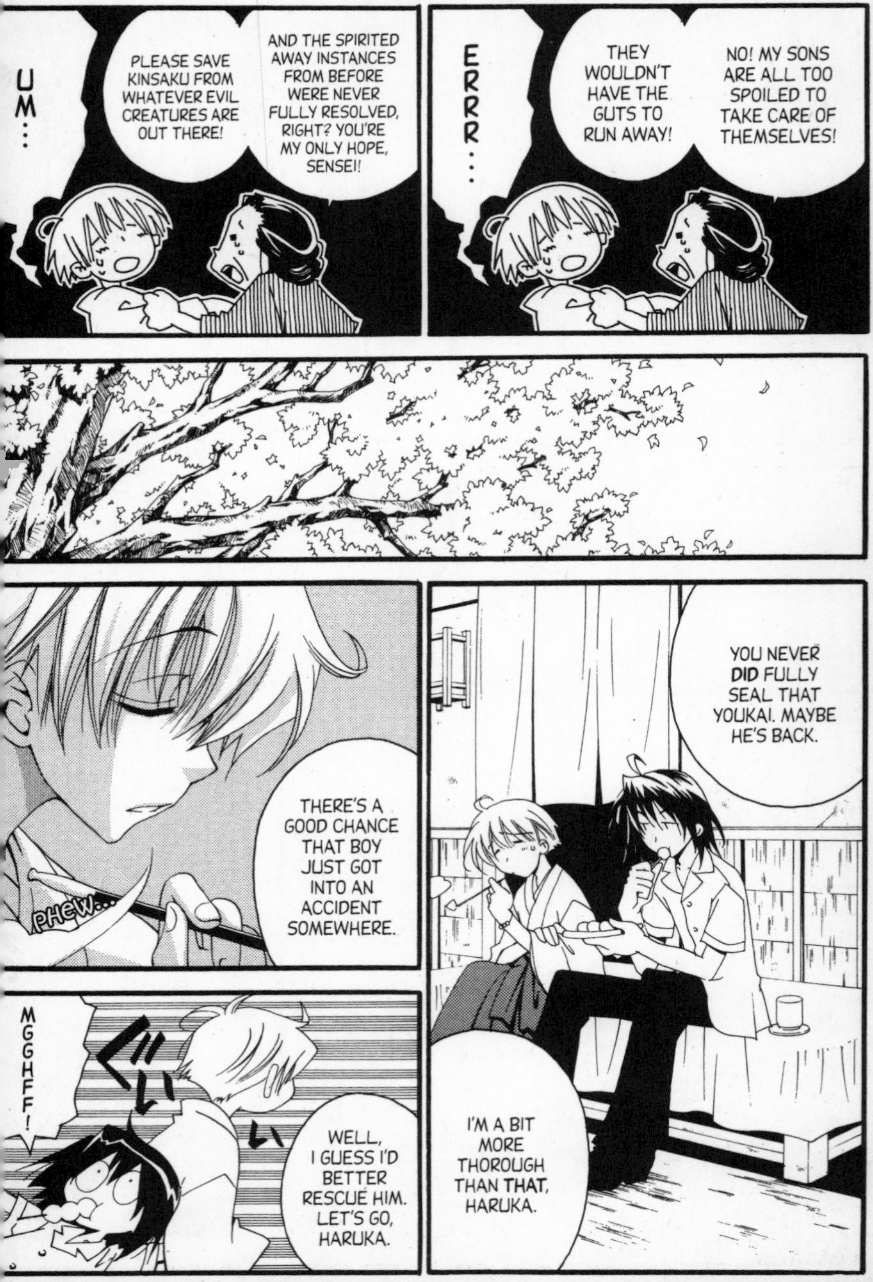
NO! MY SONS ARE ALL TOO SPOILED TO TAKE CARE OF THEMSELVES!
THEY WOULDN'T HAVE THE GUTS TO RUN AWAY!
ERRR...
AND THE SPIRITED AWAY INSTANCES FROM BEFORE WERE NEVER FULLY RESOLVED, RIGHT? YOU'RE MY ONLY HOPE, SENSEI!
PLEASE SAVE KINSAKU FROM WHATEVER EVIL CREATURES ARE OUT THERE!
UM...
YOU NEVER DID FULLY SEAL THAT YOUKAI. MAYBE HE'S BACK.
I'M A BIT MORE THOROUGH THAN THAT, HARUKA.
THERE'S A GOOD CHANCE THAT BOY JUST GOT INTO AN ACCIDENT SOMEWHERE.
PHEW...
WELL, I GUESS I'D BETTER RESCUE HIM. LET'S GO, HARUKA.
MGGHFF!

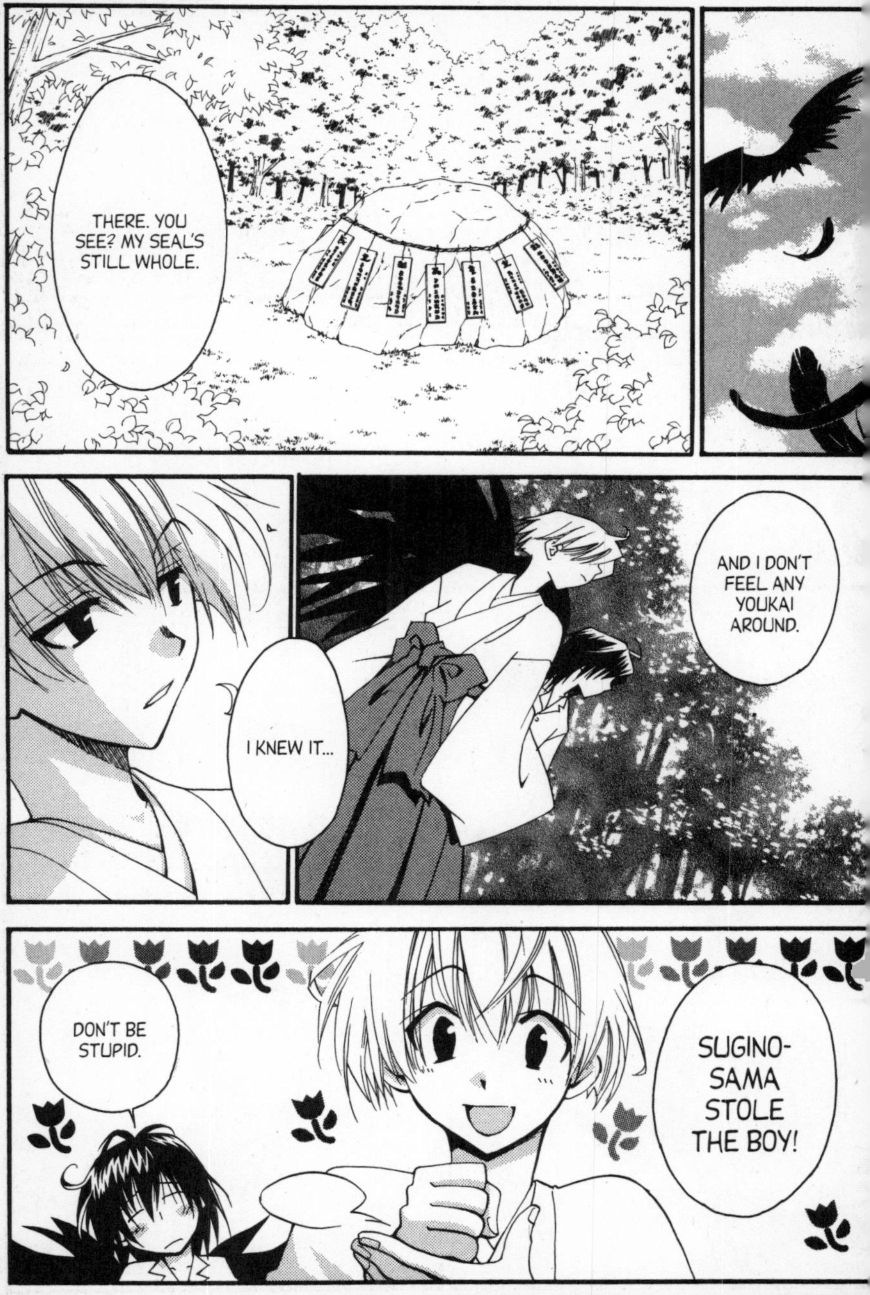
THERE. YOU SEE? MY SEAL'S STILL WHOLE.
AND I DON'T FEEL ANY YOUKAI AROUND.
I KNEW IT...
SUGINO-SAMA STOLE THE BOY!
DON'T BE STUPID.

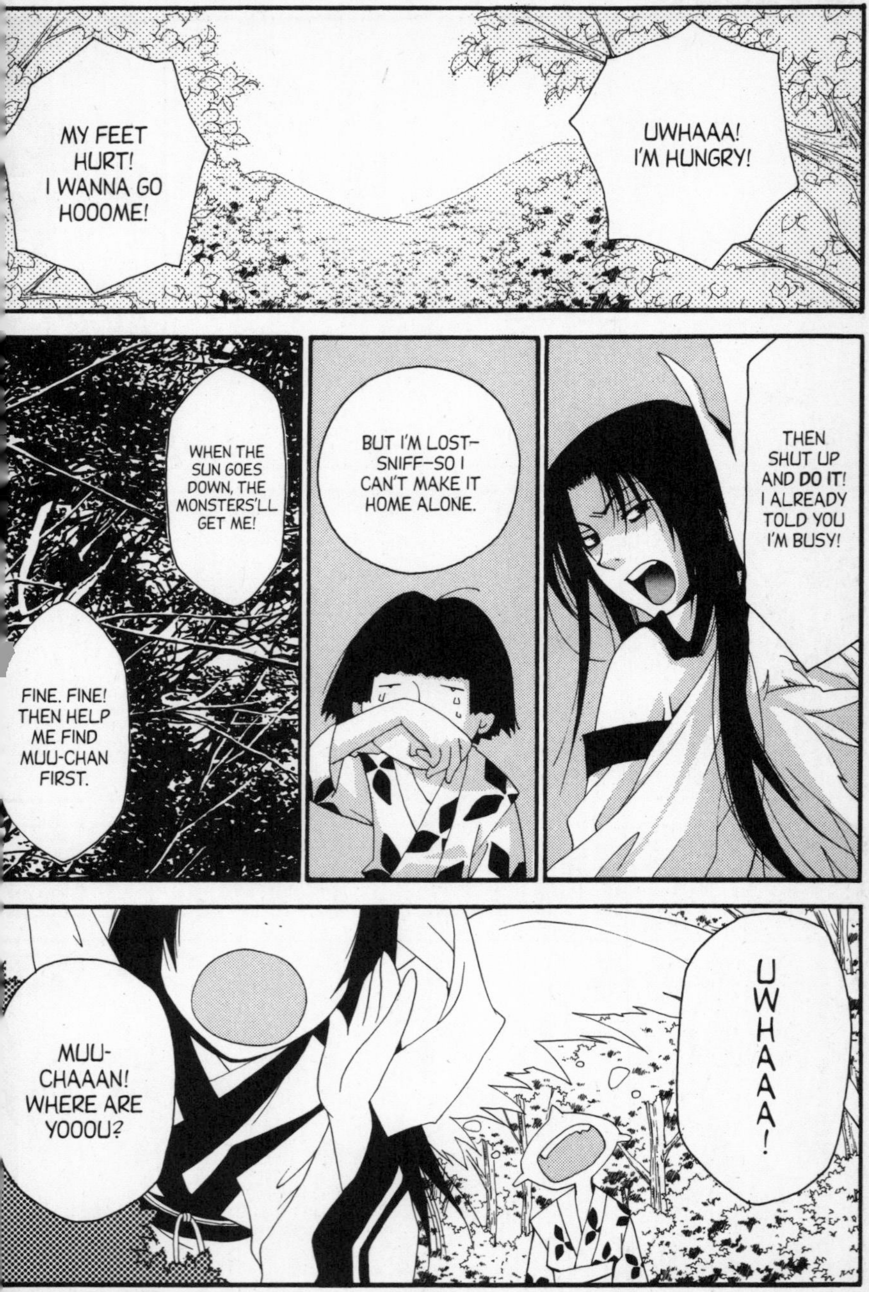
UWHAAA! I'M HUNGRY!
MY FEET HURT! I WANNA GO HOOOME!
THEN SHUT UP AND DO IT! I ALREADY TOLD YOU I'M BUSY!
BUT I'M LOST—SNIFF—SO I CAN'T MAKE IT HOME ALONE.
WHEN THE SUN GOES DOWN, THE MONSTERS'LL GET ME!
FINE. FINE! THEN HELP ME FIND MUU-CHAN FIRST.
UWHAAA!
MUU-CHAAAN! WHERE ARE YOOOU?

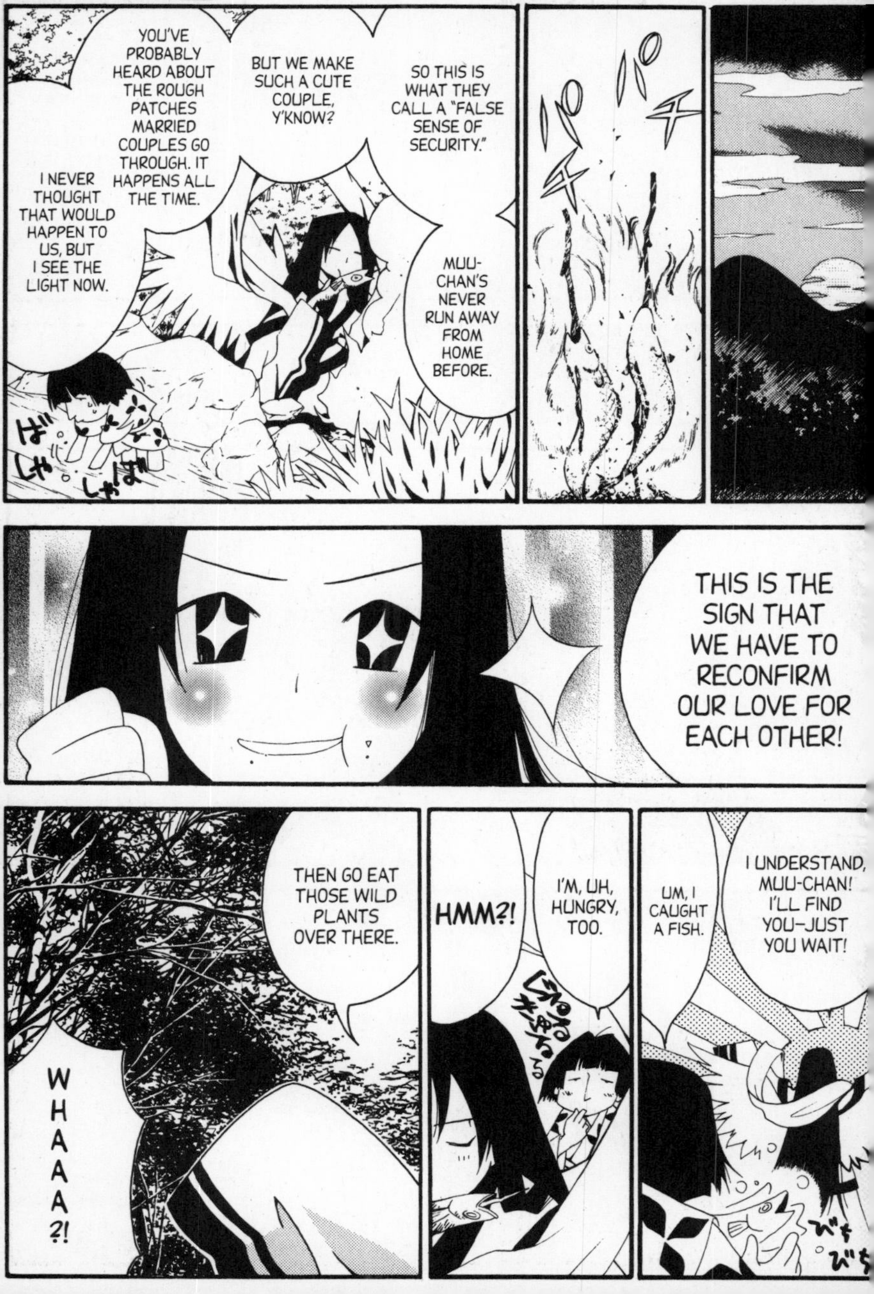
パチ
パチ
SO THIS IS WHAT THEY CALL A "FALSE SENSE OF SECURITY."
BUT WE MAKE SUCH A CUTE COUPLE, Y'KNOW?
YOU'VE PROBABLY HEARD ABOUT THE ROUGH PATCHES MARRIED COUPLES GO THROUGH. IT HAPPENS ALL THE TIME.
MUU-CHAN'S NEVER RUN AWAY FROM HOME BEFORE.
I NEVER THOUGHT THAT WOULD HAPPEN TO US, BUT I SEE THE LIGHT NOW.
THIS IS THE SIGN THAT WE HAVE TO RECONFIRM OUR LOVE FOR EACH OTHER!
I UNDERSTAND, MUU-CHAN! I'LL FIND YOU—JUST YOU WAIT!
UM, I CAUGHT A FISH.
びち
びち
I'M, UH, HUNGRY, TOO.
HMM?!
THEN GO EAT THOSE WILD PLANTS OVER THERE.
WHAAAA?!

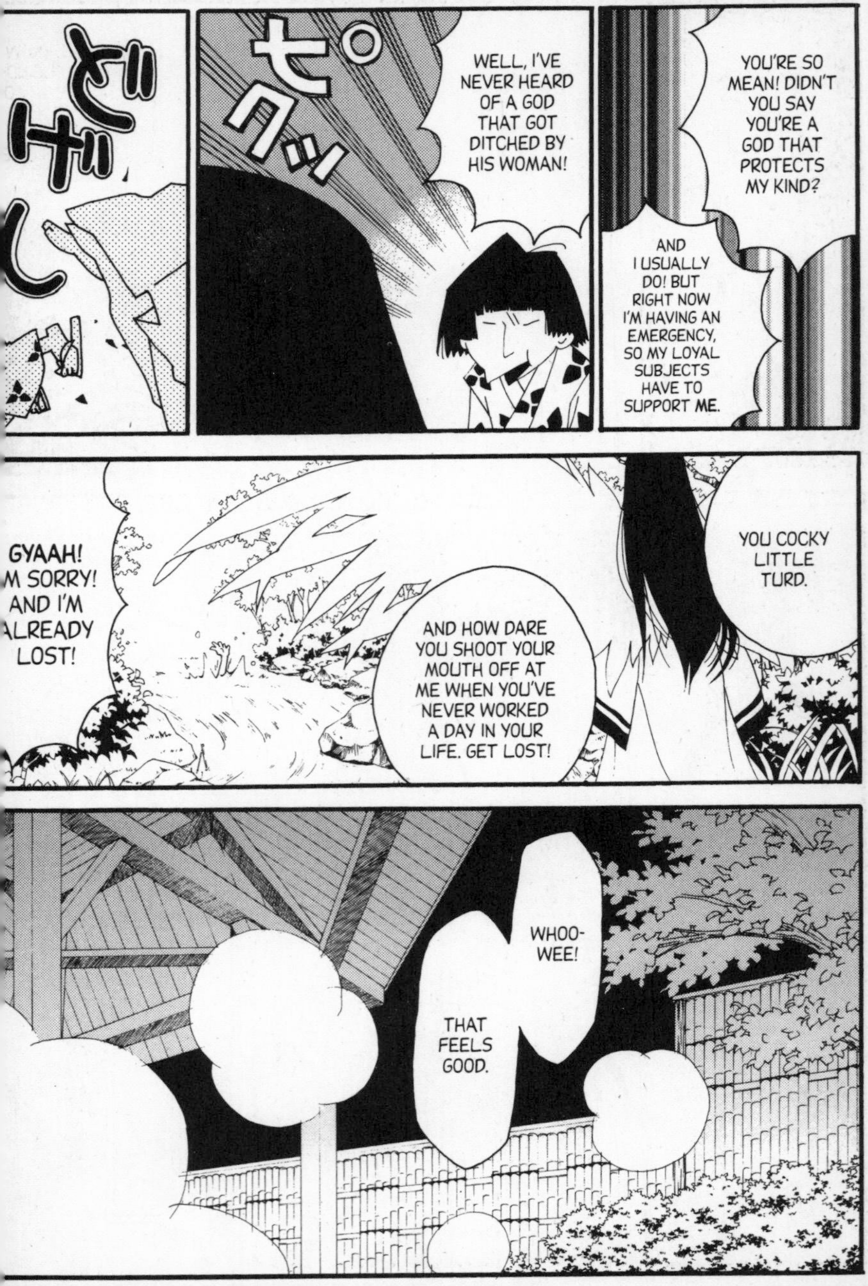
YOU'RE SO MEAN! DIDN'T YOU SAY YOU'RE A GOD THAT PROTECTS MY KIND?
AND I USUALLY DO! BUT RIGHT NOW I'M HAVING AN EMERGENCY, SO MY LOYAL SUBJECTS HAVE TO SUPPORT ME.
WELL, I'VE NEVER HEARD OF A GOD THAT GOT DITCHED BY HIS WOMAN!
ピクッ
どげし
YOU COCKY LITTLE TURD.
AND HOW DARE YOU SHOOT YOUR MOUTH OFF AT ME WHEN YOU'VE NEVER WORKED A DAY IN YOUR LIFE. GET LOST!
GYAAH! M SORRY! AND I'M LREADY LOST!
WHOO-WEE!
THAT FEELS GOOD.

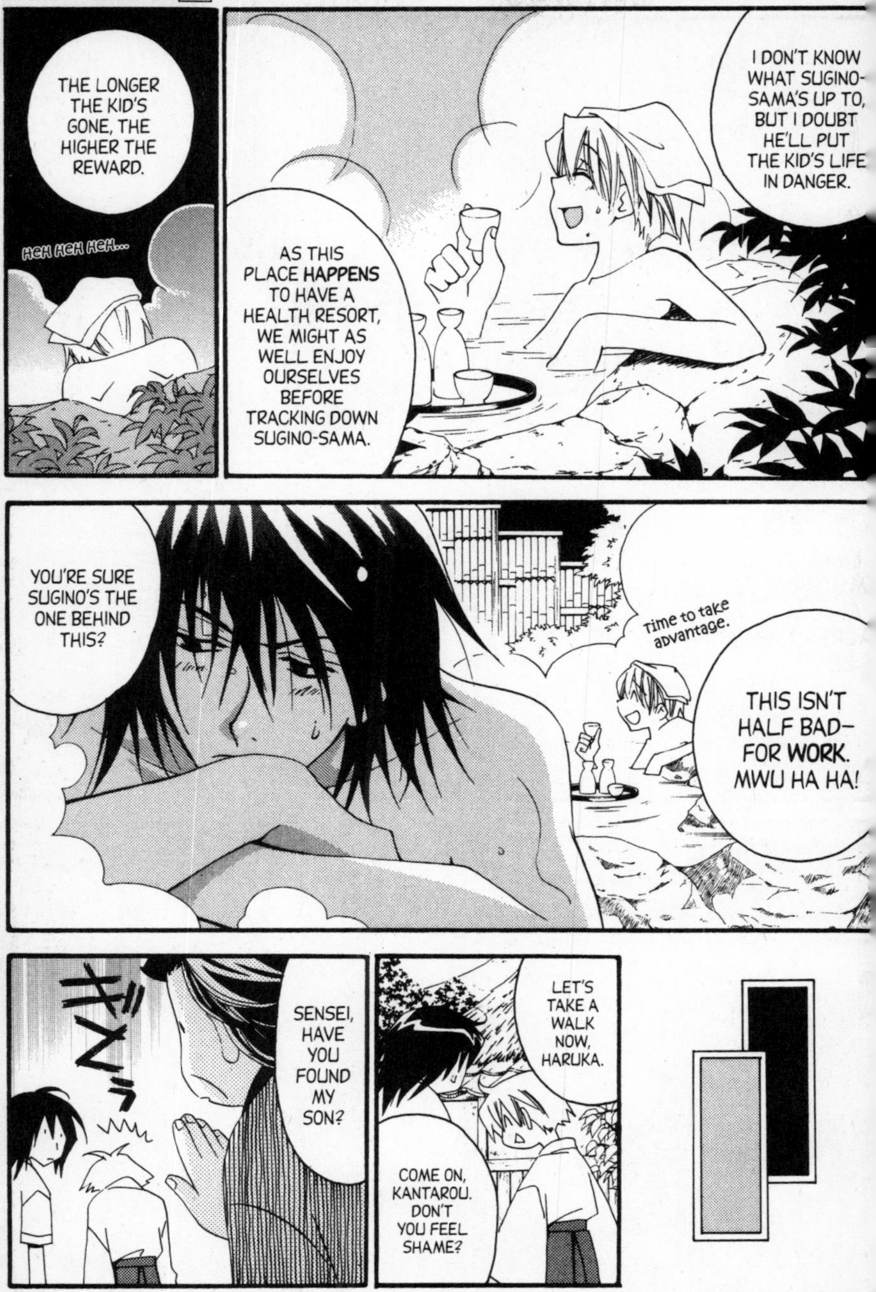
I DON'T KNOW WHAT SUGINO-SAMA'S UP TO, BUT I DOUBT HE'LL PUT THE KID'S LIFE IN DANGER.
AS THIS PLACE **HAPPENS** TO HAVE A HEALTH RESORT, WE MIGHT AS WELL ENJOY OURSELVES BEFORE TRACKING DOWN SUGINO-SAMA.
THE LONGER THE KID'S GONE, THE HIGHER THE REWARD.
HEH HEH HEH...
THIS ISN'T HALF BAD— FOR **WORK**. MWU HA HA!
Time to take advantage.
YOU'RE SURE SUGINO'S THE ONE BEHIND THIS?
LET'S TAKE A WALK NOW, HARUKA.
COME ON, KANTAROU. DON'T YOU FEEL SHAME?
SENSEI, HAVE YOU FOUND MY SON?

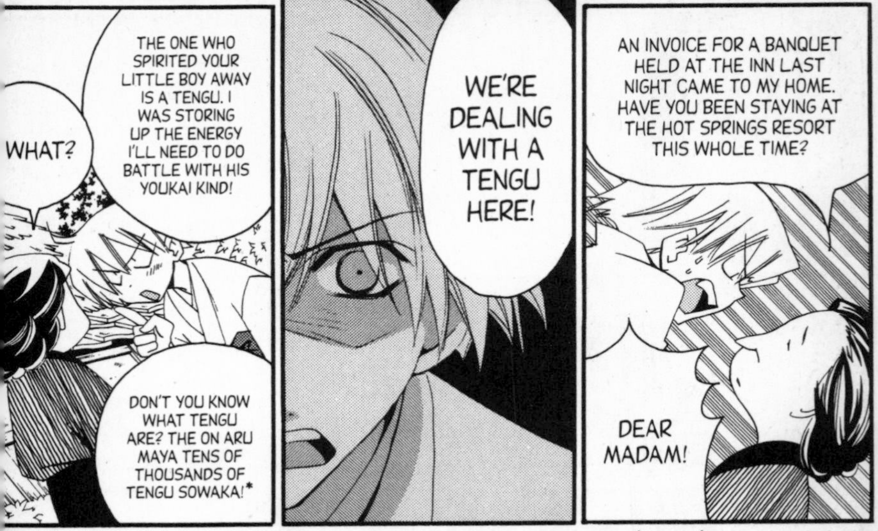
AN INVOICE FOR A BANQUET HELD AT THE INN LAST NIGHT CAME TO MY HOME. HAVE YOU BEEN STAYING AT THE HOT SPRINGS RESORT THIS WHOLE TIME?
DEAR MADAM!
WE'RE DEALING WITH A TENGU HERE!
THE ONE WHO SPIRITED YOUR LITTLE BOY AWAY IS A TENGU. I WAS STORING UP THE ENERGY I'LL NEED TO DO BATTLE WITH HIS YOUKAI KIND!
WHAT?
DON'T YOU KNOW WHAT TENGU ARE? THE ON ARU MAYA TENS OF THOUSANDS OF TENGU SOWAKA!*

*Kantarou has taken a mantra that typically goes, "on aru maya on gusuman desu sowaka," and replaced the middle part with "tens of thousands of tengu" to emphasize their horridness.

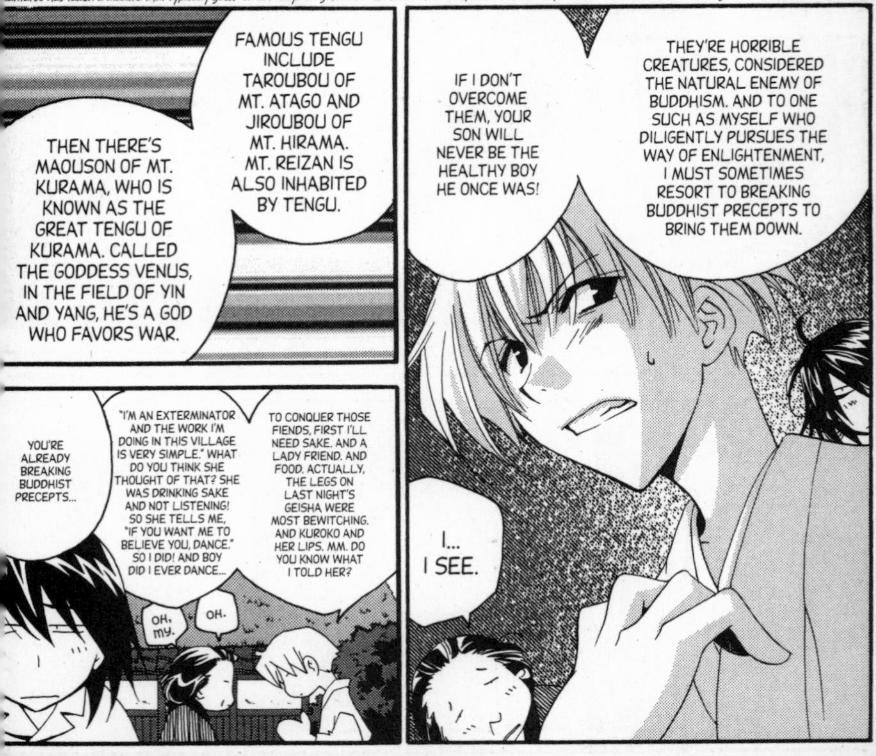
THEY'RE HORRIBLE CREATURES, CONSIDERED THE NATURAL ENEMY OF BUDDHISM. AND TO ONE SUCH AS MYSELF WHO DILIGENTLY PURSUES THE WAY OF ENLIGHTENMENT, I MUST SOMETIMES RESORT TO BREAKING BUDDHIST PRECEPTS TO BRING THEM DOWN.
IF I DON'T OVERCOME THEM, YOUR SON WILL NEVER BE THE HEALTHY BOY HE ONCE WAS!
I... I SEE.
FAMOUS TENGU INCLUDE TAROUBOU OF MT. ATAGO AND JIROUBOU OF MT. HIRAMA. MT. REIZAN IS ALSO INHABITED BY TENGU.
THEN THERE'S MAOUSON OF MT. KURAMA, WHO IS KNOWN AS THE GREAT TENGU OF KURAMA. CALLED THE GODDESS VENUS, IN THE FIELD OF YIN AND YANG, HE'S A GOD WHO FAVORS WAR.
TO CONQUER THOSE FIENDS, FIRST I'LL NEED SAKE. AND A LADY FRIEND. AND FOOD. ACTUALLY, THE LEGS ON LAST NIGHT'S GEISHA WERE MOST BEWITCHING. AND KUROKO AND HER LIPS. MM. DO YOU KNOW WHAT I TOLD HER?
"I'M AN EXTERMINATOR AND THE WORK I'M DOING IN THIS VILLAGE IS VERY SIMPLE." WHAT DO YOU THINK SHE THOUGHT OF THAT? SHE WAS DRINKING SAKE AND NOT LISTENING! SO SHE TELLS ME, "IF YOU WANT ME TO BELIEVE YOU, DANCE." SO I DID! AND BOY DID I EVER DANCE...
YOU'RE ALREADY BREAKING BUDDHIST PRECEPTS...
OH.
OH, MY.

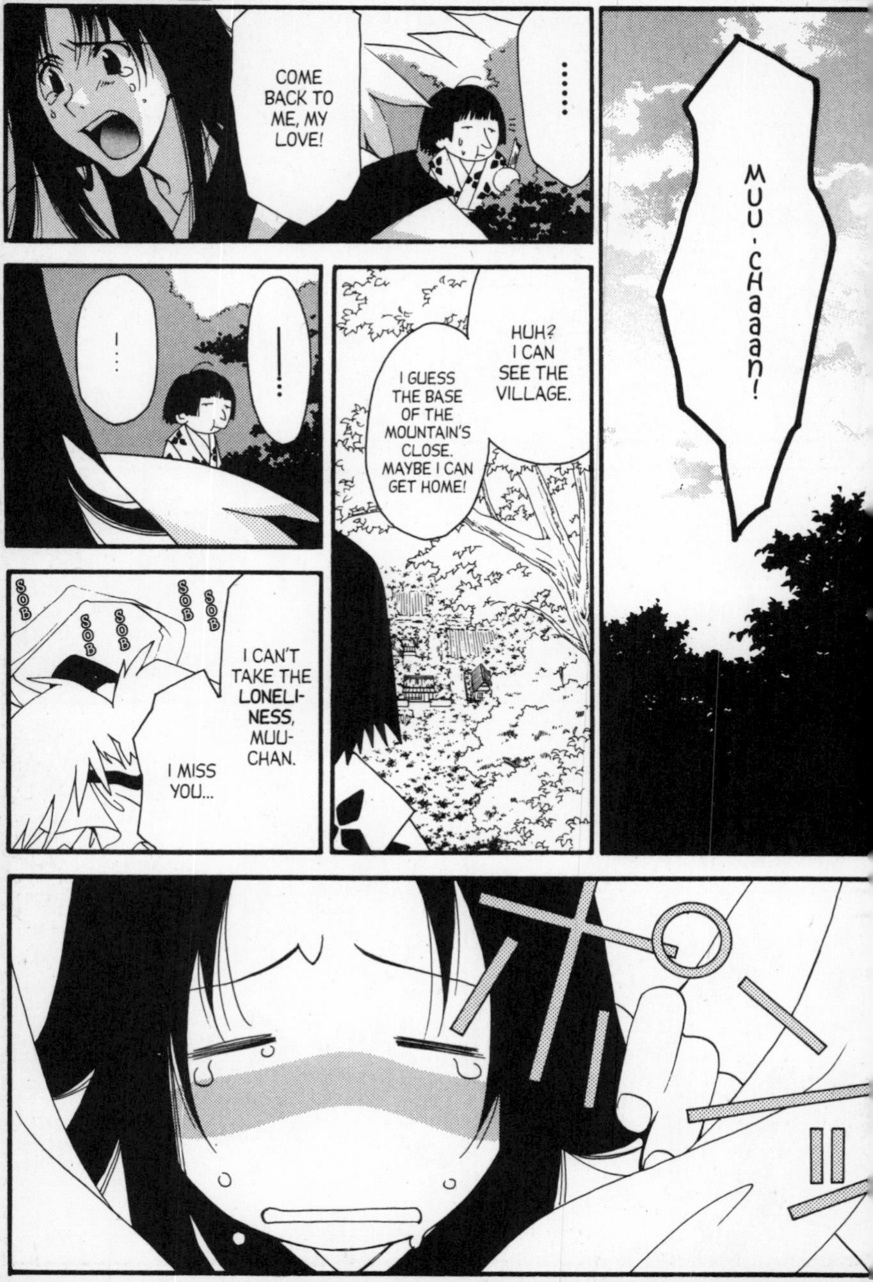
MUU-CHAaaan!
......
COME BACK TO ME, MY LOVE!
HUH? I CAN SEE THE VILLAGE.
I GUESS THE BASE OF THE MOUNTAIN'S CLOSE. MAYBE I CAN GET HOME!
!...
!...
SOB SOB
SOB SOB SOB
I CAN'T TAKE THE LONELI-NESS, MUU-CHAN.
I MISS YOU...

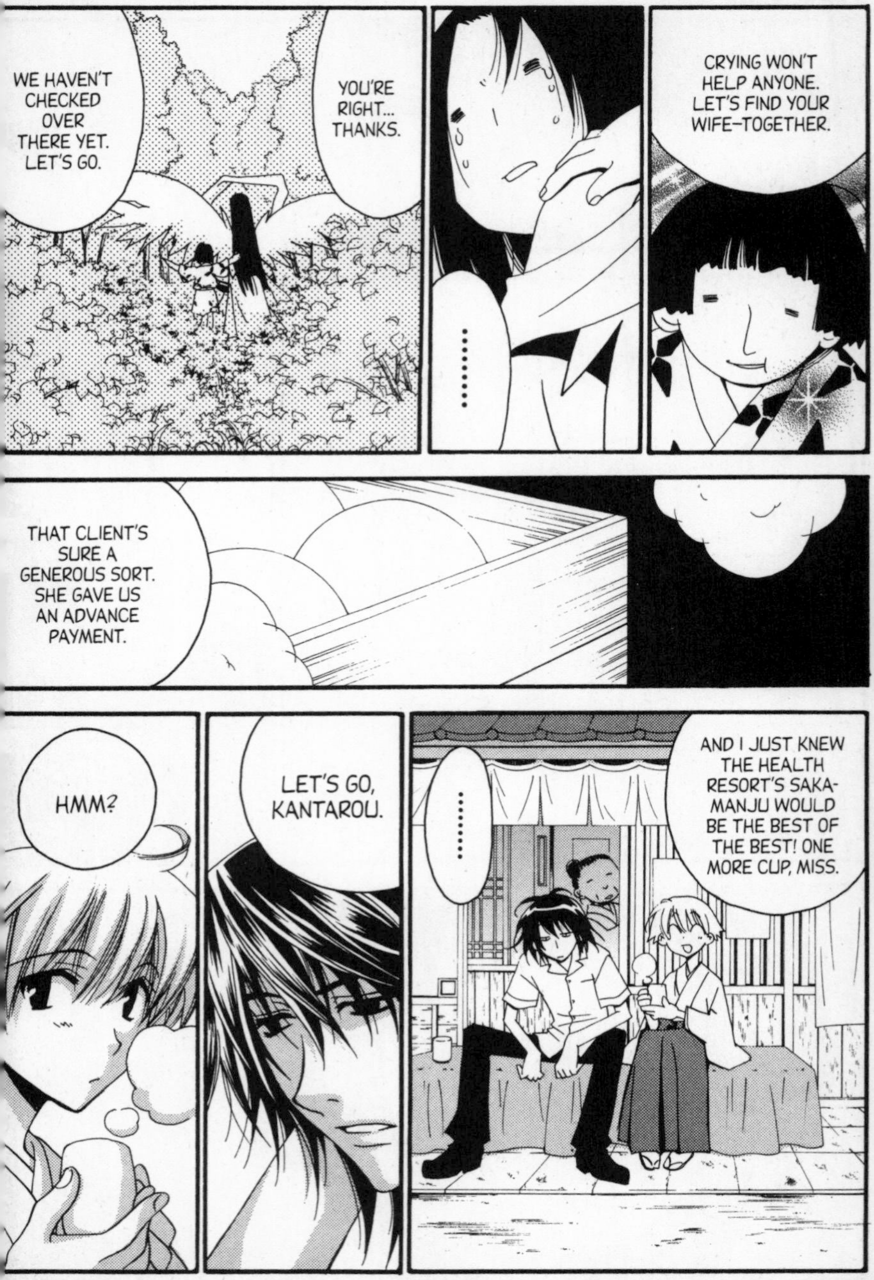

CRYING WON'T HELP ANYONE. LET'S FIND YOUR WIFE—TOGETHER.
....
YOU'RE RIGHT... THANKS.
WE HAVEN'T CHECKED OVER THERE YET. LET'S GO.
THAT CLIENT'S SURE A GENEROUS SORT. SHE GAVE US AN ADVANCE PAYMENT.
AND I JUST KNEW THE HEALTH RESORT'S SAKA-MANJU WOULD BE THE BEST OF THE BEST! ONE MORE CUP, MISS.
....
LET'S GO, KANTAROU.
HMM?

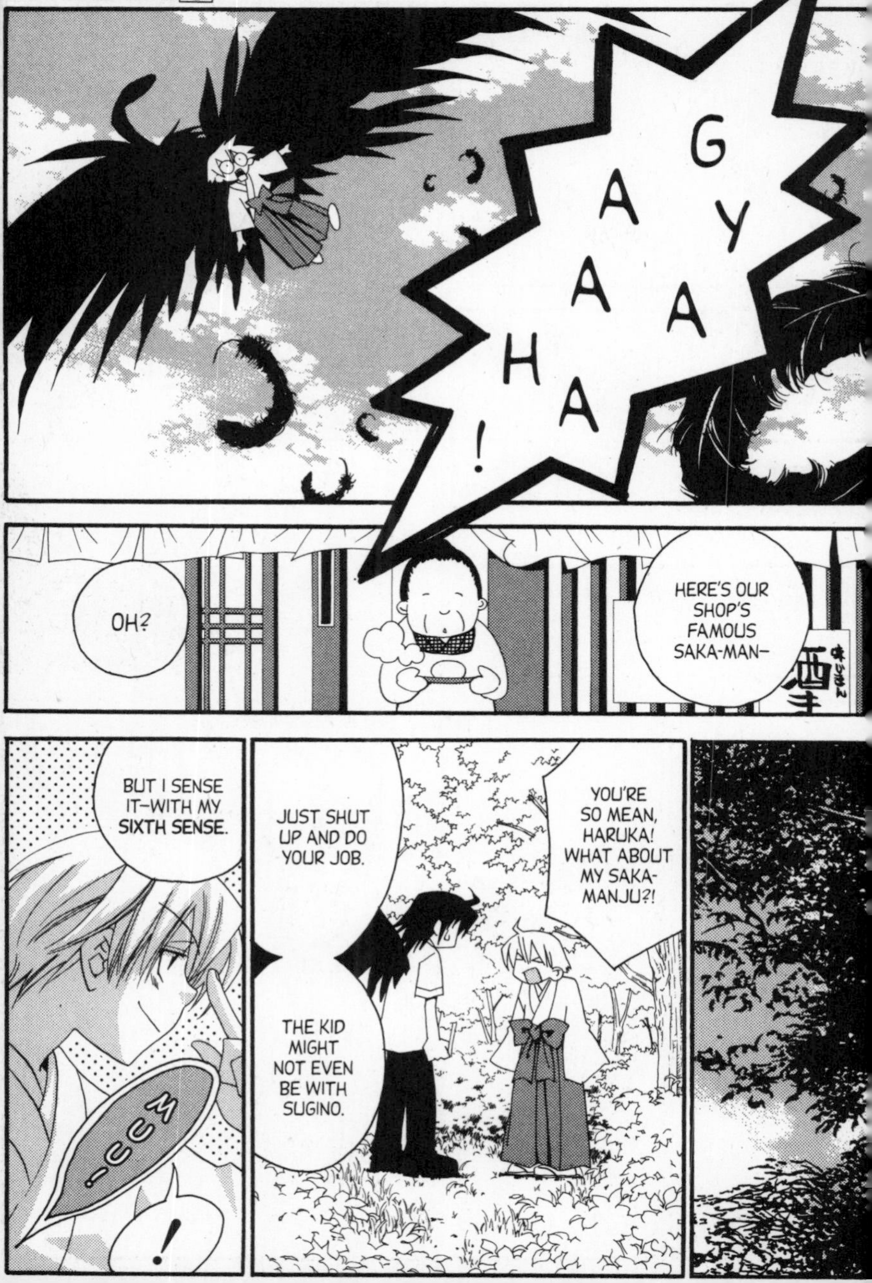
GYAAAHA!
HERE'S OUR SHOP'S FAMOUS SAKA-MAN–
OH?
YOU'RE SO MEAN, HARUKA! WHAT ABOUT MY SAKA-MANJU?!
JUST SHUT UP AND DO YOUR JOB.
THE KID MIGHT NOT EVEN BE WITH SUGINO.
BUT I SENSE IT–WITH MY SIXTH SENSE.
MUU–!
!

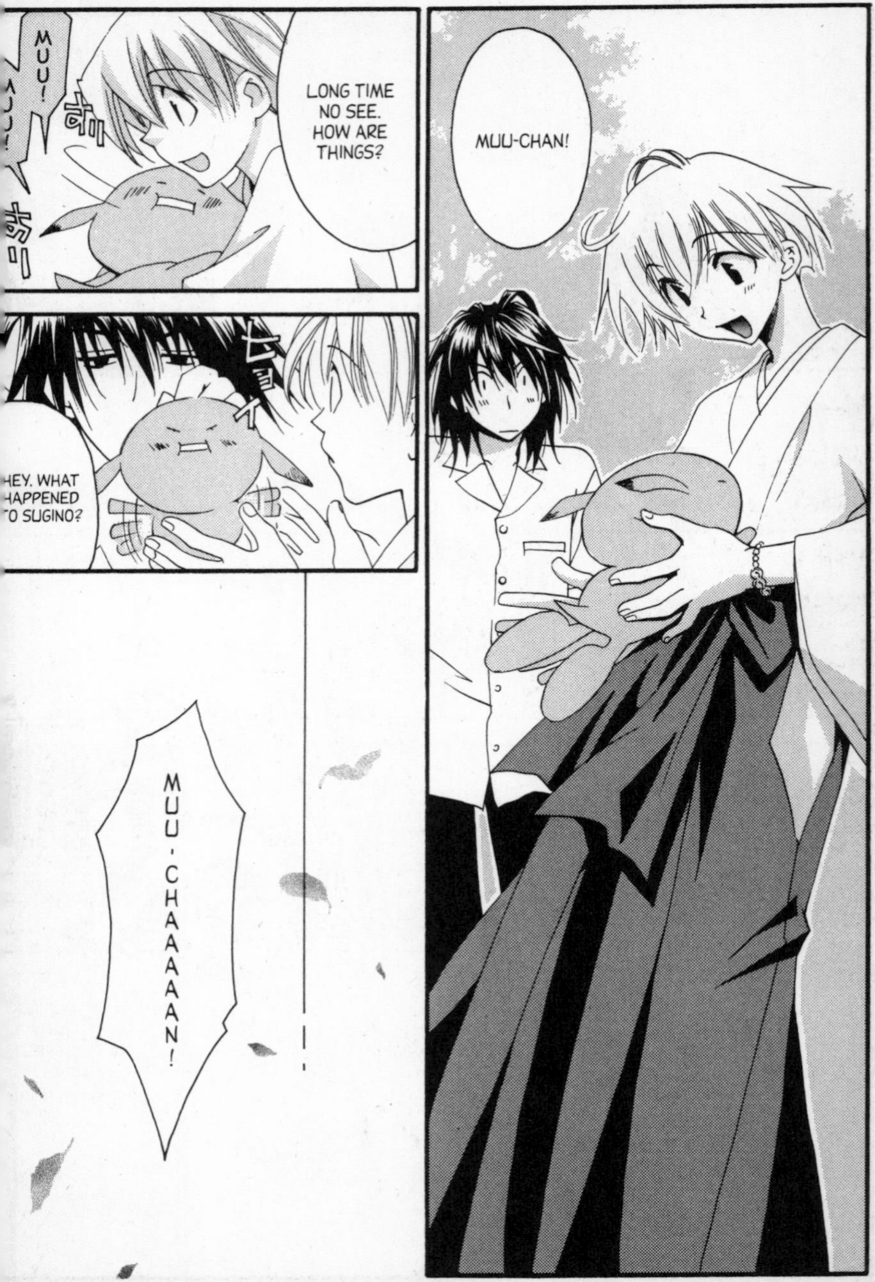
MUU-CHAN!
LONG TIME NO SEE. HOW ARE THINGS?
MUU!
HEY. WHAT HAPPENED TO SUGINO?
--!
MUU-CHAAAAAAN!

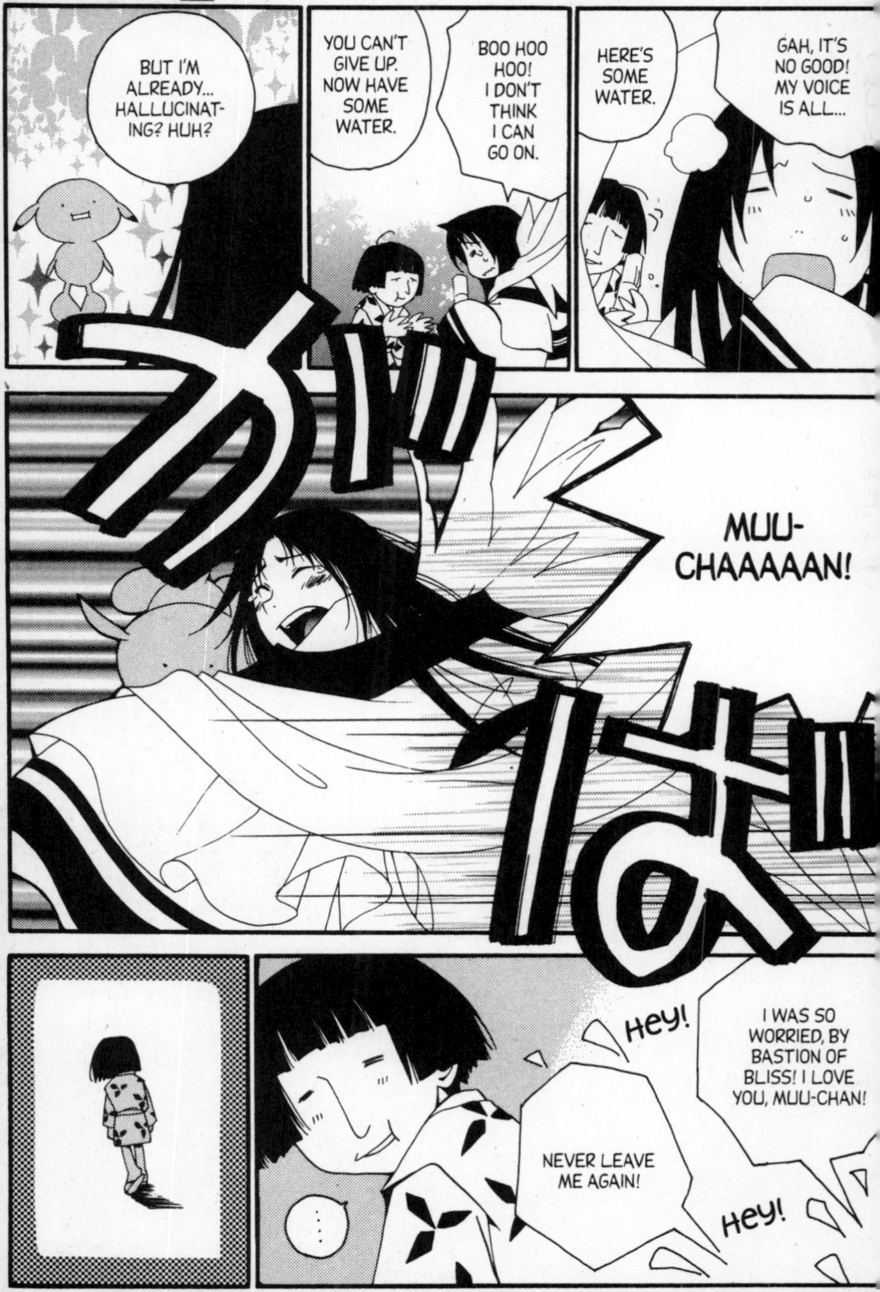
GAH, IT'S NO GOOD! MY VOICE IS ALL...
HERE'S SOME WATER.
BOO HOO HOO! I DON'T THINK I CAN GO ON.
YOU CAN'T GIVE UP. NOW HAVE SOME WATER.
BUT I'M ALREADY... HALLUCINATING? HUH?
MUU-CHAAAAAN!
I WAS SO WORRIED, BY BASTION OF BLISS! I LOVE YOU, MUU-CHAN!
Hey!
NEVER LEAVE ME AGAIN!
Hey!
...

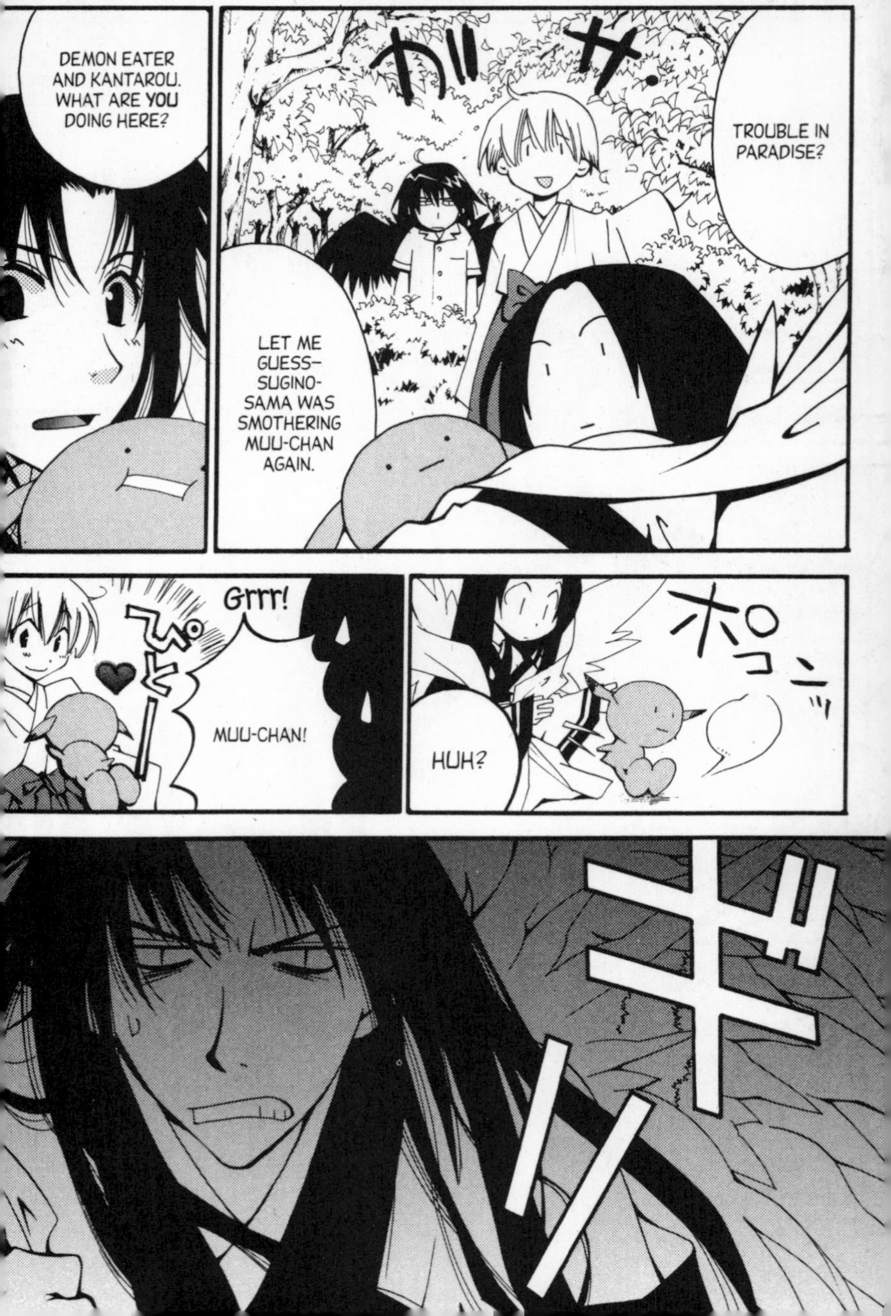
TROUBLE IN PARADISE?
LET ME GUESS— SUGINO-SAMA WAS SMOTHERING MUU-CHAN AGAIN.
DEMON EATER AND KANTAROU. WHAT ARE YOU DOING HERE?
HUH?
Grrr!
MUU-CHAN!

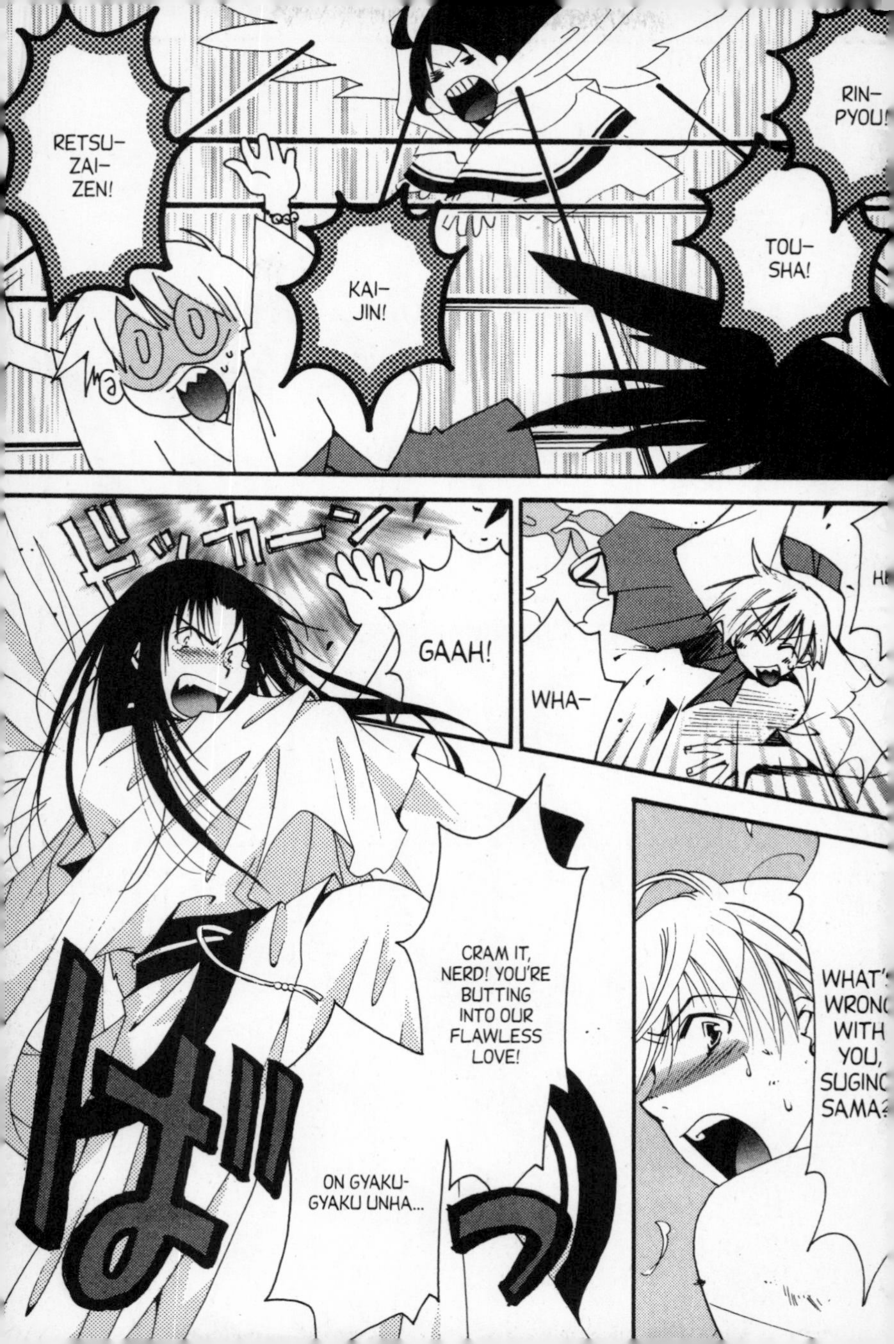
RIN-
PYOU!
TOU-
SHA!
KAI-
JIN!
RETSU-
ZAI-
ZEN!
WHA-
ドッカーン!
GAAH!
WHAT'S WRONG WITH YOU, SUGINO SAMA?
CRAM IT, NERD! YOU'RE BUTTING INTO OUR FLAWLESS LOVE!
ON GYAKU-GYAKU UNHA...
ドおっ

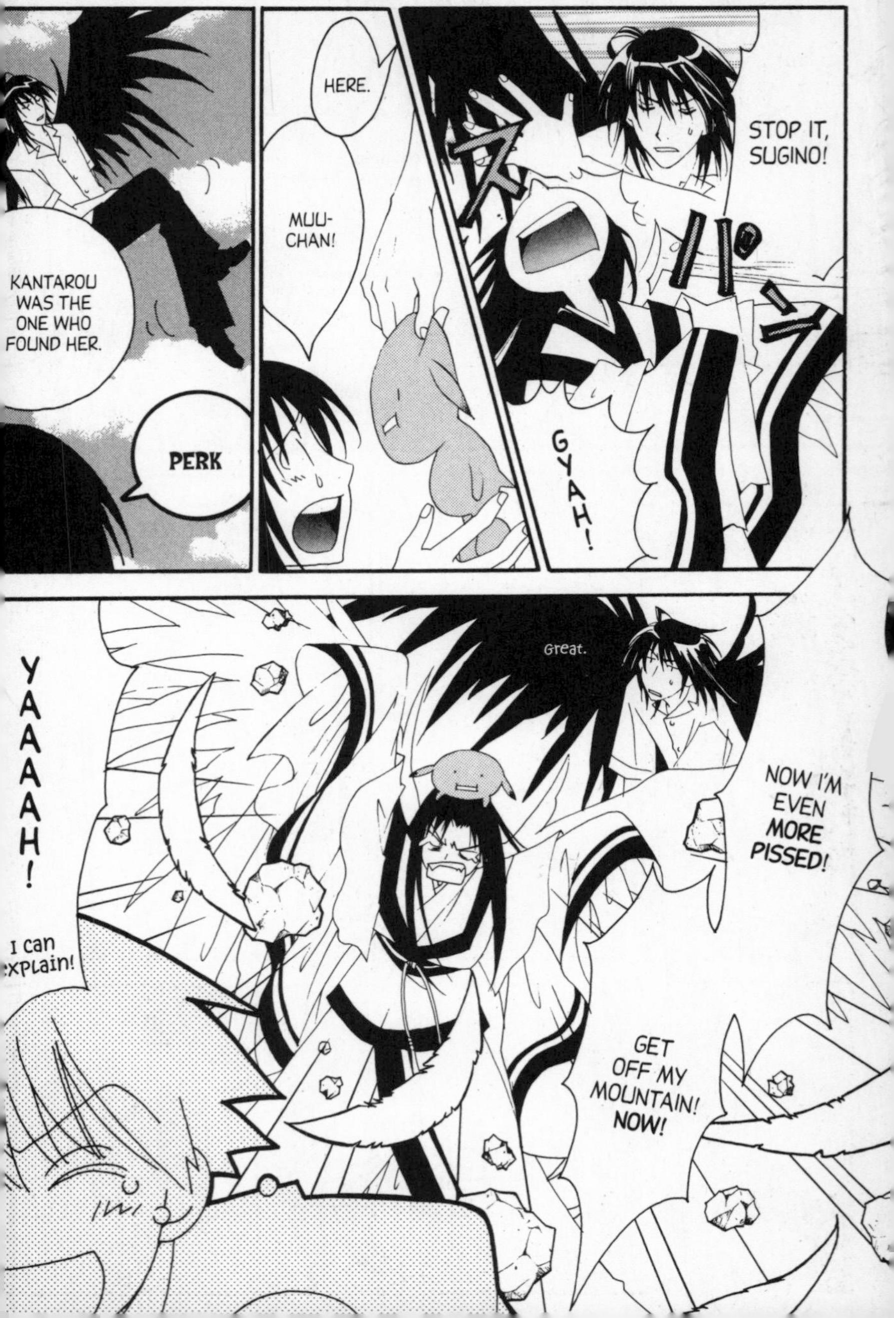
STOP IT, SUGINO!
GYAH!
HERE.
MUU-CHAN!
KANTAROU WAS THE ONE WHO FOUND HER.
PERK
Great.
NOW I'M EVEN MORE PISSED!
GET OFF MY MOUNTAIN! NOW!
YAAAAAH!
I can explain!

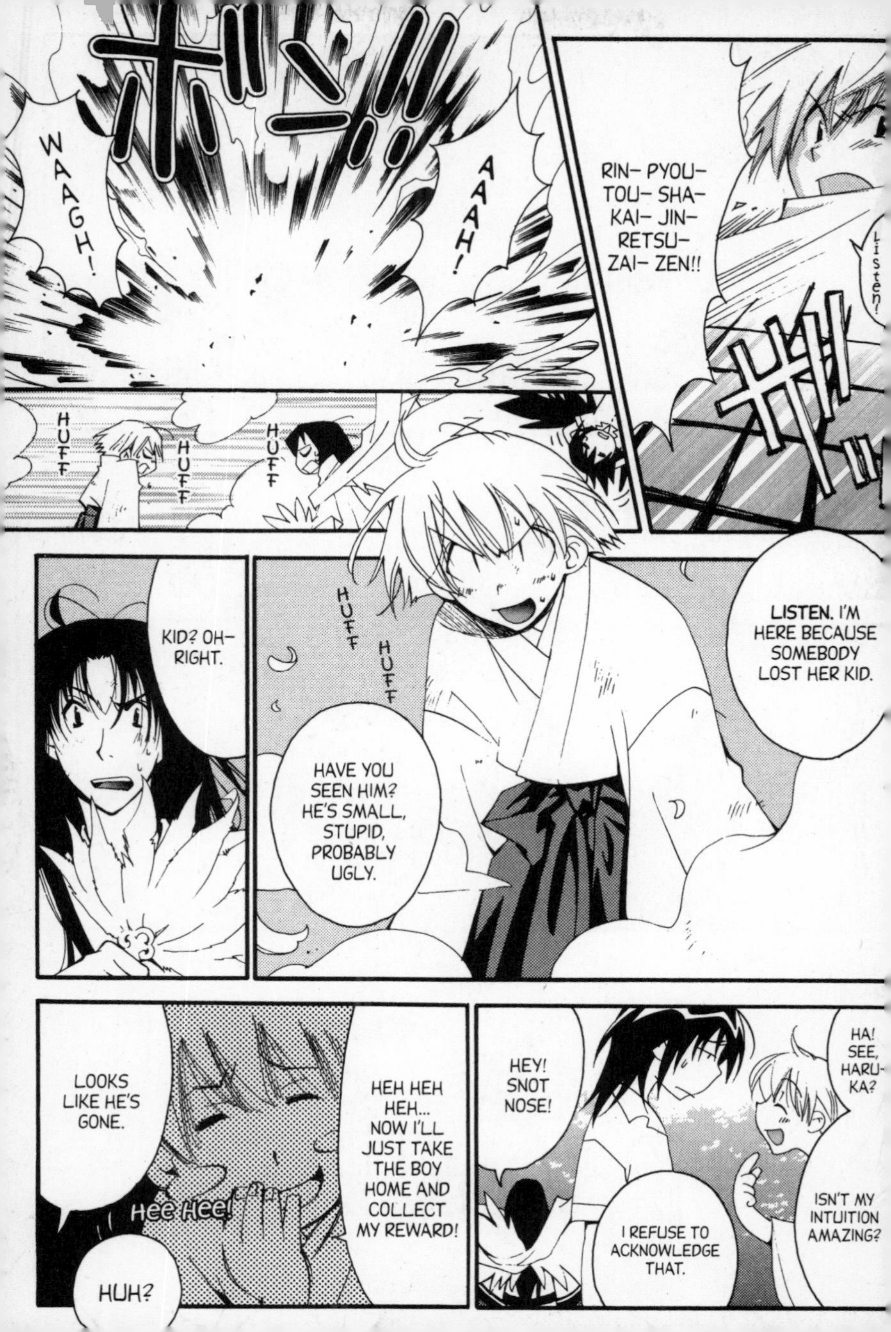
RIN- PYOU- TOU- SHA- KAI- JIN- RETSU- ZAI- ZEN!!
Listen!
AAAAH!
WAAAGH!
HUFF
HUFF
HUFF
LISTEN. I'M HERE BECAUSE SOMEBODY LOST HER KID.
HUFF
HUFF
HAVE YOU SEEN HIM? HE'S SMALL, STUPID, PROBABLY UGLY.
KID? OH- RIGHT.
HA! SEE, HARU-KA?
ISN'T MY INTUITION AMAZING?
HEY! SNOT NOSE!
I REFUSE TO ACKNOWLEDGE THAT.
HEH HEH HEH... NOW I'LL JUST TAKE THE BOY HOME AND COLLECT MY REWARD!
LOOKS LIKE HE'S GONE.
Hee Hee!
HUH?

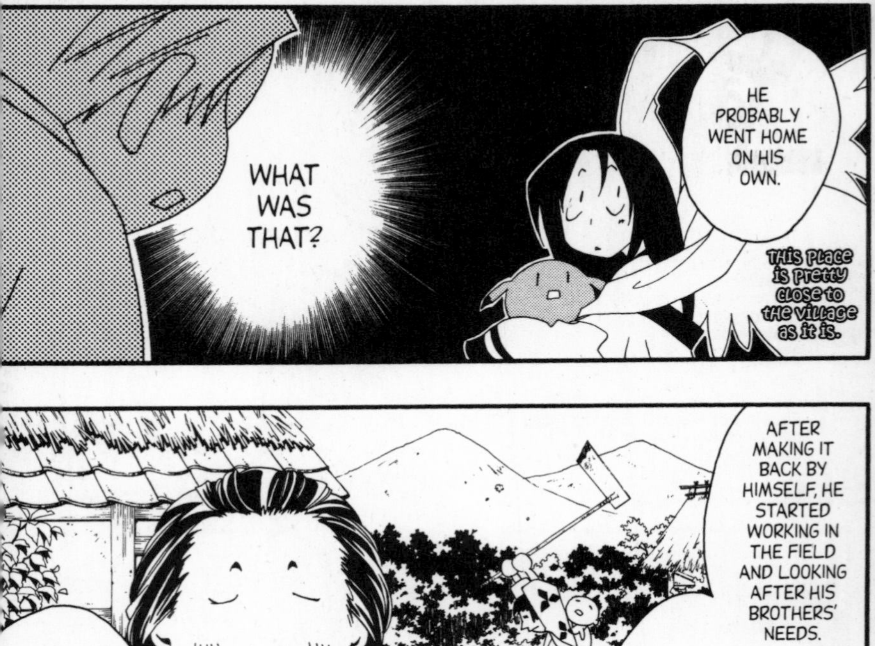
HE PROBABLY WENT HOME ON HIS OWN.
This place is pretty close to the village as it is.
WHAT WAS THAT?
AFTER MAKING IT BACK BY HIMSELF, HE STARTED WORKING IN THE FIELD AND LOOKING AFTER HIS BROTHERS' NEEDS.
THE MOUNTAIN GOD MUST'VE INSTRUCTED MY SON TO GROW UP. I'M VERY THANKFUL.
AS YOU ENDED UP NOT HELPING, I'M NOT PAYING YOU.

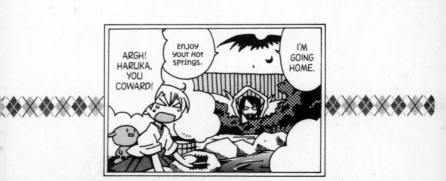

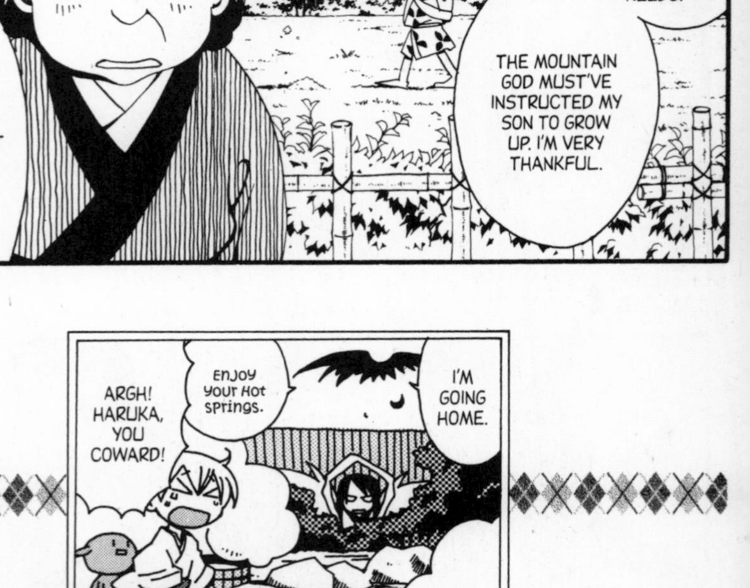
I'M GOING HOME.
Enjoy your Hot springs.
ARGH! HARUKA, YOU COWARD!

Tactics 6

Many apologies, and thanks to Kinoshita-san, who carried me on her back for much of this part of the journey as well. Then there's the bonus illustrations I did for the limited edition PC game... I really can't wait to see what it looks like when it's all done!

I'm going to do my best so that one day I can write a manga involving this tengu duo.

↑
Kino
shit
san s
she
lik
to s
tha
to

Tactics is already at Volume 6... I'm pretty surprised and impatient myself. Both Haruka-san and Kan-chan are having it pretty rough...as is Ayame, in a way. It'd make me so happy if you all continued to look after these folks. Thank you very much.

Kazuko Higashiyama

東山和子

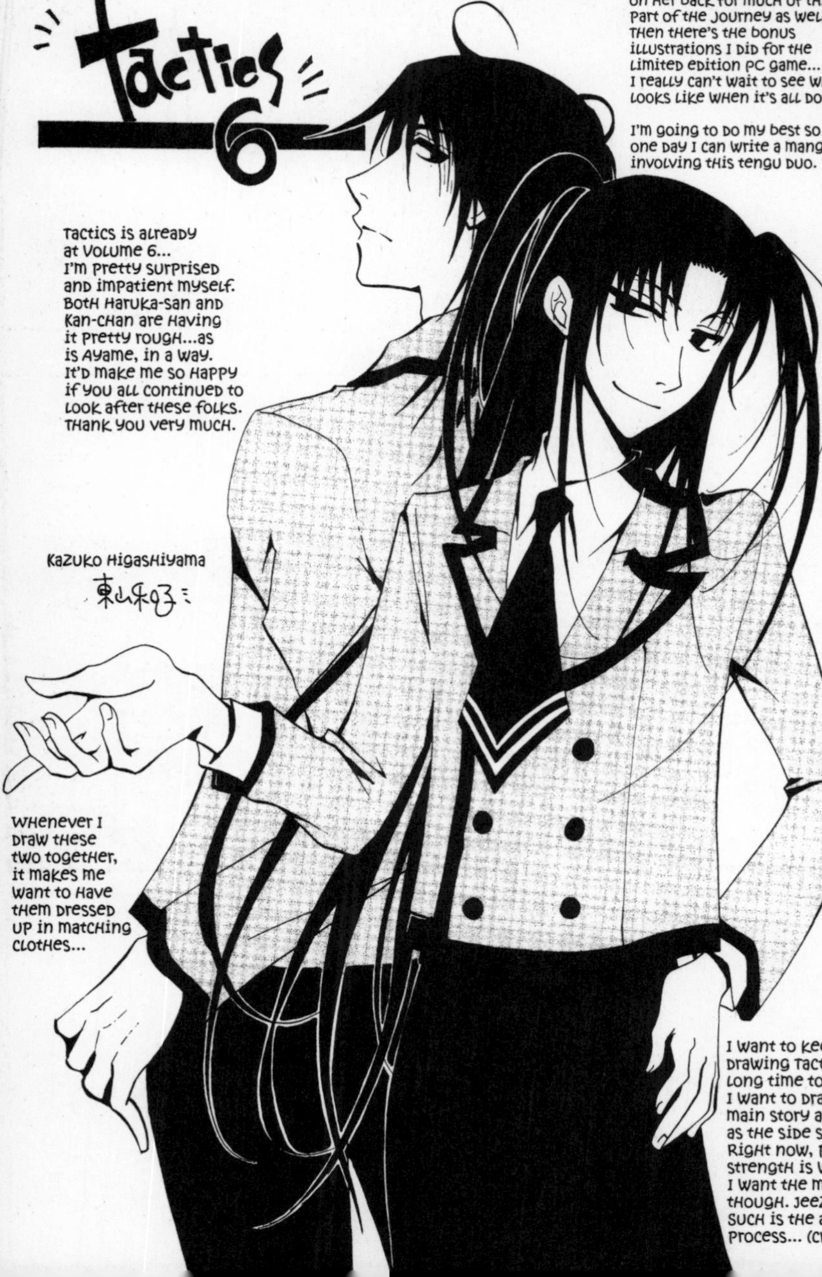

Whenever I draw these two together, it makes me want to have them dressed up in matching clothes...

I want to keep drawing Tactics fo long time to come. I want to draw the main story as well as the side stories Right now, physic strength is what I want the most, though. Jeez. Such is the aging process... (cries)

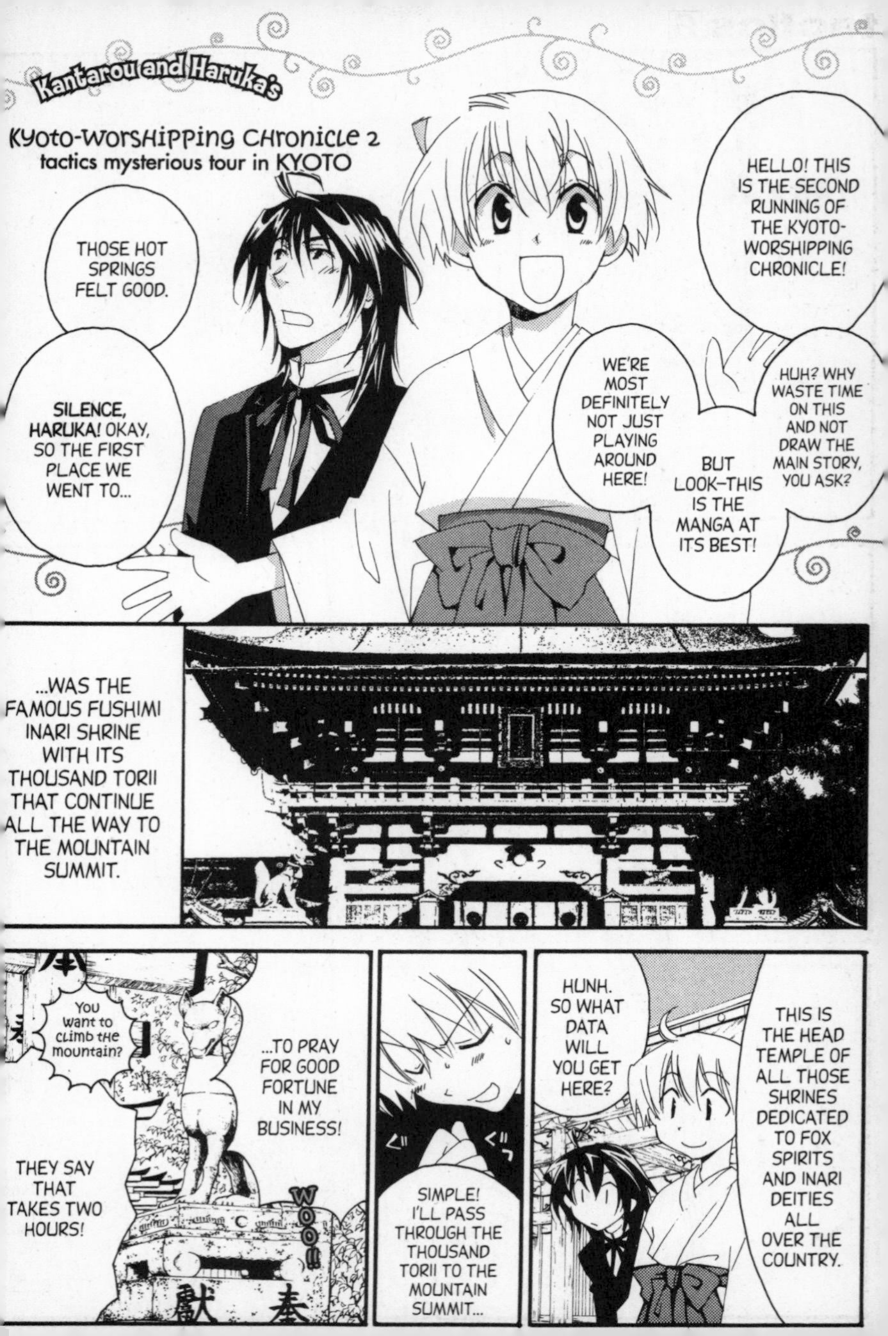
Kantarou and Haruka's
KYoto-WorsHiPPing CHronicle 2
tactics mysterious tour in KYOTO
HELLO! THIS IS THE SECOND RUNNING OF THE KYOTO-WORSHIPPING CHRONICLE!
HUH? WHY WASTE TIME ON THIS AND NOT DRAW THE MAIN STORY, YOU ASK?
BUT LOOK—THIS IS THE MANGA AT ITS BEST!
WE'RE MOST DEFINITELY NOT JUST PLAYING AROUND HERE!
THOSE HOT SPRINGS FELT GOOD.
SILENCE, HARUKA! OKAY, SO THE FIRST PLACE WE WENT TO...
...WAS THE FAMOUS FUSHIMI INARI SHRINE WITH ITS THOUSAND TORII THAT CONTINUE ALL THE WAY TO THE MOUNTAIN SUMMIT.
THIS IS THE HEAD TEMPLE OF ALL THOSE SHRINES DEDICATED TO FOX SPIRITS AND INARI DEITIES ALL OVER THE COUNTRY.
HUNH. SO WHAT DATA WILL YOU GET HERE?
SIMPLE! I'LL PASS THROUGH THE THOUSAND TORII TO THE MOUNTAIN SUMMIT...
...TO PRAY FOR GOOD FORTUNE IN MY BUSINESS!
You want to climb the mountain?
THEY SAY THAT TAKES TWO HOURS!
WOO!!

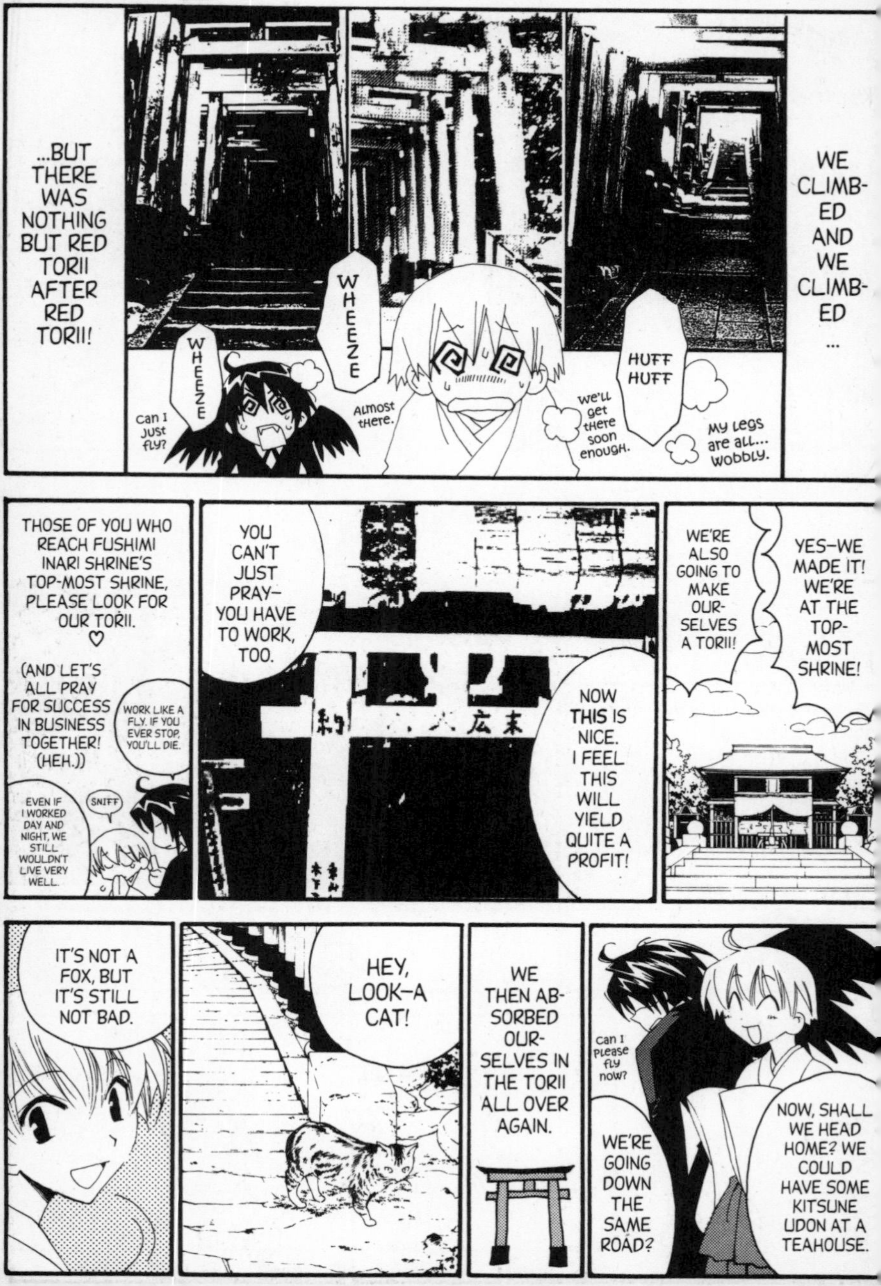
WE CLIMBED AND WE CLIMBED...
HUFF HUFF
My legs are all... wobbly.
We'll get there soon enough.
WHEEZE
Almost there.
WHEEZE
Can I just fly?
...BUT THERE WAS NOTHING BUT RED TORII AFTER RED TORII!
YES—WE MADE IT! WE'RE AT THE TOP-MOST SHRINE!
WE'RE ALSO GOING TO MAKE OURSELVES A TORII!
YOU CAN'T JUST PRAY—YOU HAVE TO WORK, TOO.
NOW THIS IS NICE. I FEEL THIS WILL YIELD QUITE A PROFIT!
THOSE OF YOU WHO REACH FUSHIMI INARI SHRINE'S TOP-MOST SHRINE, PLEASE LOOK FOR OUR TORII. ♡
(AND LET'S ALL PRAY FOR SUCCESS IN BUSINESS TOGETHER! (HEH.))
WORK LIKE A FLY. IF YOU EVER STOP, YOU'LL DIE.
SNIFF
EVEN IF I WORKED DAY AND NIGHT, WE STILL WOULDN'T LIVE VERY WELL.
NOW, SHALL WE HEAD HOME? WE COULD HAVE SOME KITSUNE UDON AT A TEAHOUSE.
Can I please fly now?
WE'RE GOING DOWN THE SAME ROAD?
WE THEN ABSORBED OURSELVES IN THE TORII ALL OVER AGAIN.
HEY, LOOK—A CAT!
IT'S NOT A FOX, BUT IT'S STILL NOT BAD.

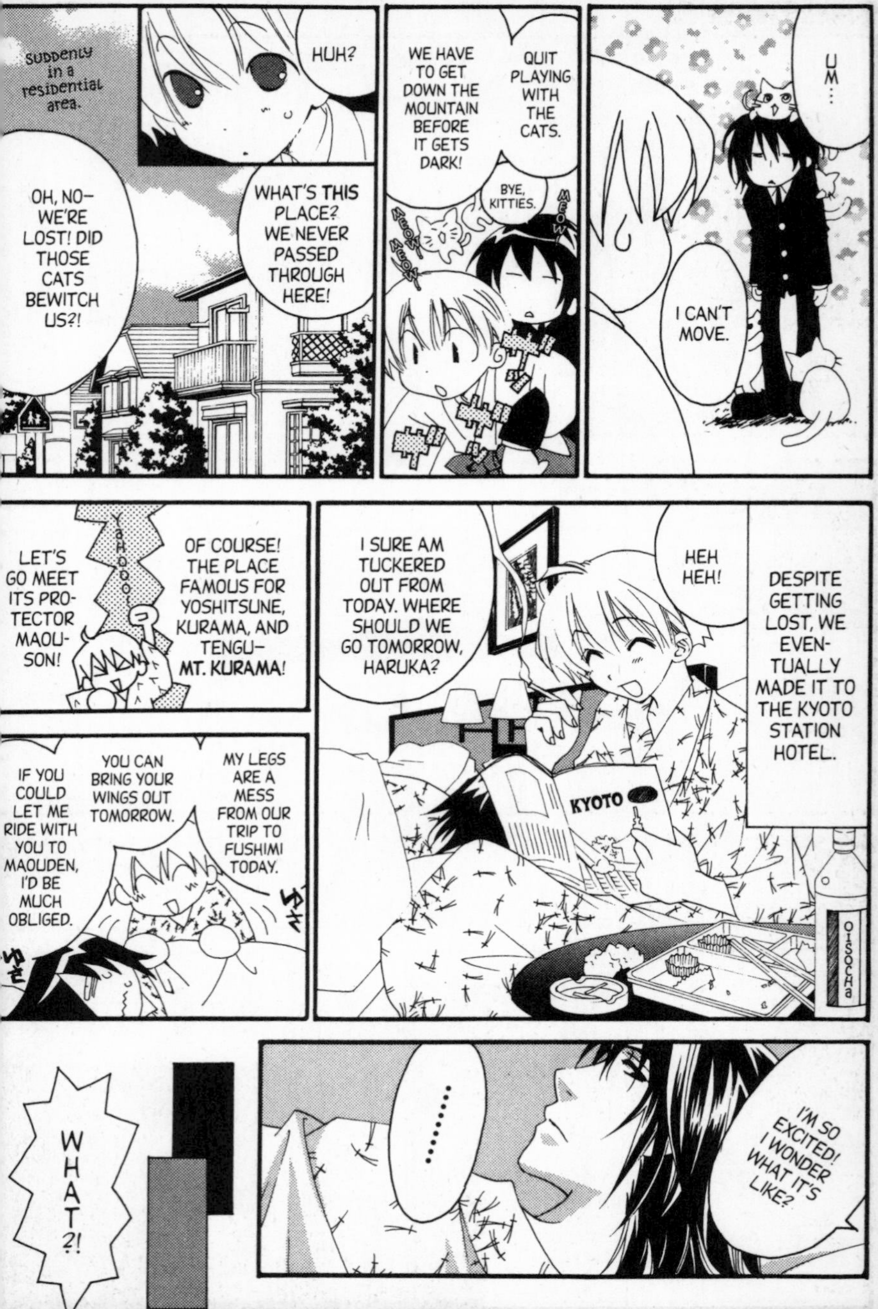
UM...
I CAN'T MOVE.
QUIT PLAYING WITH THE CATS.
WE HAVE TO GET DOWN THE MOUNTAIN BEFORE IT GETS DARK!
BYE, KITTIES.
MEOW!
MEOW! MEOW!
HUH?
Suddenly in a residential area.
WHAT'S THIS PLACE? WE NEVER PASSED THROUGH HERE!
OH, NO— WE'RE LOST! DID THOSE CATS BEWITCH US?!
DESPITE GETTING LOST, WE EVENTUALLY MADE IT TO THE KYOTO STATION HOTEL.
HEH HEH!
I SURE AM TUCKERED OUT FROM TODAY. WHERE SHOULD WE GO TOMORROW, HARUKA?
KYOTO
OISOCHA
OF COURSE! THE PLACE FAMOUS FOR YOSHITSUNE, KURAMA, AND TENGU— MT. KURAMA!
LET'S GO MEET ITS PROTECTOR MAOU-SON!
MY LEGS ARE A MESS FROM OUR TRIP TO FUSHIMI TODAY.
YOU CAN BRING YOUR WINGS OUT TOMORROW.
IF YOU COULD LET ME RIDE WITH YOU TO MAOUDEN, I'D BE MUCH OBLIGED.
I'M SO EXCITED! I WONDER WHAT IT'S LIKE?
......
WHAT?!

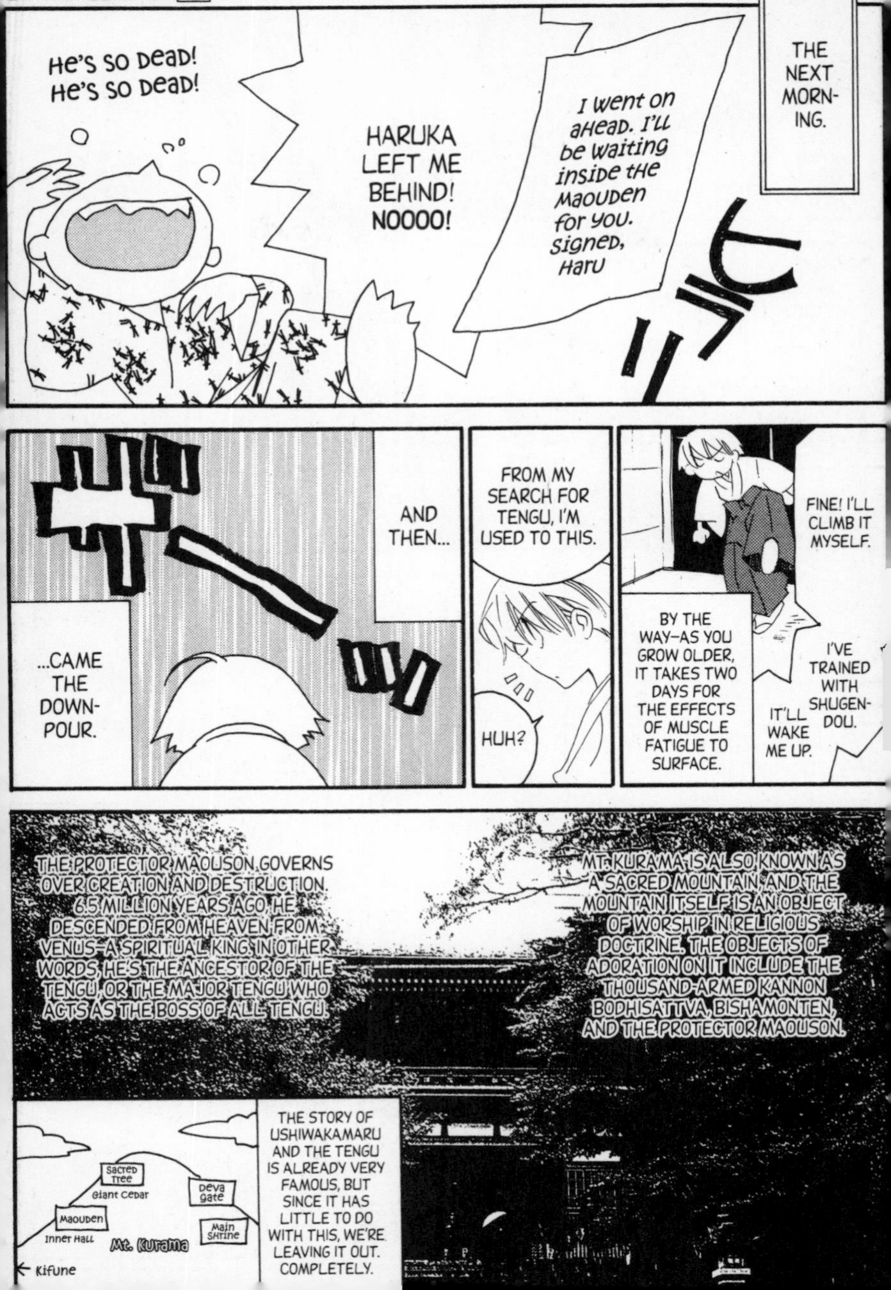
THE NEXT MORNING.
I went on ahead. I'll be waiting inside the Maouden for you. Signed, Haru
HARUKA LEFT ME BEHIND! NOOOO!
He's so dead! He's so dead!
FINE! I'LL CLIMB IT MYSELF.
I'VE TRAINED WITH SHUGENDOU.
IT'LL WAKE ME UP.
BY THE WAY—AS YOU GROW OLDER, IT TAKES TWO DAYS FOR THE EFFECTS OF MUSCLE FATIGUE TO SURFACE.
HUH?
FROM MY SEARCH FOR TENGU, I'M USED TO THIS.
AND THEN...
...CAME THE DOWNPOUR.
MT. KURAMA IS ALSO KNOWN AS A SACRED MOUNTAIN, AND THE MOUNTAIN ITSELF IS AN OBJECT OF WORSHIP IN RELIGIOUS DOCTRINE. THE OBJECTS OF ADORATION ON IT INCLUDE THE THOUSAND-ARMED KANNON BODHISATTVA, BISHAMONTEN, AND THE PROTECTOR MAOUSON.
THE PROTECTOR MAOUSON GOVERNS OVER CREATION AND DESTRUCTION. 6.5 MILLION YEARS AGO HE DESCENDED FROM HEAVEN FROM VENUS—A SPIRITUAL KING. IN OTHER WORDS, HE'S THE ANCESTOR OF THE TENGU, OR THE MAJOR TENGU WHO ACTS AS THE BOSS OF ALL TENGU.
THE STORY OF USHIWAKAMARU AND THE TENGU IS ALREADY VERY FAMOUS, BUT SINCE IT HAS LITTLE TO DO WITH THIS, WE'RE LEAVING IT OUT. COMPLETELY.
Sacred Tree
Giant Cedar
Deva gate
Maouden
Main Shrine
Inner Hall
Mt. Kurama
Kifune

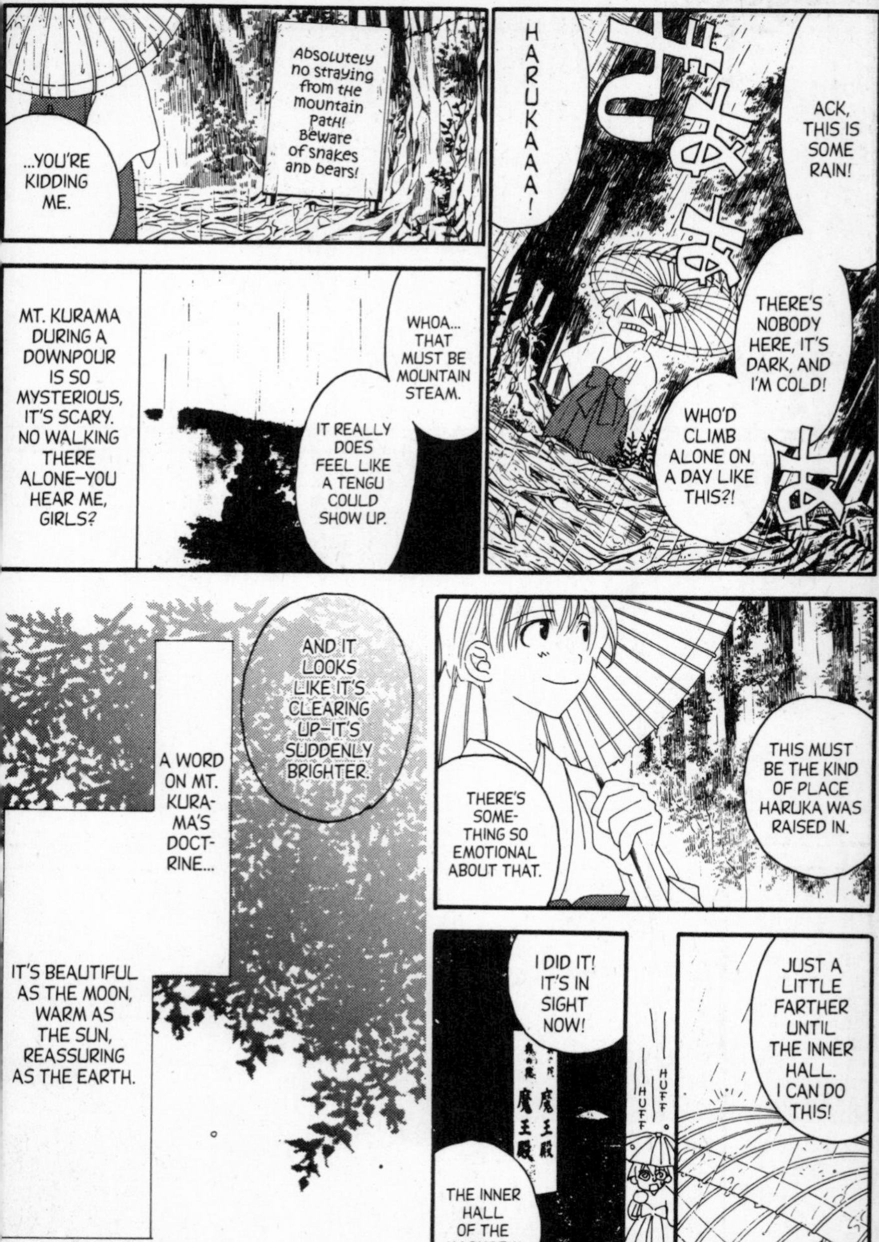
ACK, THIS IS SOME RAIN!
THERE'S NOBODY HERE, IT'S DARK, AND I'M COLD!
WHO'D CLIMB ALONE ON A DAY LIKE THIS?!
HARUKAAAA!
Absolutely no straying from the mountain path! Beware of snakes and bears!
...YOU'RE KIDDING ME.
WHOA... THAT MUST BE MOUNTAIN STEAM.
IT REALLY DOES FEEL LIKE A TENGU COULD SHOW UP.
MT. KURAMA DURING A DOWNPOUR IS SO MYSTERIOUS, IT'S SCARY. NO WALKING THERE ALONE—YOU HEAR ME, GIRLS?
THIS MUST BE THE KIND OF PLACE HARUKA WAS RAISED IN.
THERE'S SOME-THING SO EMOTIONAL ABOUT THAT.
JUST A LITTLE FARTHER UNTIL THE INNER HALL. I CAN DO THIS!
HUFF HUFF
I DID IT! IT'S IN SIGHT NOW!
魔王殿
THE INNER HALL OF THE MAOUDEN!
AND IT LOOKS LIKE IT'S CLEARING UP—IT'S SUDDENLY BRIGHTER.
A WORD ON MT. KURAMA'S DOCT-RINE...
IT'S BEAUTIFUL AS THE MOON, WARM AS THE SUN, REASSURING AS THE EARTH.

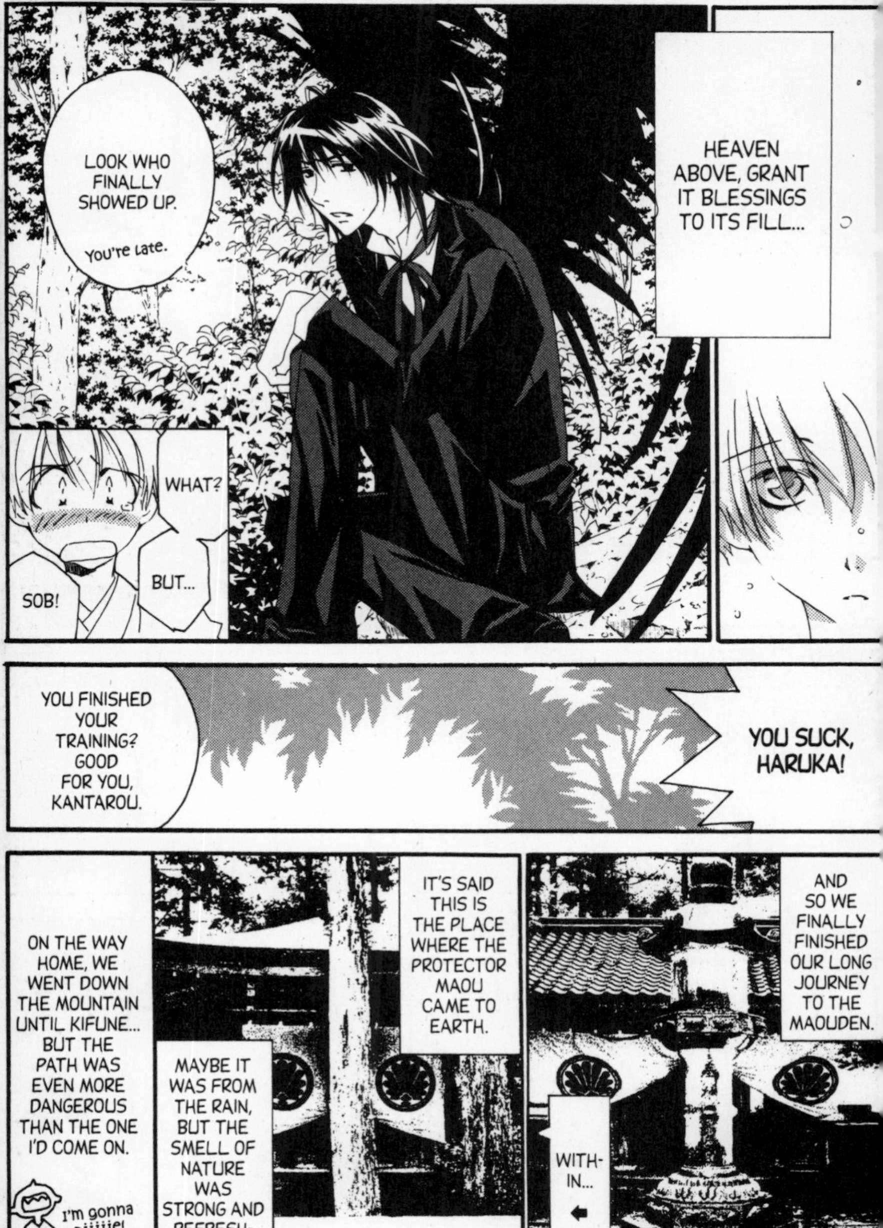
HEAVEN ABOVE, GRANT IT BLESSINGS TO ITS FILL...
LOOK WHO FINALLY SHOWED UP.
You're late.
WHAT?
BUT...
SOB!
YOU SUCK, HARUKA!
YOU FINISHED YOUR TRAINING? GOOD FOR YOU, KANTAROU.
AND SO WE FINALLY FINISHED OUR LONG JOURNEY TO THE MAOUDEN.
WITH-IN...
IT'S SAID THIS IS THE PLACE WHERE THE PROTECTOR MAOU CAME TO EARTH.
MAYBE IT WAS FROM THE RAIN, BUT THE SMELL OF NATURE WAS STRONG AND REFRESH-ING.
ON THE WAY HOME, WE WENT DOWN THE MOUNTAIN UNTIL KIFUNE... BUT THE PATH WAS EVEN MORE DANGEROUS THAN THE ONE I'D COME ON.
I'm gonna Diiiiie!

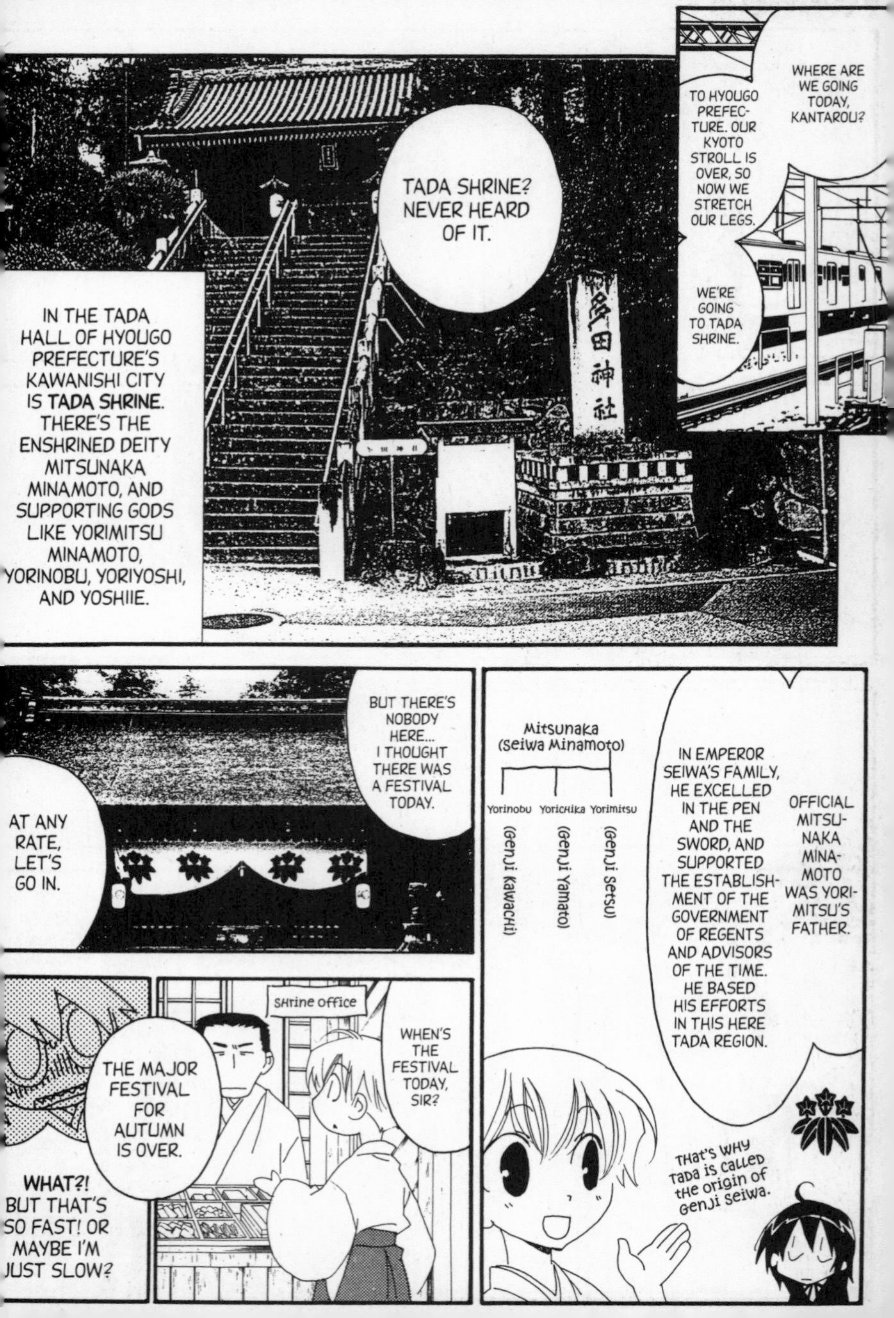
WHERE ARE WE GOING TODAY, KANTAROU?
TO HYOUGO PREFECTURE. OUR KYOTO STROLL IS OVER, SO NOW WE STRETCH OUR LEGS.
WE'RE GOING TO TADA SHRINE.
TADA SHRINE? NEVER HEARD OF IT.
多田神社
IN THE TADA HALL OF HYOUGO PREFECTURE'S KAWANISHI CITY IS **TADA SHRINE**. THERE'S THE ENSHRINED DEITY MITSUNAKA MINAMOTO, AND SUPPORTING GODS LIKE YORIMITSU MINAMOTO, YORINOBU, YORIYOSHI, AND YOSHIIE.
OFFICIAL MITSUNAKA MINAMOTO WAS YORIMITSU'S FATHER.
IN EMPEROR SEIWA'S FAMILY, HE EXCELLED IN THE PEN AND THE SWORD, AND SUPPORTED THE ESTABLISHMENT OF THE GOVERNMENT OF REGENTS AND ADVISORS OF THE TIME. HE BASED HIS EFFORTS IN THIS HERE TADA REGION.
Mitsunaka (Seiwa Minamoto)
Yorimitsu (Genji Setsu)
Yorichika (Genji Yamato)
Yorinobu (Genji Kawachi)
That's why Tada is called the origin of Genji Seiwa.
BUT THERE'S NOBODY HERE... I THOUGHT THERE WAS A FESTIVAL TODAY.
AT ANY RATE, LET'S GO IN.
Shrine Office
WHEN'S THE FESTIVAL TODAY, SIR?
THE MAJOR FESTIVAL FOR AUTUMN IS OVER.
WHAT?! BUT THAT'S SO FAST! OR MAYBE I'M JUST SLOW?

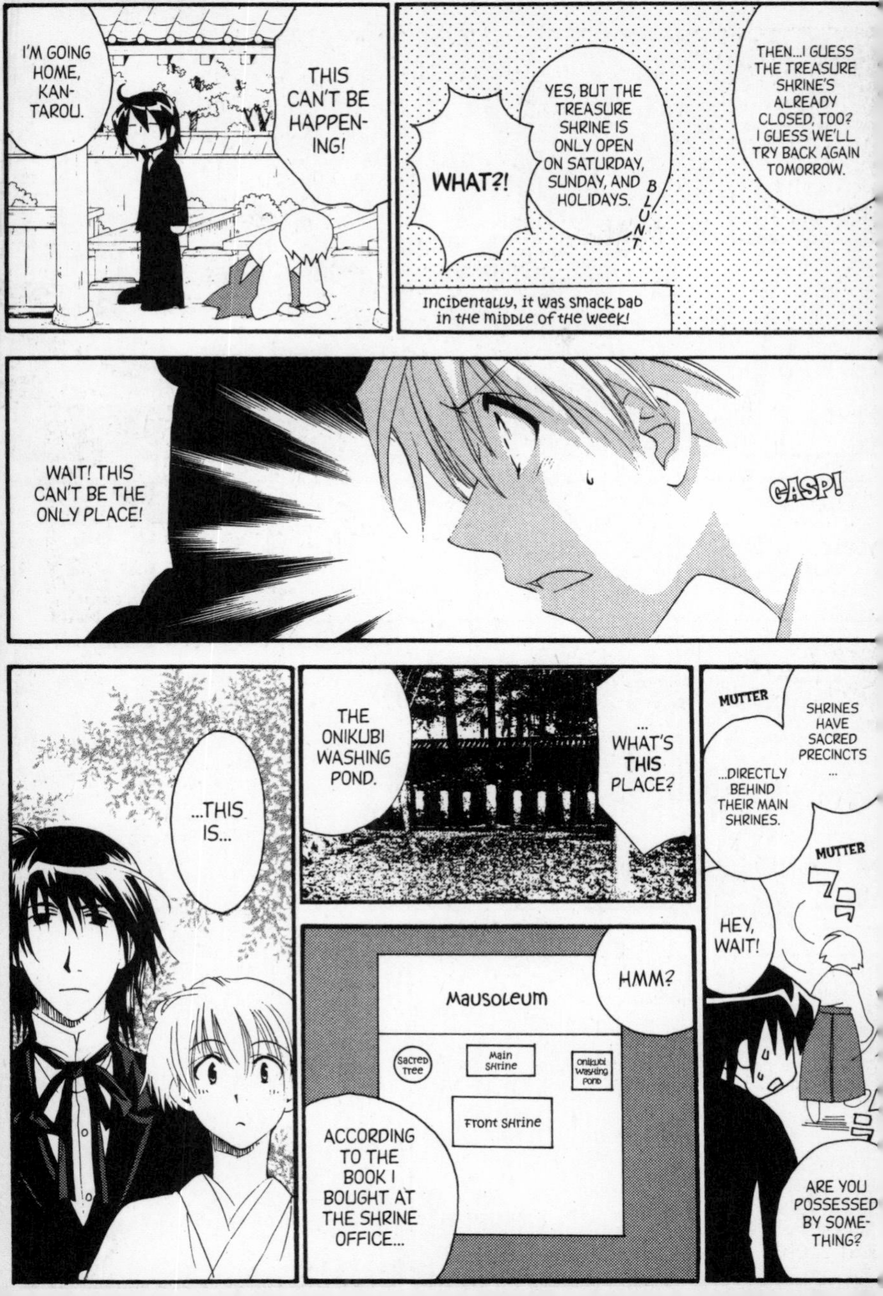
THEN...I GUESS THE TREASURE SHRINE'S ALREADY CLOSED, TOO? I GUESS WE'LL TRY BACK AGAIN TOMORROW.
YES, BUT THE TREASURE SHRINE IS ONLY OPEN ON SATURDAY, SUNDAY, AND HOLIDAYS.
BLUNT
WHAT?!
Incidentally, it was smack dab in the middle of the week!
THIS CAN'T BE HAPPENING!
I'M GOING HOME, KANTAROU.
GASP!
WAIT! THIS CAN'T BE THE ONLY PLACE!
MUTTER
SHRINES HAVE SACRED PRECINCTS ...
...DIRECTLY BEHIND THEIR MAIN SHRINES.
MUTTER
HEY, WAIT!
ARE YOU POSSESSED BY SOMETHING?
...WHAT'S THIS PLACE?
THE ONIKUBI WASHING POND.
HMM?
Mausoleum
Sacred Tree
Main Shrine
Onikubi Washing Pond
Front Shrine
ACCORDING TO THE BOOK I BOUGHT AT THE SHRINE OFFICE...
...THIS IS...

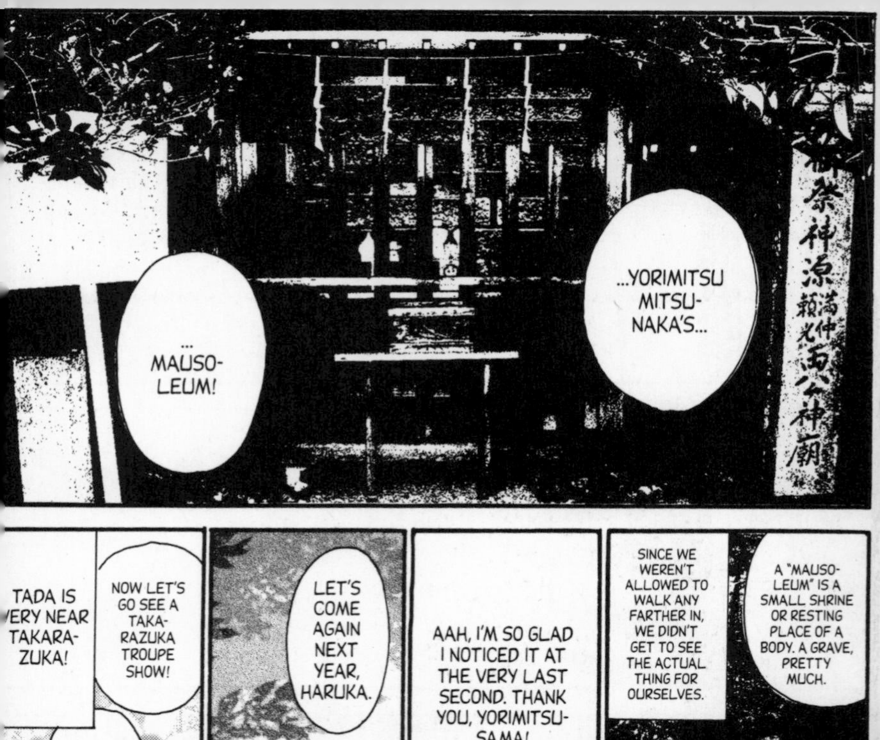
...YORIMITSU MITSU-NAKA'S...
... MAUSO-LEUM!
A "MAUSO-LEUM" IS A SMALL SHRINE OR RESTING PLACE OF A BODY. A GRAVE, PRETTY MUCH.
SINCE WE WEREN'T ALLOWED TO WALK ANY FARTHER IN, WE DIDN'T GET TO SEE THE ACTUAL THING FOR OURSELVES.
SO HE WAS ENSHRINED IN THE FOREST ON THE OTHER SIDE OF THIS HEDGE.
AAH, I'M SO GLAD I NOTICED IT AT THE VERY LAST SECOND. THANK YOU, YORIMITSU-SAMA!
LET'S COME AGAIN NEXT YEAR, HARUKA.
IS THIS THE LAST STOP ON OUR TRIP?
NOW LET'S GO SEE A TAKA-RAZUKA TROUPE SHOW!
TADA IS VERY NEAR TAKARA-ZUKA!
THAT'S NOT RESEARCH.

AT TADA SHRINE, THERE'S A FESTIVAL TO HONOR GENJI EVERY SECOND SUNDAY IN APRIL (IT'S CALLED THE GENJI FESTIVAL). I REALLY WANT TO GO TO THAT NEXT YEAR!

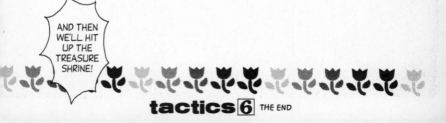

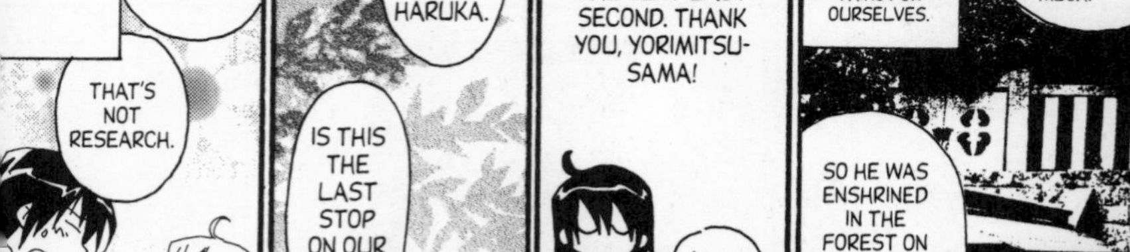
AND THEN WE'LL HIT UP THE TREASURE SHRINE!

tactics 6 THE END

The limited edition of the 6th volume of the manga came with a CD-ROM (for Windows) containing a visual novel! Wow. I used to make little games on my own just for kicks, but to think that I'd get to put that hobby to actual use here! This one involves Haruka's tea bowl turning into a tsukumogami and running away. That's why I think it worked out perfectly that this bonus manga also involves tsukumogami.

by Sakura

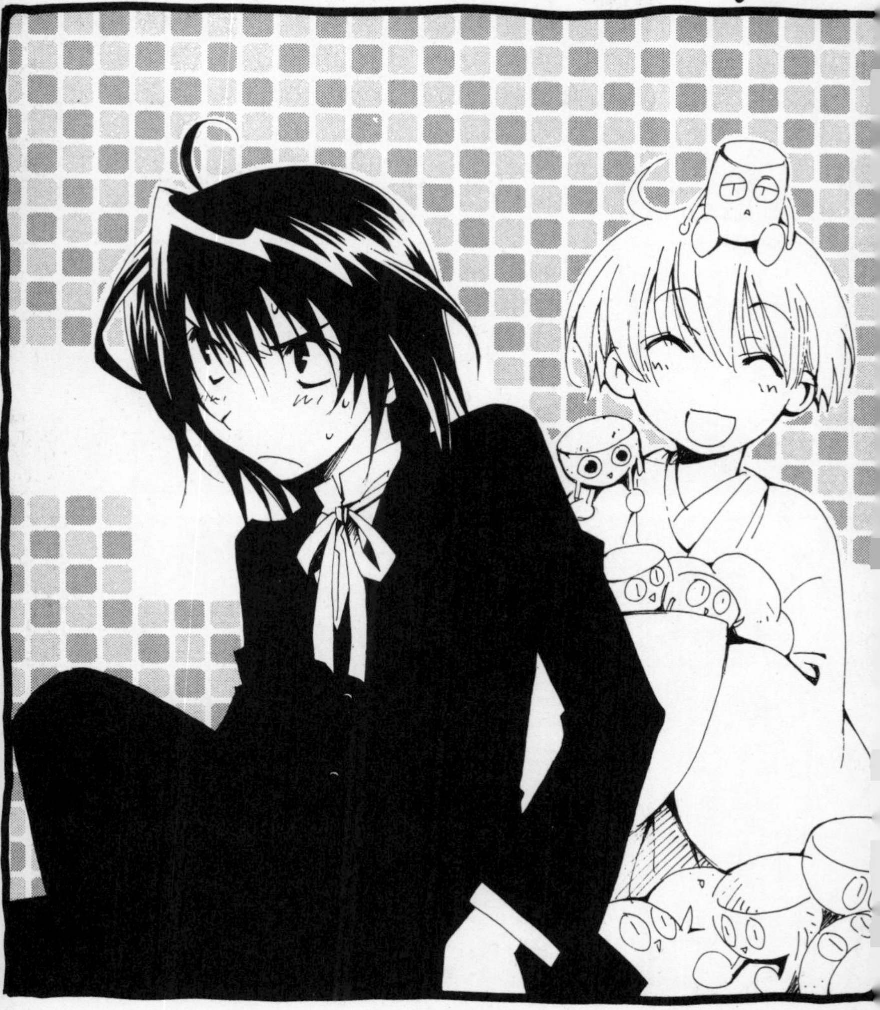

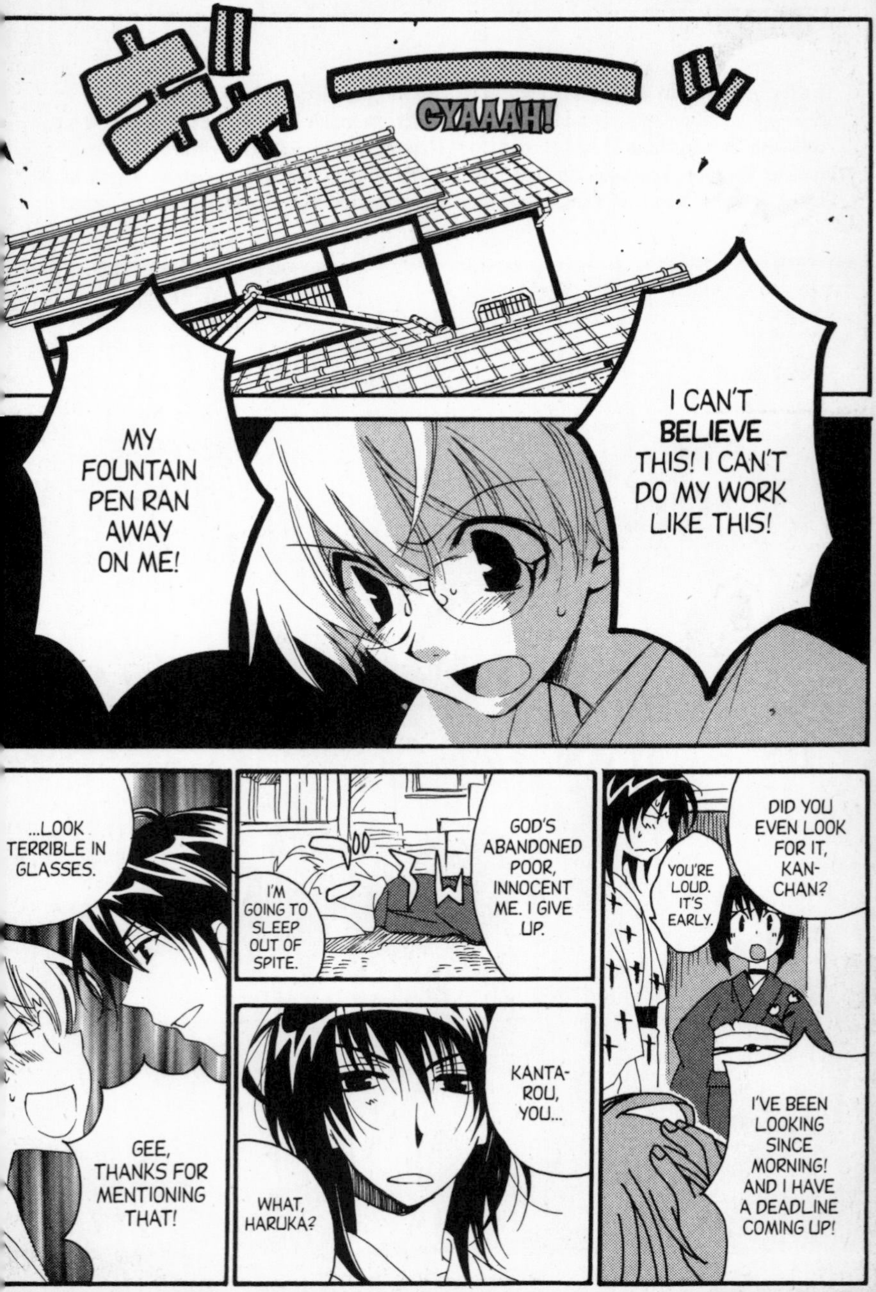
GYAAAH!
I CAN'T BELIEVE THIS! I CAN'T DO MY WORK LIKE THIS!
MY FOUNTAIN PEN RAN AWAY ON ME!
DID YOU EVEN LOOK FOR IT, KAN-CHAN?
YOU'RE LOUD. IT'S EARLY.
I'VE BEEN LOOKING SINCE MORNING! AND I HAVE A DEADLINE COMING UP!
GOD'S ABANDONED POOR, INNOCENT ME. I GIVE UP.
I'M GOING TO SLEEP OUT OF SPITE.
KANTA-ROU, YOU...
WHAT, HARUKA?
...LOOK TERRIBLE IN GLASSES.
GEE, THANKS FOR MENTIONING THAT!

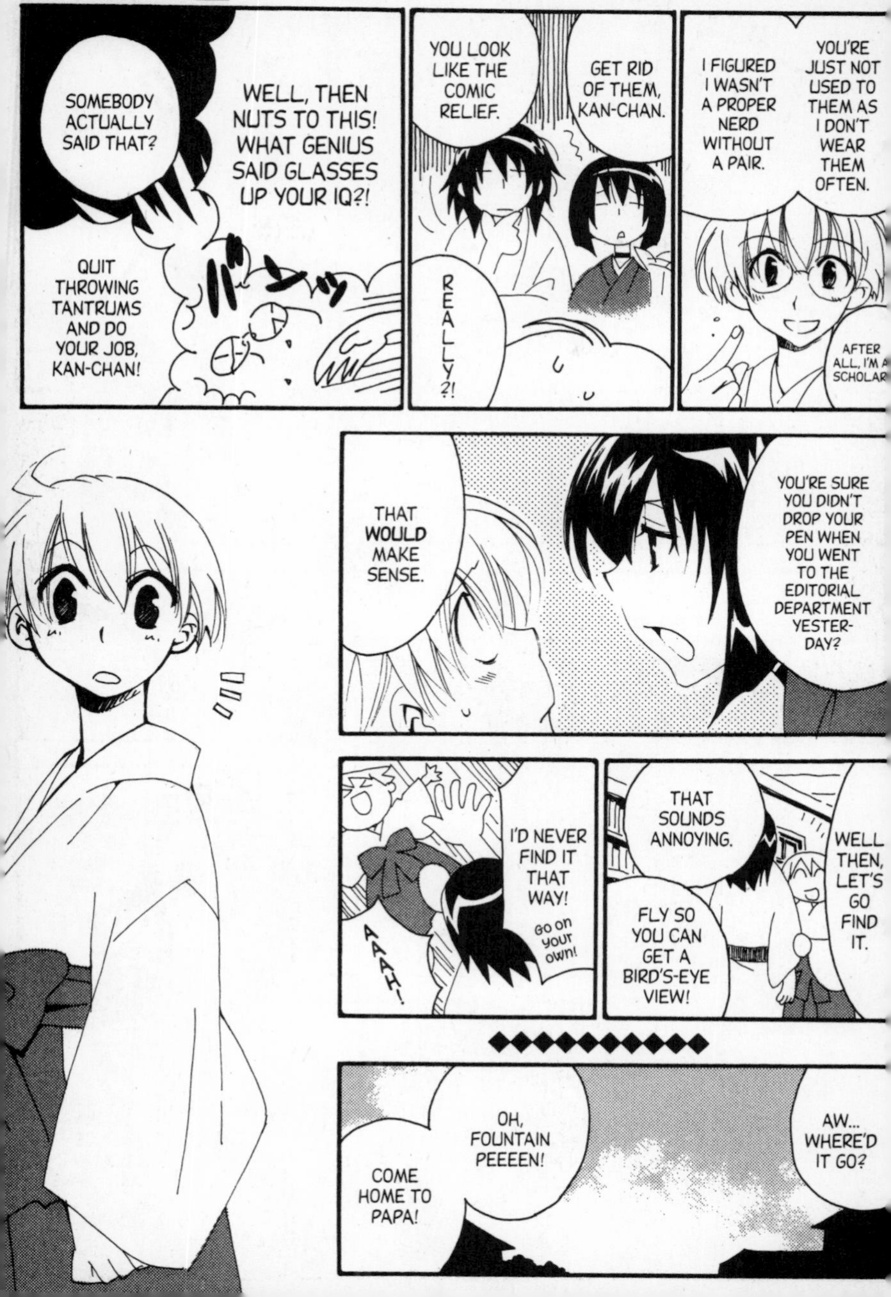
YOU'RE JUST NOT USED TO THEM AS I DON'T WEAR THEM OFTEN.
I FIGURED I WASN'T A PROPER NERD WITHOUT A PAIR.
AFTER ALL, I'M A SCHOLAR
GET RID OF THEM, KAN-CHAN.
YOU LOOK LIKE THE COMIC RELIEF.
REALLY?!
WELL, THEN NUTS TO THIS! WHAT GENIUS SAID GLASSES UP YOUR IQ?!
SOMEBODY ACTUALLY SAID THAT?
QUIT THROWING TANTRUMS AND DO YOUR JOB, KAN-CHAN!
YOU'RE SURE YOU DIDN'T DROP YOUR PEN WHEN YOU WENT TO THE EDITORIAL DEPARTMENT YESTER-DAY?
THAT WOULD MAKE SENSE.
WELL THEN, LET'S GO FIND IT.
THAT SOUNDS ANNOYING.
FLY SO YOU CAN GET A BIRD'S-EYE VIEW!
I'D NEVER FIND IT THAT WAY!
Go on your own!
AAAH!
AW... WHERE'D IT GO?
OH, FOUNTAIN PEEEEN!
COME HOME TO PAPA!

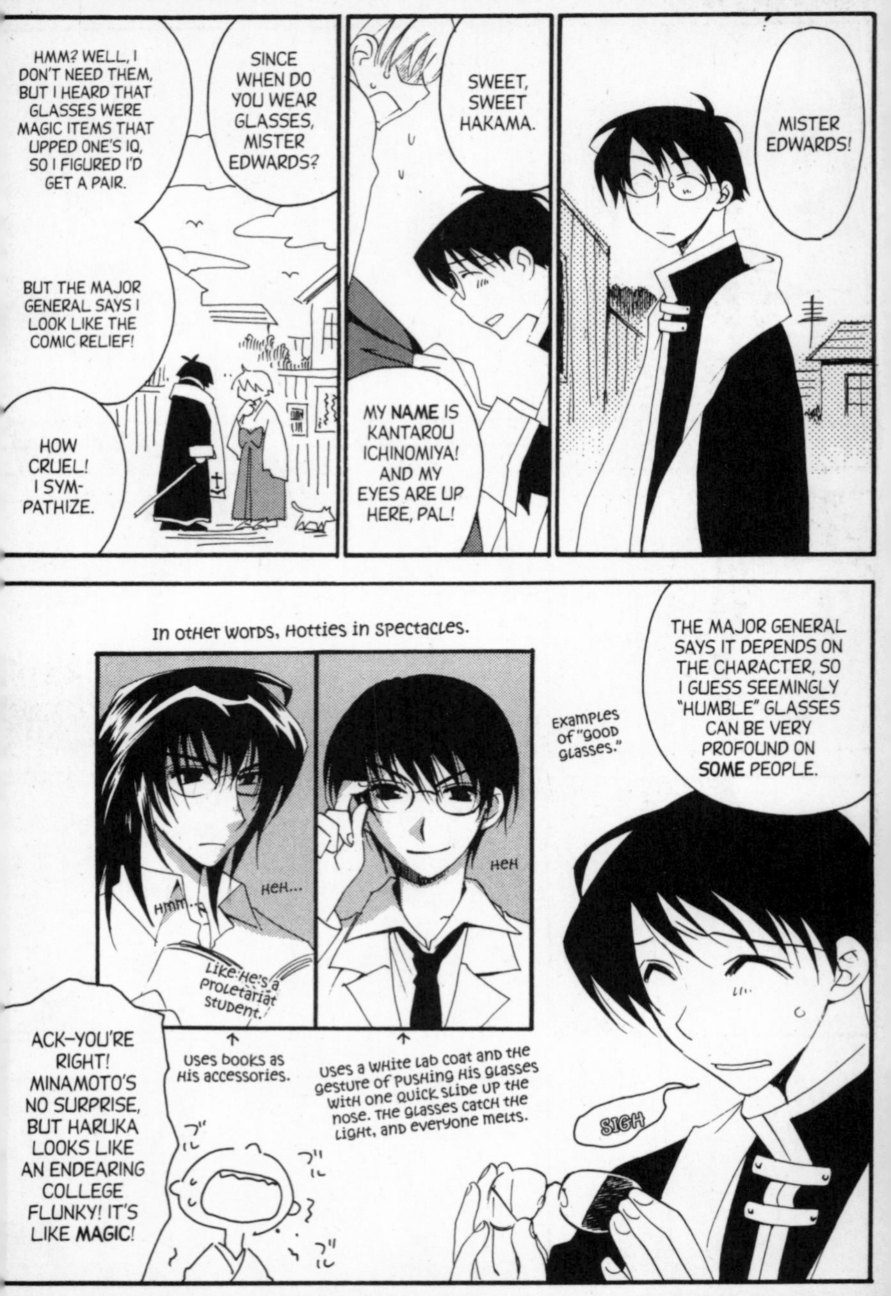
MISTER EDWARDS!
SWEET, SWEET HAKAMA.
MY NAME IS KANTAROU ICHINOMIYA! AND MY EYES ARE UP HERE, PAL!
SINCE WHEN DO YOU WEAR GLASSES, MISTER EDWARDS?
HMM? WELL, I DON'T NEED THEM, BUT I HEARD THAT GLASSES WERE MAGIC ITEMS THAT UPPED ONE'S IQ, SO I FIGURED I'D GET A PAIR.
BUT THE MAJOR GENERAL SAYS I LOOK LIKE THE COMIC RELIEF!
HOW CRUEL! I SYM-PATHIZE.
THE MAJOR GENERAL SAYS IT DEPENDS ON THE CHARACTER, SO I GUESS SEEMINGLY "HUMBLE" GLASSES CAN BE VERY PROFOUND ON SOME PEOPLE.
SIGH
In other words, Hotties in spectacles.
Examples of "good glasses."
HEH
Uses a white lab coat and the gesture of pushing his glasses with one quick slide up the nose. The glasses catch the light, and everyone melts.
HEH...
HMM...
Like he's a proletariat student.
Uses books as his accessories.
ACK—YOU'RE RIGHT! MINAMOTO'S NO SURPRISE, BUT HARUKA LOOKS LIKE AN ENDEARING COLLEGE FLUNKY! IT'S LIKE MAGIC!

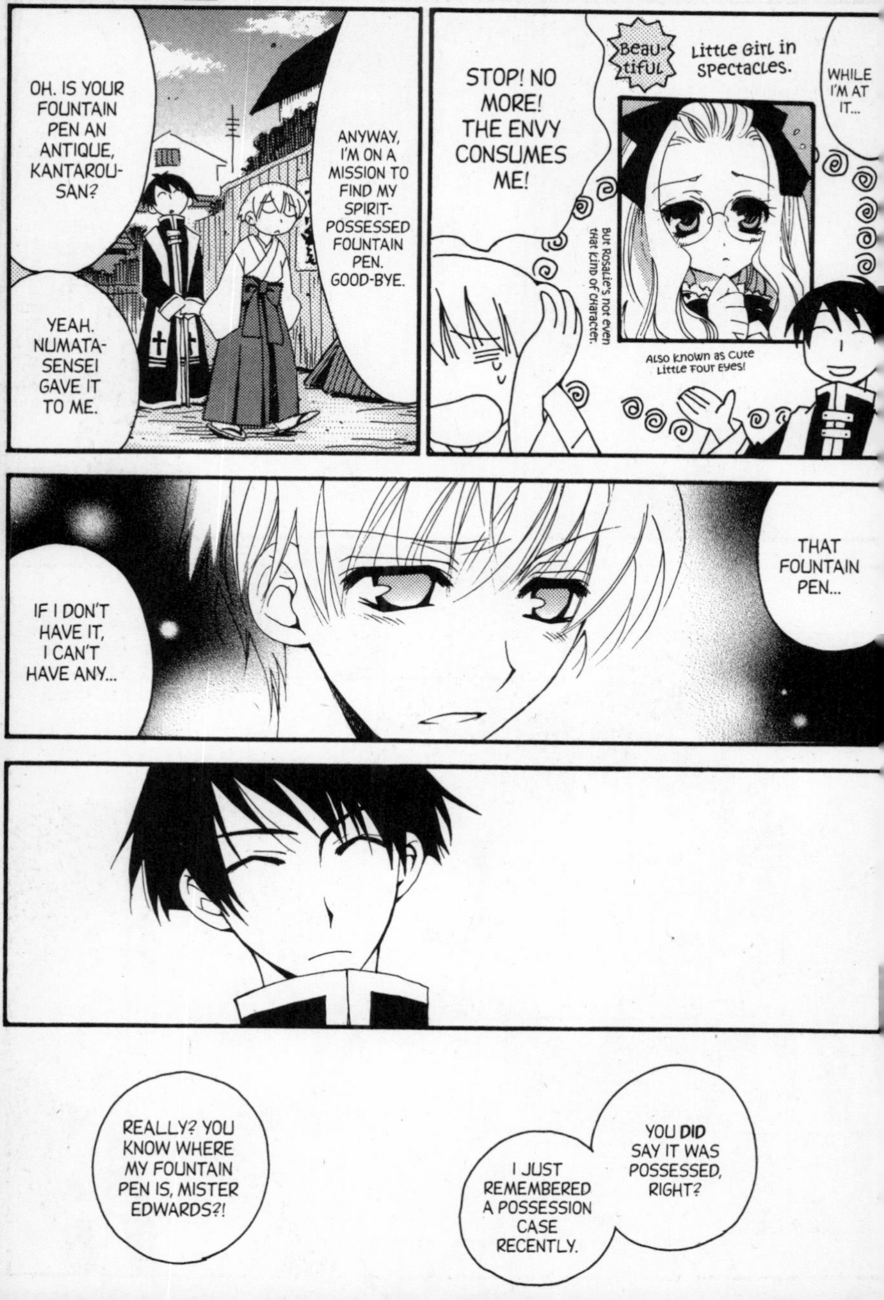
WHILE I'M AT IT...
Beau-tiful Little Girl in Spectacles.
STOP! NO MORE! THE ENVY CONSUMES ME!
But Rosalie's not even that kind of character.
Also known as Cute Little Four Eyes!
ANYWAY, I'M ON A MISSION TO FIND MY SPIRIT-POSSESSED FOUNTAIN PEN. GOOD-BYE.
OH. IS YOUR FOUNTAIN PEN AN ANTIQUE, KANTAROU-SAN?
YEAH. NUMATA-SENSEI GAVE IT TO ME.
THAT FOUNTAIN PEN...
IF I DON'T HAVE IT, I CAN'T HAVE ANY...
YOU **DID** SAY IT WAS POSSESSED, RIGHT?
I JUST REMEMBERED A POSSESSION CASE RECENTLY.
REALLY? YOU KNOW WHERE MY FOUNTAIN PEN IS, MISTER EDWARDS?!

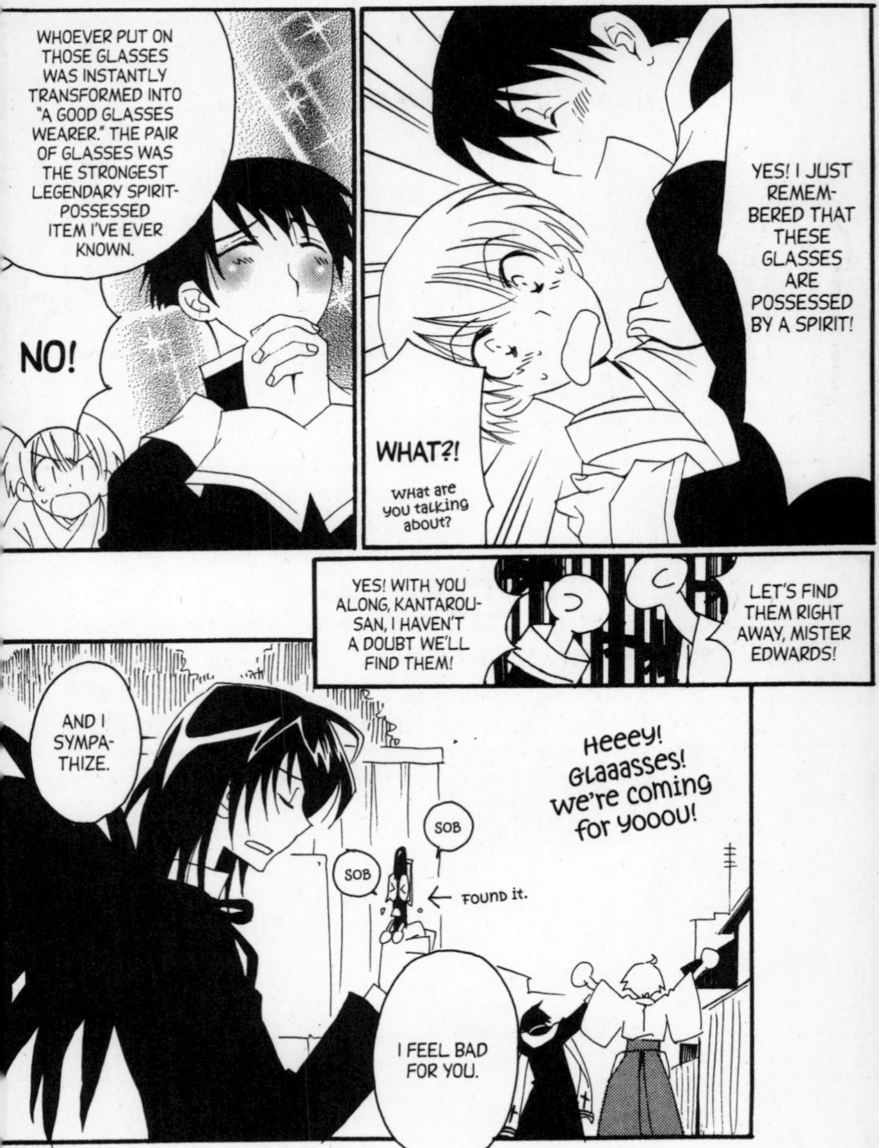
YES! I JUST REMEMBERED THAT THESE GLASSES ARE POSSESSED BY A SPIRIT!
WHAT?!
What are you talking about?
WHOEVER PUT ON THOSE GLASSES WAS INSTANTLY TRANSFORMED INTO "A GOOD GLASSES WEARER." THE PAIR OF GLASSES WAS THE STRONGEST LEGENDARY SPIRIT-POSSESSED ITEM I'VE EVER KNOWN.
NO!
LET'S FIND THEM RIGHT AWAY, MISTER EDWARDS!
YES! WITH YOU ALONG, KANTAROU-SAN, I HAVEN'T A DOUBT WE'LL FIND THEM!
Heeey! Glaaasses! We're coming for yooou!
SOB
SOB
Found it.
AND I SYMPATHIZE.
I FEEL BAD FOR YOU.

END

IN THE NEXT VOLUME OF

tactics

Kantarou takes on a case of finding a missing person that leads him to an ironworking village affiliated with a mysterious organization called the Toratsugumi Society. But they soon find out this Society is bringing back dead people! Meanwhile, Raikou Minamoto reveals more of his plan...

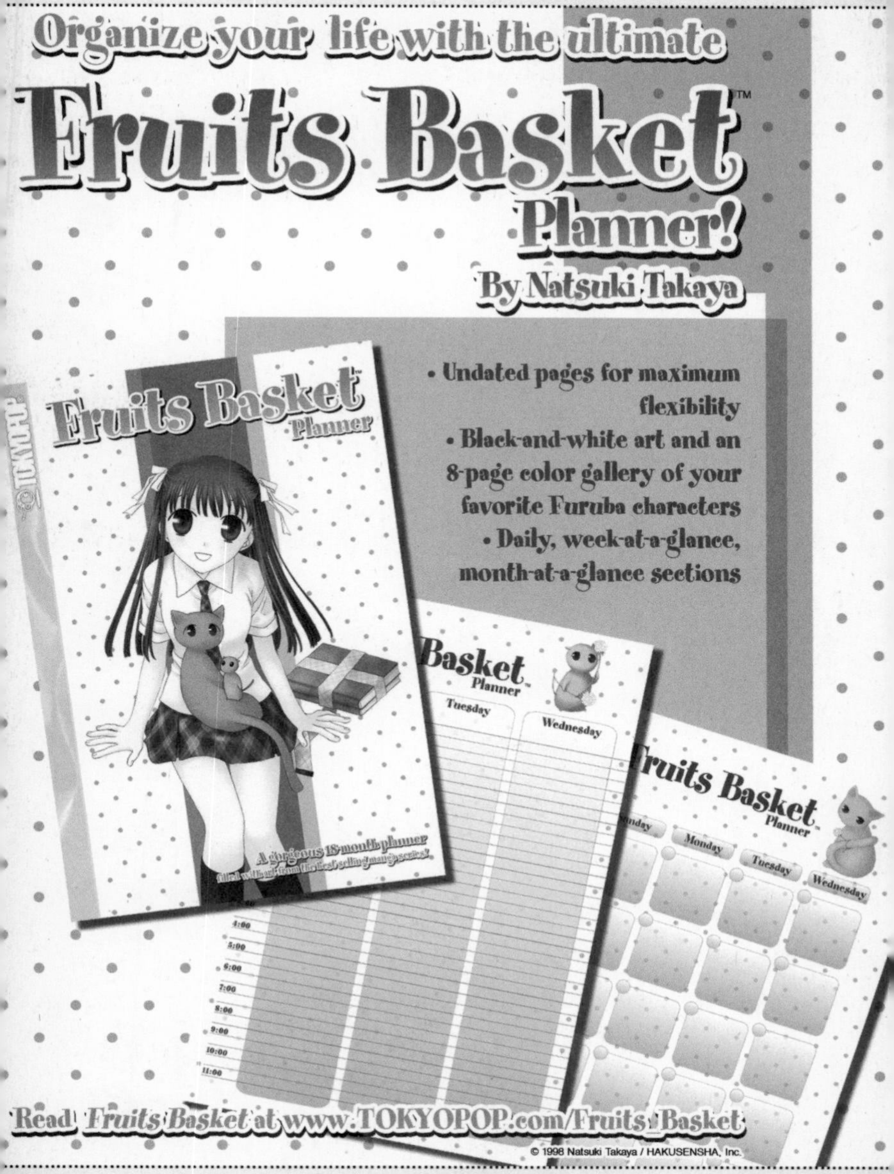
Organize your life with the ultimate
Fruits Basket™
Planner!
By Natsuki Takaya
• Undated pages for maximum flexibility
• Black-and-white art and an 8-page color gallery of your favorite Furuba characters
• Daily, week-at-a-glance, month-at-a-glance sections
Fruits Basket Planner
TOKYOPOP
Basket Planner
Tuesday
Wednesday
4:00
5:00
6:00
7:00
8:00
9:00
10:00
11:00
Fruits Basket Planner
Monday
Tuesday
Wednesday
Read Fruits Basket at www.TOKYOPOP.com/Fruits_Basket
© 1998 Natsuki Takaya / HAKUSENSHA, Inc.

STOP!

This is the back of the book.
You wouldn't want to spoil a great ending!

This book is printed "manga-style," in the authentic Japanese right-to-left format. Since none of the artwork has been flipped or altered, readers get to experience the story just as the creator intended. You've been asking for it, so TOKYOPOP® delivered: authentic, hot-off-the-press, and far more fun!

DIRECTIONS

If this is your first time reading manga-style, here's a quick guide to help you understand how it works.

It's easy... just start in the top right panel and follow the numbers. Have fun, and look for more 100% authentic manga from TOKYOPOP®!

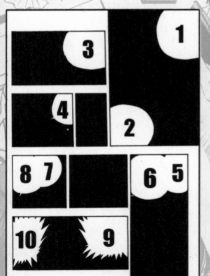